When Souls Had Wings

When Souls Had Wings

Wings

Pre-mortal Existence in Western Thought

TERRYL L. GIVENS

UNIVERSITY PRESS

2010

OXFORD
UNIVERSITY PRESS

Oxford University Press, Inc., publishes works that further
Oxford University's objective of excellence
in research, scholarship, and education.

Oxford   New York
Auckland   Cape Town   Dar es Salaam   Hong Kong   Karachi
Kuala Lumpur   Madrid   Melbourne   Mexico City   Nairobi
New Delhi   Shanghai   Taipei   Toronto

With offices in
Argentina   Austria   Brazil   Chile   Czech Republic   France   Greece
Guatemala   Hungary   Italy   Japan   Poland   Portugal   Singapore
South Korea   Switzerland   Thailand   Turkey   Ukraine   Vietnam

Copyright © 2010 Oxford University Press, Inc.

Published by Oxford University Press, Inc.
198 Madison Avenue, New York, NY 10016

www.oup.com

Library of Congress Cataloging-in-Publication Data
Givens, Terryl.
When souls had wings: pre-mortal existence in Western thought / by Terryl L. Givens.
p. cm.
ISBN 978-0-19-531390-1
1. Soul.   2. Pre-existence.
I. Title.
BL290.G58 2009
129—dc22
2009007369

9 8 7 6 5 4 3 2 1

Printed in the United States of America
on acid-free paper

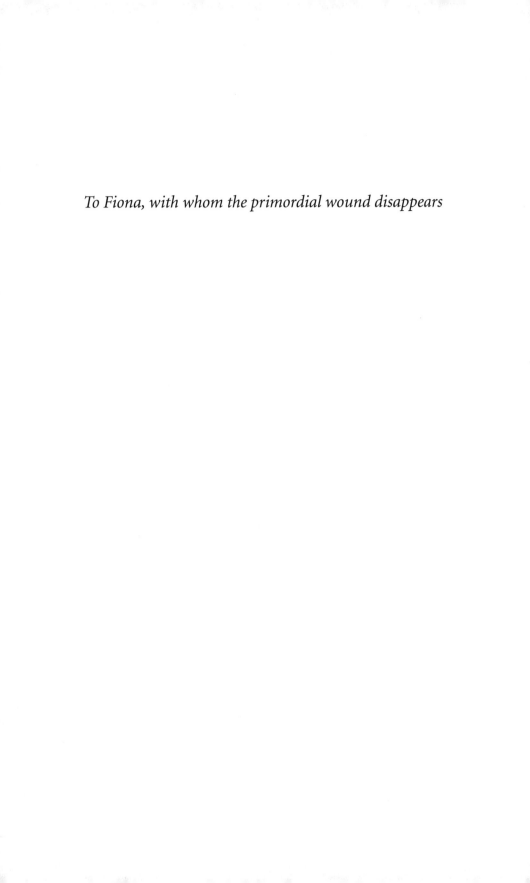

To Fiona, with whom the primordial wound disappears

Contents

Prologue

The Chaldeans represent the Soul as originally endowed with wings, which fall away when it sinks from its native element, and must be reproduced before it can hope to return. Some disciples of Zoroaster once inquired of him, "How the wings of the Soul might be made to grow again?"—"By sprinkling them," he replied, "with the Waters of Life."—"But where are those Waters to be found[?]" they asked. "In the Garden of God," replied Zoroaster.

—Thomas Moore[1]

So long as its wings are in perfect condition it flies high,...but a soul that sheds its wings wanders until it lights on something solid, where it settles and takes on an earthly body, which then, owing to the power of this soul, seems to move itself. The whole combination of soul and body is called a living thing, or..."mortal."

—Plato[2]

So long as a soul continued to abide in the good it has no experience of union with a body....But by some inclination towards evil these souls lose their wings and come into bodies.

—Origen[3]

In Michelangelo's Sistine masterpiece, the right hand of God extends majestically yet languorously to imbue the newly formed Adam with the gift of life, the divine finger touching, but not quite touching, mortal

Creation of Adam (1512, detail), by Michelangelo Buonarroti, Scala/Art Resource, New York.

man. Prominent against a light background, the gesture is sublime in its capture of that electric moment that inaugurates the whole of human history. Under God's left arm, by contrast, all is dark and mysterious, as crowded figures huddle in the shadow of the divine. Foremost in the group sheltering beneath the protective embrace of God is a strikingly lovely personage, who gazes fixedly, if somewhat apprehensively, at the reclining Adam. Critics have perceived in this figure an array of characters, from the figure of Sophia mentioned in the book of Wisdom, to the Virgin Mary, to "an angel of masculine build." Those stubbornly resistant to what most observers would consider the obviously feminine features of the person may be averse to the intuitive reading of the figure as the pre-mortal Eve, because of the theological problems this raises. Such a reading would flatly contradict Catholic theology, which holds that the soul is created at the moment of conception. Theology notwithstanding, such resistance is, writes Leo Steinberg, "a lost cause." And so it has been, ever since Walter Pater identified the group as Eve and her progeny in the nineteenth century. Seen as symbolic iconography or subversive literalism, this is the most magnificent artistic rendering of pre-mortal humans (as well as the premortal Christ child) that any era has produced.[4]

When Souls Had Wings

Introduction

And this is
Life?—Toil! and wherefore should I toil?—because
My father could not keep his place in Eden?
What had *I* done in this?—I was unborn:
I sought not to be born.

—Lord Byron,
Cain, act 1, scene 1

If there is one assertion that every disgruntled mortal seems safe in making, it is the petulant insistence, "I didn't ask to be born." Birth has, in the West at least, usually been seen as the result of forces that operate entirely independently of what those forces produce. Whether engendered by spontaneous passion or parental planning, and viewed as the consequence of strict biological laws or a divine procreative power—it has seemed self-evident to generation after generation of humanity that newborns are the passive objects of another's will, springing into being at someone else's behest—or careless instigation—set "naked and miserable upon the shores of this great ocean of the world."[1]

In this version of events, most people have generally assumed that the human individual comes into existence at the time of birth as, in the Judeo-Christian tradition at least, a combined physical body and immaterial soul or spirit.[2] In such a case, immortality is a ray, not a line, starting at a moment between conception and birth and extending into an infinite future. The process of physical procreation, as miraculous as it may be, provides a generally sufficient explanation of how our body comes to exist. (Though even here, delightful variations exist that ascribe, for example, the simultaneous physical presence of all future generations in miniscule form in the eggs of Eve or the sperm of Adam.) The origins of the soul, however, have been subject to rather more speculation. This would seem to be inevitable, given the immediate problem that emerges: the logic of physical parents producing physical progeny becomes complicated when those physical parents are considered to produce offspring possessed of an immortal and nonphysical dimension as well. The procreation of physical bodies is relatively straightforward. How and when a spirit is created and joined to that body is more problematic.

In early Christian thought, two theories evolved to resolve this conundrum. The spirit or soul was held to be either generated from the parents in the same way as the body (traducianism), or it was believed to be formed by a special act of creation on God's part for each and every individual (creationism). Traducianism (from the Latin *tradux*, "shoot" or "sprout"; *traducere*, "convey" or "lead across") can be traced at least to the church father Tertullian (b. 160) and was later embraced by the Eastern Orthodox Church and Luther. Since Adam begat a son in his own likeness and image (Gen. 5:3), and since he comprised a body and soul, then begetting a combined body and soul appears to be compatible with, if not clearly indicated by, Holy Writ.

Before the term was co-opted to refer to biblical literalists in the aftermath of Darwin, creationism was an alternative version of the soul's creation. Creationism was perhaps first taught by the African apologist Lactantius (245–325 CE) and by the Middle Ages was being proclaimed by prominent church teachers. The theory relies principally upon the biblical account of Adam's creation, at which time the spirit was infused or breathed into a body prepared for it. Creationism came to be embraced by the majority of early church authorities. This view avoids the metaphysical difficulties of how spirit and body interact in the human individual to jointly sire a combined body and spirit. At the same time, the doctrine reserves to God alone the capacity to produce that which is immortal. Catholics (like most Protestants) subscribe to creationism, based on their belief that the human soul is simple and indivisible, hence it cannot generate spiritual germs or seed; and the body, being physical, cannot generate that which is spiritual.[3]

Both doctrines are encumbered with profound theological problems. If the soul originates with the body, as the traducianists hold, then why does it not perish with the body? In what manner can a human be thought capable of generating a soul? Creationism presents, if anything, even more intractable problems. If God creates the soul afresh in every human, how can it be imperfect, as a soul of fallen nature necessarily is? If it is created pure and innocent, how and when does it come to acquire the burden of Adam's sin and guilt? And what justice can there be in immediately consigning a purely created spirit to the incubus of guilt, sin, and fallenness?

There is, however, an altogether different conception of the soul's creation which has held sway at various times and places throughout the world. According to its several formulations, every living soul existed in a former realm, either there created or eternally uncreated. Belief in the soul's pre-mortal existence has a long if currently obscured history in Western thought. It has been articulated in virtually every age, from ancient times to the present. It has been adumbrated in many forms in philosophy, theology, poetry, and popular culture. It has been anathematized as Christian heresy and defended as a true doctrine known to the ancients. Some have deployed the idea to buttress arguments for the immortality of the soul. Others have adduced it to account for individual differences evident at birth, still others to explain the existence of innate ideas, and many have used it as the basis of a more compelling solution to the problem of God's apparent injustice.

The expression "preexistence" encompasses a range of meanings, and that very richness and vagueness are both a reflection of, and a reason for, the concept's dogged persistence through time, in spite of religious anathemas, shifting philosophical trends, and the vagaries of poetic fashion. Purists might prefer the term "pre-mortal existence" to the illogical-sounding "preexistence," but it is the latter term that has far and away predominated in the history of the concept and the one that will be largely employed in this book. In general, the term refers to the existence of the soul before it was incarnate in its present human form. "Before" can in some contexts and traditions mean logically, rather than temporally, prior to creation. And preexistence can itself refer to the soul and to a galaxy of related concepts, from emanations and hypostases (essential realities rooted in the divine) like "the church," to the Logos, or the figure of Sophia. Though sometimes found in conjunction with metempsychosis (transmigration of souls, or reincarnation), preexistence is a distinct doctrine and neither entails nor is entailed by a doctrine of cyclical rebirth or multiple lives. On the one hand, the spirit may have an existence prior to its one and only incarnation, and on the other, multiple mortal lives may include no prior or independent existence of the spirit that animates those sequential versions of mortality. Scholar of esoterica G. R. S. Mead registered this point a century ago, noting:

> [T]his general hypothesis of pre-existence...by no means necessarily includes the special doctrine of reincarnation or transcorporation proper, that of repeated incarnations in physical bodies on this earth. It is somewhat necessary to insist on this distinction at the outset, for the two theories are not infrequently confused in the popular treatment of the transmigration-doctrine.[4]

And though proponents of one often championed the other, it was at least as common for the defenders of preexistence to explicitly reject transmigration. Geddes

MacGregor suggests one particular reason for this fact: in early Christianity, at least, preoccupied as it was with the imminence of Christ's return, a theory of past spiritual existence was perfectly reasonable and often compelling. A theory involving future reembodiments, on the other hand, was largely obviated by the nearness of the world's end and the rapturous contemplation of a heavenly life in Christ or with him.[5] There was also the dilemma that transmigration raises for physical resurrection (which of multiple incarnations would be the immortal form?) and the fact of explicit New Testament language declaring that "it is appointed unto men once to die" (Heb. 9:27).

In general, I am taking preexistence as the positing of the existence of humankind's spiritual identity in a state and place that preexist mortal life. In some versions, the soul is a fully self-aware moral agent seemingly possessing most of the attributes and characteristics of the later, embodied self. In other versions, since personhood is considered to be a composite of spiritual core and bodily nature, the preexistent self is only a partial self. And in yet other, early versions, the preexistent self is the raw material out of which the spirit will itself be formed. This volume will encompass the entire range and variety of beliefs that trace the origins of individual identity to some kind of nonphysical state before birth.

The idea appears to have more than one point of origin, and influence and inheritance are in any case notoriously difficult to establish with certainty where the history of ideas is concerned. Most early appearances of the concept in the Western world are traceable to a classical setting where Greek, Egyptian, Persian, and even Indian streams of thought intermingled just the other side of clear historical genealogies. Some would trace the ancestry of the idea further backward, even to Central Asia, but those paths lead well outside the realm of documented transmission.[6] For this reason, and for simple reasons of practicality, I begin the present study with the first appearances of the idea in Semitic traditions and in Greek antiquity and then trace the tradition as it developed and was manifested in subsequent Western culture.

Belief in the soul is generally a function of religious belief, and Christianity has long consigned the doctrine of a pre-mortal soul to the realm of heresy. That fact itself only adds to the questions surrounding the rich and tempestuous history of this idea. Definitive prohibitions generally dampen ardor for all but the most recalcitrant religious tenets. Belief in preexistence, on the other hand, has persisted across millennia and across cultures. It resurfaces as a religious doctrine in spite of orthodox proscription, affirmed by theologians, prophets, and mystics alike. It recurs as a philosophical idea from Plato into modernity, in mythological formulations and contemporary argumentation. Poets from antiquity to Robert Frost and Polish Nobel laureates have limned the features of a human preexistence, as literary trope and as apparently earnest, polemical description.

Although the breadth and variety of versions of preexistence are enormous, the focus of this book is not to merely trace a tradition or track sources. One student of preexistence (as it pertains to Christ) has written that "it is not sufficient to ask of a passage that reflects the idea of pre-existence, What is its source? Even if the source were known, the same questions must be asked of the source that are asked of the text: What is the function of the idea of pre-existence within the context where it is found?"[7] R. G. Hamerton-Kelly refers to general agreement that a conception of preexistence "involves and presupposes a whole view of reality."[8] Such belief structures, like all enduring myths and paradigms, persist because of their explanatory power. The most successful are those that are more effective than others in the interpretation of human experience.[9] Such paradigms do important intellectual and cultural work, which is to say, they order reality, satisfy emotional yearning or longing, rationalize the incongruities and traumas of existence, or simply explain why the sky is blue, birds fly, and things are the way they are.

Pre-mortal existence is such a paradigm. In the case of Christ's preexistence, the doctrine is most simply read as the necessary consequence of an incarnate deity also conceived of as eternal, transhistorical, and to be identified with God himself. He must, in some sense, have predated his mortal birth. Alternatively, as in continental dogmatic theology, Christ's preexistence can be taken to emphasize not continuity but his utter transcendence as "an alien intruder into a world with which he has no ontological connection."[10] He exists, in other words, not so much before time as outside time. Applied more generally to entities besides Christ, the theme of preexistence has been attributed to a desire to impute special value, "express divinity or ultimacy," or convey a transhistorical hope in the midst of apocalyptic circumstances.[11]

I hope to go beyond such sparse conjectures to elaborate an entire series of motivations and purposes behind an idea that has flourished well outside and beyond the early Christian contexts that frame many studies of the topic.[12] Preexistence has been invoked to explain "the better angels of our nature," including the human yearning for transcendence and the sublime; it suggests a reason for the frequent sensation of alienation and the indelible sadness of human existence. Preexistence has been offered to account for why we know what we should not know, whether in the form of a Greek slave's grasp of mathematics, the moral sense common to humanity, or the human ability to recognize universals. The belief has salved the wounded sensibility of a host of religious thinkers and people of good conscience, who could not otherwise account for the unevenly distributed pain and suffering that are humanity's common lot, and has been triumphantly invoked to rescue God's justice and honor. Lives lived in pre-mortal realms have explained convincingly the uncannily instantaneous bonds between friends and between lovers, forged so profoundly that they seem to possess their own mysterious prehistory. An origin in the eternal realms has been found philosophically more credible than human hormones and happenstance to ground the existence of a soul that is held to be immortal and an image of divinity. And many philosophers have found in human pre-mortality the necessary precondition for a will that is genuinely free and independent. Finally, preexistence has been advocated for reasons as unanticipated as its aesthetic and logical symmetry, in comparison to orthodoxy's asymmetrical notions of eternity and the unidirectionality of the soul's immortality. It even provides, as we shall see, a lyrical etiology for the appearance of the gentle groove, the philtrum, that graces the upper lips of the entire human family.

Given the breadth of the cultural and intellectual work that the paradigm of preexistence performs, it is no surprise to find the concept such a durable one, resistant to anathemas, the changing fortunes of poetic fashion, and the vanquishment of Plato, metaphysics, and spiritual anthropologies generally. The surprise, rather, is that the idea met such determined and vociferous opposition in the early Christian world, forcing the doctrine into the peripheries and underground of Western thought. As we shall see, the arguments adduced in opposing the doctrine were almost invariably logically inferior to those invoked in its support. The explanation for its suppression must therefore be found rather in the galaxy of weighty theological concerns and political stakes on which the doctrine impinged. Emerging Christian doctrines of God's sovereignty, the creation of the cosmos, human relation to the divine, the doctrines of grace and original sin, the meaning and significance of incarnation and physicality—these and particular moments of historical crisis, like the Pelagian controversy, the Gnostic menace, the Origenist debates, all combined to render the dangers inherent in preexistence weightier than its virtues. That the ideas with which preexistence was associated and interconnected, rather than the inherent deficiencies of the doctrine, caused its official banishment seems evident in the resilience with which preexistence not only survived but proliferated in succeeding centuries in myriad forms and genres.

In the 1930s, Albert Einstein attempted to bequeath the religious and theological papers of his only serious intellectual rival, Sir Isaac Newton, to some of the greatest universities in the Western world. Incredibly, Harvard, Yale, and Princeton, like Cambridge, the British Museum, and the Royal Society before them, were not interested.[13] For Newton's personal papers revealed the embarrassing fact that the father of classical mechanics was also a devout student of alchemy, esoteric wisdom, Solomonic mysteries, and biblical prophecy. The same sense of modern intellectual reasonableness, a jealous concern for the reputation of the deceased, and a cultural deference to canons of Christian orthodoxy that are only now succumbing to more militantly secular critical standards can also be seen at work in the long history of preexistence. Since Newton's era especially, the divide between religious and scientific investigations has become more and more pronounced. Newton's contemporary and teacher Henry More, who positioned himself as a foremost defender of the new scientific spirit of the age, who proselytized for Descartes and embraced Copernicus even while Newton hedged, was already becoming an anachronism as he simultaneously and comfortably acknowledged that he was a believer in witchcraft and demons.

The moral here is that wishing away Newton's religious papers does not simply inhibit our understanding of the man by denying a more complex portrait of him as a product of earlier historical conditions. Those papers also illuminate a powerful point about the ways that paradigms serve to make experience intelligible, mirror the still ongoing struggle to find a synthesis of the material and suprasensible realms, and prompt questions as to exactly which religious and philosophical yearnings those models were thought to successfully address. In a similar way, historical tendencies to suppress, downplay, or deliteralize the centuries-long belief in preexistence miss the point. Whether the human soul precedes birth is a religious question, and whether Plato really believed it is a trivial one. What the paradigm portends for the larger intellectual, religious, and literary worlds it engages is immensely illuminating. This point is clear in the case of a historically pervasive paradigm like the great chain of being. That vision of the cosmos as a scale of existence with infinite gradations arranged in hierarchical fashion both informed and reflected profoundly held beliefs that ranged from humans' relationship to deity, to legitimate ways of ordering society, to the assumed purpose and standards of artistic representation. Questions about the chain of being's metaphysical status in the minds of its adherents or the literalness with which they embraced it would obscure the larger fact of its ideological and practical significance, its enormous historical impact as a model that helped to order personal, religious, and political life. The same principle may be urged in regard to preexistence. Nietzsche championed this insight when he chose, in his own investigations into the history of morals, to reconfigure the problem of good and evil's ontological status and revolutionized the study of ethics in the process. Hitherto, he wrote, the independent reality of evil had been a given, and philosophers and theologians had only plumbed the question of its origin in the world. Nietzsche's project was to approach the subject with a different set of questions:

> What was at stake was the *value* of morality.... Under what conditions did man devise these value judgments good and evil? *and what value do they themselves possess?* Have they hindered or furthered human prosperity? Are they a sign of distress, of impoverishment, of the degeneration of life? Or is there revealed in them, on the contrary, the plenitude, force, and will of life, its courage, certainty, future? (emphasis in original)[14]

Similarly, we might ask, what are the conditions, agendas, and purposes under which philosophers, theologians, and poets have turned time and again to explore and develop the theory of preexistence?

The history of preexistence is far from linear or straightforward. The idea assumes the form, at various times and even in the same proponent, of any combination of theological conviction and poetic trope, literal belief and allegory, crude myth and philosophical abstraction. Motives range from earnest to speculative to playful, and the idea's appeal can extend far beyond the simple set of themes I have chosen to emphasize. These themes in any case blur into each other and fail to fully capture the scope and richness of the formal defenses, poetic celebrations, and implicit apologies for preexistence. But they recur often enough to suggest that serious thinkers over a span of more than two millennia have believed that significant intellectual, religious, and emotional ends were well served by the notion of a human soul that arrived in mortality, "trailing clouds of glory," having originated in a time and place the other side of birth.[15]

1

Ancient Near Eastern Traditions

Pre-existence in and of itself appears as a matter almost of idle speculation. But the biblical writers make it for us an essentially religious affirmation.... Paul and others were not introducing a startling innovation.

—Paul E. Davies[1]

Mesopotamian Myth

Quite obviously, the concept of the soul had to itself evolve before questions of its origin could arise. The idea that the body is possessed of some animating principle or some entity that is the seat of life is thousands of years old. Different traditions have accorded this soul or spirit varying degrees of substantial existence separate and apart from the body. Not all traditions conceived of the soul as immaterial, and not all accorded it survival beyond the death of the body. In the earliest creation accounts of which we have record, on the other hand, ideas about the human soul are found with intimations that the soul is traceable to a pre-mortal origin. "The oldest religion we are aware of," writes Jean Bottéro, "is the religious system of ancient Mesopotamia, dating from the fourth millennium B.C. to shortly before the birth of Christ."[2] One of that civilization's creation narratives recounts an assembly of gods, who are convened to plan the making of humans under extraordinary circumstances. Both the ensuing narrative and the etymology of the characters involved provide a window into the emergence of the idea of a human soul, its genesis in the heavens, and its ambiguous status in the universe. A panoply of threads are present that will weave in and out of subsequent mythologies of the soul's origins and potential destiny.

The cosmos of Mesopotamian mythology is populated by two races, both divine but vastly unequal. It is the lesser of these deities, rather than humans, who populate the earth. According to *Atrahasis*, an Akkadian poem dating to circa 1700 BCE, it is they who

> bore the work and suffered the toil—
> The toil of the gods was great,
> The work was heavy, the distress was much—
> The Seven great Anunnaki
> Were making the Igigi suffer the work.[3]

They sculpt the mountains, dig the rivers, and irrigate the land. So burdensome does their toil grow that they unite in protest and threaten war against the seven ruler gods. These greater gods convene a council to consider the problem, and one of their number, Enki, proposes a brilliant solution: they will create a race of humans, made of clay, to perform the undesirable tasks that provoked the first strike in cosmic history. To animate this new creation and make it capable of fulfilling work previously performed by gods, it is deemed necessary to infuse it with a divine element. This necessary ingredient, it is proposed, will come from a slain god. Not just any deity will suffice. They choose one named We for the sacrifice and stress the particular reasons for selecting that god:

> From [We's] flesh and blood
> Let Nintu mix clay
> That god and man
> May be thoroughly mixed in the clay....
> Let there be a spirit [*etemmu*] from the god's flesh.
> Let it proclaim living [man] as its sign,
> So that this be not forgotten, let there be a spirit [*etemmu*]....
> We-ila, who had personality [*temu*],
> They slaughtered in their assembly.
> From his flesh and blood
> Nintu mixed clay.
> From the flesh of the god [there was] a spirit.[4]

We is selected, in other words, because he is both divine (*ilu*) and possessed of a spirit (*temu*). The etymology of the resulting product reflects the theological reasoning behind this creation myth, writes Bottéro:

By adding to We the mention of his divine nature, *ilu*, one obtained the Akkadian word for "human being": (*a*)*welu*, or *awilu*. And if one also joined to the name We the reminder of his "spirit" [*temu*], the combination gave (*w*)*etem*(*m*)*u*, which designated everything that remained of a person after death: "ghost."[5]

The derivation Bottéro asserts of *awilu* (human) from We (a god only appearing in this epic) and *ilu* (god) may be a folk etymology, but the author of *Atrahasis* almost certainly invented or invoked We in order to suggest such a linguistic connection. (Other scholars agree on the deliberate "similarity in sound and punning.")[6] The author, at any rate, finds in the very name for human the echo of both a god and the divinity he imparted to humans. Myth and etymology alike, then, confirm that primal humans consist of an element traceable to the divine. As Tzvi Abusch concludes, the god We is the source of the "soul that imbues the individual with life and consciousness."[7] Likewise with the second etymology, *etemmu* (human spirit or ghost), which Bottéro sees as deriving from We (the god) and *temu* (which can mean personality, inspiration, intelligence, or rationality—whatever it is that constitutes the essence of divine beings).[8] It is clear that man's *etemmu*, or spirit, derives from We's *temu*, or essence, mythically if not etymologically as well. The human *etemmu* and the divine *temu*, with their close ontological and linguistic affinity, maintain nonetheless one crucial distinction. The word *etemmu*, in Mesopotamian belief, signified that which remained of a person after death. It was an immortal spirit, rooted in a preexisting *temu*. But in the process of its mortal incarnation, it becomes "a distant and pale shadow of divine immortality, so that he would never seek immortality further."[9]

As W. G. Lambert and A. R. Millard point out, "it was a common Mesopotamian view that man had a spirit that survived death." However, *Atrahasis* is the only surviving creation narrative in either Akkadian or Sumerian that attempts to explicate the origin and nature of this spirit.[10] In this particular case, the conditions of human origins and the semantics themselves suggest not just the seeds of a conception of human preexistence, but also that very ambivalence about human origins that will haunt the entire history of preexistence and inform critiques and debates from Tertullian to the present. In this Akkadian word for human being, we see human identity as a divine-human hybrid, with roots in the realm of the gods. But in the word for man's post-mortal essence, we find, as Bottéro reminds us, a derivative at one remove from the immortal spirit of the god. Or, as Abusch writes, the myth suggests that this "creation of the human from a slain god imparts not only immortality or divinity to man but also mortality,"[11] reflecting an implicit wariness or apprehension about humans reading into their divine origins an invitation to theosis (or elevation to god-like status). And thus are clearly foreshadowed in this formula both the allure and the danger of human aspirations toward the divine.

Western history records multiple versions of this tension between divine nature and human limitations, between portentous origins and dangerous presumption. The fall of Icarus, the fall of Lucifer and myriad angels, the tragedy of Eden, the Faustian yearning for transcendence can all be read as the playing out of this millennia-long contest between simple apokatastasis, or restoration, on the one hand, and vaulting ambition and the path to perdition, on the other. This early anthropology of the human condition explains the mortal striving for deification as both natural destiny and supreme blasphemy. In fact, virtually all of the seeds for subsequent philosophical elaboration and theological controversy regarding the prehistory of the human soul are here. The spirit is specifically invoked as that which distinguishes humans from other beings in the created order of things and makes them nearer the gods than all other creatures. The spark of divinity in the human breast beckons to a heavenly home, even as it is a temptation to hubris, to step beyond the assigned link in the great chain of being, and incur divine displeasure or even wrath.

The council of the gods approves Enki's plan, and the creation of the human proceeds. The exact wording of the plan's actual execution establishes a precedent not just for the kind of dualism that will develop in Judeo-Christianity, but also for a creation of spirit and body that lacks perfect simultaneity. Conception, says *Atrahasis*, occurs as a "deposit" of an already existing divine substance, taken from the god, into the "matrices" of the clay "prototype."[12] Sharing the very blood of the gods, the human is both kin and threat. And the deposit that inaugurates life and guarantees immortality precedes that life, having its origin in the heavens among the gods themselves. Such origins are portrayed here as simple myth, and the spirit or soul itself is not yet developed to the point of constituting the core identity of humankind; it is but a vague shadow of selfhood. But it is a start. For the language and mythology of this poem suggest that it was thought necessary, in order to create this species called human, to have recourse to a divine entity possessed of spirit, and the union of the preexistent, divine aspect and the created shell together constitute "man."

Divine Assemblies

The council of the gods, the divine assembly, is a common motif in Mesopotamian texts. It will pass into the Ugaritic tradition (fl. 14th–13th century BCE) and survive clearly in Hebraic religious texts. The motif is important to the subject of pre-mortal existence in two ways besides the thematic foreshadowings discussed above. First, in addition to planning the creation of the cosmos or of humankind in particular, divine assemblies sometimes did the work of foreordaining mortals. And the object of such foreordination is at times intimated to be pre-mortal humans. And second, the divine assemblies themselves embody a sophisticated organization that will later take the form of complex hierarchies involving gradations of angels, spirit powers, and, in some later variants, humans.

The creation of a human being following council deliberation in *Atrahasis* is not far removed from the image of the first human featured in the biblical book of Job. The questions presented to Job by his antagonist, Eliphaz, concerning the primal human reflect an early notion that the first human being existed prior to the creation of the earth:

> Are you the firstborn of the human race?
> Were you brought forth before the hills?
> Have you listened in the council of God? (Job 15:7–8)[13]

The interrogation suggests that the first human was in fact "brought forth" before the formation of the hills. This person therefore participated, at least from Eliphaz's perspective, in the planning session of the heavenly council. As Dexter Callender has observed regarding the query: "The allusion to the primal human in Job does not give us explicit details concerning his incorporation into the sacred world; it is clear, however, that the idea is present in the reference that the primal human, 'listened' in the council of God."[14]

Foreordination

The election by the gods of human beings for particular tasks or positions is a frequent motif in Near Eastern texts.[15] A prominent example of election that involves foreordination occurs in the prologue to the Babylonian Laws of Hammurabi, roughly contemporaneous with the Akkadian poem cited above:[16]

> When the august god Anu, king of the Anunnaku deities, and the god Enlil, lord of heaven and earth, who determines the destinies of the land, allotted supreme power over all peoples to the god Marduk, the firstborn son of the god Ea, exalted him among the Igigu deities, named the city of Babylon.... At that time, the gods Anu and Enlil, for the enhancement of the well-being of the people, named me by my name: Hammurabi, the pious prince, who venerates the gods, to make justice prevail in the land, to abolish the wicked and the evil, to prevent the strong from oppressing the weak, to rise like the sun-god Shamash over all humankind, to illuminate the land.[17]

Three events are described as transpiring in this divine assembly. The deity Marduk is accorded his dominions, the city of Babylon is given its name, and the unborn Hammurabi is foreordained to his earthly throne. This prologue is clearly political in nature and does not in any case necessitate that Hammurabi existed at the time— long before his birth—that he was divinely elected to his mortal office. Such appointment is likely based on divine foreknowledge, rather than the actual pre-mortal existence of Hammurabi. The purpose here is apparently to endow Hammurabi with the authority and prestige such divine foreordination conveys, not to propound an anthropology of the human soul. Still, foreordination and divine assemblies, like the divine substance that animates creatures formed of clay, will be incorporated and elaborated more fully in the biblical narratives of the Hebrew Bible. They thus constitute part of the repertoire of motifs and settings that will be developed into or associated with the actual creation of the human soul before birth.

Near the end of Israel's First Temple period (roughly 1000–600 BCE), the theme of foreordination of mortals that we saw in the prologue to Hammurabi's code finds its clearest echo in the book of Jeremiah. "Before I formed you in the womb I knew you, and before you were born I consecrated you; I appointed you a prophet to the nations" (Jer. 1:5). Such an allusion (and the kindred calling of the Lord's servant Israel "before [he] was born" and from his "mother's womb"; Isa. 49:1), as in the Babylonian instance, could merely suggest foreknowledge. But it is certainly at least as possible, in this case, that while foreknowledge can be interpreted as divine prescience, sanctifying and ordaining require an entity to be sanctified and ordained. A passage in Psalms, while not as clear in its language, similarly suggests a pre-mortal origin to humans. "My frame was not hidden from you," the psalmist says, "when I was being made in secret, intricately woven in the depths of the earth" (139:15). Phillip Johnson has observed that this verse "unusually locates individual origin in 'the depths of the earth,' though whether this is mother earth or the underworld is unclear."[18] That the latter is intended as a possibility has both biblical and linguistic support. The Hebrew word used here, 'ares, or earth, is related to the Akkadian word ersetu, which denotes both earth, in a cosmic sense, and the netherworld.[19] Even more closely related to the Hebrew term is the Ugaritic 'eres, which likewise refers to both earth and the underworld.[20] A biblical passage that implies the latter is Jonah's statement that he "went down to the land ['ha'ares] whose bars closed upon me forever,"—or so it seemed, until, he rejoices, "you brought up my life from the Pit, O Lord my God" (Jon. 2:6). Psalm 139 therefore evinces the belief that the human soul was created in a different, under- or otherworldly sphere to which it will someday return. And the possibility of new light on the curse of Adam is raised: "By the sweat of your face you shall eat bread until you return to the ground, for out of it you were taken" (Gen. 2:19).

Heavenly courts and preexistence come into closer contact, at least according to some readers, in a contested passage of Deuteronomy. E. Theodore Mullen describes the setting of the poem of chapter 32 as yet another instance where "the assembly is gathered....The setting is clearly that of a law court."[21] It was in this setting that "the Most High apportioned the nations, when he divided humankind, he fixed the boundaries of the peoples according to the number of the gods." There seems little doubt that these gods ("sons of God" in some translations, like the New English Bible [NEB]) are heavenly beings, whether members of the divine assembly or not. The expression "sons of Israel" in the King James (KJV) translation (or "Israel" in the Jewish Publication Society [JPS] version) reflects manuscript traditions (the Masoretic text has "yisrael") that were stripped of any polytheistic implications, writes Ronald Hendel. The original reference is "indeed divine beings."[22] The Septuagint, the oldest Greek translation of the Hebrew Bible, agrees about the divine entities, though with different language: when God separated the sons of Adam, it reads, the division took place "according to the number of the angels of God" (*kata arithmon angellon theou*). These translational differences reflect the progressive excision of traditions that described heaven as being peopled by more divine beings than God. It would seem, for example, that the "sons of god" (*bene elyon, bene elim,* or *bene elohim*), who had formerly been considered of divine rank, have by the last centuries BCE been demoted to the status of mere angels in Jewish thought.[23]

But the real question that this particular passage raises is, why apportion land in accordance with the number of the heavenly hosts—or of Israel? Church father Origen read the Septuagint and seemed to find in the verse an indication that these "angels" referred to the pre-mortal souls who would inhabit the various nations.[24] And he found that unsurprising since he was sure that men and angels both preexist the earth and in fact can refer to the same kind of being. In glossing the Deuteronomy passage, he finds these particular angels to be an example of "certain different orders" that pertain to human beings. Elsewhere, Origen repeated this point, writing that the "third order of rational creatures" consists of "the souls of men [who are] assumed in consequence of their moral progress into the order of angels."[25]

Taking the text to refer instead to "Israel" or "sons of Israel" may have led just as inevitably to a conception of preexistence—either ideal or actual. This is because the point of the apportionment described in the passage is to make of Jacob (or the people of Israel) "the Lord's own portion,...his allotted share," according to God's divine wisdom or foreknowledge (32:9). As Adolf Harnack pointed out, the logic, if not the exact language, of passages like this, which saw Israel's inheritance as divinely apportioned in a distant past, led Jewish thought to preexistence. "If the world was created for the sake of the people of Israel, and the Apocalyptists expressly taught that, then it follows, that in the thought of God Israel was older than the world. The idea of a kind of pre-existence of the people of Israel follows from this."[26]

Populous Heavens

The divine assembly, peopled by gods in Ugaritic texts, appears as a grouping of various heavenly figures in several passages of the Hebrew Bible. While Jeremiah's foreordination is the most explicit Old Testament instance suggesting a preexistent past for a particular individual, an equally striking and even more contested passage is Psalm 82. The court of heaven is referred to by name, a plurality of gods is mentioned, and an explicit connection between those divinities and mortal humans is indicated:

> God has taken his place in the divine council;
> in the midst of the gods he holds judgment:
> How long will you judge unjustly
> and show partiality to the wicked?...
> I say, "You are gods,
> children of the Most High, all of you;
> nevertheless, you shall die like mortals,
> and fall like any prince." (Ps. 82:1–7)

The translation and meaning of this psalm, which was invoked by Jesus in the New Testament (John 10) and apparently refers to a plurality of deities, are vigorously disputed. Accused by his Jewish audience of making himself the equal of God, Jesus responds by saying, "is it not written in your law, I said, Ye are gods. If he called them gods,... [do I blaspheme] because I said, I am the son of God?" (John 10:34–36). The exact significance of Jesus's allusion to gods is unclear, but in context this citation of the passage can only be effective if he is affirming the psalmic reference to other gods or god-like beings.[27] Otherwise, it would hardly serve to soften or justify his own claim to divinity.

Who these pre-mortal sons of God are or how the gods in the divine assembly will come to die as men are likewise far from clear. Yet Yahweh is here condemning the sons of God, the *bene elohim*, to mortality. As another scholar writes, the passage "means that they must forfeit completely their original, divine nature, and with it undoubtedly whatever divine powers and prerogatives they possessed, and take on the nature of human beings and in particular become subject to death, become mortal."[28] The sons of God appear in another pre-mortal scene, in which Job is asked where he was when God "laid the foundation of the earth," "when the morning stars sang together and all the heavenly beings shouted for joy" (38:4, 7).

Another vivid description of a divine assembly in the Hebrew Bible is found in the story of the wicked King Ahab (871–852 BCE) in the book of Kings. A prophet named Micaiah appears before the king and forecasts divine retribution for Ahab's misdeeds. He describes the remarkable conditions under which God decreed Ahab's fate:

> Then Micaiah said, "Therefore hear the word of the Lord: I saw the Lord sitting on his throne, with all the host of heaven standing beside him to the right and to the left of him." And the Lord said, "Who will entice Ahab, so that he may go up and fall at Ramoth-gilead?" Then one said one thing, and another said another, until a spirit came forward and stood before the Lord, saying, "I will entice him." "How?" the Lord asked him. He replied, "I will go out and be a lying spirit in the mouth of all his prophets." Then the Lord said, "You are to entice him, and you shall succeed; go out and do it." (1 Kings 22:19–22)

Angelic emissaries sent to do the bidding of God are not unusual in the Bible. Striking in this case is the picture presented of a heavenly council peopled with entities whom God consults before taking important steps pertaining to human affairs. Similar, though less detailed scenes appear when God countenances the temptation of Job in another convocation of the court of heaven involving the "sons of God" (*bene elohim*) along with "the accuser" (*ha-satan*; Job 1); surrounded by several "attendants," God asks for a volunteer to go forth to his people and commissions Isaiah, after asking, "Whom shall I send, and who will go for us?" (Isa. 6:8). Job 15:8, as we saw, also posits a primal human in the divine council before the world was created ("Have you listened in the council of God?").[29]

Other heavenly characters are intimated in the words of Moses:

> The Lord came from Sinai,
> and dawned from Seir upon us;
> he shone forth from Mount Paran.
> With him were myriads of holy ones;
> at his right, a host of his own. (Deut. 33:2–3)

Theodore Mullen argues that these "Holy Ones…are the members of Yahweh's court," whom we also see in Psalm 68:18 and in several other Old Testament scenes.[30] In addition to these "holy ones" (*qedosim*), other terms for the various members, some of which we have already encountered, include "sons of gods/gods" or "sons of El" (*bene elim*), "sons of the Most High/Elyon" (*bene elyon*), and "sons of God" (*bene ha elohim*).[31] Against the background of the heavenly council, such beings appear as more than simple angelic hosts who provide filler for Renaissance artists. They will provide the basis for what Mullen calls "the development of an elaborate angelology wherein there were specific ranks and hierarchies of divine beings."[32]

Not all divine beings that populate the Hebrew Bible are of the angelic variety. Moving in the other direction from angels is what one scholar calls "the bald allusion to the *Nephilim* (lit. fallen ones) in Gen[esis] 6," where sons of god ("divine beings" in the JPS) mingle with daughters of men, producing strange progeny translated as "giants" in the KJV. This passage has long proved daunting to commentators, but it unarguably raises again the specter of a breach of the divine-human divide. The episode accomplishes this by a kind of hierarchical miscegenation that produces a monstrous hybrid. But the actions of these purported "sons of God" themselves reveal, as much as they engender, a profound fall from divine station. As Moses Aberbach holds, misleading translations (fallen ones = giants) and official targums cannot entirely obscure a "'fallen angels' tradition which exploited the plain etymology of the word, from *npl* 'to fall.'"[33] Here, then, we find a powerful reinforcement for some of those traditions which will later feature intersecting angels and men, pre-mortal deeds and earthly repercussions. The ambiguity surrounding their origin collides with the clear implications of the etymology. P. W. Coxon asks:

> Were these superhuman creatures,...or can they be regarded as completely human[?]...The NT notion of the fallen angels who like Satan (Luke 10:18) plummeted to earth because they failed to recognize their position in the divine hierarchy (2 Pet. 2:4; Jude 6) has clear allusions to the Nephilim.... Etymologically, the basis of Nephilim is transparent. This explains the wealth of allusions which exploits the *fall* from heaven.[34]

Such references to fallen ones, morning stars, angels, and sons of God are but ghostly remnants of an entire cosmology now mostly lost to us. Moshe Halbertal and Avishai Margalit point out that, in early monotheistic traditions:

> [T]he gap between God and human beings is filled by the intermediary forces of angels, constellations, and demons. The world of divinity becomes a kind of complex bureaucratic system, or an emanated chain of being.... Hierarchical and organic conceptions of the world of divinity stand in opposition to the picture of simple unity of the philosophers.[35]

But most biblical translations render a vast array of different terms as "angels," blurring the original distinctions and collapsing an intricately tiered and variously populated heaven into a monochromatic landscape. We have here the mythic material that either resurfaces as or is refashioned into a number of cosmologies in which various pre-mortal beings—including humans—participated in heavenly scenes of foreordination, consultation, rebellion, and expulsion. These latter themes of divine beings who descend, out of punishment or challenge, to take upon themselves human bodies become firmly established in the early Christian era. By then, myriad cultures and influences have become disseminated and interfused by the Hellenistic revolution. Mesopotamia, whence we traced the earliest attestations of these ideas,

was one of many kingdoms to find its religious system utterly reinvented in the aftermath of Alexander's conquests. One of these systems, called astral religion, rendered
the vague mythology of the Akkadians much more explicit and pronounced about
the origins of human identity and the purpose of life:

> The human was not, as had been thought, simply a body, a carnal mass: to
> animate and enhance him he above all had a "spirit," in itself independent
> from the body, a "soul" existing by itself, created foremost by the divine
> stars in their celestial dwellings....At birth the soul descended to join the
> material body....At the time of death, freed from its carnal attachments
> to the body, which then returned to matter, the soul returned to its celes-
> tial homeland, gradually becoming more enriched by the luminous and
> beatific attributes that were conferred upon it by the sovereign stars.[36]

How did such a transition occur, from the vague intimations of a human spirit
with a divine provenance in *Atrahasis*, to the independent and preexistent human
soul of astral religion described above? These may have been internal developments; it is also possible that they resulted from the Greek conquests. The general
consensus of scholars is that the versions of preexistence appearing in the Jewish
and Christian traditions at this time derive from Plato and from the utter transformation of religious thought in the wake of Hellenization. However, significant
differences between the Hellenic and Hebraic versions are apparent, one of which
was noted a century ago by Frank Porter: "To the Greek the soul that pre-exists was
or tended to be the personality, the man's real thinking self; while to the Jew it was
only a part of the coming man."[37] Porter pointed out that the core scriptural text in
this regard is Genesis 2:7, according to which a human is constituted dualistically,
of earthly clay and divine breath or spirit. As he reasoned, "this breath or spirit
of God seemed to the Hebrews to belong to God to such a degree that for a long
time they did not even individualize each man's share in it, still less connect with
it the man's personal consciousness." Only gradually does the idea emerge that the
breath of God "was also for each man in some sense a distinct entity." The different
paths of development, Porter postulated, were reflected in (or conditioned by) the
incommensurate terms with which we are dealing here:

> There is scarcely a greater cause of confusion and difficulty in the compre-
> hension of Hebrew modes of thought than the tendency—in part, to be
> sure, the necessity—that impels us to translate *nephesh* by the word "soul."
> The *nephesh* is the life or the self of man, the living man himself, just as
> he is here and now. The older Hebrews had no word for body (*soma*) and
> what we call body was not to them the opposite of *nephesh*, but was insep-
> arable from it....The pre-existence of the *neshamah* [breath or spirit] is a
> very different thing from the pre-existence of the *psyche*.[38]

Adolf Harnack also argued that Jewish and Hellenic conceptions of preexistence were "as wide apart as the poles."[39] In the former case, he wrote, "according to the theory held by the ancient Jews and by the whole of the Semitic nations, everything of real value that from time to time appears on earth has its existence in heaven." True enough, its existence is bound up in God—but he is at pains to insist that this does not reduce it to the status of the merely foreknown. "It has a real being....It exists beforehand with God in the same way as it appears on earth, that is with all the material attributes belonging to its essence. Its manifestation on earth is merely a transition from concealment to publicity." With Greek conceptions, on the other hand, the objects themselves are "meant to be ennobled" by their preexistence. They have no relation to God. And their material appearance is regarded as derivative and inferior.[40] Only slightly more recently, Paul Davies insisted that the Hebrew emphasis on the unity of body and spirit precluded an independent or prior existence for that spirit. Apparent references to such, as in Psalm 139 and Jeremiah, he relegated to "ideal existence in the mind and purpose of God."[41] Ideal existence may be one form that Jewish preexistence could assume, but we will see myriad examples that suggest alternative conceptions which impute something closer to autonomy to the pre-mortal spirit.

Jewish thought would develop under increasing Greek influence, but Hamerton-Kelly also points to three distinctly Jewish ideas that give to the Jewish conception of preexistence its particular cast. The theology of "promise and fulfillment" suggested that the future was already present in God's mind. The almost material presence of God's name is a "foreshadowing of the later idea of pre-existent hypostases." And, perhaps most powerfully, the visions of the prophets (he mentions our case of Jeremiah) imply the existence of a "heavenly world which contains the pre-existent things."[42] Other scholars agree that the notion that everything which is to be revealed in the eschaton preexists in heaven is "a commonplace of apocalyptic thought."[43]

The Platonic influence on Judeo-Christianity notwithstanding, a confused but consistent picture emerges of a Semitic tradition that was already populating heaven with various orders of beings and assemblies and that engendered, if it did not already involve, a conception of human participation in a heavenly realm. At least, as Gerald Bostock asserts, "it can reasonably be argued that the Platonic and Pythagorean view of pre-existence was already akin to Jewish thought, and was duly incorporated into it."[44] All we know for sure is that, when we encounter Semitic treatments of human preexistence in the early Christian era, they are within a Jewish culture that has been affected by a host of influences, including Babylonian myth, Ugaritic traditions, and most important, the philosophy of the classical world.

2

Classical Varieties

One of the chief perils in the exegesis of ancient writings is that we should take figuratively that which in origin was meant quite realistically.... Even the professed student will often take the short cut of calling the ancient usage a figure of speech. That can be perilous.

—H. Wheeler Robinson[1]

Pythagoras and Orpheus

In the world of Roman Palestine, whatever Semitic and Eastern sources and influences infiltrated the West were largely swallowed up in the fervently cosmopolitan culture of Hellenism, which had its own admixture of religious, philosophical, and esoteric ingredients circulating throughout the Mediterranean world. The paternity of the ideas related to preexistence becomes hopelessly entangled as a result. Of course, and this is a crucial fact, even if we had recourse to earlier Greek religious texts than those available to us, it is unlikely we could trace Hellenic ideas about preexistence of the soul much further into the past. This is because the idea of the soul as an entity that is at least to some degree self-aware and independent probably developed in classical thought between the ages of Homer and Plato. As Werner Jaeger reminds us:

> [W]e look in vain in the Homeric epics, the *Iliad* and the *Odyssey*, for the view that men survive their bodies. The Trojan war sent

to Hades the ψυχαί [psyches, spirits] of many heroes, whereas "they themselves" were thrown to the dogs and birds of prey. "They themselves" means their bodies; some modern interpreters have concluded that the ψυχή that goes to the underworld must be something like the soul, especially since "soul" is the later meaning of the word ψυχή. But Homer describes the ψυχαί of the dead as mere shadows without conscious life or mental activity.[2]

The soul that in Homer's view survived death was far from synonymous with the seat of personality or individual human identity. In Homer and many subsequent literary works, the "shades" that visitors to Hades encounter are eerily and disturbingly incomplete vestiges of personhood. Only over time did the belief expressed by Plato of the soul as an immaterial entity, the true self temporarily housed in a material body, take shape.

Two more or less associated religious systems, Orphism and Pythagoreanism, figure as precursors to Plato's ideas concerning the soul's prehistory. The first translator of Plato's entire corpus into English, Thomas Taylor, flatly asserted that "all the Grecian theology is the progeny of the mystic doctrines of Orpheus; Pythagoras first of all learning from Aglaophemus the orgies of the gods, but Plato in the second place receiving an all-perfect science…from the Pythagoric and Orphic writings."[3] William Guthrie finds in these two Greek sources, originating in close proximity in the second half of the sixth century BCE, the first evidence of "the sharply dualistic conception of body and soul, according to which the former is no more than the tomb or prison of the latter."[4] These two philosophies are also the first, not coincidentally, to use "psyche" to denote "the essential human 'self': not only the life-principle, and thus the principle of growth and motion, but also the seat of feeling, thought, and decision."[5]

Still, Pythagoras and Orpheus are only two of the most celebrated figures in the classical world associated with authoritative doctrines in this regard. Plato's student Aristotle gives us a picture of a Hellenic world energetically divided among competing conceptions of human nature and the soul's origins. Faced with a sprawling array of creative mythologies and what he sees as silly speculations on the subject, Aristotle judges most of them to be sorely deficient—including the popular pair mentioned above.

> But the following absurdity goes with both this account and most of those that concern the soul. They attach the soul to the body and set it into it, determining no further what the cause of this is or what the condition of the body is,…as though, in the manner of the Pythagorean myths, any random soul were to be clothed in any random body. [But] each body seems to have its own proper look and form.…[A different problem

arises] with the account given in the so-called Orphic verses, for they say that the soul comes in from the whole when things breathe, carried by the winds, but it is impossible for this to happen to...some of the animals, if not all of them breathe; but this has escaped the notice of those who have had this conception.[6]

The ideas of a number of pre-Socratics and even the more durable theories of Plato, we shall see, were not immune to Aristotle's skepticism. The philosopher's attack on contemporary opinions about the soul, which he wrote sometime in the fourth century BCE, is a valuable window into the Greek world. It reveals just how complicated an idea like soul can be and how diverse its uses even within a relatively circumscribed cultural tradition like ancient Greece. Along the way, Aristotle raises a critique of the soul/body paradigm that will resurface centuries later. Far from embracing the dualism of his mentor, Aristotle argues that the soul is not a spiritual being separate from the body, but the form of a particular body, and it thereby constitutes the individual in a total way. He emphatically rejects, accordingly, systems which imagine a preexistent soul capable of inhabiting other kinds of bodies. What immortality he does envision emerges in his discussion of the difference between passive and productive intellect (*nous*) in *De Anima* (III.5). Speaking of productive intellect, he says, "when separated it is just exactly what it is, and this alone is deathless and everlasting (though we have no memory, because this sort of intellect [the productive intellect] is not acted upon, while the sort that is acted upon [the passive intellect] is destructible, and without this nothing thinks)."[7] In other words, even Aristotle recognizes an aspect of the soul that is immortal, but the immortality of this aspect may not amount to a personal immortality, because, as he says, this durable aspect (not being passive) is not susceptible to memories. It would seem, then, that this immortal, productive intellect is one in which we jointly share as rational creatures.

About the origins of those doctrines Aristotle contests, especially Orphism, we know little for certain. But we do know something about the myths in which the figure of Orpheus appears. Shakespeare's Hamlet may have referred to death as "the undiscovered country from whose bourne no traveller returns," but if the poets are to be believed, a good number of travelers have done just that. Alcestis, Odysseus, Dionysus, and Psyche in the Greek world alone visited Hades and returned to tell the tale. Heroes, poets, and Hebrews from Aeneas to Dante to Lazarus would follow in their footsteps. In antiquity, however, the most famous visitor to the underworld was Orpheus, in unsuccessful pursuit of his beloved, Eurydice. His fame and vaunted knowledge of what lies beyond the veil of death engendered one of the mystery cults—Orphism—of the ancient world. Whether it even existed as a discrete religious system is doubtful; Orphism may have been simply a practice of invoking

Orpheus as an authority for any number of teachings. What rites the Orphics may have practiced were based on a set of poems attributed to the mythic hero, but written probably in the late sixth century BCE.[8] While its mysteries centered on the post-mortal existence of the soul, Orphism apparently involved teachings about its preexistence as well. Before Aristotle, Plato had made reference to Orphism, writing that members of the cult believed "that the soul is being punished for something, and that the body is an enclosure or prison in which the soul is securely kept…until the penalty is paid."[9]

Plato's extensive writings on preexistence are generally attributed to the influence of Pythagoras, but Pythagoras had little to say about preexistence per se, teaching rather a doctrine of transmigration of souls (metempsychosis). Transmigration can be one variety of preexistence, but does not necessarily entail the idea of the soul as having an independent existence prior to mortal incarnation. Neither does the preexistence of the soul imply a theory of multiple incarnations. Most classical scholars tend to conflate the two and write as if the ancients necessarily equated them as well;[10] Walter Burkert, for example, writes that if, as the Orphics professed, a person breathes in a soul at birth, "it is an almost unavoidable supplement to suppose that other living creatures, at their death[s], have 'breathed out' these same souls." However, it is not at all clear why death and subsequent births must involve these "same souls" in a kind of eternal recycling program; Burkert's logic would make reincarnationists of all Judeo-Christians, since they too generally believe that a soul enters a body sometime in the process of birth, or quickening, and leaves at the time of death. And, as Burkert himself asserts, "metempsychosis is not attested directly for in Orphism in any ancient source—only the pre-existence of the soul."[11]

One philosopher reputedly influenced by Orphic doctrines was Empedocles (c. 495–435 BCE), the originator of the idea that earth, air, water, and fire are the four primal elements of the universe and famous in antiquity for hurling himself into the volcano at Etna to confirm his godhood. Empedocles was thought to have imbibed his religious doctrines from Orphic streams, and he conflated the two ideas of preexistence and metempsychosis in his own writings. He calls the soul, writes Jaeger, "of divine origin,…the daemon that dwells upon this earth in exile from God," and believed that "from the unspeakable bliss of its heavenly home the soul came down to the confinement of this cave."[12] Empedocles' poem "On Purification" reflects his position in the tradition of theurgy, a spiritual process involving the soul's ascent (back) to God through successive stages tied to rites, knowledge acquisition, and spiritual refinement. Theurgy frequently, though not always, characterizes the ascent as a return to a condition of primordial bliss and purity, back to a time when the fallen human soul had wings.

It is in this context that metempsychosis attaches to the idea of preexistence, since successive incarnations represent progressive rungs of the ladder by which human beings recuperate a lost splendor. For Empedocles, then, it stands to reason that "I was born once a boy, and a maiden, and a plant, and a bird, and a darting fish in the sea."[13] The successive incarnations of the cycle of metempsychosis seem to have emerged in Orphic religion and elsewhere by way of reflecting the many layers of the great chain of being, which have come to separate the soul from its true home and to facilitate the laborious, incremental process necessary to recapture a faded glory. The point, in other words, is to draw the human mind to the initial state of preexistence as both memory of painful loss and promise of eventual destiny. This is why the contrast between a newfound embodiment and memory of the soul's first habitation provokes an initial shock and horror that at best can only dissipate into a tragic sense of the human condition. "And I wept and shrieked," wrote Empedocles, "on beholding the unwonted land where are Murder and Wrath, and other species of Fates, and wasting diseases, and putrefaction and fluxes....From what honor and how great a degree of blessedness have I fallen here on the earth to consort with mortal beings."[14]

About Pythagoras, we know little more than about Orphism. This is not surprising, for he lived in a "twilight period" between the shadows of myth and the light of Greek rationalism and came to fame "in an atmosphere of miracle, secrecy, and revelation."[15] Born in the early sixth century BCE on the island of Samos, he was reputed to have spent time in temples and centers of learning from Italy to Egypt to Phoenicia. (Wrongly) famous for the mathematical theorem that bears his name and probably wrongly credited with being the first to expound musical scales in mathematical terms, his historic role is most certain in relation to a number of mystical ideas and practices to which he gave shape and leadership.[16]

Pythagoreanism became not just a mathematical school, but a religious cult, with a set of rules and restrictions involving speech, diet, and behavior. His disciples included both general followers and an inner circle privy to the secret, higher truths he taught them personally. All in all, it seems rather too dismissive to write, as one scholar does, that his "ethical and religious teachings were...often bizarre and of little philosophical interest."[17] His teachings on the soul's origin and destiny exerted a profound influence on Plato and, through him, on the subsequent history this study unfolds. His particular doctrine of metempsychosis is "the one most certain fact in the history of early Pythagoreanism."[18] Just how that doctrine was related to, or if it involved, other claims about the human soul or its previous existence is a matter of conjecture. Almost no details about Pythagoras's teachings on the soul are verifiable. We know little more for certain than that Plato gathered either general inspiration or particular details from doctrines associated with Pythagoras. We may also trace to Orpheus and Pythagoras a doctrine that appears recurrently in connection with preexistence, a particular view of mortality's burden as necessary for the purification of the soul, to fit it for a return to its heavenly place of origin. Guthrie calls this the doctrine of *katharsis*, or purification;[19] it can imply preexistence to the extent that the purification is seen as recuperative or restorative. Plato, however, goes well beyond mere implication in his treatment of human preexistence.

Plato

With Plato himself, we may at last trace something that approaches a detailed prehistory of the soul. What sources he relied upon other than Pythagoras, or perhaps Orphic teachings, is impossible to discern. Augustine wrote that Plato "went even to Egypt, and studied whatever great things were held and taught there. Thence, he came to those parts of Italy where the fame of the Pythagoreans was celebrated, and there, studying under the most distinguished teachers, he very easily mastered whatever in Italian philosophy was then flourishing."[20] Similarly, the ancient Greek biographer of philosophers Diogenes Laertius wrote that Plato was personally familiar with several Pythagoreans whom he visited in southern Italy. It is perhaps telling

Plato, the most influential Western philosopher of antiquity, developed the motif of preexistence in several of his dialogues. *Herm of Plato*, c. 350 BCE, Bildarchiv Preussischer Kulturbesitz/Art Resource, New York.

that the interlocutor who opens the discussion in Plato's *Phaedo*, where Socrates invokes the doctrine of preexistence in the face of his own imminent death, is Echecrates, a Pythagorean philosopher.

To this synthesis of earlier ideas, Plato gives both poetic form and philosophical foundations in several of his dialogues, written sometime in the fourth century BCE. His commanding presence as the most important philosopher (along with Aristotle) of antiquity has two important repercussions for the subsequent history of the idea. First, the unequaled respect accorded him by both the early church and subsequent philosophers ensured that preexistence would—at least through the early Christian centuries—be accorded legitimacy as a respectable doctrine even if it was eventually to fall outside both intellectual and theological orthodoxy. That most of Western philosophy is a series of footnotes to Plato is particularly true in the case of preexistence. Most of the Christian philosophers and church fathers of the first Christian centuries, through and including Augustine, were committed Platonists. By and large, they found his metaphysics not just conformable with, but foundational to, the Christian theology they were in the process of elaborating. Second, Plato's commanding dominance as a philosopher and the authority, not to say the broad exposition, he lent the idea has meant that virtually all subsequent discussions of preexistence assume—often without specific evidence—Platonic inspiration or influence.

Plato first raises the specter of a preexistent realm of souls in *Meno*. The principal subject of the dialogue is virtue, but the immediate occasion is a statement Meno makes about human knowledge. Meno has been operating under the assumption that, in a philosophical exchange such as the one he entertains with Socrates, he will either prevail in defending his view of a principle or, more likely, be persuaded of the falseness of his position and be instructed in or guided to the truth by his mentor. In typical fashion, Socrates effectively discombobulates Meno in his earnest attempts to define virtue. Meno is perplexed, however, when instead of simply guiding him to his own version of the truth, the great teacher offers to "examine and seek together" for an understanding of virtue. He is perplexed because, as Socrates phrases his dilemma, "a man cannot search either for what he knows or for what he does not know. He cannot search for what he knows—since he knows it, there is no need to search—nor for what he does not know, for he does not know what to look for."[21]

This particular formulation of the problem may not be the most compelling; it is typically Platonic in its sophistical oversimplification. Obviously, a person may inquire the time, which he does not know, and be informed by one who does, and then both will know. And if neither person knows, they may take a reading from a sundial, and both will know. Plato's point, however, seems rather to be this: in cases where the subject is not a contingent fact, like the time of day or length of a board, but a conceptual apprehension or a knowledge of universals, then how can we "recognize" as true that of which we have no prior knowledge and for which no empirical verification is conceivable? This is a more genuinely compelling dilemma, one that will resonate for centuries across the philosophical tradition. In slightly transmuted form, it will become for Augustine the question: how can we hunger and search for a God, unless we have already known and loved him? For Descartes, it will be a problem to be solved by invoking innate ideas, the only alternative he can see to giving over the field of human knowledge entirely to the vagaries and inadequacies of sensory experience or inventions of the mind. Kant will reconstitute modern philosophy in navigating the same dilemma.

Socrates' solution to the quandary expressed by Meno is simple: strictly speaking, he agrees, we cannot recognize that of which we have no prior experience. Therefore, if we go in search of knowledge and find it, it must be like finding anything else that we once possessed and lost. It is rediscovery or, in his language, recollection (*anamnesis*). In introducing his recollection theory of knowledge, Plato refers to it as a "divine matter" that has come to him from certain priests and priestesses as well as from Pindar and "others of the divine among our poets." He summarizes the doctrine in these words: "as the soul is immortal, has been born often and has seen all things here and in the underworld, there is nothing which it has not learned; so it is in no way surprising that it can recollect the things it knew before, both about virtue and other things."[22]

His famous demonstration of this point follows in his interrogation of a slave boy who, with proper prodding, manages to recreate a proof of the Pythagorean theorem (that the sum of the squares of the two legs of a right triangle is equal to the hypotenuse squared). The boy blunders at first but is guided to a solution with apt questions, and Meno admiringly concedes, "I know that no one has taught him." "Yet he has these opinions, or doesn't he?" "That seems indisputable, Socrates." "If he has not acquired them in his present life, is it not clear that he had them and had learned them at some other time?" "It seems so."[23]

The debate continues as to whether Plato himself seriously maintained this theory of knowledge as recollection and the preexistence of souls.[24] It is possible that Plato merely finds the doctrine to be a powerful hypothesis, an account that functions as many myths do, employing an imaginative prehistory in order to make sense out of present realities. Certainly, he must have been aware of the weakness of his particular brand of evidence. Leading questions may, of course, convey implicit information rather than reveal latent knowledge. However, Plato appears to be quite serious in his presentation of the doctrine itself. Invoking a preexistent past to explain the human capacity for recognizing truth is not of the same order as weaving fanciful tales about how the leopard got his spots. There is profound philosophical earnestness surrounding Plato's employment of this paradigm, both here when he is trying to understand the nature of human virtue and plumb the wellsprings of human knowledge of divine things, and later, when he reintroduces the topic in the context of Socrates' impending execution and his accompanying quest to ascertain the reasonableness of self-consolation in the face of death. He also incorporates into this initial treatment of the theme an unusual testimonial: "Somehow, Socrates, I feel that what you say is right," says Meno of Socrates' argument for pre-mortal recollection. Then, confessing that his theory may have more affective appeal than rational proof behind it, Socrates adds, "I do not insist that my argument is right in all other respects, but I would contend at all costs both in word and deed as far as I could that we will be better men, braver and less idle, if we believe that one must search for the things one does not know."[25]

Plato returns to the theme of the soul's preexistence in *Phaedo*, his dialogue describing the death of Socrates. Here, too, there is a tone of moral earnestness, with Socrates saying that no one "who heard me now, not even a comic poet, could say that I am babbling and discussing things that do not concern me."[26] As before, Plato credits other sources for this "ancient theory" that our souls exist in the underworld and are born, apparently recurrently, into this one. He adds a new argument in this dialogue, that opposites are always generated out of opposites. So, as more comes from less and less from more, and sleep proceeds from waking and waking from sleep, so must the dead be generated from the living and, therefore, the living from the dead. If such is true, then living souls must come from a world below where they currently exist. Socrates' friend Cebes at that point reintroduces what he tellingly refers to as Socrates' pet doctrine: "for us learning is no other than recollection," which necessarily implies a previous time in which we have learned that which we now recollect. But this is only possible, he adds, "if our soul existed somewhere before it took on this human shape."[27]

For the probable benefit of those readers unfamiliar with *Meno*, Cebes recapitulates as evidence of the validity of this doctrine the example of the slave boy who is unconsciously proficient in math. Pressed to offer additional support, Cebes turns to more persuasive evidence than a too-compliant, mathematically inept youth. And in the argument that follows, Socrates puts the doctrine of preexistence on a new trajectory. Until now, his concept, which he obliquely credited to the Pythagoreans, had little to distinguish it from those roots and seemed but another variety of the transmigration of souls, multiple embodiments. It could for that reason be considered more a doctrine of multiple existence than preexistence, or pre-mortal existence. But when Socrates merges the Pythagorean conception with his distinctive brand of idealism, a new variety of human anthropology altogether emerges, one that establishes a sharp bifurcation and a qualitative distinction between mortal existence and a different kind of existence that came before it.

Plato reasons that, as rational beings, we all have knowledge of certain absolutes (the forms or ideas)—like Equality or Justice or the Beautiful. These ideal
absolutes are prior to, independent of, and in every way superior to the world
of phenomenal reality. The dualism that results—a universe divided between
the shadowy world of physicality and imperfection and a transcendent realm of
perfection, immutability, and immateriality—is the essence of Plato's whole philosophical system. And the task of philosophy itself is to elevate us from the particular to the universal, from the material to the spiritual, principally by overcoming
the allures and obstacles represented by the human body and its senses.[28] For "the
body keeps us busy in a thousand ways" and "makes for confusion and fear, so that
it prevents us from seeing the truth."[29] On the other hand, bodily perception of
the particular can lead us toward the universal, as when (he argues in *Symposium*)
the love of a particular beautiful body evolves in us to a love of all beautiful bodies, and then to a love of the beauty of institutions and laws. Eventually, we can
approach Beauty itself in its absolute, perfect ideality. In Cebes' simpler example,
"we see an equality in material things, like sticks and stones, and move as a consequence to the idea of equality itself."[30]

In *Meno*, Socrates points to certain mental acquisitions which cannot be
traced to one's particular mortal experience. The slave knows math, but he was
never taught. Therefore, he must have learned it somewhere previously, possibly
in another incarnation as allowed for by Pythagorean transmigration of souls. But
now Socrates is saying that, by our ability to intuit universals, we reveal faculties
of understanding which cannot be accounted for by this, or by any conceivable
previous, incarnation in human form. That launches us into a new realm, one of
pre-mortal, rather than merely prior, existence. In Socrates' summary of the case
for pre-mortal existence:

> Before we began to see or hear or otherwise perceive, we must have pos-
> sessed knowledge of the Equal itself if we were about to refer our sense
> perceptions of equal objects to it. . . . We must then have acquired the knowl-
> edge of the Equal . . . before birth. . . . Therefore, if we had this knowledge, we
> knew before birth and immediately thereafter not only the Equal.

We also knew the Good, the Beautiful, and all ideas or essential realities. As a consequence, "our souls also existed apart from the body, before they took on human
form, and they had intelligence."[31]

Plato develops his theory of the human soul and its origins yet further in his
Phaedrus. He clearly establishes the soul as unbegotten, indestructible, and immortal. Whereas the soul was described as unitary in *Phaedo*, in this dialogue it is tripartite. The highest faculty of soul, reason, is compared to a charioteer who struggles
to maintain control over and harmony between two horses. The first is "beautiful

and good and from stock of the same sort, while the other is the opposite and has the opposite sort of bloodline."[32] Not all charioteers succeed, and the resulting disharmony drags the chariot earthward. "A soul that sheds its wings wanders until it lights on something solid, where it settles and takes on an earthly body, which then, owing to the power of this soul, seems to move itself. The whole combination of soul and body is called a living thing, or…'mortal.'"[33] With this myth, Plato characterizes mortality as a demotion from heavenly realms and every human incarnation as an individualized fall.

No rebellious souls, these, no Luciferian revolts. For all souls aspire to remain in the heavenly realms, where they can behold "the plain where truth stands." Pasturage is found there "which is the right food for the best part of the soul, and it is the nature of the wings that lift up the soul to be nourished by it."[34] But falling short, some of these souls drop to the ground to be reborn according to the degree of truth they have beheld. To be human, in this conception, is to be assured of actually, at one time, having "seen reality; otherwise, no soul could have entered this sort of living thing [mortal form]. But not every soul is easily reminded of the reality there by what it finds here."[35] Implicit in this Platonic scheme is a view of mortality as educative rather than simply punitive, though there is no question that incarnation is a form of debasement. Plato also foreshadows the nostalgia of Milton's fallen Lucifer, when he wistfully invokes

> [that] time when the souls, along with the glorious chorus (we were with [God]…) saw that blessed and spectacular vision…and we gazed in rapture at sacred revealed objects that were perfect.…That was the ultimate vision, and we saw it in pure light because we were pure ourselves, not buried in this thing we are carrying around now, which we call a body, locked in it like an oyster in its shell.[36]

If Plato originally presents his theory of preexistence for reasons of epistemology, in order to explain human apprehension of universals or the capacity to make judgments moral or mathematical, or for reasons of etiology, to explain how the divine soul came to occupy material reality in the first place, or even to explain the capacity for language, as he does in *Phaedrus*,[37] he eventually finds in the paradigm a powerful tool for rationalizing the human condition itself. The apparent disconnect between the all-too-apparent inequalities and injustices of individual circumstances and human notions of justice was powerful fuel for the development of Greek tragedy. The very pity that Aristotle thought such staged ritual could effectively purify, or aesthetically condition us to suffer, was predicated on the terrifying disproportion between human misjudgment, such as the dogged blindness of Oedipus, and the apocalyptic consequences that minor misdeeds could precipitate, such as the death, blindness, and generational mayhem his family experienced.

Plato was likewise struck by the problematic imbalance between merit and circumstance, accountability and punishment. In the last book of the *Republic*, Plato invokes preexistence to offer compelling new possibilities for reevaluating the most intractable of human conundrums. He tells of one hero, Er, a soldier who returns from death to narrate to mortals the journey of the soul. This character describes a beautiful meadow which is framed by a pair of portals, a heavenly and an earthly. Judges send newly arrived souls to a kind of purgatory, the just being directed heavenward and the unjust to the underworld. Through an adjacent opening, souls return either clean and bright or dusty and travel weary. After tarrying in the meadow for seven days, those returning souls who have expiated their crimes or reaped their rewards are required to proceed on their journey until they reach a shaft of light, the spindle of Necessity, piercing the center of heaven and earth. The spot turns out to be the staging area for reentry into mortal life.

Upon the arrival of Er and his fellow spirits, a prophet comes forward holding "lots and a number of models of lives" and says, "Ephemeral souls, this is the beginning of another cycle that will end in death. Your daemon or guardian spirit will not be assigned to you by lot; you will choose him. The one who has the first lot will be the first to choose a life....The responsibility lies with the one who makes the choice; the god has none."[38] The sample lives exhibit different conditions ranging from royalty to beggary, health to sickness, ugliness to beauty, and every other quality. Intuitively, of course, those who pick winning lots would opt for the conditions of life most congenial to comfort and happiness. But, as we learn, the wisest choice may turn out to be other than the obvious one. Only the precipitous would rashly choose the easy and attractive path through mortality. For, as Plato reminds us, the purpose of life and the end of cyclical rebirth are the acquisition of virtue. Therefore, a wise soul will consider carefully

> what the good and bad effects of beauty are when it is mixed with wealth, poverty, and a particular state of the soul. He will know the effects of high or low birth...and all the things that are either naturally part of the soul or acquired, and he will know what they achieve when mixed with one another. And from all this he will be able, by considering the nature of the soul, to reason out which life is better and which worse and to choose accordingly, calling a life worse if it lead[s] the soul to become more unjust, a[nd] better if it leads the soul to become more just.[39]

Three important ends are powerfully accomplished through this mythology, in a preview of the cultural work that such innovations can perform. First, the story comports with a Christian theology of suffering. Though Stoicism provides a powerful model that Christianity will appropriate, this Platonic scheme reinforces the Christian emphasis on suffering as sanctifying. If earthly life is intended as morally educative, then pain and misery might more appropriately be measured against the standard of edification than of justice. Second, the myth connects present circumstance to a kind of narrative preview or outline glimpsed before mortality. Though the first act of the play was obscure, its hidden details make cursory judgments of this second act seem hasty and ill informed. Third and most important, the prominent role given to personal choice in the account of Plato absolves God, fate, and chance alike of the charge of eclipsing moral agency and human accountability in the pageant of human life. Human beings are active coparticipants, rather than passive victims, in the scripting of human circumstance. The myth is therefore a potent source of consolation and self-definition, affirming as it does God's goodness, freedom of the will, and human dignity.

Elsewhere, Plato turns to an altogether different question that again drives him (through a surrogate) to construct fanciful pre-mortal mythologies: how to explain the origins and power of human love? Through the person of Aristophanes, Plato presents one of the most comical yet poignant myths in his whole repertoire in order to resolve this question. Aristophanes may have been one of the greatest comedic writers of antiquity, but his contribution to Plato's theory of love mingles comic myth with profound pathos. In *Symposium*, guests compete to offer the most elegant encomiums on the subject of the god Eros (embodiment of love or desire). The first speakers address the god's antiquity, the beneficent consequences of love, desire's heavenly and earthly varieties, and Athenian customs that govern its expression. But when Aristophanes' turn comes, he weaves a fanciful myth of human origins to explain human love. The hunger for love, he suggests, is a quest to heal a primordial wound in human nature. Our condition in a time belonging to the mythic past was of three types: male, female, and androgynous. Human creatures in this primordial age were roundish like eggs, with two heads, four arms, and four legs. With the strength and power they then possessed, they were tempted to scale heaven and to assault the very gods themselves. They were soundly defeated, and in reprisal, Zeus decided not to annihilate the race, but rather to split them all asunder and let them suffer perpetually in their humbled and unnatural condition. In this severed state of incompleteness, mortal men and women walk the earth.

So great is the yearning to be restored to an original wholeness that humans spend their entire lives seeking out their other half. Yet even when they find true love and companionship in the rediscovered other, the restoration is never complete; the intractable intimation of a prior state of organic wholeness lends an indefinable melancholy to the present imitation of a more perfect past:

> And so, when a person meets the half that is his very own,...the two are
> struck from their senses by love, by a sense of belonging to one another,
> and by desire, and they don't want to be separated from one another, not

even for a moment. These are the people who finish out their lives together and still cannot say what it is they want from one another. No one would think it is the intimacy of sex....It's obvious that the soul of every lover longs for something else; his soul cannot say what it is, but like an oracle it has a sense of what it wants, and like an oracle it hides behind a riddle.[40]

Plato was not alone in representing human love in terms of a bond so powerful that it demands a mythic representation, one that pushes love's origins into an imagined epoch preceding human history. A similar myth appears in Philo and in Gnostic, rabbinic, and, later, Kabbalistic texts. The *Apocalypse of Adam*, for instance, refers to an unnamed offense committed by the heavenly Adam/Eve, for which "God...divided us in wrath, and then we became two beings."[41] Such original androgyny is really not that far removed, of course, from the Genesis account of Eve's physical derivation from Adam.

In *Phaedrus*, Plato records Socrates as formulating his own version of soulmate love, basing it on a personal, rather than a racial, memory of preexistence. In this case, it is not reunion with a severed half that we experience, but a hopeful embrace of a human surrogate for divine entities remembered only dimly:

Beauty was radiant to see at that time when the souls, along with the glorious chorus,...saw that blessed and spectacular vision....Now beauty, as I said, was radiant among the other objects; and now that we have come down here we grasp it sparkling through the clearest of our senses....A recent initiate,...one who has seen much in heaven—when he sees a godlike form that has captured beauty well, first he shudders and a fear comes over him like those he felt at the earlier time; then he gazes at him with the reverence due a god....The stream of beauty that streams into him through his eyes warms him up and waters the growth of his wings....(Long ago, you see, the entire soul had wings.)[42]

Having clearly articulated through these dialogues and myths a vision of the human soul as an immortal entity, whose timelessness extends into pre- as well as post-mortality, Plato will subsequently turn this vision into a full-blown cosmology. And here he will account for the origins of the visible and invisible order of things in such a way as to elaborate fully the genealogy of the human soul before it embarks upon its cycle of incarnations. The work where this occurs, one of Plato's last, is *Timaeus*. In this dialogue, Timaeus, who is "our expert in astronomy and has made it his main business to know the nature of the universe," gives an account of the creation of the universe through its several stages and including the creation of humans.[43]

In explaining the divine motives behind creation, Timaeus envisions a deity of greater magnanimity than the insecure and jealous God of the Eden story: the

Creator or demiurge "was good, and one who is good can never become jealous of anything. And so, being free of jealousy, he wanted everything to become as much like himself as was possible." Timaeus then clearly specifies the purpose of creation. Finding in the visible sphere disorder and irregularity, the Creator brought order to the chaos. He organized, rather than created, the universe in accordance with an unchanging and eternal pattern. Since that which is intelligent is more fair than that which is not, and the Creator only fashions that which is fair, he would naturally endow the created world with intelligence. But "it is impossible for anything to come to possess intelligence apart from soul. Guided by this reasoning, he put intelligence in soul and soul in body, and so he constructed the universe." And so the god "gave priority and seniority to the soul, both in its coming to be and in the degree of its excellence, to be the body's mistress and to rule over it as her subject."[44]

The soul and body referred to here are not human, but cosmic. And by this process, "our world [came] into being as a truly living thing, endowed with soul and intelligence." Next in order, the fixed stars were created, also as "divine living things," along with the wandering stars and earth itself. Finally, the Creator (or demiurge) supervised the creation of mortal beings, at this point suddenly revealing the same apprehensions about unfettered human potential seen in *Atrahasis*:

> There remain still three kinds of mortal beings that have not yet been begotten....But if these creatures came to be and came to share in life by my hand, they would rival the gods. It is you [lesser deities], then, who must turn yourselves to the task of fashioning these living things, as your nature allows. This will assure their mortality.

And so:

> [H]e turned again to the mixing bowl he had used before, the one in which he had blended and mixed the soul of the universe. He began to pour into it what remained of the previous ingredients....And when he had compounded it all, he divided the mixture into a number of souls equal to the stars....Then he would sow each of the souls into that instrument of time suitable to it.

And thus, "the souls were of necessity implanted in bodies." In accordance with the commands of the demiurge, the lesser deities set to work and welded together the materials of the body—not with indissoluble bonds but with "copious rivets so small as to be invisible," which would admit of dissolution—and invested these bodies "with the orbits of the immortal soul."[45]

As for the terms and conditions of mortality, the Creator "described to them the laws that had been foreordained: They would all be assigned one and the same initial birth, so that none would be less well treated by him than any other." He indicated as well that humans will be born alike with the same faculties of sensation and with the same mix of emotions—love, fear, and anger. The purpose of life, in this Platonic version, is for man to master the passions and, through virtue thus attained, "at the end return to his dwelling place in his companion star, to live a life of happiness that agreed with his character." Failing in this endeavor, he is fated to be reborn as a woman, and so on down or back up the chain of being through successive incarnations. But cyclical rebirth is clearly neither the intention nor the inevitable course of existence. For, as Plato has Timaeus conclude:

> [W]e ought to think of the most sovereign part of our soul as god's gift to us, given to be our guiding spirit....It raises us up away from the earth and toward what is akin to us in heaven, as though we are plants grown not from the earth but from heaven. In saying this, we speak absolutely correctly. For...heaven [is] the place from which our souls were originally born.[46]

Plato's unabashed misogyny raises the obvious question about the role of gender in constructions of pre-mortal identity. That a male could be reborn as a female, but with the same soul, initially suggests that the soul itself is male (hence the "demotion" would function effectively as punishment). However, it is unlikely that, for Plato, the soul is sexually differentiated—or that categories of sex or gender even apply. Bodily form is itself contrary to the true nature of the soul, and thus man, woman, and animal simply represent places on a scale of being at increasing levels of remove from perfection. The later Gnostic Exegesis on the Soul depicts the soul, confusingly, as "female in her nature," possessed of a womb and originally virginal, but "in form androgynous."[47] In Kabbalistic versions, the soul will be depicted as dual-gendered. And in at least one nineteenth-century variant we shall see, human identity is (constantly) gendered from its pre-mortal beginnings and throughout eternity. For Plato, the gender of the soul may be unaddressed; it will, however, generally be identified with a masculine principle in the aggressively male intellectual universe of antiquity.[48]

As these dialogues, *Timaeus* especially, demonstrate, Plato's medium for the promulgation of his philosophical and ethical views is largely mythopoeic. As for the value of such methods in rational discourse, it is well to keep in mind the last speech of Socrates before his death. Having outlined his version of the afterlife, with its rivers and chasms, its place of judgment and torments of Tartarus, he concludes: "No sensible man would insist that these things are as I have described them, but I think it is fitting for a man to risk the belief—for the risk is a noble one—that this, or something like this, is true about our souls."[49] Similarly, Timaeus justifies his mythopoesis rather defensively by insisting that Socrates should not be surprised

> if it turns out repeatedly that we won't be able to produce accounts on a great many subjects, on gods or the coming to be of the universe—that

are completely and perfectly consistent and accurate....If we can come up with accounts no less likely than any, we ought to be content....So we should accept the likely tale on these matters. It behooves us not to look for anything beyond this.[50]

Timaeus will prove to be one of the most important texts to the subsequent development of Platonism and Neo-Platonism. It will be the only Platonic dialogue known in its entirety during the Middle Ages. Positing as it does claims about God, the creation, and human origin, it is a text that will present special appeal as well as special challenges to early Christian philosophers. Whereas the account in Genesis leaves ambiguous the question of whether God organized or introduced into existence physical matter, *Timaeus* makes matter clearly preexistent. Over the next centuries, the dialogue will be invoked time and again to fill in the voids left in the Judeo-Christian creation narrative, offering an account, no less plausible than Noah's flood and Babel's tower, of divine motives, human origins, and life's purpose.

One final point is worth making about Plato's philosophy, because it is generally overlooked and because it corroborates the remarkably common connection between preexistence and a corollary. David Sedley has remarked that, if you asked any well-educated citizen of antiquity "to name the official moral goal, or *telos*, of each major current philosophical system... [y]ou will hear that Plato's is *homoiosis theoi kata to dunaton*, 'becoming like god so far as is possible.'" And yet, Sedley marvels, "*Homoiosis theoi*, universally accepted in antiquity as the official Platonic goal, does not even appear in the index to any modern study of Plato."[51] Implicit in several of Plato's dialogues, including *Timaeus*, the ideal is most explicitly stated in *Theaetetus*, where Socrates tells Theodorus, "a man should make all haste to escape from earth to heaven, and escape means becoming as like God as possible."[52] Not only is this idea central to Platonic philosophy, it is inextricably connected in his thought with pre-mortal origins. Preexistence and theosis will increasingly be linked, to the eventual detriment of both, in the subsequent thought of Origen, the Neo-Platonists, and a host of others.

3

Philo to Christian Beginnings

A hundred years or so after Ezra and Nehemiah the whole Jewish
community changed its overlord. In an unprecedented victory march
the Macedonian king, Alexander the Great (334–323), drove through
Asia Minor, Syria, Palestine and Egypt to Babylon and across the
Indus....The whole oriental world was thus drawn into another cultural
province, whose power and influence they had no capacity to resist.

—Werner Foerster[1]

Philo of Alexandria

The culture of classical Greece was absorbed and assimilated into the
larger world of Alexander's conquests and produced the Hellenistic
fusion: the richest synthesis of cosmopolitan cultures and religion the
ancient world would ever know. Much of the intellectual energy of
the empire would come to center in a city designed by the conqueror
himself. Within a hundred years of its founding in 332 BCE, Alexandria
had become one of the largest and most prosperous trading centers of
antiquity. It was not commerce, however, but learning that soon gave the
city its great fame. A center of both Greek and Semitic intellectualism,
Alexandria was home to a library and museum founded by the
Ptolemies, Alexander's successors, and would be the cradle or the nursery
of many of the greatest scholars of the ancient world, including Euclid,
Ptolemy, Archimedes, and Eratosthenes. The library was famed for its

half million volumes, perhaps the greatest Western collection of knowledge till then assembled. Jews had settled in Egypt from earliest times, and they were concentrated in Alexandria; two of the five city districts were dominated by Jewish inhabitants, and Jewish thought thrived in its politically and intellectually liberal atmosphere. The translation of the Hebrew Bible into Greek, a symbol of the great synthesis of classical and Hebraic learning, was accomplished here in the third century BCE, answering both the needs of increasing numbers of Hellenized Jews, who were not always conversant in Hebrew, and the appetite of Greek intellectuals for access to the texts of Jewish culture.

After the Romans mastered the Mediterranean world, Alexandria continued as the intellectual center of the empire. It was inevitable, then, that after its birth in Palestine and subsequent diaspora, Christian thought would find significant intellectual articulation and flowering in that city. Some of the strongest foundations for a bridge from classical to Christian culture were laid not by a Christian but by one of those Hellenized Jews not even skilled in Hebrew, Philo of Alexandria (c. 20 BCE–50 CE). Thoroughly versed in Greek philosophy, Philo revered Plato as much as he reverenced the prophets of his own Hebrew past. In his desire to merge philosophical rationalism with religious concerns, he essentially paved the way for one of the first fully fledged versions of a religious philosophy. Ironically, perhaps, his efforts exerted little influence on subsequent Jewish or Greek thinking. Instead, it was Christian theology that grew out of the soil Philo cultivated. Tremendously influential in his syncretism, he was a major aqueduct through which the disparate waters of Greece and Judea were combined and channeled into the Christian world.

The role and influence of Greek thought—and Platonic philosophy in particular—on Christian theology are indisputably great. What is more controversial is the extent to which that influence approaches contamination or corruption of the gospel preached by the apostles. As Platonic thought wove in and out of Christian doctrine, two subtly interconnected ideas saw their fortunes rise and fall: they concerned the creation of the universe and of the human soul. Philo was profoundly committed to Platonism, but he clearly believed that it reaffirmed, rather than negated, the contributions to spiritual anthropology of his own Jewish heritage. Edwin Hatch noted that, in these first formulations of a Christian philosophy, "precisely those elements are dominant which were dominant in Jewish philosophy": an allegorical method of interpretation and cosmological speculation.[2] Those elements were certainly present in Philo's thought. And he brought both to bear in ways that profoundly affected the development—and transmission—of the idea of preexistence.

Philo follows Plato's *Timaeus* in writing, "This world consists of all earth, and all water, and all air, and all fire, not a single particle, no not the smallest imaginable atom, being omitted."[3] Though he is sometimes associated with the idea of creation *ex nihilo*, Philo nowhere explicitly credits God with the creation of primordial matter, as in the later formulation of that classic doctrine.[4] In fact, it seems clear that "Philo postulates a pre-existent matter alongside God."[5] He does not consider Plato to be superior to biblical authority but actually credits Moses with the doctrine Plato merely develops. Moses, he believes, anticipated the philosopher in teaching that the original elements existed before the world itself was given form. Philo states:

> God…has invested with shape the essence of all things which was previously devoid of shape, and has stamped with a particular character that which previously had no character, and has endowed with form that which had previously no distinctive form, and having perfected the entire world, he has impressed upon it an image and appearance.[6]

It was the Logos that transformed the raw, unshaped, and unorganized preexistent matter, which Philo describes as "destitute of arrangement, of quality, of animation, of distinctive character and full of disorder and confusion,"[7] into the building blocks of the world, in roughly the same way as was indicated by Plato.

In his account of human origins, Philo again follows the lead of Plato, with modifications. According to Philo, God created two types of rational souls. The first are creatures of purity and virtue that serve God as unembodied angels. A second class, of less purity and excellence, are attracted to earthly things and thus descend to be embodied in human forms. Following Plato, Philo describes the souls of these lesser beings as composite. One part, of divine origin, he calls "mind" (*logos* or *pneuma* or *nous*). The lower, or irrational, part of the soul Philo divides between a passionate dimension (*thumikon*) centered in the chest and a sensual aspect (*epithumatikon*) located in the abdomen.

A common interpretive strategy when faced with doctrines of preexistence has been to assume a nonliteral meaning. This tendency is pronounced when scholars deal with Philo's version of the theory.[8] One case in point is Philo's commentary on the account of Eve's creation, which he reads allegorically. However, preexistence is what Philo's allegory points us toward, not part of the allegory to be interpreted away or dismissed as mere literary invention. Philo's interpretation of the creation narrative of Genesis reads this way:

> For there was a time when Mind neither had sense perception, nor held converse with it.…It was but half the perfect soul, lacking the power whereby it is the nature of bodies to be perceived, a mere unhappy section bereft of its mate without the support of the sense perceiving organs.…God, then, wishing to provide the Mind with perception of material as well as immaterial things, thought to complete the soul by weaving into the part first made the other section, which he called by the general name of "woman" and the proper name of "Eve," thus symbolizing sense.[9]

Philo may or may not be asserting a literal "time before" when he alludes here and elsewhere to "a time when the world was not"[10]—though the locution seems unambiguous. The focus is on seeing through or beyond the literal creation of Eve to find the larger or greater truth to which it points. Her creation out of Adam's rib was metaphorical. The higher meaning, according to Philo, concerned the reason for human incarnation. Unembodied mind was incomplete, "half the perfect soul," bereft of physical form and "perceiving organs." We find here a highly significant departure from Plato's conception of mortality as punitive, in favor of a view of corporeality as moving in the direction of more perfection—human life as beneficial and educative. In Philo's reading of the biblical myth of creation, a greater capacity to perceive the plenitude of creation follows from the soul's progress into mortality. His reading is also important as perhaps the clearest indication to date of the classical association of the spirit (in this case, intellect or mind) with the masculine, and the body with the feminine. Philo's model is at some remove from Plato's radical sexism; he sees the feminine principle as completing and perfecting the masculine. Still, the male is here primary, essential, and identified with the soul or spirit, and the female is secondary, supplemental, and identified with the physical. This male-female dichotomy, with its privileging of the masculine soul over the feminine body constitutes an enduring and pervasive intellectual tradition in the West. It draws upon three powerful currents.

First, in Plato's dualism, the intellect is primary, and physical reality is ontologically inferior. The noetic realm of pure *nous*, or intellect, is the only reality worthy of the name, as he argues in the *Republic*.[11] Second, Greek ideas about conception portray the embryonic body as a male form that gives shape to a female material. In Aristotle's fetology, it is the woman who provides the physical substance which is acted upon and formed by the male principle. Aristotle is emphatic on this point: "it is plain that the contribution which the female makes to generation is the *matter* used therein":

> [But] the female, *qua* female, is passive, and the male, *qua* male is active—it is that whence the principle of movement comes....The one thing which is formed is formed *from them* only in the sense in which a bedstead is formed from the carpenter and the wood, or a ball from the wax and the form. It is plain, then, that there is no necessity for any substance to pass from the male; and if any does pass, this does not mean the offspring is formed from it as from something situated within itself.

Or, more bluntly, "the contribution which the male makes to the young has to do not with bulk but with specific character," just as milk is curdled by the action of rennet in his famous example.[12] And then he makes the hierarchy emphatic and definitive: "Thus the physical part, the body, comes from the female, and the Soul from the male, since the Soul is the essence of a particular body."[13] Finally, in the Christian theology of the incarnation, the divine Logos, substance of the Father, comes to inhabit a mortal body through the vehicle of the woman. Thus, the gendered hierarchy of soul-body is reinforced through philosophy, science, and dogma alike.

Elsewhere, Philo provides a model of preexistence that reflects early Jewish ways of thinking about pre-mortal realities in ideal terms:

> When any city is founded…it happens at times that some man coming up who, from his education, is skillful in architecture,…first of all sketches out in his own mind nearly all the parts of the city which is about to be completed—the temples, the gymnasia, the…markets, [etc.]. Then, having received in his own mind, as on a waxen tablet, the form of each building, he carries in his heart the image of a city, perceptible as yet only by the intellect, the images of which he stirs up in memory which is innate in him.…Engraving them in his mind like a good workman, keeping his eyes fixed on his model, he begins to raise the city of stones and wood, making the corporeal substances to resemble each of the incorporeal ideas.…So in the same manner neither can the world which existed in ideas have had any other local position except the divine reason which made them.[14]

The affinity of this conception with the Platonic forms is obvious. But where Plato situated his ideas in a realm populated by souls, thus linking eternal forms, or a noetic reality, with human preexistence, Philo is doing something different. He is locating preexistent forms in the Logos, or "divine reason," in a move that emphasizes God's infinite sovereignty, not humankind's anthropology. In this version of preexistence, then, the emphasis is on a reality that is logically prior, rather than temporally prior, to mortality. This shift from a temporally pre-mortal realm to a noetic reality that logically precedes creation has been deployed by a number of modern philosophers.

It would clearly be a mistake, however, to generalize this instance of ideal preexistence, or to rule out of Philo's conception preexistence in the plain sense of the word. Invested as he is in the allegorical mode of scriptural exegesis, Philo seems aware of the porous boundaries among scriptural narrative, allegory, and myth. So when he returns to the theme of human souls in *The Giants* (a commentary on Gen. 6:2–4), he makes a special plea. The angels referred to by Moses in these verses, he tells us, "are souls that fly in the air." He insists (as if to forestall modern critics), "And let no one assume that what is said here is a myth." They are real, he continues, if supersensible: "We ought not to conclude,…inasmuch as our vision is incapable of forming images of souls, that there are consequently no souls in the air, but they must be apprehended by the mind, that like may be discerned in conformity with its similars."[15]

Then, in a manner roughly similar to Plato, Philo describes the differing origins and status of these souls, according to their dispositions and choices.

> Now some of the souls have descended into bodies, but others have never deigned to associate with any of the parts of earth. Since the latter are consecrated and devoted to the service of the Father, they customarily serve their Creator as ministers and helpers in his care for mortal man. The former, however, descend…into the body as though into a stream.

Some are swallowed up in the waters, weighed down by attachment to "that corpse which was our birth-fellow, the body." Others, the souls of those who prove themselves to be genuine philosophers, "soar…back up to the place whence they had set out."[16]

Philo recapitulates this scenario in his work on the biblical figure of Noah, explicitly bringing Greek mythology into harmony with Jewish scripture. He declares that God made to inhabit the air both "the winged animals capable of being perceived by the eternal senses, and other powers which can by no means be comprehended in any place by the external senses; and this is the company of incorporeal souls." And then he elaborates:

> Some are assigned to mortal bodies,…others which have received a more divinely prepared habitation, look down upon the regions of the earth, and that in the highest place, near the other itself, the purest souls are placed, which those who have studied philosophy among the Greeks call heroes, but which Moses…entitles angels.[17]

In yet a third text, Philo finds it useful to invoke preexistence in his effort to fit angels into a Platonic cosmology, which he does in the context of the dream vision of Jacob. The ladder the patriarch saw (in Gen. 28:12), with its angels ascending and descending between earth and heaven, Philo interprets as an image of suprasensible realities, reflecting two intersecting realms of spirit, comprising both human souls working out their destinies and messengers appointed to assist them. The former either "descend upon the earth with a view to be bound up in mortal bodies, those namely which are most nearly connected with the earth, and which are lovers of the body," or ascend, pronouncing the body "a prison and a grave, and, flying from it as from a house of correction or a tomb, have raised themselves aloft on light wings towards the aether." Others, "the purest and most excellent of all," never having fallen through mortal craving into bodily form, serve as "lieutenants of the Ruler of the universe," conveying human needs to God and the divine will to his children.[18]

In Philo, the earlier Semitic strands and Hellenic conceptions thus marry, as the preexistent soul of Plato merges with the populous heavens of Hebraic precursors: "this air is the abode of incorporeal souls, since it seemed good to the Creator of the universe to fill all the parts of the world with living creatures." In a rhapsodic version of the great chain of being, he describes ethereal oceans teeming with life: "for not only is [the air] not alone deserted by all things besides, but rather, like a populous city, it is full of imperishable and immortal citizens, souls equal in number to the stars."[19]

Philo also incorporates into his scheme earlier ideas of embodiment as a kind of fall, as in Plato, but he is ambiguous about the precise reasons for the fall of certain angels into mortality. Glossing the Levitical dietary approval of flying reptiles (Lev. 11:21), Philo writes:

> [T]hese are symbols of the souls that, though rooted like reptiles to the terrestrial body, have the power, once purified, to haunt the heights, exchanging earth for heaven and corruption for immortality. We must accordingly believe that a heavy dose of sheer ill luck has infected those souls that, nourished in air and the purest ether, migrated to earth…because they were unable to endure the satiety of divine goods.[20]

More cryptically yet, he suggests that incarnation might be due to a law of necessity, in order to educate the soul or in order to comport with its true nature as a created and therefore imperfect being. "Why does Abraham say, 'I am an immigrant and sojourner among you'?" he asks, reading the scripture (Gen. 23:4) as a statement about the unnatural lodging of the soul in a human shell. And he answers:

> [D]oes not every wise soul live like an immigrant and sojourner in this mortal body, after having for habitat and country the most pure substance of heaven, from which it migrates to this habitat by a compelling law? Perhaps this was in order that it might carefully inspect terrestrial things, that even these might not be without a share in wisdom to participate in the better life, or in order that it might be akin to created beings and not be continuously and completely happy?[21]

Certainly not an optimistic assessment of the human condition or the grand design behind it, this last thought. But then, this is not surprising in a thinker who called pleasure "of itself evil."[22] In addition to quoting Abraham in support, he also finds Moses's creation narrative an allegory of a pre-mortal fall, seeing in the coats of skin with which God clothed Adam and Eve clear reference to the incarnation of their preexistent souls.[23] Though the reasons for this descent into the world may be unclear, the way back is, as it was for Plato, straightforward: the purification of the soul. And just as "to be separated from the contemplation of the Existent One is the most complete of Evils,"[24] return to that heavenly place of origin is the most supreme happiness. The process of ascent begins, according to Philo, with "migration out of three regions, body, sense perception and speech."[25] Philo's version of theurgy thus incorporates ascetic discipline and renunciation. Humans must "escape…from the abominable prison, your body, and from the pleasures and lusts that act as its jailers." But his mystic bent entails as well that the disciple

> escape also your own self and stand aside from yourself, like persons pos-
> sessed and corybants [pagan priests] seized by Bacchic frenzy and carried
> away by some kind of prophetic inspiration. For it is the mind that is
> filled with the Deity and no longer in itself, but is agitated and maddened
> by a heavenly passion, drawn by the truly Existent and attracted upward
> to it.[26]

To some extent, of course, all mysticism, insofar as it aspires to union with the divine—and the divine is devoid of parts—presupposes this blurring of person-hood and individualism. The consummation of the mystical ascent therefore tends toward an emphasis on the paradox of a self that both originates in, and is eter-nally constituent of, God himself. In Philo's case, he invokes the paradox of a finite human being contemplating eternity to argue for an essential connection that links the individual mind to something itself infinite. "For how was it likely," he asks, "that the human mind being so tiny, hemmed in by such puny masses as brain or heart, should be able to contain such an immense magnitude of sky and universe, had it not been an inseparable portion of that divine and blessed soul? For noth-ing is severed or detached from the divine, only extended."[27] Plotinus will further develop this paradoxical relation between the soul and its origin in God.

Like Plato, Philo sees mortality as a kind of exile. It is the task of the mind, where reason and will are centered, to establish dominion over those senses and appetites that are allied with the physical body. Life is also the academy in which the soul acquires the dominion and purity that enable it to return to God. Those who triumph over the flesh inherit their pre-mortal abode in the heavens. Excep-tionally purified souls ascend to the world Plato called the realm of ideas, and the most perfect of all attain the presence of God himself. Those souls who fail, dying in bondage to physical appetite, descend to Hades or even oblivion.

Apocrypha and Pseudepigrapha

Philo's was a self-conscious and deliberate effort to synthesize the learning of his Jewish forebears, and biblical texts in particular, with the forms of Platonism that reached him in the early Christian era. But the larger intellectual world of which he was a part comprised hopelessly complicated lines of cultural transmission. Most scholars, as Harnack did, assume that any Semitic antecedents were relatively incon-sequential or overwhelmed by Hellenization. As one writes simply, "the Platonic and Neo-Platonic doctrine [that] individual souls…are pre-existent and merely enter the physical body destined for them was adopted by the ancient rabbis."[28] However, Semitic motifs figure prominently in texts produced in the centuries just before and after Christ. One such motif is the heavenly assembly, which appears in a number of pseudepigraphal works, such as the apocryphal text of *2 Enoch*. In these same texts, pre-mortal humans frequently make their appearance. Extant only in Slavonic, *2 Enoch* is thought to derive from Hebrew that was translated into Greek and then Slavonic, but other origins are possible, and likely dates range from the first century BCE to the Middle Ages.[29] In this text, which expands upon the Enoch story briefly narrated in Genesis 5:21–32, Enoch is taken up by divine messengers and tours the several heavens. At the culmination of the ascension, he is ushered into God's presence as into a royal court, where Michael, Gabriel, and other heavenly attendants wait upon the Lord. Enoch is anointed and dressed in "the clothes of [God's] glory," and he becomes like one of the glorious ones, with "no observable difference." Immediately following this scene, he is commanded to write all the things he has learned. Singled out for special mention in his record is the following: "Sit down and write—all the souls of men, whatever of them are not yet born, and their places, prepared for eternity. For all the souls are prepared for eternity, before the composition of the earth."[30]

Other works of the era clearly indicate that human souls, if not present in pre-mortal councils, are nonetheless products of a pre-mortal creation. Sometimes, the patriarchs in particular are singled out as having a pre-mortal existence, if not an actual presence in divine assemblies. In the *Prayer of Joseph*, a first- or second-century CE fragment that Origen quoted with approval, Jacob declares simply, "Abraham and Isaac were created before any work."[31] This text describes some of the patriarchs as great souls, even angels, who descended to assume human nature. Says the patriarch: "I Jacob, who speak to you, and Israel, I am an angel of God, a ruling spirit, and Abraham and Isaac were created before every work of God.…I am the first-born of every creature which God caused to live."[32] Whether Origen was interpreting the document freely or relying upon portions of the *Prayer of Joseph* no longer extant, he understood it to say that Jacob was a chief captain among the angels before his birth, who had to be reminded of that heritage by the archangel Uriel "while doing service in the body."[33] James Charlesworth notes that, while not widespread, Jewish claims that "the patriarchs or Moses were pre-existent" were not uncommon.[34]

In the *Assumption of Moses* (also known as the *Testament of Moses*), a text of unknown authorship dating to the first century CE, we find Moses declaring that he was "prepared from [*before*, in R. H. Charles's translation] the foundation of the world, to be the mediator of the covenant."[35] Charles glosses the passage as a clear indication that "Moses is here assigned pre-existence as is the Son of Man in 1 Enoch."[36] Other figures mentioned as peopling the preexistent world are Isaac, Jacob, Jeremiah, and, in later traditions, the twelve apostles.

At other times, preexistence is imputed to the entire covenant people, or even to the whole human race. Pseudepigraphal works like the *Assumption of Moses*, ostensibly authored by major biblical figures, claim to convey God's word and held great authority in early Jewish and Christian communities. Another such work, *Jubilees*, recounts matters revealed to Moses during his forty days on Sinai. Written in the second century CE by a Palestinian Jew, the text offers a fuller account of creation than the version extant in Genesis. We learn, among other details, that on the very first day of creation, God made "all of the spirits which minister before him," several angelic beings, and "all of the spirits of his creatures which are in heaven and on earth."[37] From the same general era, we also have the *Apocalypse of Abraham* (70–150 CE). Caught up in a heavenly vision, Abraham sees multiple firmaments, legions of angels, and "a great crowd of men and women and children":

> And I said, "Eternal, Mighty One! What is this picture of creation?" And he said to me, "…Whatever I had decreed was to exist had already been outlined in this and all the previously created [things] you have seen stood before me." And I said, "O sovereign, mighty and eternal! Why are the people in this picture on this side and on that?" And he said to me, "These who are on the left side are a multitude of tribes who existed previously.…Those on the right side of the picture are the people set apart for me of the people with Azazel; these are the ones I have prepared to be born of you and to be called my people."[38]

One of the Jewish apocalyptic works most influential in Christian history was the *Fourth Book of Ezra*, composed around 100 CE. Portions of it inspired Bishop Latimer at the stake and Milton in his poetry, Christopher Columbus to set sail, and William Whiston, Newton's successor at Cambridge, to conclude that the end of time approached. Parts of it still appear in Roman Catholic liturgy.[39] Preexistence hovers in the background throughout Ezra's third vision (seven are recorded in the document). The world was created for "the righteous," where they go in order to experience "the contest which every man who is born on earth shall wage." The Most High feels compassion for "those who have not yet come into the world." And upon death, Ezra is reminded, "the spirit leaves the body to return again to him who gave it."[40]

Even more authoritative—especially in the early Christian centuries—was the *Wisdom of Solomon*, dating from the first or second century BCE and included in the first known listing of Christian canonical writings, the Muratorian canon of the second century. It has since been considered a deuterocanonical book of the Bible (apocryphal to the Protestants). Describing his own quest for true *sophia*, the author writes:

> I loved [wisdom] and sought her from my youth;
> I desired to take her for my bride,
> and became enamoured of her beauty....
> I went about seeking how to get her for myself.
> As a child I was naturally gifted,
> and a good soul fell to my lot;
> or rather, being good, I entered an undefiled body.
> But I perceived that I would not possess wisdom unless God gave her to
>   me. (8:2, 18–21)

The author describes the human condition thus: "a perishable body weighs down the soul, and this earthy tent burdens the thoughtful mind." And as for the souls of the just, "their hope is full of immortality. Having been disciplined a little, they will receive great good, because God tested them and found them worthy of himself; like gold in the furnace he tried them" (Wisd. 9:15; 3:5–7).

Several points are worth making here. First, there is no indication of any metempsychosis, or cyclical rebirth. The time line is linear. Second, the structure of the comment makes clear that the soul is the seat of personal identity—a point the self-correction seems intended to emphasize. (He goes from referring to himself as receiving a noble soul—"a good soul fell to my lot"—to being the noble soul himself: "rather [I], being good.") Finally, the purpose of mortal incarnation is not, at least not primarily, here related to punishment; incarnation is not a fall. Rather, incarnation is an educative and probationary time.

As we saw, few such explicit allusions to preexistence survive in the Hebrew Bible itself. Divine assemblies and sons of the gods appear liberally, but the strongest claim for explicit reference to mortal preexistence we have already seen in Jeremiah. But an entire tradition developed around one preexistent entity alluded to in the Hebrew Bible, the figure of Wisdom. Personified in Greek as Sophia, considered the consort of God by the Canaanites, Wisdom is by any measure a figure of great complexity and of primary importance for Gnostics, Jews, and some early Christians. Helmer Ringgren finds one of the earliest allusions to this entity in Job 15:7–8, where Eliphaz asks Job, "was thou born the first of men, or wast thou brought forth before the hills? Hast thou listened in the council of God, and drawn Wisdom to thyself?" In this case, Ringgren reasons, "Wisdom has been conceived as a kind of independent entity, which...is on the way to becoming something other than an inherent quality of God."[41] The most famous and fully developed treatment of this figure is Wisdom's hymn in Proverbs 8, which strikingly suggests not just her preexistence, but humankind's as well:

> The Lord created me at the beginning of his work,
> the first of his acts of long ago.
> Ages ago I was set up,
> at the first, before the beginning of the earth.
> When there were no depths I was brought forth,
> when there were no springs abounding with water.
> Before the mountains had been shaped,
> before the hills, I was brought forth—
> when he had not yet made earth and fields,
> or the world's first bits of soil.
> When he established the heavens, I was there,
> when he drew a circle on the face of the deep,
> when he made firm the skies above,
> when he established the fountains of the deep,
> when he assigned to the sea its limit,
> so that the waters might not transgress his command,
> when he marked out the foundations of the earth,
> then I was beside him, like a master worker;
> and I was daily his delight,
> rejoicing before him always,
> rejoicing in his inhabited world
> and delighting in the human race. (22–31)

Hamerton-Kelly holds that the figure of Wisdom is "not a person," though it is clearly "a pre-existent personified being" and "an uncreated, independent entity."[42] Roland Murphy points out that, though personification is a frequent trope in the Old Testament, the quality of Wisdom's personification is entirely unique.[43] Ringgren emphasizes that "it is obvious that Wisdom is here not an abstraction or a purely poetic personification but a concrete being, self-existent beside God."[44] In the apocryphal book of *Ecclesiasticus* (*Wisdom of Jesus Son of Sirach*), Wisdom narrates a similar autobiography, but moves from a pre-mortal existence to embodiment in or among Israel:

> I dwelt in the highest heavens,
> and my throne was in a pillar of cloud.
> Alone I compassed the vault of heaven
> and traversed the depths of the abyss....
> Then the Creator of all things gave me a command,
> and my Creator chose the place for my tent.

He said, "Make your dwelling in Jacob,
and in Israel receive your inheritance."
Before the ages, in the beginning, he created me,
and for all the ages I shall not cease to be.
In the holy tent I ministered before him,
and so I was established in Zion.
Thus in the beloved city he gave me a resting-place,
and in Jerusalem was my domain.
I took root in an honored people,
in the portion of the Lord, his heritage. (24:4–5, 8–13)

As Ringgren points out, we find Wisdom here "a personal being, raising her voice in the council of God," coming into existence "in the beginning of time."[45] In one line of Jewish thought, this figure of Wisdom will metamorphose into the Torah as a preexistent entity, the agent and blueprint of creation, embodiment of eternal wisdom. Among Alexandrian Jews, as is apparent in the writings of Philo, Wisdom merges with the Logos, the classical Greek term for the divine intelligence that orders the cosmos. As the agent of creation, this identification comfortably comports with the Johannine treatment of the Son of God as Logos. The preexistent Wisdom, or word, becomes fully identified in this way with the preexistent Christ. This concept of a preexistent Christ adds an important new dimension to the doctrine of preexistence, with implications that contribute to both a broadening of the concept and, in subsequent centuries, its sharp decline.

Early Christianity

By the New Testament era, Peter can write of Christ as in some sense having been preexistent, as when he refers to Christ's being "foreknown before the creation of the world" (1 Pet. 1:20). The Gospel of John, with its opening declaration that "the Word was made flesh," similarly evokes, or recuperates, the Greek ideas of dualism and pre-mortal, nonmaterial existence. This will be a major impetus to the elaboration of preexistence in accordance with the developing Christology at the heart of the new faith. Scholars like Harnack have found no hint of Platonic dualism in earlier Jewish conceptions of preexistence:

Precious things and persons, so far as they are now really manifested, were never conceived as endowed with a double nature. No hint is given of such an assumption; the sensible appearance was rather conceived as a mere wrapping which was necessary only to its becoming visible, or, conversely, the pre-existence of the archetype was no longer thought of in the presence of the historical appearance of the object.[46]

On the other hand, George A. Barton, Emil Schürer, R. H. Charles, and Alfred Edersheim interpreted the Jewish belief of the early Christian era that "all souls were
pre-existent" in its plain, or Platonic, sense.[47] In any event, Christ's reputed preexistence adds new impetus to a more general conception of human preexistence.

As the great exemplar, Christ was understood by Christians to be the ultimate
role model for human behavior and morality. It would seem inevitable that his
status as the supreme instance of humanity should serve as a prototype for human
anthropology as well as for human striving. Harnack probably overstated the case
when he read conceptions of human preexistence in early Christianity as a simple
extrapolation of Christ's preexistence. ("They may be regarded as the working out
of the original conception attaching to Jesus Christ.")[48] But it would be just as inaccurate to underestimate the theological clout that Christ's preexistence would give
to the more general theory. Yet, surprisingly few scholars confront the theological implications of the confluence of the early Christian tendency to view Christ
as typifying human anthropology and destiny and the developing doctrine of the
preexistent Christ. The particular nature of Christ's preexistence continues to be
debated. John's Logos, after all, does not strictly entail a concept of Christ as a preexistent personality. But Simon Gathercole is merely one of the scholars to argue
that Paul himself usually assumes rather than argues such a belief, and he goes
further than most in finding Christ's preexistence in all three synoptic Gospels as
well as in Paul and John.[49] Philippians 2 is perhaps the most emphatic among Paul's
writings that depict Jesus as the incarnation of the preexistent Christ:

> Who, though he was in the form of God,
> did not reckon equality with God
> as something to be exploited,
> but emptied himself,
> taking the form of a slave,
> being born in human likeness.
> And being found in human form,
> he humbled himself
> and became obedient to the point of death—
> even death on a cross. (2:6–8)

No wonder, in light of this and other Pauline passages, that H.-C. Kammler can
write that "the pre-existence of Christ in Paul…is conceived as *absolute, real* and
personal" (emphasis in original).[50]

Bostock's recognition of the attendant difficulty is an exception:

> [W]e have to face, as a matter of logical necessity, the fact that we cannot
> defend the pre-existence of Christ without at the same time defending the
> pre-existence of every human soul. Without such a defense Christ will not

be one with humanity and humanity, which needs to be *homoousios* with Christ in order to be saved, will remain separate from Christ....[That is why] the problem of pre-existence is not a peripheral academic question, but a central and crucial issue for the Christian Faith.

Origen is unusual among Christian thinkers, he adds, in avoiding "the dichotomy which haunts modern discussions of Christology. But he can do so only by defending the pre-existence of the soul as a literal truth."[51]

Origen had written:

[T]he faculty of free-will, variety and diversity characterized the individual souls, so that one was attached with a warmer love to the Author of its being, and another with a feebler and weaker regard, that soul [of Jesus]...inhering, from the beginning of the creation, and afterwards, inseparably and indissolubly in Him,...was made with Him in a preeminent degree.

Jerome's version of Origen's words is slightly different but suggests the same essential fact of Christ's pre-mortal rise to eminence: "No other soul which descended into a human body has stamped on itself a pure and unstained resemblance of its former stamp."[52] As one nineteenth-century commentator read Origen's logic, "Christ's soul also must be of like nature with ours: however exalted Christ may have been above other men, however distinguished and unique was His appearance,...He could not have enjoyed this exceptional position from the very beginning, but must have attained it as the reward of His virtue."[53] The explosive, heretical potential of the preexistence of Christ, if read as typical of a broader human pre-mortality, is clear. (It will flare up with the Origenists in later centuries.) Any paradigm which subsumes mortals and Christ into the same anthropological trajectory finds itself careening between the Charybdis of making God's divinity developmental and the Scylla of making man's divinity inevitable.

The expansion of Christ's preexistence to embrace humanity's, which Harnack saw as simple movement from the particular to the general, has plenty of materials to draw upon for its elaboration. As we have seen, Jewish conceptions of preexistence were already widespread in the early Christian world, and traditions of a populous heavenly assembly persisted into the rabbinic era. One scholar sees that motif as an especially fruitful source of new developments regarding the preexistent church. "The council of Yahweh," writes H. Wheeler Robinson, "opens out into such conceptions as that of Hebrews xii ('the general assembly and church of the firstborn') or of Rev. iv and v, with the circle of worshippers expanding to the furthest horizon."[54]

Bostock suggests that Robinson is on the right track in seeing the heavenly council as an antecedent to the idea of the preexistent church. He believes that preexistence arose as a Jewish concept independently of Platonism, one indication of this being the "corporate dimension" of Jewish preexistence. He finds its roots in the ancient Semitic belief in the preexistence of the Tabernacle, and of Jerusalem itself, which appears most explicitly in the first-century *Apocalypse of Baruch* (or *2 Baruch*), as we have seen (where God speaks of the Jerusalem "prepared beforehand...from the time when I took counsel to make Paradise," and shown to Adam, Abraham, and Moses).[55]

Among the early Christians, the idea of a preexistent church appears explicitly in the hugely influential text the *Shepherd of Hermas*. Harnack described the development as a natural segue from Jewish antecedents:

> If the world was created for the sake of the people of Israel, and the Apocalyptists expressly taught that, then it follows, that in the thought of God Israel was older than the world. The idea of a kind of pre-existence of the people of Israel follows from this. We can still see this process of thought very plainly in the shepherd of Hermas, who expressly declares that the world was created for the sake of the Church. In consequence of this he maintains that the Church was very old, and was created before the foundation of the world.[56]

This second-century text was considered scriptural by many of the earliest Christians and was even bound with the New Testament in some codices. Here, in this account of five visions, interspersed with several parables and commandments given to the former slave Hermas, we find the most emphatic ancient expression of the preexistent church. Appearing in a vision, a beautiful lady addresses the shepherd with this preface: "Hear the words which I am going to speak to you. God, who dwells in the heavens, and made out of nothing the things that exist,...multiplied and increased them on account of His holy Church." That the church here referred to has its roots in the pre-mortal world is explicitly stated soon after. Hermas mistakes a different female figure for a sibyl, but a messenger of the revelation quickly corrects him: "It is the Church." Hermas asks, "Why then is she an old woman?" and is told, "Because...she was created first of all. On this account is she old. And for her sake was the world made."[57]

The allusion seems to be to Ephesians 4:11–13, which describes the purpose of the church which Christ instituted, with its apostles, prophets, evangelists, pastors, and teachers, as nothing less than "the building up the body of Christ," till the saints all come to "maturity, to the measure of the full stature of Christ." Indeed, the intertextual allusion seems confirmed by Hermas's subsequent vision of the construction of a tower, with stones representing "apostles, bishops, teachers, and deacons," and a summary explanation of God's dispensation of mercy and righteousness, intended to make the shepherd "righteous and holy."[58] In this version, it would appear that we have a Christian institutional counterpart to the vague theurgy we saw in Plato: life is a school for moral betterment, but the established church is the particular medium envisioned for the amelioration of the human spirit.

That the Shepherd (or Pastor) of Hermas espoused these views carried enormous weight. Irenaeus, one of the earliest of the church fathers, was instrumental in defining the New Testament canon. He endorsed the four Gospels, Acts, Revelation, and all of the epistles except four minor ones (Philemon, 2 Peter, 3 John, and Jude). But in addition, he considered *1 Clement* of value and went so far as to refer to Hermas as scripture and quoted it in his own apologetic writings.[59] So did Tertullian consider it, and both Origen and Clement reverenced this 160 CE composition.

The spurious letter called *2 Clement* is by an unknown author, writing about the same time as the author of the *Shepherd of Hermas*. An exhorter to righteousness who frequently invokes New Testament passages, the author also admonishes his audience that, if they will but "do the will of God our Father, we shall be of the first church, that spiritual one, that was created before the sun and the moon." Seeming to recognize that this might surprise his hearers, he adds that "the books and the apostles say that the church not only exists now, but has done so from the beginning. For she was spiritual as our Jesus also was."[60]

Of course, comparing the church's preexistent status to Christ's hardly clarifies the exact nature of either, although this seems to be an instance of what Harnack referred to as the extension of the idea of Christ's actual preexistence to a whole community of individuals. That the analogy carries so far as to move beyond the community as a collective, to those individuals who constitute it, is made clear in what follows. "This flesh," the author of *2 Clement* writes, is the "counterpart and copy of the spirit." In glossing this passage, J. B. Lightfoot can only avoid the homily's implications of Christian belief in the preexistence of the church by resorting to a lawyer's argument in the alternative. On the one hand, his notes refer to this church made before the sun or the moon as a "celestial" or "spiritual" church, rather than a preexistent one. And then, rather inconsistently, he attributes these notions to Platonic influence rather than, for example, Jewish conceptions of a covenant or soul that preceded birth.[61]

Intimations of a chosen, preexistent people also surface in a first-, second-, or third-century production, the *Odes of Solomon*. Some scholars find a Gnostic dimension to this collection of psalms, alongside its Jewish and Christian elements, especially from the Gospel of John.[62] Christ is often taken to be a speaker in the songs, but at times his preexistence spills over to others. In the seventh ode, the speaker writes, "He who created me when yet I was not, knew what I would do when I came into being."[63] In the eighth ode, preexistence becomes more general when the Lord says of his people, "And before they had existed, I recognized them;

and imprinted a seal on their faces [and] I fashioned their members." Having established the pre-mortal election of his chosen, the (presumed) Messiah then pronounces, "Grace is for the elect ones. And who will receive it but they who trusted in it from the beginning? Love is for the elect ones. And who will put it on, but those who possessed it from the beginning."[64]

R. G. Hamerton-Kelly, in the most exhaustive study of the idea of preexistence in the New Testament, writes that "the main pre-existent entity,...as far as Paul is concerned, is the Church. It is the heavenly city or heavenly temple, to be revealed at the end but pre-existent now in heaven." In fact, the idea is "constitutive of his whole soteriological scheme." (He cites 1 Cor. 2:6–16 and 3:9–17 as examples.)[65] Albert Schweitzer agreed that "the Pauline mysticism is therefore nothing else than the doctrine of the making manifest in consequence of the death and resurrection of Jesus, of the pre-existent Church."[66] The Pauline (or, as is more generally believed in the case of Ephesians, Deutero-Pauline) conception of a righteous people "chosen before the foundation of the world" (1:4) could be taken to suggest both foreknowledge and predestination. It could also, as Bostock pointed out, be seen as referring to a "pre-existent assembly of the righteous."[67]

This idea possibly found support or inspiration in Old Testament allusions to a people whom God had foreordained to the covenant: "Have you not known? Have you not heard? Has it not been told you from the beginning? Have you not understood from the foundations of the earth?" and "I am the Lord your God, who stirs up the sea so that its waves roar—the Lord of hosts is his name. I have put my words in your mouth, and hidden you in the shadow of my hand, stretching out the heavens and laying the foundations of the earth, and saying to Zion, 'You are my people'" (Isa. 40:21, 51:16). Zion, in other words, appears to be the name for the covenant people the Lord prepared, or at least envisioned, before they were born. Lucien Cerfaux goes further. Paul's concept, he writes, is but a development of "the idea of the pre-existing Jerusalem, both heavenly and future, made by God at the time he created paradise," as we saw in the *Apocalypse of Baruch*.[68]

Origen hints at such a notion as well. In exploring first things, he argues that we can look to the future to divine the past, "for the end is always like the beginning." This idea is integral to his influential version of the principle of apokatastasis, or restoration, in which the future recapitulates the past. (This leads to the dangerous inference of a universal salvation that includes even Satan—later to be condemned as an Origenist heresy.) Those of the righteous whom the scripture predicts will end in blessedness must, therefore, have "obtained, in the ordering and arrangement of the world, the rank of angels" in some previous time. And the church of which Paul spoke in his epistle to the Corinthians (1:10) is likewise "the form of that kingdom which is to come."[69] As Crouzel describes the doctrine, "all rational creatures, those which would later become angels, men, demons,...were absorbed in the contemplation of God and formed the Church of the pre-existence, united like the Bride to the Bridegroom with the pre-existent intelligence that was joined to the Word."[70]

By the third century, this idea of the preexistent church had been assimilated by Christian Gnostics as well, an association that has often been the death knell for disputed doctrines. As recently as 2001, the nature of this preexistent church was still being debated in Catholic circles. Pope Benedict (then Cardinal Ratzinger) and Cardinal Walter Kasper differed on the relationship between the universal church and the particular church, i.e., actual congregations of flesh and blood. Kasper objected to Ratzinger's claim that, "in its essential mystery, the universal church is a reality ontologically *and temporally prior* to every individual church" (my emphasis). Of course, any argument like this can boil down to a dispute about the validity of universals or the reality of ideal forms, as in Plato. But, as described by Kasper, this argument takes an interesting turn:

> Surprisingly, Cardinal Ratzinger grounds his theory of the ontological primacy in a thesis about the pre-existence of the church. He finds justification for this thesis in the words of Paul the Apostle, who speaks of the heavenly Jerusalem from above as our mother, as the city of the living God, the community, *ecclesia*, of the firstborn whose names are written in heaven (see Heb. 12:22ff.).

Significantly, Kasper mentions in passing that Clement and Origen also paid particular attention to this passage.[71]

His response to Ratzinger's alleged Platonism and to his preexistent thesis is simple. "The pre-existence of the church must be understood as the concrete church that consists 'in and from' particular churches." In other words, in his curious logic, preexistence means postexistence. But in a post-Justinian church, one in which Origen is now a heretic, Clement's ideas about preexistence generally ignored, and his theory of creation *ex materia* superseded, Ratzinger will of course stop short of reading preexistence too literally. And in any event, as he makes clear in his response to Kasper, he invokes the New Testament motif of the preexistent church in order to emphasize its ontological, rather than chronological, primacy.[72] Still, it is a rare instance of preexistence taking center stage in a contemporary debate between theological heavyweights.

Within the New Testament record, as we have seen, some form of Christ's preexistence appears to be implicit in Pauline thought. On human preexistence, the record is silent or, at best, unclear. Some New Testament passages intimate, as does Jeremiah 1:5, a type of foreordination, but most are plausibly read as reflecting more on God's foreknowledge—or predestinating—than on the individual's preexistence. Paul refers to "those who love God, who are called according to his purpose. For those whom he foreknew [*proegno*] he also predestined to be conformed to the image of his Son" (Rom. 8:28–29). Yet, in this case, as Hamerton-Kelly points out:

> [T]here is some reason…to believe that something more "concrete" than "foreordination" is in mind here. [William] Sanday and [A. C.] Headlam suggest that *proginosko* ("I know beforehand") is being used in a sense…where it means "to take note of," "to fix regard upon" something, preliminary to selecting it for some special purpose. Such a meaning would entail that the believers existed in some form more substantive than an idea.[73]

We saw a similar case in the passage of Ephesians referring to a people chosen "before the foundation of the world" (1:4).

The exchange between Christ and his disciples in John's Gospel appears more clearly reliant upon a premise of individualized pre-mortal existence. Passing by a blind man, the followers ask Jesus, "who did sin, this man or his parents, that he should be born blind?" (John 9:2). Jesus expressly states that the man's sins were not the cause of his inherited condition—thus implicitly condoning the presupposition. In order to avoid the obvious implications of the verse, commentators have employed arguments not always the strongest. John Peter Lange, for instance, writing in the nineteenth century, averred that while some would see here a reference to preexistence, this was not "a national tenet of orthodox Jews, although it had forced an entrance from Platonism into Alexandrian Jewish theology." He finds it more reasonable to believe that "the man may already have sinned in the womb, as an embryo."[74] Writing earlier in the century, Adam Clarke, on the other hand, found in the episode a plain reference to metempsychosis and saw the disciples as here under the sway of Pythagoreanism. "The Jewish rabbis have had the same belief from the very remotest antiquity," he writes, citing Origen, Philo, and Josephus by way of confirmation. He also anticipates Lange in imputing to the Jews a belief that "it was possible for an infant to sin in the womb."[75] A hundred years earlier, Matthew Henry judged the very raising of the question to be an impertinence. (One is reminded of Augustine's alleged answer to the question, "What was God doing before creating the universe?" "Preparing hell for such as would ask!") Although Henry acknowledged the question's clear implication—that a man can commit sin before his birth—the disciples' question on that subject he called "very odd" and "unnecessarily curious."[76]

Roughly contemporaneous with the New Testament writings, Josephus gave an account of the Essenes' doctrine of the soul that, as he suggested, had evident similarities to Platonic conceptions that privileged spiritual over physical existence. For the Essenes, Josephus wrote, believed:

Souls are immortal, and continue for ever; and that they come out of the most subtile air, and are united to their bodies as to prisons, into which they are drawn by a certain natural enticement; but that when they are set free from the bonds of the flesh, they then, as released from a long bondage, rejoice and mount upward. And this is like the opinions of the Greeks.[77]

Josephus receives some support from one document from the Dead Sea Scrolls, found near the Essene site of Qumran:

> These are those you fou[nded before] the centuries,
> to judge through them all your works before creating them,
> together with the host of your spirits and the assembly of [the gods,]
> with the holy vault and all the hosts,
> with the earth and all its produce.[78]

The Dead Sea Scrolls were discovered in 1947 and, except for this one passage, contribute little to our understanding of doctrines of preexistence in the early Christian world. They shed light principally (assuming the connection is correctly made, which some scholars doubt) on the religious beliefs and practices of the Essenes, a reclusive group of religious ascetics. The find was of signal importance to the study of messianic and mystic varieties of Judaism and in pushing the date of the earliest biblical manuscripts back a thousand years. But two years earlier, another ancient library was discovered in upper Egypt that would revolutionize modern scholarship on the subject of Christian origins and development. And preexistence featured very prominently indeed among those believers.

Gnosticism

"Out of the mist of the beginning of our era," wrote the great German scholar of antiquity Hans Jonas, "there looms a pageant of mythical figures whose vast, superhuman contours might people the walls and ceiling of another Sistine Chapel." This cast of "strangely familiar" characters, he continued, people a drama whose action unfolds "in the heights, in the divine or angelic or daimonic realm, a drama of pre-cosmic persons in the supranatural world, of which the drama of man in the natural world is but a distant echo."[79]

Jonas was referring to Gnosticism—a set of diffuse and fragmented beliefs, notoriously difficult to define. This may be because, as some scholars argue, it is difficult "in the post–Nag Hammadi age, to come up with a single definition that does justice to the diverse data that by scholarly convention have come to be lumped into this category."[80] Karen King agrees that "no widely accepted consensus has resulted from the many recent attempts to define Gnosticism, to characterize its nature and essence, to list its essential characteristics, or to establish its origins and trace its development."[81] What scholars have been calling Gnosticism for centuries has, over the years, been traced to "Hellenic, Babylonian, Egyptian, and Iranian origins and every possible combination of these with one another and with Jewish and Christian elements." Those writers generally considered Gnostic were usually seen, by the church fathers especially, as representing a deviant form of early Christian thought. Jonas maintained that "there was abroad in the Hellenistic world Gnostic thought and speculation entirely free of Christian connections."[82] Indeed, in the melting pot of the Hellenic world, even Hindu and Buddhist influences were felt, as commercial contacts between the East and the Greco-Roman world exploded at the very moment of Gnosticism's flowering (80–200 CE).[83]

The main limitation to our understanding of Gnosticism has been the fact that, for most of modern history, scholars only had access to its leading figures and teachers through a group of writers bitterly hostile to them—those church fathers who attacked the Gnostics as heretics. No record remains of how the Gnostics replied to those attacks, what misconceptions or misrepresentations they might have objected to or rebutted. The situation changed dramatically in 1945 when the so-called Nag Hammadi library was discovered in upper Egypt north of ancient Thebes. This find of manuscripts dating from 100 CE to 250 CE revolutionized modern understanding of Gnosticism by revealing many of its revered texts—but it by no means presents a clear picture. It may be true, on the one hand, as James Robinson argues in introducing the first complete English translation of the texts, that "the coming to light of the Nag Hammadi Library gives unexpected access to the Gnostic stance as Gnostics themselves presented it."[84] On the other hand, the discovery included texts from an array of traditions—Gnostic, Christian, hermetic, and Platonic—that were, perhaps precipitously, assumed to represent a self-consistent collection of Gnostic thought.[85] Kurt Rudolph suggests that it is most accurate to consider Gnosticism as having, "strictly speaking,…no tradition of its own but only a borrowed one. Its mythology is a tradition consciously created from alien material, which it has appropriated to match its own basic conception."[86] Michael Williams proposes that a term like "biblical demiurgical traditions" would unify most texts in the old rubric under a designation that draws attention to the distinctive aspect of the Gnostic cosmology—the making and supervising of the cosmos by a class of deities subordinate to or distinct from the highest God.[87] The dominant mode of what scholars have called Gnostic, however, is, in the words of Elaine Pagels, "Christian terminology, unmistakably related to a Jewish heritage."[88]

In appropriating texts from traditions like Christianity and Platonism to its own purposes, Gnosticism offended disciples of both. "Gnostic schools," writes Robinson, inheriting "the ancient world's religious and philosophical traditions and mythology…began to emerge within Christianity and Neo-Platonism, until both agreed in excluding them as the 'heresy' of Gnosticism."[89] In the early Christian centuries, boundaries among Jewish, Christian, Neo-Platonic, and esoteric traditions were permeable and shifting. Ideas later identified as Gnostic were a considerable part of the mix and emerged as one of the greatest, if somewhat amorphous, threats to a developing Christian orthodoxy. However, whenever one deals with religious historiography, in which a stable orthodoxy punctuated by eruptions of schism and heresy is considered the norm, it is good to remember the criticism of Walter Bauer, who faults the assumption that, "where there is heresy, orthodoxy must have preceded. For example, Origen puts it like this: 'All heretics at first are believers; then later they swerve from the rule of faith.'" In reality, Bauer suggests, heresy is simply the orthodoxy that lost in the battle over competing doctrines.[90] What is known for certain is that the church fathers whose positions became dominant considered the Gnostics to be a principal threat to their definition of orthodoxy. Preexistence featured in many of the Gnostic texts and traditions. And that fact suggests one reason that this doctrine became a polarizing topic in the early Christian centuries.

Although Gnosticism may be a grouping of many traditions (or an amalgam, what Rudolph calls a "product of Hellenic syncretism"), a number of core elements persist through many of the texts. One common feature is suggested by the Gnostic teacher Theodotus in the mid-second century. The Gnostic, meaning one who "knows," has come to a knowledge of "who we were, and what we have become, where we were or where we were placed, whither we hasten, from what we are redeemed, what birth is and what rebirth."[91] Gnosticism, in other words, ambitiously lays out to the initiate the full range of the soul's history, from pre-mortal realms in the divine presence, through imprisonment in a degraded tabernacle of flesh, and on to a sublime reintegration into the heavens. Rudolph agrees that the first common principle of Gnosticism is this religious knowledge oriented around "the divine nature of man, his origin and his destiny."[92] The knowledge takes the form of a special revelation, or a kind of remembering or recovery of something forgotten. As the *Gospel of Truth*, a second-century CE text from Nag Hammadi, claims, "Those who are thus going to have knowledge know whence they came and whither they are going. They know it as someone who, having become intoxicated, has turned from his drunkenness and, having come to himself, has restored what is his own." Or, in another metaphor, one who comes to a gnosis of one's true origins and nature is like "the one who comes to himself and awakens." Eventually, the same gospel continues, "each one will speak concerning the place from which they have come forth, and to the region from which they have received their essential being they will hasten to return again and receive from that place, the place where they stood before, and they will taste of that place, and be nourished, and grow."[93]

Theodotus provides a brief but telling account of creation, where he writes that a human consists of two souls. The one "according to the image of God" is fashioned of earthly matter. But the soul "according to the likeness of God" is the one God placed in man by means of angels and is "something consubstantial with himself."[94] A historic Congress on the Origins of Gnosticism gave ampler expression to this central myth, which centers on "the presence in man of a divine 'spark' [or spirit, *pneuma*]…which has proceeded from the divine world and has fallen into this world of destiny, birth and death and which must be reawakened through its own divine counterpart in order to be finally restored." The myth further includes the idea of "a downward development of the divine whose periphery (often called *Sophia* or *Ennoia*) has fallen victim to a crisis and must—even if indirectly—produce this world."[95]

Several other elements follow from this core narrative. First is what Rudolph calls "dualism on a monistic background." The dualism is inherent in the idea of a fall from spirit into matter; the monism is implicit in the primal (and eventual) identification of the human with God, the divine spark or spirit of humankind being the guarantor of ontological continuity with the Father and of destiny as a return to origins. (This runs counter both to Jewish hostility to such ontological continuity with God and to similar resistance in Christian theology.) The "pledge of redemption," Rudolph calls this; it is essentially related to the doctrine of apokatastasis.[96] Metaphysical dualism is consistent with both Plato and Pauline Christianity, though the Gnostic variety will be more radical, equating as it does materiality and the created world with unequivocal evil; the monism is a more vexed and vexing orientation, creating both the promise and the specter of human approximation to the divine, which worried the Mesopotamian gods and the church father Tertullian, as we shall see. In Gnosticism, that tension is raised to the level of actual friction and contestation. Building on the Genesis story of human creation, but dividing the God of the Hebrew Bible into a lesser Creator (like Plato's demiurge) and a greater, unknown God, Gnostics saw Adam as a composite of earthly materials and the divine spirit given to him "in a secret or mediated fashion." This divine inheritance "exalts him above the creator God….Redemption consists in the awakening of Adam to the knowledge of his true origin." This true knowledge is none other than knowledge of himself "as a being related to God." The Creator God imposes restrictions on the potent Tree of Knowledge in order to thwart Adam's greater potential. In Gnostic texts, the serpent of Eden thus performs the good work of enticing humans to eat the tree's fruit, which "imparts to Adam his appropriate god-like status."[97]

It would be hard to overstate the significance of this anthropology in Gnosticism and its typification of what is at stake in doctrines of preexistence. This "doctrine of the God 'Man'" is, says Rudolph, one of the more important of the complex of ideas in Gnosticism and is rooted in "the close relationship or kinship of nature between the highest God and the inner core of man." In one principal version of this idea, the first or primal man is the highest being himself and precedes the physical man, serving as his prototype. In another version, God first produces man as a heavenly being of a nature like himself, who then becomes the pattern for earthly beings. In this latter version, heavenly man is sometimes seduced or tricked into taking up his abode in an earthly shell. The basic motif remains the same in both versions and forms "one of the basic conceptions of Gnosis": the "idea of the fall of a heavenly being and his dispersal in the earthly world."[98] Hans Jonas wrote that "this exaltation of 'man' into a supramundane God who…is…earlier and more exalted than the Demiurge, is one of the most important aspects of gnostic mythology in the general history of religions."[99]

The journey of the human spirit from pre-mortal beginnings through earthly descent and on to eventual glory is represented lyrically and clearly—if allegorically—in the *Hymn of the Pearl*, which appears in the *Acts of Thomas*. The reading of Bentley Layton is probably the most common; the hymn recounts, he writes, "the soul's entry into bodily incarnation and its eventual disengagement from the body."[100] The first stanza tells of a son of royal parents who is required to leave his father's kingdom to seek a pearl. His parents bless him, clothe him, and send him away:

> When I was a little child living
> in my father's palace in his kingdom,
> happy in the glories and riches
> of my family that nurtured me,
> my parents gave me supplies
> and sent me on a mission
> from our home in the east.…
> They took off my bright robe of glory,
> which they had made for me out of love,
> and took away my purple toga,
> which was woven to fit my stature.
> They made a covenant with me
> and wrote it in my heart so I would not forget:
> "When you go down into Egypt
> and bring back the one pearl
> that lies in the middle of the sea
> and is guarded by the snorting serpent,
> you will again put on your robe of glory
> and your toga over it,
> and with your brother, our next in rank,
> you will be heir in our kingdom."

In this new realm, he is soon distracted from his mission. Once among the many strangers, he recalls, "I put on a robe like theirs" and

> fell into a deep sleep.
> I forgot that I was a son of kings
> and served their king.
> I forgot the pearl
> for which my parents had sent me.
> Through the heaviness of their food,
> I fell into a deep sleep.

His alarmed parents, together with his crown prince brother, send him a letter reminding him of his mission. Their message, delivered by an eagle, rouses him from his spiritual lethargy and spurs him to defeat the serpent.

> I seized the pearl
> and turned to carry it to my father.
> Those filthy and impure garments
> I stripped off, leaving them in the fields,
> and went straight on my way
> into the light of our homeland in the east.

His "robe of glory" is offered to him again, and in its reflection he sees himself as "two entities in one form…Therein I clothed myself and ascended to the gate of salutation and adoration."[101]

The *Gospel of Philip* presupposes a less individualized preexistence. According to the author of this text, the names we give to worldly versions of what is real are "very deceptive," including our naming of "'the Father' and 'the Son' and 'the Holy Spirit'…and 'the Church.'" The implication, according to Coptic scholars, is that all of these "worldly things" have their true essence in preexisting forms.[102] The Christian Gnostic text *A Valentinian Exposition* similarly makes reference to an "Uncreated Tetrad" of word, life, man, and church that produced begotten forms of each.[103] It seems that this preexistent church is more than an unrealized heavenly template. For the Gnostics, there were two (or sometimes three) types of humans: the earthly or fleshly (*choic* or *sarkic*); the spiritual (pneumatic from *pneuma*, "spirit"); and the psychic (from *psyche*, "soul"), which could constitute a middle group. According to this doctrine, the "church" consisted of the elect, that is, the pneumatic or spiritual beings. As Rudolph writes, the earthly church "is limited to the 'spirits' which existed already with the primeval Father before the creation and are reborn in the pneumatics."[104] Therefore, the true church has both pre-mortal and earthly versions. Finally, echoing the early Christian logic described above by Harnack, the *Tripartite Tractate* argues by analogy from the Son to the church as a whole:

> Not only does the Son exist from the beginning, but the Church, too, exists
> from the beginning….The matter of the Son exists just as something

which is fixed. His offspring, the things which exist, being innumerable, illimitable, and inseparable have, like kisses, come forth from the Son and the father....Such is the Church consisting of many men, which exists before the aeons....Such is the nature of the holy imperishable spirits upon which the Son rests.[105]

The *Apocryphon of John* contains many of those Gnostic mythological elements, which were unpalatable to the Christian orthodoxy that prevailed. Sophia figures as a prominent entity, an emanation from the Supreme Being, whose unauthorized actions bring about calamity. "She wanted to bring forth something like herself, without the consent of the spirit," but her misguided initiative only succeeds in producing a monstrous subdeity named Yaldabaoth. He in turn creates numerous angels, and then, assuming the role that Genesis assigns to God, Yaldabaoth in this text creates the race of humans in the Father's image. Then he is duped ("because he lives in ignorance") into bestowing spirit upon the body he has fashioned, whereupon "he breathed his spirit into Adam," and "the body moved and became powerful. And it was enlightened." Jealous deities unite to destroy the creation, but God sends Epinoia (Reflection), also named Zoe (Life, which is Eve's name, according to the Septuagint), to be man's companion and to help the creature by "restoring it to its fullness, teaching it about the descent of the seed, teaching it about the way of ascent, which is the way of descent." Thus, an antidote to man's imprisonment in a material body, forged with "the fetter of forgetfulness," is provided by Epinoia, or "enlightened afterthought within."

Epinoia, Adam's gift of afterthought or reflection, is then given human embodiment in a lovely counterpart to Eve's creation story in Genesis. In this Gnostic version, Adam's initial apprehension of Eve creates a shock of recognition. Either her supernal beauty or the form's familiarity temporarily suspends the mists of forgetfulness in which he has until then labored. "At once enlightened afterthought appeared and removed the veil that covered his mind. He sobered up from the drunkenness of darkness. He recognized his counterpart and said, This is now bone from my bones, and flesh from my flesh."

The text then reaffirms that the human condition is marked by obliviousness to our pre-mortal state, even as it hints of a Christ who will be the instrument of the eventual restoration (or apokatastasis) of the entire human race:

The human beings were made to drink water of forgetfulness by the first ruler, so that they might not know where they had come from. For a time the seed remained and helped so that when the spirit descends from the holy realms, it may raise up the seed and heal what it lacks, that the entire realm of fullness may be holy and lack nothing.[106]

The ignorance imposed by the Mesopotamian gods out of jealousy and self-pres-
ervation becomes in some later variations an act of compassion and mercy. In this
Gnostic version, just why humans should forget their primeval home is unclear.

The author of the letter to the Colossians makes passing reference to Christ
as having created "things visible and invisible, whether thrones or dominions or
rulers or powers" (1:16). The *Revelation of Adam* (or *Apocalypse of Adam*), like
John's *Apocryphon*, elaborates this multitiered cosmology, peopled by preexistent
angels and aeons (supernatural entities emanating from the Supreme Being), but
also humans—though the details are sometimes garbled and incomplete due to
manuscript damage. In the variety of Gnosticism represented by this document
(composed before 350 CE), Seth is the great progenitor of the righteous. Adam
explains to his son how Adam and Eve came from "the eternal realm," where they
resembled "the great eternal angels." After their fall into mortality, various other
groups follow. Some, presumably the righteous descendants of Seth, will become
"like the cloud of great light." Others, cast out from "the great eternal realms and
the angels," apparently become the descendants of Cain. In this tradition, there is
no undifferentiated fall of humans into mortality, but an apportionment of earthly
lineages that depend upon different preexistent scenarios. Eternal destiny as well is
linked to these various origins. Seth's descendants, the true Gnostics, will be saved
for "they have not received spirit from this kingdom" but from a place "eternal,
angelic."[107]

The *Exegesis on the Soul* is a brief treatise whose purpose is to recount the
fall of the soul into mortality and encourage its repentance and return. Consistent
with so much of Platonic thought, corporeality is seen as a degradation, rendered
metaphorically in this case as prostitution. "As long as [the soul] was alone with the
Father," the anonymous author writes, "she was virgin....But when she fell down
into a body and came to this life,...she fell into the hands of many robbers." At
first forcibly defiled, in the end "she prostituted herself and gave herself to one
and all."[108] In this mythical treatment, the soul repents "abandoning [the Father's]
house," which suggests an element of choice in the soul's descent into the world.
The Father takes pity on her and assists her soul to "regain her proper character."
Forsaking her lovers, the soul returns to the bridegroom and finds in the union
both personal renewal and the power to conceive and bear "good children." The
culmination, now familiar to us, is of reintegration into remembered, heavenly
realms through a kind of mystical ascent (epistrophe, or the return of something
to its original source):

> Now it is fitting that the soul regenerate herself and become again as she
> formerly was. The soul then moves of her own accord.[109] And she received
> the divine nature from the Father for her rejuvenation, so that she might be

restored to the place where originally she had been.... This is the upward journey of ascent to heaven. This is the way of ascent to the Father.[110]

Other Gnostic texts do not just assert the pre-mortality of the soul, but fully justify the fears later expressed by Tertullian and other apologists that such doctrines tend toward the dangerous glorification of human potential, insofar as they assert that the human soul both outlasts and predates the heavenly rulers themselves. Some of these are variants on the divine assembly motif we saw in Kings and Psalm 82. One of these texts, the *Hypostasis of the Archons*, is an extended gloss on Colossians 1:13 and Ephesians 6:12. The author of Colossians refers to our "rescue from the power of darkness," and the author of Ephesians notes the human struggle against "the rulers, against the authorities, against the cosmic powers of this present darkness, against the spiritual forces of evil in the heavenly places." The long dominance in Protestantism of the King James Version of the Bible, with its reference to the "power of darkness" and "spiritual wickedness in high places" made it easy to see the combat as a metaphorical one against abstract wickedness or corrupt rulers in church or government. The Gnostics, like the character Ransom in C. S. Lewis's *Perelandra*, find such watered-down evasions to be dangerous self-deception. Hence the title's "hypostasis," that is, the *essential* or *substantive reality*, of the heavenly rulers.[111] ("Hypersomatic beings at great heights," Ransom calls them.)[112]

In the *Hypostasis*, we are introduced to myriad archons (rulers), one of whom misguidedly boasts, "it is I who am God; there is none other apart from me." The narrative follows these lascivious rulers as they are outwitted by Eve, conspire to drown the human race, and threaten the righteous woman Norea. She is finally accosted by a wise angel, who reveals the origin and destiny of humans and archons alike. Inquiring, "am I also from...Matter," like the archons? she is told that "you, together with your offspring, are from the Primeval Father, from Above, out of the imperishable Light, their souls are come." Even the archons will pass away, but those imbued with the spirit of truth (the Gnostics) will be "deathless in the midst of dying mankind."[113]

Another text found in Nag Hammadi, *On the Origin of the World*, closely parallels the *Hypostasis*. One of the archons, the arrogant demiurge Yaldabaoth, creates the world and boasts that he "is god and no other one exists." He is rudely corrected by Pistis, who informs him that "an enlightened, immortal man [or humanity, *anthropos*] existed before you. This will appear within your molded bodies." Eventually, as in the *Hypostasis*, the enlightened ones triumph over Yaldabaoth and his cohorts, and return to their place of origin, "for it is necessary that every one enter the place from whence he came." As for the humanity that exists before even the archons, little more is said. Sabaoth, the righteous son of Yaldabaoth, learns of "the deathless man and his light" and creates "an angelic church" like the church that is in the eighth heaven. Pistis teaches him "about all those which exist in the eighth [heaven]," but we hear nothing more of them. Only Jesus and "a first born called Israel" are mentioned by name as existing in these contested courts on high.[114]

Also found at Nag Hammadi were texts linked to a tradition closely associated with Gnosticism, known as hermeticism.[115] The *Corpus Hermeticum* is a compilation believed since antiquity to have been written by the ancient Egyptian Hermes Trismegistus, a name that blends the Greek god of communication with the Egyptian god of wisdom. In actuality, the works were not written by Egyptians in remote antiquity, but derive from the Hellenized Egypt of the second and third centuries and contain "popular Greek philosophy of the period, a mixture of Platonism and Stoicism, combined with some Jewish and probably some Persian influences." The *Corpus Hermeticum*'s particular cast comes from what Frances Yates saw as a second-century weariness with Greek philosophy generally and a lively belief that the true home of all knowledge was in Egypt. This most famous scholar of hermeticism saw it as "a religion, a cult without temples or liturgy," that shared with Gnosticism generally the belief that inner illumination, rather than rational dialectic, held the key to knowledge of the divine.[116] The principal texts of hermeticism purport to describe an Egyptian religion, its rites and methods of theurgy (drawing down the powers of divinity to enable the soul to re-ascend through the spheres to the heaven whence it came).

Many early Christian writers believed that the *Corpus* was produced at the time of the biblical Moses or even earlier (Noah, Shem, and Japheth or even Enoch and Adam were all candidates for authorship).[117] The church fathers explained the unexpectedly inspired nature of its pagan writings by asserting that God had revealed eternal truths to the *Corpus*'s authors, albeit in limited fashion. Such precious morsels of inspired truth therefore represented part of a *prisca theologia*, or "ancient wisdom."[118] Some of these hermetic teachings echoed *Timaeus*, such as the belief that "[a]ll the souls...come from the one soul of the all," and that "when the body gets its bulk and drags the soul down to the body's grossness, the soul, having separated from itself, gives birth to forgetting."[119] Yet the imputation of these doctrines to Moses via Egypt gave them a pedigree that was immune to charges of pilfering from the Greeks. (And, in at least one regard, that of Hebrew wisdom literature, scholars have been arguing since 1924 over evidence that Hebrew writings do indeed show evidence of borrowing from Egyptian models.)[120] Augustine had his doubts about Hermes as the best example of an inspired predecessor to the prophets. He held that, even though "Hermes, indeed, says many things concerning the Maker of this world which have the appearance of truth," ultimately "it was not the Holy Spirit Who revealed these things to him, as He did to the holy prophets."[121] But earlier authorities, like the Christian apologist Lactantius, placed Hermes in ancient Egypt before the time of Pythagoras and considered his teachings to be "a divine testimony."[122]

The most fundamental doctrine of the *Hermetica*, perhaps, is that the soul is a prisoner of matter. One of the most important texts in the *Corpus Hermeticum* is the *Poimandres*. It recounts how "the Father of all" brought forth a child in his own image, the primal man. He bestowed upon him authority and dominion over all of God's creatures. Descending through the spheres of heaven to look upon the world, the man becomes enamored of Nature and she of him. The consequence is described as a tragic fall that explains man's human condition and bifurcated nature: "And this is why the human, of all creatures on the earth, is twofold: mortal in his body but immortal through the eternal human.... Though above the world of spheres, he is a slave of destiny."[123] The text then tells how this primal man gradually re-ascends through seven spheres, shedding all unholy attributes, until "stripped naked by the force of the harmony, he enters the eighth sphere of the fixed stars." There, he and unnamed "others" "move in order up to the father. They surrender to the powers, and become the powers, and are in god. This is the good, the aim of those who have gnosis: to become god."[124] Hermes Trismegistus himself appears as a character in a similar-themed text found at Nag Hammadi, the Discourse on the Eighth and Ninth, wherein he instructs a pupil about the heavenly ascent back to the place of origin.

In the Renaissance, not only neglected classics of Greece were rediscovered and enthusiastically promoted. Hermetic, along with Platonic, texts were translated and celebrated by the influential humanist Marsilio Ficino, lending impetus to a resurgence of the idea of preexistence found in both sources. In the early Christian centuries, however, it is not surprising that Neo-Platonic, Gnostic, and hermetic texts met with a mixed reception nor that the church fathers massed their greatest intellectual energies against the Gnostic heresies in particular. This is because heresy has always represented a more acute danger to orthodoxy than radical difference, and contamination is more difficult to combat than outright opposition. Some Gnostic doctrines were quite obviously beyond the pale of Judeo-Christian monotheism, seeming to represent overzealous and creative attempts at theodicy. For example, Jonas did not explain exactly what he meant in saying that Gnosticism "fed on the impulses of a widely prevalent human situation." But certainly the problem of evil and suffering in a world created by an all-good and all-powerful God has been a perennial challenge for Christian theology. Some of the earliest dissenters from Christian orthodoxy were those, like the second-century Gnostic Marcion, who found a single, omnipotent God irreconcilable with a world of pain and sorrow. Taking his cue from the seeming dichotomy of the biblical deity—the harsh and vengeful God of the Old Testament and John's New Testament God of love—Marcion concluded that two gods, not one, ruled the universe.

One nineteenth-century writer holds that, in the history of theology, three less radical theodicies have been propounded to address this "great question of the ages"—why God did not preserve the world from the "overshadowing of evil," or "why he permitted the beauty of the world to become disfigured, as it has been, by the dark invasion and ravages of sin." And the author indicates that the first theory invoked to at least "mitigate the stupendous darkness" enveloping the world was the hypothesis of the soul's preexistence.[125] The power of preexistence to function as theodicy would be one explanation for its proliferation among the Gnostics. But while not clearly proscribed by Judeo-Christian scriptures, the doctrine still had the distinct potential to offend a certain religious sensibility. As Elaine Pagels points out, "Orthodox Jews and Christians insist that a chasm separates humanity from its creator: God is wholly other. But some of the Gnostics who wrote these gospels contradict this: self-knowledge *is* knowledge of God; the self and the divine are identical."[126] Believing the human soul to originate in heavenly realms rather than terrestrial wombs clearly threatens the Creator-creature divide. An evangelical scholar has noted the proclivity of moderns to continue to react defensively to cosmologies that threaten narrowly conceived versions of monotheism. He is writing in the context of early Jewish ideas about deity, but his point is clearly applicable to pre-mortality. We, too, commonly operate, he argues, on the basis of a priori assumptions about what monotheistic belief entails. And accordingly, "there seems to be an implicit agreement...that more than one transcendent being of any significance complicates or constitutes a weakening of or threat to monotheism."[127] Situating the soul in a pre-mortal sphere, among a panoply of other heavenly beings in the presence of and capable of embracing the divine, portends just such a collapse of sacred distance.

Tertullian, one of the earliest of the church fathers, attacked as heretical any system or thinker that encouraged this collapse, and Gnosticism's view of the human soul was seen as especially pernicious in this regard. As Hans von Campenhausen notes, the Gnosis represented "a spiritual and idealistic overestimate of the self which blurs the fixed limits that separate the creature from the deity."[128] We will witness time and again that this concern is a principal cause of objections to preexistence. Not fearing to blur the Creator-creature divide, the Gnostics find no reason to shun the Platonic solution. Ultimately, the impact of the Gnostics on the history of preexistence will be a negative one. As the greatest threat to orthodoxy in the early church, Gnosticism—and those doctrines it promoted that were not indisputably germane to Christianity—will be definitively banished by the time of the first councils. The guilt by association imputed to preexistence will add a burden of suspicion that—allied to other objections to preexistence—will prove decisive.

4

Neo-Platonism and the Church Fathers

What indeed has Athens to do with Jerusalem?
—Tertullian[1]

In the early Christian centuries, Platonism was undergoing dramatic developments, profoundly influencing—even as it was shaped by—Christian theology. In about 230 CE, at a time when Christianity was still a persecuted sect, a man of uncertain birth—perhaps Egyptian—named Plotinus (205–270) traveled to Alexandria to study philosophy. There, he fell under the influence of a teacher of Platonism named Ammonius Saccas. Together with his mentor, Plotinus forged a brand of philosophy sufficiently distinct from Plato's original to constitute a new variety that would be called Neo-Platonism.[2] After years in Alexandria, Plotinus moved to Rome, where he attracted a number of students. The most prominent of these, Porphyry, edited his teacher's vast collection of notes and lectures and published them as the *Enneads*. That work became the most important text through which Platonism, in modified form, was disseminated to subsequent generations. As one scholar writes, "Neo-Platonism is not only the final flowering of ancient Greek thought but also the mode in which it was transmitted to the Byzantine, Western European and Islamic civilizations. It remained influential even after the Enlightenment," and it appears in the writings and philosophy of Jacob Boehme, the Quakers, the Jewish Kabbalah, Thomas Aquinas, Dante, Spenser, the Romantics, the Cambridge Platonists, Hegel, and Emerson, as well as in Renaissance art, new science, and mysticism.[3]

Plotinus is generally referred to as the father of Neo-Platonism, though it is difficult to know how much he contributed to the version of Platonism taught by his mentor. The *Enneads* (meaning "nines," reflecting the book's organization by groupings of nine) covers a spectrum of topics from virtue and beauty to cosmology and free will. To read the *Enneads* is to be immersed in a world radically unlike the relatively straightforward dialogues Plato typically wrote. The mysticism of *Timaeus*, with its nebulous cosmogony involving transcendent forms, the demiurge, and the world soul, is here heightened and elaborated, as concepts and cosmological origins especially become ever more ineffable, resistant to concrete articulation, and relegated to the realm of metaphor and analogy.

For Plotinus, all existence is rooted in the One, which is outside all possibilities of language to describe and so transcendent that it is better understood as the possibility of all being than as a being or in fact anything that exists. (We see here an anticipation of the later, creedal attempts to describe God through an always inadequate language.) As Plotinus writes, "the One is all things and not a single one of them: it is the principle of all things, not all things....It is because there is nothing in it that all things come from it: in order that being may exist, the One is not being, but the generator of being." What eventuates from this One is not so much an act of creation as what Neo-Platonists will call "emanation." "The One, perfect because it seeks nothing, has nothing, and needs nothing, overflows, as it were, and its superabundance makes something other than itself."[4]

This new emanation is intelligence, mind, or intellectual principle (*nous*), which is the source of all existence. The possibilities or templates of all reality are present to it as thoughts in the divine mind—what Plato called the forms or ideas (*eidoi*). It is this second hypostasis that Plotinus refers to as the divinity, the demiurge, or God (*theos*).

The third hypostasis in this cosmological hierarchy is soul (analogous to the world soul of *Timaeus*), which is effectively the agent of creation and a kind of mediator between two versions of a dichotomized soul. The higher, contemplative aspect of soul remains associated with the divine mind, while the inferior aspect of soul descends to create, order, and inhabit a material world. In Plotinus's language, the soul is thus both divisible and indivisible at the same time: "it is divided and not divided, or rather it is not itself divided and has not become divided; for it remains whole with itself, but is divided in the sphere of bodies by the peculiar divisibility of bodies." In other words, the "Soul of All" always abides in the heavens, "but the particular souls themselves go to the things. So they have departed to the depths; or rather, a great part of them has been dragged down...to the lower existence." That is why he can say that "the soul is composed of that which is above and that which is attached to that higher world but has flowed out as far as these parts, like a line from a centre." In that sense, it is with the second hypostasis, or level of reality, that the souls of humankind originate. "That world has souls without bodies, but this world has the souls which have come to be in bodies."[5]

Having souls that originate in and are identical with the indivisible soul, human beings in that sense "possess God." Plotinus explains the precise sense in which human souls are related to their divine origin: though there is a sense in which souls are individual entities, in fact the soul is "present to bodies since it shines in them and makes them living creatures," not by physically imparting its substance, but by remaining itself "and giving images of itself, like a face seen in many mirrors." Accordingly, birth involves a "descent of the Soul, when something else comes to be from it which comes down in the soul's inclination."[6] The metaphor he reverts to time and again is of a light casting a shadow. The shadows come into existence by virtue of a light and therefore can be said to originate in that light and depend for their subsistence on that light; still, a shadow is not physically a portion of that light and does not, by its existence, represent a diminishing of the original light in the way a graft represents a diminishing of the original tree from which it is taken. Human souls in this model are thus both part of and synonymous with the world soul; the world soul, in turn, which we also saw in *Timaeus*, is itself a product of the divine mind, universal intelligence, or intellectual principle (*nous*), which is the totality of all being, containing the forms or ideas of all things that exist in the universe. And this *nous* is itself an emanation of the One, just as the sun gives light and illumination to the universe, without itself being diminished thereby.

In this transformation of Platonism into Neo-Platonism, the philosophy articulated by Plotinus acquires an emphatic religious dimension; he never mentions Christianity by name, and his God is still far from the personal being of perfect love and benignity. But Plotinus does emphasize the absolute transcendence and divinity of the One, and his highest aspiration as a philosopher is to articulate—and personally enact—the means by which a human soul achieves a kind of ecstatic union with that source of all being. For this reason, in the very first book of the *Enneads*, he poses the question, "What art is there, what method or practice which will take us up there where we must go? Where that is, that it is to the Good, the First Principle, we can take as agreed."[7] In this case, he anticipates the theurgy that comes to be a hallmark of Neo-Platonism. "Try to bring back the god in you to the divine in the All" were reportedly his dying words.[8] If Platonism seemed to many Christians an inspired version of Christian principles, Plotinus's innovations made a synthesis even easier, by situating human beings firmly within a scheme of divine origins, earthly purification, and reintegration with the divine in a mystical union.

Moving from theory to praxis, Plotinus personally embodied Neo-Platonism's contribution to Christianity's mystical side. Four times, he achieved the goal of union with the divine "in an unspeakable actuality and not in potency only," according to his biographer, who was with him on those occasions.[9] He also added to Christianity's ascetic impulses, by outdoing even Plato in his devaluation of the physical in favor of the spiritual. For Plotinus, the soul, originally divine and pure, becomes evil through the fact of its incorporation into the body.[10] His biographer seemed to think his self-contempt in this regard to be the most notable aspect of his life and teachings, since he began his account with the words "Plotinus…seemed like one who felt ashamed of being in a body."[11] As philosophy was for Plato the instrument of purification from all bodily desires and attachments, so for the Neo-Platonists it is the vehicle through which the soul draws upon divine powers to re-ascend the levels of being in pursuit of unity with the One.

Having declared that the human soul is at once a part of the world soul and an independent entity housed in flesh, Plotinus devotes considerable attention to this latter dimension of the self. His fourth *Ennead* purports to illuminate the question of "how soul comes to be in a body. What is its way of entering?"[12] It is clear that, for Plotinus, mortality is a kind of fall, though what form this fall took is obscure. "The souls of men," he writes, "have entered into [mortality] in a leap downward from the Supreme." Alliance with a physical body makes that descent a kind of degradation, "but Father Zeus, pitying them in their troubles, makes the bonds over which they have trouble dissoluble by death and gives them periods of rest, making them…free of bodies."[13] The fall appears to be universal and involves both choice and preordained destiny (unlike Plato's scheme). On the one hand, no spirit is arbitrarily forced into the lower plane of existence. "If the souls came willingly," he asks, "why do you blame the universe into which you came of your own free will, when it gives you leave, too, to get out of it, if any of you dislike it?"[14] And yet, choice and destiny are vaguely conflated:

> Each soul comes down to a body made ready for it according to its resemblance to the soul's disposition.…The inescapable rule and the justice ["which govern the descent of souls," adds the translator]…compel…each to go to its proper order to that to which it originally tends, the image of its original choice and disposition.[15]

But the resulting tragic human condition is not entirely one of deserving:

> The individual souls, certainly, have an…impulse to return to…the principle from which they came into being, but they also possess a power directed to the world here below.…Those which are able to be more in the company of Intellect live the life there more, but those whose normal condition is, *by nature or chance*, the opposite, live more the life here below.[16] (my emphasis)

Plotinus realizes the tension he has depicted, but insists there is "no contradiction…between necessity and free-will," since the law of nature justly punishes not just actions, but also the principle from which such actions spring. Therefore, he argues, the soul inevitably comes to earth "by a spontaneous inclination, its own power," and the unfolding of its nature is "the cause of its descent." Thus, "the souls go neither willingly nor because they are sent." The soul, when it goes forth, does so in both "willingness and unwillingness." Besides, he adds weakly, no serious harm is done if the suffering spirit escapes the bonds of mortality quickly. (Ingenious but unsuccessful, judges R. T. Wallis of Plotinus's attempts to resolve the ambiguity.)[17]

No angels or escorts usher the soul to its incarnation in Plotinus's system, but the occasion is momentous even without chiming bells or guiding heralds:

> There is no need of anyone to send it or bring it into the body at a particular time, or into this or that particular body, but when its moment comes to it[,] it descends and enters where it must as of its own accord. Each has its own time and when it comes, like a herald summoning it, the soul comes down and goes into the appropriate body, so that what happens is like a stirring and carrying away by magic powers and mighty attractions.

The end result is a scene of cosmic splendor: souls burst into existence, like trees filling bare ground, "breaking out into spots in excessive numbers." And "because all this has happened this universal order of ours, which has many lights and is illuminated by souls, is being further set in order and adorned, receiving new beauties over and above its former ones, from the gods of that other world and the other intellects which give souls."

Plotinus's account of the journey earthward itself becomes the seed that subsequent poets and mystics will elaborate in great detail. "The souls when they have peeped out of the intelligible world go first to heaven, and when they have put on a body there go on by its means to earthier bodies." The rate and extent of the descent depend on their nature, their degree of self-mastery, and their susceptibility to heaviness and forgetfulness.[18]

Surprisingly perhaps, Plotinus explicitly resists the occasion his own anthropology gives him for theodicy. Though he earlier tried to find a place for freedom in a system of cosmic order and determinism, he now attributes the fall of some souls to the best of intentions. From their place above, given stewardship over earthly counterparts, they find that their charges need more care than they anticipated. Then, like sailors trying to save a storm-tossed vessel, these souls get pulled down and "fettered with bonds of magic" by the very charges they were intent on saving. Plotinus poses the question of cosmic justice directly: what of unmerited "punishments or poverty or sickness[?]...Are these to be said to have come upon them because of previous sins?" No, he answers simply. They are accidental consequences in a larger order of things, much as innocent occupants of a house will perish if the structure falls.[19]

Even if pre-mortal existence provides relief for the dilemma of an innocent humanity consigned to a world of suffering, any temporal origin of the human soul can defer but not escape other theological quandaries. This is because, for an omniscient and omnipotent God, any act of creation is itself problematic, insofar as it suggests acting out of need or desire—both of which imply inadequacy, insufficiency, or change in the divine perfection. As Aristotle had already seen, things must be either better or worse after the world's creation. If worse, God is flawed. If better, then God was previously responsible for an imperfect universe, and he is likewise flawed.[20] (The creation of God the Son would create its own, even more vexing theological dilemmas, hence the crucial creedal insistence on Christ as "begotten, not made.") Philo had confronted the problem and to preserve God's unchangingness argued that "God's creative action has no extension in time; the distinction of the days of creation in the biblical creation story represents an order, not a succession in time. The creation of the world is achieved once [and] for all and is not amenable to temporal categories." Gerhard May's comment is pertinent: "Frankly such statements cannot hide the problems which arise for the concept of God from the acceptance of a beginning of the world: The creative act in time implies that God is not eternal creator; and so through the creation we come to a change in God."[21]

The Neo-Platonists acted to resolve the dilemma and in so doing provided a formula that will prove to be an integral ingredient in early Christian theology and, much later, philosophical attempts to resolve the problem of free will. Neo-Platonism does this by establishing the origin of the world in terms of causal relation, rather than chronological coming into being. This explains why the One must be outside of being itself. For, as Plotinus reasons, if the true whole "really is a whole, [it] must not only be whole in the sense that it is all things, but it must have its wholeness in such a way that it is deficient in nothing. If this is so, there is nothing that is going to be [in the future] for it, for if something is going to be, it was lacking to it before; so it was not whole." Therefore, he concludes, that which is self-existent and unengendered cannot be subject to change or futurity, else it "will fall from the seat of being."[22] And so we have here a version of transcendence that lays a foundation for the emphatic separation of the human and the divine (the "non-engendered" cannot be touched by those temporal processes that we humans inhabit); the distinction also rescues God from the charge of changeability that any act occurring in time would entail.

Proclus will develop this idea in an eighteen-point argument in *On the Eternity of the World*. But far from using it to develop the Creator-creature divide of subsequent theology, he extends this concept of chronological timelessness to the human soul itself. In his seventh argument, Proclus takes the soul's preexistence as a premise, rather than as a conclusion. This soul itself, in other words, though in some sense a product of intellect, as emanation, is taken by definition not to have an origin in time. As Proclus puts the case (following Plato's lead in *Phaedrus*):

> [T]he definition of the soul...is "that which moves itself." And everything
> that moves itself is an "origin and source of motion." If, therefore, the soul
> of the all is eternal, then the all, being moved by the soul, must be eternal;
> and because the all is not either earlier or later, the motion of the all has
> soul, which is eternal, as its source of motion.[23]

Plotinus laid the foundations of Neo-Platonism, but his ideas received substantial modifications and additions through his disciple Porphyry, his successor Iamblichus, and Proclus, who is considered to be the last great philosopher out of ancient Greece. Porphyry's major contribution, in addition to editing the *Enneads*, was to work Aristotle into the Neo-Platonic system. Porphyry believed that the mind was capable, through its own exertions, of lifting the spirit to the requisite levels of self-transcendence. Porphyry also provided one of the most original variations on the Platonic hypothesis concerning the descent into mortality:

> As a fruitful field, though it may for a certain period of years yield good
> Grain, yet at length it is exhausted and grows barren, and then if it be laid
> fallow though it brings forth nothing but weeds and tares, yet it thereby
> recovers its ancient vigour and fruitfulness; so our Souls having been
> for many ages impregnated with the seed of Divine Ideas, by degrees
> spent themselves in bringing forth large returns of contemplation, till
> at length their Intellectual powers decaying, the higher part falls into
> a swoon, and they can exert no acts but of Imagination, whence spring
> forth the powers of the Vegetal life, which cause in them strong and irre-
> sistible propensities to an union with those inferior and terrestrial Bod-
> ies, in order to the awakening of the higher Powers, for because every
> thing in the Etherial Regions is too calme and serene to awake them,
> they are therefore conveyed to this place of noises and disturbance, and
> invessel'd in a body full of rude and impetuous passions, by which they
> may be chased into life and sensation again.[24]

So, intellectual fatigue and boredom, rather than the simple gross appetite of Plato, or the satiety which Origen will describe, account for a fall from heaven. And earthly life is provocation and stimulus, rather than punishment or purgatory.

Regarding the nature of the soul, the version of Iamblichus is more compli-cated. He will refer to man's "two souls," "two lives," and "two powers."[25] But, as Martin Laird explains, for Iamblichus, "the essence of the soul is descended in the body, with the result that, of the soul's two functions—animating the body and uniting with the divine—the soul can only perform the former. It is the precise role of theurgy to make up for what the soul cannot do."[26] This is because, for Porphyry (and Plotinus, as we saw), the soul's real essence remains in the divine realm; for Iamblichus, on the other hand, the soul is not just preexistent but fully individuated and embodied upon mortal descent. He therefore saw it as necessary to draw down heavenly powers to assist in the soul's ascent, thus developing the hugely influential idea of theurgy, giving shape to those rites and rituals which, conjoined with mental and spiritual exercises, enable the soul to re-ascend to its heavenly home. The removal of the soul's essence from the divine to the fallen realm therefore complicates, but does not preclude, the full realization (or recuperation) of its divine potential. Theurgy blurs into theosis when the culmination of this upward ascent, assisted by heavenly powers, becomes participation in or emulation of the divine itself.

Theology, for Iamblichus, was merely *theion logos*—a discourse about God or gods. He saw theurgy, on the other hand, as a "*theion ergon*, a 'work of the gods' capable of transforming man to a divine status.... Theurgy fulfilled the goal of philosophy understood as *homoiosis theo* [assimilation to the divine, or God resembling]."[27] The roots of such a goal we saw in Plato himself, when he admonished Theodorus that "a man should make all haste to escape from earth to heaven; and escape means becoming as like God as possible."[28] And Plotinus had quoted this passage with approval, developing it into his treatise "On Virtue," where he asked, "What could be more fitting than that we, living in this world, should become like to its ruler?"[29] This concept of theosis, also called theopoesis or deification, Aharon Lichtenstein summarizes, "became one of the dominant themes of the Platonic and Neo-Platonic traditions."[30] And thus we see yet another example of how those same philosophical currents that, by positing a preexistence, celebrate the spark of divinity in human beings almost invariably intimate a corresponding destiny that will prove problematic to Christian orthodoxy.

Over the next centuries, the fortunes of human preexistence will rise and fall with the shifting appraisals of Platonic philosophy generally. As the Christian fathers work to resolve the status and value of Plato's thought, preexistence will be alternately prized as ancient wisdom, reviled as a pernicious myth, and, by some of the coming age's most influential thinkers, tolerated as promising—if dubious—speculation.

Church Fathers and *Prisca Theologia*

In the early Common Era, Christianity was a small but growing cultic presence in the Roman world; Greek philosophy was synonymous with culture, enlightenment, and civilization itself. And yet by the fourth century, the world had been turned upside down. It was not so much that Christianity had vanquished pagan religion and philosophy as that Christianity had arrogated to itself, in addition to the reins of political power, the right to dictate the terms of philosophical and religious orthodoxy. In so doing, Christianity managed even to claim much of the credit for the very paganisms it had once excoriated but now appropriated and rehabilitated. "A victory in which the victors were the vanquished," Edwin Hatch described it. As he observed, the Sermon on the Mount "belongs to a world of Syrian peasants," the Nicene Creed of the fourth century "to a world of Greek philosophers."[31] The borrowings from and incorporations of secular thinkers into the Christian mainstream were too conspicuous to ignore, and Christians developed a range of explanations, some apologetic and some critical, for how Greek thought had come to occupy such a central place in Christian belief.

In the first Christian centuries especially, the relationship between the philosophies of Plato, Aristotle, the Stoics, and other classical thinkers, on the one hand, and the words of Holy Writ, on the other, was a continual subject of debates, church councils, fierce polemics, anathemas, and edicts. According to Hatch, the history of the second Christian century essentially *is* "the history of the clash and conflict between these new mystical and philosophical elements of Christianity and its earlier forms."[32] Many Christian thinkers were not, by either inclination or background, enamored of or even respectful toward those classical authorities once revered as paragons of wisdom and virtue. Those opposed to the amicable marriage of pagan and Christian thought saw only contamination and corruption in any compromise with paganism, an invitation to an array of apostasies of which Gnosticism was the most pervasive and hydra-headed. On the other side of the balance, enthusiasts engaged in at least three strategies to legitimize the Great Synthesis. They invoked the precedent of the "spoiling of the Egyptians," when the children of Israel "borrowed" the wealth of their captors in order to found their own exodus and cultural renewal; more dubiously, they could insist that the Christians were merely reclaiming what the Greeks had earlier stolen from the Hebrews. Or, they argued the theory of *prisca theologia*, the idea that a generous and just God had inspired the ancients with hints and shadows of inspired truth that anticipated the fullness of Christian doctrine.

Writing at a time when Greek philosophy still dominated the classical intellectual universe, Justin Martyr, one of the earliest church fathers (100–165 CE), defended a besieged Christianity by insisting on its similarity to Greek philosophy. As he asked his Roman audience in *First Apology*, "If, therefore, on some points we teach the same things as the poets and philosophers whom you honor, and on other points are fuller and more divine in our teaching,…why are we unjustly hated more than all others?"[33] In later centuries, some apologists continued to implicitly admit the priority of Greek culture over Christian, but justified their plagiarism as a modern-day version of Israel's studied plundering of its Egyptian masters.[34] Just as the Israelites had pilfered gold and silver to build the wealth that they would carry into the exodus, so would Milton and a host of other writers appropriate pagan models from Homer and Virgil to expound a Christian aesthetic. Beginning with Justin, however, daring voices asserted that, appearances notwithstanding, it was really the people of God who had been plundered of their inspired philosophy.

Justin insists that the Hebrew conception of creation predates the Platonic:

> It was from our teachers—we mean the account given through the proph-
> ets—that Plato borrowed his statement that God, having altered matter
> which was shapeless, made the world....Moses...was the first prophet
> and of greater antiquity than the Greek writers....So that both Plato and
> they who agree with him, and we ourselves, have learned, and you also can
> be convinced, that by the word of God the whole world was made out of
> the substance spoken of before by Moses.[35]

A generation later, Clement would clarify exactly what that chain of transmission was:

> Since the Scriptures having perished in the captivity of Nabuchodonosor,
> Esdras the Levite, the priest, in the time of Artaxerxes king of the Per-
> sians, having become inspired in the exercise of prophecy restored again
> the whole of the ancient Scriptures. And Aristobulus, in his first book
> addressed to Philometor, writes in these words: "And Plato followed the
> laws given to us, and had manifestly studied all that is said in them." And
> before Demetrius there had been translated by another, previous to the
> dominion of Alexander and of the Persians, the account of the departure
> of our countrymen the Hebrews from Egypt, and the fame of all that hap-
> pened to them, and their taking possession of the land, and the account
> of the whole code of laws; so that it is perfectly clear that the above-
> mentioned philosopher derived a great deal from this source, for he was
> very learned, as also Pythagoras, who transferred many things from our
> books to his own system of doctrines. And Numenius, the Pythagorean
> philosopher, expressly writes: "For what is Plato, but Moses speaking in
> Attic Greek?"[36]

Elsewhere, Clement said of the philosophers simply, "They have plagiarized and falsified (our writings being, as we have shown, older) the chief dogmas they hold."[37] This was especially thought to be true of *Timaeus*. Clement's contempo-rary Tertullian was equally audacious in charging the Greeks with stealing from the Jewish and Christian writings. "What poet or sophist," he wrote, "has not drunk at the fountain of the prophets? Thence, accordingly, the philosophers watered their arid minds."[38] For those inclined to Platonic notions about the soul and its origins, this scenario validated their ideas by labeling them as thinly disguised versions of the truths revealed to Israel's prophets. So Numenius of Apamea (fl. 150 CE) could implicitly suggest that his teachings, like the doctrine of the soul's descent into the world, while found in Greek philosophy, were actually biblical in origin.

Two centuries later, Christianity is the religion of the realm, not a persecuted cult, so Augustine can develop this version of the chain of influence more fully. Plato, he writes, received his "understanding of God…in many respects consistent with the truth of our religion" from reading the Jewish scriptures while traveling in Egypt. (Later, Augustine revised his account, suggesting that Plato probably gained his knowledge of Genesis by conversing with those knowledgeable about those scriptures.)[39] Plato's writings were sometimes supportive of, and sometimes contrary to, the true faith. But in sum, "no one has come closer to us than the Platonists…who, as we see, are not undeservedly raised above the rest [of the philosophers] in fame and glory."[40] Augustine's idea of the relative merits of classical learning and the Christian revelation allows him to downgrade the Greeks to just one people in a whole cavalcade of shadowy forerunners of the gospel fullness. "That which is called the Christian religion," he writes, "existed among the ancients, and never did not exist, from the beginning of the human race until Christ came in the flesh, at which time the true religion which already existed began to be called Christianity."[41] For a scholar like Augustine, classical learning is still to be admired— but it is now cast as one precursor rather than as a prime exemplar or immediate stepfather to inspired truth.

The Christians, of course, had learned how to confound paternity to their own purposes from Jewish predecessors. In the years of the amalgamation of Jewish and Greek ideas taking place in Alexandria, Jewish writers were already alleging that Orpheus was but a disciple of Moses, and Philo claimed Moses was the teacher as well of Pythagoras and all of the Greek philosophers. The Jewish historian Arta-panus of Alexandria (second century BCE) identified Moses as the teacher of Orpheus, and Aristobulus of Paneas in the same era claimed Moses as the source for much of what was found in Homer and Hesiod.[42] All of these mixed intellectual bloodlines enabled the justification as Christian of many philosophical traditions of dubious provenance—including preexistence.

Church Fathers

Out of this mix of philosophy and revealed religion, the first generations of church scholars and writers struggled to elaborate a theology that would iden-tify what was doctrinal, what was speculative, and what was clearly outside the pale. Depending on who was writing, preexistence would find a place in all three categories. Clement of Rome is sometimes called the first father of the Christian church. One of the earliest bishops of Rome (Peter's third successor, according to Irenaeus), Clement authored the oldest existing Christian text outside the bible—the epistle known as *1 Clement*. Also attributed to Clement, erroneously according to most scholars, was a document known as the *Recognitions of Clement*, of unknown date but quoted by Origen already in the early third century. One authority writes that "there is scarcely a single writing which is of so great importance for the history of Christianity in its first stage."[43] And at this stage, and from this writer, there is apparent affirmation of the pre-mortal existence of the soul. From his earliest youth, the author says, he has been preoccupied with "the condition of mortality" and has asked himself "whether I did not exist before I was born." His answer is evident when he hears the apostle Peter rehearse the phases of creation, starting with the "in the beginning" of Genesis and proceeding in abbreviated form through light, the firmament, plants, animals, and paradise. At last, God creates man, "on whose account He had prepared all things, whose internal species [*soul*, interpolates the editor] is older, and for whose sake all things that are were made, given up to his service, and assigned to the uses of his habitation."[44]

In the context of that soul's preexistence and the habitation prepared for it, mortality becomes the occasion for a probation based on free exercise of the will associated with that soul. The second and third books of the *Recognitions* reproduce a dialogue between Peter the apostle and Simon Magus. Their conversation turns to the nature of good and evil and human free will. Peter affirms the dependence of moral goodness upon individual choice and recognizes the problem of causality in diminishing human freedom. "Every motion is divided into two parts," he reasons, "so that a certain part is moved by necessity, and another by will; and those things which are moved by necessity are always in motion, those which are moved by will, not always." It is an early version of the quest for an "unmoved mover" to ground human moral agency. Peter locates the faculty of choice in that soul which, if not uncreated and therefore outside causality, he has already posited as at least prior to incarnation: "The power of choice is the sense of the soul, possessing a quality by which it can be inclined towards what acts it wills." Simon asks if it is not possible to create a man who would be good, with no power to be otherwise. Peter answers that, under such conditions, "we should not be really good, because we could not be aught else....What we did would not be ours, but of the necessity of our nature....And on this account the world required long periods, until the number of souls which were predestined to fill it should be completed." Following a period of apparent testing, "the souls of the blessed, being restored to their bodies, should be ushered [back] into light."[45]

Justin Martyr

Justin Martyr in the second century describes his own spiritual trajectory as an odyssey through a number of philosophical systems that prepared him to embrace the Christian gospel as a young man of about thirty. With his background in classical philosophy, especially Platonism, he endeavored to reconcile or at least to find points of agreement between Hellenistic philosophy and Christianity. Given the disadvantaged position Christianity then occupied, it made good sense to compare the new religion to the much-admired classical systems. And so Justin is unabashedly admiring: "I will tell you…what seems to me; for philosophy is, in fact, the greatest possession, and most honorable before God, to whom it leads us and alone commends us; and these are truly holy men who have bestowed attention on philosophy."[46]

Justin's ideas about the human soul are difficult to determine. He admires Plato and accepts his doctrine that "the soul [is] also divine and immortal, and a part of that very regal mind." Some modern sources refer to Justin as one of the "pre-existiani," or supporters of belief in human preexistence.[47] He appears initially to hold this view in his *Dialogue with Trypho*, affirming that human souls "are begotten wholly apart, and not along with their respective bodies." However, he is at the same time persuaded by Trypho that there is no advantage falling to the one who has seen God, or seen more than other persons, "unless he remember this fact, that he *has* seen." He seems to disallow both metempsychosis and the version of preexistence Origen will shortly champion, in agreeing with Trypho that wicked souls embodied in wild beasts, or subject to any other punishment, can "reap no advantage from their punishment…unless they are conscious of the punishment." The implication for Plato's system is clear. As Trypho concludes, and Justin concurs, "souls neither see God nor transmigrate into other bodies."[48] Even Plato and Pythagoras, Justin learns, "who have been as a wall and a fortress of philosophy," must defer to the prophets.

The first father to produce a substantial apologetics, Justin called himself a Samaritan but settled in Rome. By the rise of the next generation of church fathers, a new center of intellectual activity was firmly established. And there, preexistence would find fertile ground.

Clement of Alexandria

The confluence of Christian theology and Platonic metaphysics was shaped by the fact that what scholars call the "golden age of Christian theology" unfolded in the city of Alexandria. Alexandria, as we have seen, was a thriving and intellectually vibrant metropolis with a sizable population of well-educated Jews and Christians, and it was pervaded by philosophical and religious cross-currents from a host of traditions. Philo, the Hellenized Jew who thought he saw Platonism throughout Hebrew scripture, had been from this metropolis, and the Neo-Platonic school, as we saw, blossomed at the end of the second century there under the leadership of Ammonius Saccas and his disciple Plotinus. Even earlier, Gnostic Christianity had taken firm hold in Alexandria, associated with names that the Ante-Nicene fathers would later make famous: Basilides, Isidore, Valentinus, and others.

According to tradition, the apostle Mark founded a Christian school in the city. More likely, a private catechetical school was established there for religious study and the training of priests in the mid- to late second century. Its earliest instructor of record was one Pantaenus, but it was Clement (c. 150–215) who while head of the school became the first in a line of immensely influential Alexandrian theologians. The writings of Clement perfectly capture the uncertainties and theological dragons that lurked at the peripheries of any discussion of the world's creation and the soul's origin in this era of unsettled dogma. He seems to follow Justin in affirming creation *ex materia*. In his hymn "To the Paedagogus," he refers to the God who "out of a confused heap…didst create / This ordered sphere, and from the shapeless mass / of matter didst the universe adorn."[49] Clearly, he is profoundly influenced by Plato's *Timaeus*, yet leery of its implications for God's sovereignty. So in his *Stromata*, he takes a more cautious middle ground. Accepting the Platonic version of creation, Clement yet points out that "what is called matter by [the philosophers] is said by them to be without quality, and without form, and more daringly said by Plato to be non-existence."[50] As Henry Chadwick glossed Clement's doctrine of the creation, the world "is made not from that which is absolutely non-existent, but from relative non-being or unformed matter, so shadowy and vague that it cannot be said to have the status of 'being,' which is imparted to it by the shaping hand of the Creator."[51]

Clement was even more equivocal on the question of the human soul. Plato, once again, seems a principal influence, or at least support, for his inclination to embrace the idea. Clement finds the Attic philosophical tradition itself to be a handmaid and precursor to the true Christian religion. In fact, he writes, it was "a schoolmaster to bring 'the Hellenic mind,' as the law [did] the Hebrews, to Christ."[52] And "the Greek preparatory culture, therefore, with philosophy itself, is shown to have come down from God to men."[53] Greek philosophy in particular, he continues, derived in great part from the barbarians. And at this juncture, he cites a specific example of "barbarian" thought: "For according to Plato, 'they think that good souls, on quitting the supercelestial region, submit to come to this Tartarus, and assuming a body, share in all the ills which are involved in birth, from their solicitude for the race of men.'"[54] Henry More in the seventeenth century will cite this passage as proof of Clement's assent to the principle of preexistence since "he is so far from exploding" this opinion here. More recently Jaroslav Pelikan agrees that "passages in the writings of Clement do suggest the preexistence of the human soul."[55] Clement does follow his restatement of the mythic descent of noble souls with an apparent affirmation of the idea: "And these [embodied souls] make laws and publish philosophy, 'than which no greater boon ever came from the gods to the race of men, or will come.'" And then he seems to reaffirm this cluster of ideas when he writes that both Plato and Pythagoras "learned the most and the noblest of their dogmas from the barbarians."[56] That preexistence ranks among these most noble dogmas is nowhere stated but is suggested by Clement's recurrent invoking of that Platonic idea in his refutation of the Marcionites in book 3 of *Stromata*. In his *Exhortation to the Pagans*, Clement asserts, again with some equivocation, that the Phrygians, Arcadians, and Egyptians all claim ancient descent:

> Yet none of these existed before the world. But before the foundation of the world were we, who, because destined to be in Him, pre-existed in the eye of God before,—we the rational creatures of the Word of God, on whose account we date from the beginning; for "in the beginning was the Word."…He did not now for the first time pity us for our error; but He pitied us from the first, from the beginning.[57]

Elsewhere, however, perhaps recognizing the grave difficulties to which belief in a preexistent soul could lead, Clement holds that "the soul, which is produced along with the body, is corruptible." He clarifies his position somewhat when he writes that "the soul is not naturally immortal; but is made immortal by the grace of God."[58] It may seem unusual for a Christian father to insist that the soul is of finite duration. But an eternal past or an immortal future posed equal theological problems in this age in which Christian thinkers considered innate immortality to be God's monopoly. A preexisting soul, like an eternally subsisting one, can be seen to threaten that monopoly. Writing about the same time as Clement, Tertullian explains the problem more fully:

> That which has received its constitution by being made or by being born, is by nature capable of being changed…whereas that which is not-made and unborn will remain for ever immoveable. Since, however, this state is suited to God alone, as the only Being who is unborn and not-made (and therefore immortal and unchangeable), it is absolutely certain that the nature of all other existences which are born and created is subject to modification and change.[59]

This early Christian understanding of immortality explains the otherwise enigmatic insistence, in the letter to Timothy, that it is God "alone who has immortality" (1 Tim. 6:16).

Irenaeus, a generation older than Tertullian, had found these arguments convincing enough to decide conclusively against preexistence. He wrote, "[S]ome persons…maintain that souls, if they only began a little while ago to exist, cannot endure for any length of time." They must, therefore, either be eternally preexistent or perish with the body. The problem with that argument, Irenaeus reasoned, was that it would require the soul to be eternal in both directions, and "God alone, who is Lord of all, is without beginning and without end." Elsewhere, he declared simply, "the soul was not anterior to the body in its essence, nor, in regard to its formation, did the body precede the soul: but both these were produced at one time."[60]

Despite Clement's caveats and his own vagueness on the subject, he has repeatedly been invoked as a supporter of the doctrine of pre-mortal existence. Some of the confusion arises from Clement's ambiguous position regarding the Gnostics, who were a major force in transmitting the doctrine of a fall from preexistence. Clement found much worthy of admiration and assimilation in Gnostic thought, though he had in mind an idealized version, a "true Gnosis" as a Christian ideal, rather than the varieties his fellow church fathers so vociferously opposed. Clement even opens a book in one of his three major treatises by defending rather than attacking Gnosis. "It is now time to show the Greeks," he begins *Stromata*, "that the Gnostic alone is truly pious,…and worships the true God in a manner worthy of Him."[61] And in his scrapbook of Valentinian Gnosticism, *Excerpta ex Theodoto*, his sympathy with theories of an ante-mortal existence might be inferred from his taking note of the knowledge that those Gnostics found "liberating," i.e., the "knowledge of who we were" and "what birth is."[62]

To the extent that Clement accedes to the possibility of preexistence, he hints that it is righteousness, not sinfulness, that precedes human incarnation—at least of this world's faithful. Invoking the clearest indication of preexistence in the Hebrew Bible, Jeremiah's call before being formed in the belly (1:5), Clement considers this case pertinent to the Christians, who are likewise "destined in the eye of God to faith before the foundation of the world."[63] And so, he goes on to combine the language of Platonic *anamnesis* with this doctrine of foreordination to recast the sanctified life as one motivated by memory. In the process, Clement precludes the dilemma that will arise from an emphasis on human depravity. If men are totally corrupt and depraved, it is difficult to logically account for their first inclinations toward God. The concept of prevenient grace evolves to explain how an act of grace precedes and enables the act of will that responds to such grace. But in Clement, the turn of a fallen person to God is prompted by a Christian version of recollection and thus is cast as an act of reversion rather than conversion:

> Nor were it absurd to employ the expressions of those who call the reminiscence of better things the filtration of the spirit, understanding by filtration the separation of what is baser, that results from the reminiscence

of what is better. There follows of necessity, in him who has come to the recollection of what is better, repentance for what is worse. Accordingly, they confess that the spirit in repentance retraces its steps. In the same way, therefore, we also, repenting of our sins, renouncing our iniquities, purified by baptism, speed back to the eternal light, children to the Father.[64]

Ultimately, it seems that Clement, like Augustine in a later era, was not wholly committed to a doctrinal position on human preexistence, since such a doctrine falls outside the area of revealed truth. He was trying to negotiate a stance that showed a full appreciation for Hellenic culture and an expansive view of divine revelation and that condemned the heretical excesses of the Gnostics while defending them against mischaracterization. He was faced, moreover, with the delicate task of repudiating the metempsychosis of Basilides and Valentinus without denying the whole Platonic/Pythagorean heritage from which it largely derived. In these difficult circumstances, Clement exhibited sufficient ambiguity to leave his ultimate position on the doctrine in doubt. His most famous student, Origen, will show neither his indecision nor his subtlety.

Tertullian

If Justin was the first church father to attempt a marriage of classical learning and religion, pagan philosophy and scripture, then Tertullian was most adamant in urging a divorce. Like other church fathers, Tertullian protested the impertinence of the philosophers in theorizing about matters not clearly articulated in the scriptures—which for him clearly includes preexistence. The heretics and philosophers, Tertullian notes, are always asking, "what is the origin of man? and in what way does he come?" Those are the very kinds of questions, he concludes, "which make men heretics."[65] Indeed, he lists a whole rogues gallery of Gnostic heretics (all inspired by Plato, he says) who "suppose that they came down from heaven," including Saturninus the disciple of Menander, Carpocrates (who endows the human soul with "such supernal qualities" to intimate "an equality with Christ"), Apelles (who "tells us that our souls were enticed by earthly baits down from their supercelestial abodes by a fiery angel"), and Valentinus (who thinks the soul, fortified with divine Wisdom, can recognize in earthly objects echoes of deific powers [*aeons*]).[66] None of these heresies are surprising, given that "the apostle, so far back as his own time, foresaw, indeed, that philosophy would do violent injury to the truth."[67] For Tertullian, inquiries into the soul's origin are rendered needless by his reading of Genesis: when God breathed on Adam, Adam became a living soul. So the soul, as far as Tertullian is concerned, "originates with the breath of God" and dates to the birth of the body; at the same time, "all souls are derived from one."[68] In this view, Adam alone received his soul from God. His descendants derive theirs from their parents, in the same way their physical bodies derive. This version of the soul's origins, traducianism, also has the great virtue of simplifying the mystery of original sin. Since "from the one (primeval) man comes the entire outflow and redundanc[y] of men's souls," the sin of Adam becomes a literal, physiological inheritance of all successive generations. Therefore, it is no empty abstraction to claim, as he does, that "every soul, then, by reason of its birth, has its nature in Adam." So, in addition to any evil introduced into or freely chosen by a morally responsible soul, there is "an antecedent, and in a certain sense natural, evil which arises from its corrupt origin."[69]

Tertullian considered philosophy, operating outside the domain of scripture, as nothing other than "the material of the world's wisdom, the rash interpreter of the nature and the dispensation of God. Indeed heresies are themselves instigated by philosophy." The specific intellectual evils against which Paul warned us, he continues, "he expressly names *philosophy*." And then Tertullian famously asks, in a radical challenge to the direction of early Christian theologizing, "what indeed has Athens to do with Jerusalem? What concord is there between the academy and the church? [Quid ergo Athenae et Hierosolymis? Quid academiae et ecclesiae?]."[70] He adds, with profound irony, "Our instruction comes from 'the porch of Solomon,' who had himself taught that the Lord should be 'sought in simplicity of heart.'" Ironic, because he is here citing the *Wisdom of Solomon* (1:1), which, as we already saw, provided a principal basis for the Christian adoption of Platonism in general and preexistence in particular.

The irony is lost on Tertullian, who elsewhere did not hesitate to condemn Plato's theory in no uncertain terms. The stakes, he realizes, are high, because Plato's reputation among early Christian thinkers was considerable, and he was appropriated both by those well outside an evolving orthodoxy, as well as by many who considered themselves devout Christian apologists (like Tertullian's near contemporary Origen). For Tertullian, however, to be a Platonist sympathizer *was* tantamount to being a heretic. That is why he could hopefully write, "I shall sufficiently refute the heretics if I overthrow the argument of Plato."[71]

The Achilles' heel of Plato's doctrine of preexistence, according to Tertullian, is its concomitant idea of the imperfectly and unevenly intuited memories we carry with us into this life. "I cannot allow that the soul is capable of a failure of memory," he says and then elaborates a series of related objections. Instinctual knowledge is indelibly embedded even in animals. How does it happen, then, that "the knowledge of the intellectual faculties fails, to which the superiority is ascribed?" If the soul is eternal, how can its passage into mortality make it suddenly subject to the passage of time and its vicissitudes, which forgetfulness implies? Why and how does the soul forget, only to remember again? How can the body impede recollection, if it does not impede divination? How can forgetting be equally universal, and recollection erratic and unequal? If children have the best memories, with their "fresh, unworn souls," then why is it to philosophers that Plato imputes the greatest power to recollect?[72]

These criticisms notwithstanding, to refute *anamnesis* is not to refute preexistence. For that, Tertullian must address Plato's idea of the soul itself. "For when we acknowledge that the soul originates in the breath of God," he writes in *Treatise on the Soul*, "it follows that we attribute a beginning to it. This Plato, indeed, refuses to assign to it, for he will have the soul to be unborn and unmade."[73] The problem with such a scenario is not that a soul's eternal nature is philosophically implausible. It is, rather, the implications of such a conception for Tertullian's ideas concerning God's supreme divinity and absolute sovereignty. Plato, he writes, has conceded to the soul

> so large an amount of divine quality as to put it on a par with God. He makes it *unborn*, which single attribute I might apply as a sufficient attestation of its perfect divinity; he then adds that the soul is immortal, incorruptible, incorporeal—since he believed God to be the same—invisible, incapable of delineation, uniform, supreme, rational, and intellectual. What more could he attribute to the soul, if he wanted to call it God? We, however, who allow no appendage to God (in the sense of equality), by this very fact reckon the soul as very far below God: for we suppose it to be born.[74]

This statement may be the most emphatic—and ultimately the most influential—objection to the doctrine of preexistence in the early church. The battle against preexistence turns recurrently on the implications of the doctrine for God's sovereignty. Recognizing the tendency for such theological spillover, Adolf Harnack was at pains to absolve Jewish thought of a kindred sin. He emphasized that Jewish preexistence was never intended to promote any idea of preexistent human autonomy. The Jewish conception of preexistence, he insisted, "is founded on the religious idea of the omniscience and omnipotence of God" and "brings to light the wisdom and power of God."[75] Preexistence was therefore seen primarily as a statement about God's nature, before it was a statement about humanity's nature or origin. It was meant to ennoble God in our conception, not humans, he suggested. Augustine, though less prone to see in human preexistence a threat to divine sovereignty, evinced a similar sensibility about the stakes involved. "What could be worse pride," he asked in his *Confessions*, referring to his Manichaean past, "than the incredible folly in which I asserted that I was by nature what [God is]?"[76] Joseph Campbell's summation in this regard is pertinent: Augustine's conversion to Christianity represented his repudiation of "the Manichaean doctrine of the immanence of divine light" for "the Christian doctrine of the absolute transcendence of divinity."[77] What is at stake for all of these fathers is the creeping disintegration of the creature-Creator divide, a divide absolutely foundational to their cosmology.

For an opponent of the Platonic spiritual anthropology like Tertullian, it should be conceivable that a soul could be created prior to the body, without entailing the actual doctrine of self-sufficient immortality or creation prior to the world itself. But Tertullian does not allow even so much, refuting all those who "suppose that they came down from heaven" or that "the soul had formerly lived with God," insisting that both body and soul "are conceived, and formed, and perfectly simultaneously, as well as born together; and that not a moment's interval occurs in their conception, so that a prior place can be assigned to either." In the absence of scriptural clarity, Tertullian has recourse to personal experience, even at "the risk of offending modesty....In that very heat of extreme gratification, when the generative fluid is ejected, [do we not] feel that somewhat of our soul has gone from us?"[78] And yet, even in the steadfast Tertullian, we find inconsistencies and equivocation. In a treatise written probably slightly earlier, *The Soul's Testimony*, he had not been so sure about the soul's prehistory, seeing strength and weakness in both positions:

> Stand forth, O soul, whether thou art a divine and eternal substance, as most philosophers believe—if it be so thou wilt be the less likely to lie,—or whether thou are the very opposite of divine...whether thou art received from heaven, or sprung from earth...whether thine existence begins with that of the body, or thou art put into it at a later stage.[79]

Tertullian eventually settles into a stance of opposition to Plato's doctrine, declaring by the time of his work on the resurrection (c. 208) that the theory of traducianism is correct, even while he leaves himself an out: "The flesh and the soul have had a simultaneous birth, without any calculable difference in time; so that the two have been even generated together in the womb....The two are no doubt produced by human parents....They are so entirely one, that neither is before the other *in point of time*." But this seeming certainty is rendered suspect by his proviso that "even if the soul was a good deal prior to the flesh, by the very circumstance that the soul had to wait to be itself completed, it made the other really the former."[80] Such vacillation and caution reveal a church in which burgeoning heresies made orthodox boundaries imperative, even as scriptural resources often proved inadequate to the task. The consequent debating, negotiating, and fluidity of doctrine was as often within as among heresy hunters. The ironic coda to Tertullian's own career in the church was that, having placed himself on the right side (historically speaking) of the preexistence controversy, the scourge of heretics was himself later denounced as a heretic for joining the Montanist sect in North Africa, then broke with that group to found his own variety of ascetic Christianity.

Origen

Origen (185–254) represents the most dramatic—though complicated and contested—example of the converging worlds of Christianity and a newly formulated Platonism. His contribution goes beyond the mere integration of classical culture into Christian philosophy. As Paul Johnson characterizes his accomplishment, "With Origen, Christianity ceased to be an appendage of the classical world and became, intellectually, a universe of its own."[81] Born into a devout Christian family, and educated in both classical culture and biblical studies, Origen was only seventeen, Eusebius writes, when he took over as head teacher of the same catechetical school in Alexandria where Clement had taught. In that city, apparently even as he headed up Christian instruction, he began to attend the lectures of Ammonius Saccas, as did Plotinus. That would mean that the same figure taught both the founder of Neo-Platonism and the greatest church father of the age. (At least, that is the general view, going back to antiquity. Some scholars argue that there were two Ammoniuses and two Origens, the Christian Origen and the Platonist Origen.)[82]

As the primary force behind the development of Neo-Platonism, Plotinus was primarily concerned to resurrect the heritage of Plato and defend it against corruption by the Gnostics and others. He did not set out to provide a philosophical model more amenable to Christian theology, though that is what ended up happening. Origen, on the other hand, expressly aimed to combine the best elements of Christian doctrine and Platonism. Even as he worked to bring into fruitful union the Hellenic and Judeo-Christian traditions, he worked for an overall synthesis that would have the rigor and coherence of the pagan philosophies. The fruit of Origen's labors was successful enough in this regard to earn him a reputation as "the founder of philosophical theology."[83] Yet his exact relationship to Platonism and to orthodoxy has also earned him a designation as "the most astonishing sign of contradiction in the history of Christian thought."[84]

Jerome famously considered Origen to be the most important church teacher after the apostles themselves. At least, he did until he denounced Origen as a heretic. Ranked with Augustine and Aquinas, Origen was indisputably "the greatest theologian the Eastern Church has produced" by one reckoning;[85] "the most learned and able divine of the ante-Nicene period, the Plato...of the Greek church," according to Philip Schaff;[86] and second only to Paul, according to another scholar.[87] Yet Origen's name would stand at the center of swirling controversies in the late fourth century and again in the sixth as a term of reproach, which eventuated in a condemnation of so-called Origenism in 543 and 553. Exactly what brought about his change of fortunes is a complicated story.

Writing at a time of religious and philosophical turbulence in the Christian world, Origen is distinguished not only for his learned refutation of the Gnostic

Origen, an early church father, wrote the first philosophical treatment of Christian doctrine that included a theory of preexistent souls and other teachings later declared to be heretical. Twelfth-century pen-and-ink drawing; MS Clm 17092, fol. 130v, Bayerische StaatsBibliothek, München, Germany.

heresies, but for his authorship of numerous letters, homilies, and commentaries. His most important work, however, is *On First Principles*. It has been called the first systematic account of Christian belief, though one scholar argues that it is only "systematic in the sense that Origen opposes to the Gnostic…theology a coherent and self-consistent view of Christian doctrine...[whose] essential character is exploratory rather than dogmatic."[88]

On First Principles is exploratory in that some of the questions Origen asks had not, in those infant years of church history, received scriptural elucidation or authoritative resolution. The text itself has a complicated history, which renders interpretation equally complicated.[89] Origen begins by opening an important window on the church of the third century, differentiating nonnegotiable teachings of the apostles ("delivered...with the utmost clearness on certain points which they believed to be necessary to every one")[90] from those questions that are not adequately addressed by scripture. So, he first affirms those truths that are clearly indicated: there is one God, who created all things; Jesus Christ was born of the Father and made flesh; the Holy Spirit is "associated in honor and dignity with the Father and the Son" (although whether created or uncreated, he is unsure); and the soul as an independent entity shall be judged and rewarded according to its deserts. But this subject leads immediately to another concern that is by no means yet settled doctrine:

> With respect to the soul, whether it is derived from the seed by a process
> of traducianism, so that the reason or substance of it may be considered
> as placed in the seminal particles of the body themselves, or whether it
> has any other beginning; and this beginning itself, whether it be by birth
> or not, or whether bestowed upon the body from without or no[t], is not
> distinguished with sufficient clearness in the teaching of the church.[91]

Origen therefore lays down the principle that each person must make use of "the light of knowledge" to deduce "a connected series and body of truths agreeable to the reason of all these things...by clear and necessary statements."[92] And through a process of logical deduction, Origen conceives a scheme of vibrant cosmology that reflects his passionate preoccupation: the fluidity and dynamism of a universe peopled with rational, free beings. It is striking that, after treating in his first three chapters God, Christ, and the Holy Spirit—three nonnegotiable Christian truths—he proceeds immediately in chapter 4 to the topic "On Defection; or, Falling Away." The step that takes him there is illuminating and will lead inexorably to his theory of pre-mortal existence.[93]

God, he reasons, "bestows upon all, existence." And Christ's role in creation, as the Logos, renders all humankind "rational beings." Rationality, for Origen, means such beings "are deserving either of praise or blame, because capable of virtue and vice."[94] Absolutely fundamental to his theology, then, is the rationality, freedom, and accountability of the individual soul. Anticipating twentieth-century formulations, Origen continues that rational beings are not possessed of "goodness in them by essential being"; neither are they inherently evil.[95] They are rational and, therefore, free. The question naturally arises: given existence by God, rational natures from Christ, and holiness from the Holy Spirit, why would anyone who had "earned advancement" to this sanctified "grade" then lapse? The multiplicity and diversity of entities that people the cosmos, from divine to demonic with every gradation in between, clearly attest to the fact that choice must have been exercised in almost infinitely variable ways with almost infinitely variable consequences.

The subsequent discussion of defection, through accountable choices, becomes the logical basis for any account of this present cosmos with its myriad "species and orders" of rational beings, whose various appointments and stations proceed from their individual choices. Some (and here he shows clear borrowing from Philo) through a "satiety" of blessedness regress, while others "make progress and advance to higher degrees of perfection."[96] But a different lot falls to those who are neither wholly good nor wholly depraved in their conduct:

> Some sinned deeply and became daemons, others less and became angels; others still less and became archangels; and thus each in turn received the reward for his individual sin. But there remained some souls who had not sinned so greatly as to become daemons, nor on the other hand so very lightly as to become angels. God therefore made the present world and bound the soul to the body as a punishment.[97]

Implicit in this conception, as a necessary premise, is a sphere of action before mortality that could account for the ordering of the temporal sphere to which Origen refers. And what is implicit Origen soon makes explicit:

> If the soul of a man . . . was not formed along with his body, but is proved to have been implanted strictly from without, much more must this be the case with those living beings which are called heavenly. For, as regards man, how could the soul of him, viz., Jacob, who supplanted his brother in the womb, appear to be formed along with his body? Or how could his soul, or its images, be formed along with his body, who, while lying in his mother's womb, was filled with the Holy Ghost? I refer to John leaping in his mother's womb.[98]

Origen finds additional scriptural support in the Genesis narrative of the Fall, which, like Philo, he reads allegorically: "The expulsion of the man and woman from paradise, and their being clothed with tunics of skins . . . contain a certain secret and mystical doctrine (far transcending that of Plato) of the soul's losing its wings, and being borne downwards to earth, until it can lay hold of some stable resting place."[99]

Even if all of this is hypothetical, it is nonetheless a highly detailed theory of great scope. "Whole nations of souls," he apparently believed, "are stored away somewhere in a realm of their own, with an existence comparable to our bodily life....So long as a soul continued to abide in the good it has no experience of union with a body....But by some inclination towards evil these souls lose their wings and come into bodies."[100]

The present variety of earthly circumstances and conditions, the principle by which the future recapitulates the past, and the cited scriptural texts—all lead Origen to propound and defend a preexistence in which we freely choose our destinies.[101] Not only does Origen's scheme have the virtue of explaining the present gradients of being within a framework of human choice; it also neatly absolves God of any blame for the present, uneven distribution of pain and blessedness. The compelling problem with God's justice, assuming that souls are created at the moment of birth, was raised by both Plato and the Gnostics. The problem is worth looking at in detail, since it is one of the major rationales that will consistently inform the debates about preexistence. Origen writes:

> Certain beings are called earthly, and among them, i.e., among men, there is no small difference....And certain of them, from the hour of their birth, are reduced to humiliation and subjection, and brought up as slaves....Others, again, are brought up in a manner more consonant with freedom and reason: some with sound bodies, some with bodies diseased from their early years....And why should I repeat and enumerate all the horrors of human misery, from which some have been free, and in which others have been involved, when each one can weigh and consider them for himself?...Now, when we say that this world was established in the variety in which we have above explained that it was created by God, and when we say that God is good, and righteous, and most just, there are numerous individuals, especially those coming from the school of Marcion, and Valentinus, and Basilides,...who object to us, that it cannot consist with the justice of God in creating the world to assign to some of His creatures an abode in the heavens, and...[to make] others of second, or third, or of many lower and inferior degrees.[102]

Refusing to "nourish the insolence of the heretics by silence," Origen propounds an explanation that solves the dilemma, but only by asserting a time prior to mortality in which free will had free rein:

> When He in the beginning created those beings which He desired to create, i.e., rational natures,...He created all whom He made equal and alike, because there was in Himself no reason for producing variety and diversity. But since those rational creatures themselves...were endowed with the power of free-will, this freedom of will incited each one either to progress by imitation of God, or reduced him to failure through negligence. And this...is the cause of the diversity among rational creatures, deriving its

origin not from the will or judgment of the Creator, but from the freedom of the individual will....God, who deemed it just to arrange His creatures according to their merit, brought down these different understandings into the harmony of one world.[103]

That this merit manifested itself before mortal birth is a point on which he is emphatic: "There were certain causes of prior existence, in consequence of which the souls, before their birth in the body, contracted a certain amount of guilt," while conversely, these pre-mortal actions "furnish grounds for merit even before they do anything in the world."[104] And so, "owing to causes that have previously existed, a different office is prepared for each one in proportion to the degree of his merit."[105] If that sounds like a prototype of mortality and its subsequent final judgment, the comparison was not lost on Origen. Just as there will be an earthly probation followed by final judgment, there was a prior probation and preliminary judgment. At least, he writes, "I am of opinion some such state of things was formerly the case."[106]

In the face of such manifest disparity in condition and blessedness among the creatures of earth and heaven, the only alternative to this scheme would be a God who randomly and capriciously apportions good and evil (as the Marcionites alleged of the Christian God) or who unfairly creates souls of varying disposition and goodness (as the Valentinian Gnostics believed). So Origen's model had the additional merit of allowing him to effectively disarm the Marcionite critique and improve upon the Valentinian system.[107] The consequence is an order in heaven and earth, past, present, and future, that teems with variety and mobility and holds a potential for human spiritual evolution that will have particular appeal in Neo-Platonism and beyond:

Both in those temporal worlds which are seen, as well as in those eternal worlds which are invisible, all those beings are arranged, according to a regular plan, in the order and degree of their merits; so that some of them in the first, others in the second, some even in the last times, after having undergone heavier and severer punishments,...and for many ages, so to speak, improved by this method of training, and restored at first by the instruction of angels, and subsequently by the powers of a higher grade, and thus advancing through each stage to a better condition, reach even to that which is invisible and eternal...according to its own actions and endeavors.[108]

Improvement, rather than or in addition to punishment, is the purpose of the mortal sojourn. And throughout the entire cosmic process of differentiation, personal agency is operative: "it lies within ourselves and in our own action to possess either happiness or holiness; or by sloth and negligence to fall from happiness into wickedness and ruin."[109]

While Origen was in fundamental respects clearly Platonic, his scheme was complicated by the postulation of a transcendent God performing acts of creation in time (a problem we saw addressed in Neo-Platonism). Commenting on the *Wisdom of Solomon*, which asserts that Wisdom (which he interprets as Christ) "is a kind of breath of the power of God," Origen reasons that God's begetting of Wisdom or of the Son cannot be considered a beginning to that power. Because "if he shall grant that there was once a beginning, when that breath proceeded from the power of God," then it would mean that there was a time when he desired something he did not then possess.[110] By a parallel argument, Origen reasons that "God cannot be called omnipotent unless there exist those over whom He may exercise His power; and therefore, that God may be shown to be almighty, it is necessary that all things should exist." That he was at one time not omnipotent is unthinkable. Therefore, there was never a time when all things did not exist.[111] At the same time, of course, Christians must "confess that God…created and disposed all things."[112] On this point, Origen was emphatic: all creatures came into being. In other words, God's eternal nature and omnipotence constrain Origen to posit a God who is the Creator of all things, which things have no beginning. The solution to the conundrum appears in Origen's simple formula, "the existence of the Son is derived from the Father, but not in time."[113] Time and again, in theology, mysticism, and idealist philosophy, we find this equivocation between a preexistence posited as chronologically antecedent to physical creation, and preexistence as a state or condition altogether outside of time, necessary to preserve the paradox of a God who creates but is never deficient or desirous and a human freedom that is grounded outside of temporality.

Origen's writings on preexistence also mark a clear distinction from the Pythagorean doctrine of reincarnation. This, Origen explicitly renounced, calling "the dogma of transmigration,…foreign to the Church of God, and not handed down by the Apostles, nor anywhere set forth in the Scriptures."[114] MacGregor points to another compelling objection: in the logic of Gnosticism, which Origen rejects, a cyclical philosophy of history would suggest multiple incarnations of God along with those of humans. Transmigration, therefore, "did not seem to him to fit the Christian philosophy of history, despite what he felt was its rational appeal."[115] Origen's emphatic distinctions notwithstanding, other Christian theologians were not prepared to sever the two principles, and the presumed (and, often, actual) association of the one with the other was yet further ammunition for those who opposed and would eventually vanquish both ideas as heresy. So, while it was certainly inaccurate, there is some basis in precedent for the later assertion of Thomas Aquinas, who will insist that "all those who held souls to be created apart from bodies, believed in the transmigration of souls."[116]

The other doctrine linked with preexistence in Origen's thought is apokatastasis which, as we have seen, leads him to believe that the past anticipates the future, just as the future recapitulates the past. The two doctrines are profoundly linked in yet another way. Like Plato, Origen believed that approach to the divine was the supreme goal of human existence. And he reads Genesis 1:26–27 in such a way as to relate a supernal destiny to a celestial origin. As this connection persists through thousands of years of myth and religious history alike, it is worth citing his rationale in full. Like the Gnostic Theodotus, Origen finds the "likeness and image" of the creation narrative a portent of allegorical significance:

> The highest good, [philosophers] say, is to become as like to God as possible. But this definition I regard…as a view derived from holy Scripture…."And God said, Let Us make man in Our own image, and after Our likeness."…Now the expression, "In the image of God created He him," without any mention of the word "likeness," conveys no other meaning than this, that man received the dignity of God's image at his first creation; but that the perfection of his likeness has been reserved for the consummation,…the possibility of attaining to perfection being granted him at the beginning through the dignity of the divine image.[117]

Thus, in the "first creation," which for Origen takes us to man's pre-mortal origin in the heavens, is anticipated his full realization of perfection in God's likeness.

Origen's embrace of the fully cyclical nature of cosmic history leads him to another position with disastrous theological consequences. Origen affirmed the eventual salvation and restoration of all spirits—even that of Satan himself. It was likely the latter belief, more than the less objectionable doctrine of preexistence, that tainted Origen's reputation among orthodox theologians. Clearly, the doctrines of a preexistent fall and eventual restoration were, in his thought, interdependent. No wonder, then, that we often find his disciples embracing the two and his opponents damning the pair. By the time of the first anathemas against Origen, the two doctrines are linked in history as well as logic to justify the assumption of their interconnectedness.

As the tide fully turned against Origen and his doctrine of preexistence, the divinity and inherent immortality it attributed to the human soul were major catalysts to opposition. This is ironic given that, ultimately, Origen's anthropology blames human weakness and a tendency toward earthiness for our cosmic catastrophe. Other versions of preexistence were extant, though not as influential as Origen's, in the early Christian centuries. And it would be a century and more before the myriad versions, defenses, and attacks on preexistence would coalesce into full-blown controversy. When the final, official blow came, it would be almost anticlimactic.

5

Augustine and the Formation of Orthodoxy

O multitude of the faithful, place no faith in any of the ancients.
If Origen had some secret facts of the divine purposes, let none of
you admit them. And similarly if one of the Clements said any such
things,...yes even if they were said by the great Gregory of Pontus, a
man of apostolic virtues, or by the other Gregory, of Nazianzus, and
Didymus, the seeing prophet, both of them my teachers, than whom
the world has possessed none more deeply taught in the faith of Christ.
All these have erred as Origen has erred.

—Rufinus, paraphrasing Jerome[1]

Christianity's gradual domination of the West was not an uninterrupted
conquest or conversion of the pagan masses. Constantine's personal
embrace of the faith paved the way in 313 for his edict of toleration (the
Edict of Milan), which lifted the church out of its besieged predicament
and cleared the way for an alliance of empire and the Christian religion.
But even then, the battles between Hellenistic culture and the new
religion were far from over. A few short decades after Constantine's
conversion, the victorious general Julian (332–363) was acclaimed
emperor in 361. Julian harbored a resentment toward Christianity arising
from the murder of his family in the purges following Constantine's
death. Schooled in Neo-Platonism and an initiate in the Mithraic
mysteries, Julian (subsequently named "apostate") moved immediately
to enthrone Neo-Platonic paganism as the religion of the empire and
checked the rights and prerogatives of Christians. His reforms extended

to philosophy and rhetoric as well, insofar as he suspended the appointment of Christian teachers, thus temporarily aborting the synthesis of Greek philosophy and Christian thought that had proved to be such a productive and successful endeavor throughout the Hellenistic world. After his short reign and perhaps in part because of the bald affront to the ascendant religion of the empire that his move represented, religious syncretism lost some of its luster; over the next generations, some emperors would act to exclude pagan and Greek influences as thoroughly as he had attempted to elevate them. Near the end of the century, for instance, Emperor Theodosius would move to restrict pagans from imperial offices and banned or limited cult practices and the mystery religions.

The empire had large numbers of people steeped in the traditions of classical philosophy and the religious practices of Greece and Rome, and the cultural give and take would persist. Even so, it is true, as one scholar of the era writes, that "in the second half of the fourth century A.D. the last important battles between Hellenism and Christianity were fought."[2] Augustine would be the commanding figure of this era, and his conversion from Manichaeanism and retirement from his career as professor of rhetoric were emblematic of how difficult the road to a comfortable syncretism had become.

Augustine of Hippo (354–430) was perhaps the most important figure in the development of Christian doctrine since Paul. Converted in 386, he quickly rose in prominence and became a prolific and seminal theologian. One of four original doctors of the church, his writings are considered to be the intellectual basis for much Reformation theology as well. The first two ecumenical councils, at Nicea in 325 and in Constantinople just five years before his conversion, had thrashed out the staples of Christian dogma in regard to the Trinity, but had not addressed a question still on many minds: whence the human soul? In a work written within a decade of his conversion, Augustine provided a clear window into the contending theories regarding the soul's origin as they were held in his time. And he appeared confident that the question, even with the theological stakes as high as they were, was still an open one. But momentum had been building against the doctrine, and the outlook was not auspicious.

Tertullian, writing in the early third century, had raised an alarm against a doctrine of preexistence that threatened to put the soul "on a par with God." He was not alone in this concern. Clement and Tertullian, as we saw, had qualified the soul's immortality as gifted rather than innate, to distinguish it from God's self-sufficiency and eternity. The problem was that the idea of immortality bestowed upon a mortal creation did not comport well with Platonism. For this reason, the preexistent soul, for Neo-Platonists, was regarded as inherently endowed with immortality, which was not seen as a contingent consequence of divine grace. Alarmed that such a conception of immortality suggested divinity as well, apologists like Arnobius of Sicca (d. 330) attacked the whole idea. Writing a century after Tertullian, Arnobius lays out the entire, dangerous chain of reasoning:

> Wherefore there is no reason that that should mislead us, should hold out vain hopes to us, which is said by some men till now unheard of, and carried away by an extravagant opinion of themselves, that souls are immortal, next in point of rank to God and ruler of the world, descended from that parent and sire, divine, wise.

And then Arnobius describes how this human presumption continues an inevitable trajectory ad absurdum. As he writes with unmistakable sarcasm:

> Now, because this is true and certain, and because we have been produced by Him who is perfect without flaw, we live unblameably, *I suppose*, and therefore without blame; *are* good, just, and upright, in nothing depraved; no passion overpowers, no lust degrades us; we maintain vigorously the unremitting practice of all the virtues.[3]

Finally, comes his stinging reproach of those who hold that humankind lived in heaven as God's spirit offspring before a fall into mortality: "Will you lay aside your habitual arrogance, O men, who claim God as your Father, and maintain that you are immortal, just as He is?…What excellence is in us, such that we scorn to be ranked as creatures?"

For Arnobius, and for many Christians of his age, immortality was an attribute of the divine alone, unless it was, in the case of humans, emphatically made contingent upon God's grace. To be created was to be subject to dissolution; conversely, to be intrinsically immortal was to be divine. As Arnobius argues elsewhere, even the lesser deities, if created by God, "are also doubtless liable to annihilation." If any created thing has the appearance of immortality, it is only because, through God's grace, "they have been privileged to remain the same through countless ages, though by nature they are fleeting, and liable to dissolution."[4]

These difficulties explain why Arnobius is yet another example of a church father caught between admiration for Plato and an inclination toward belief in the soul's preexistence, on the one hand, and uncertainty about its harmony with the evolving doctrine of deity, on the other. So, even as Arnobius decries the conflation of human and divine attributes, he asks rhetorically, "To Him do we not owe this first, that we exist, that we are said to be men, that, being either sent forth from Him, or having fallen from Him, we are confined in the darkness of this body?"[5] On the one hand, then, he accedes to the Platonic and Origenist account of human origins. On the other, he rejects what he believes to be the manifest blasphemy of reading into such accounts the implicit divinization of the human soul. In the background to these concerns, Arianism, adoptionism, and kindred heresies of the era threatened to collapse the sacred distance between God and the human, making for special wariness in the face of similar developments. In this context especially, these dangerous implications of the soul's immortality may explain why the Catholic Church would not make the soul's immortality into dogma for a thousand years.[6] In the meantime, this linkage among preexistence, self-sustaining immortality, sinlessness, and divinity will prove to be a prime factor in the growing resistance to the idea of preexistence. And it will be a decisive element in Augustine's retreat from the doctrine when the Pelagian threat makes these associations and implications even more vivid.

Another problem with preexistence was the group which had earlier endorsed the doctrine: the Gnostics. Gnostic heresies—so called—became the prime impetus to early Christian apologetics and the elaboration of Christian doctrine. The Gnostics were the perennial heretics, threatening to overwhelm the fledgling faith with an array of competing divinities, cosmologies, and spiritual anthropologies. In the fathers' zeal to purge church teachings of their influence, it was natural that questionable Christian doctrines championed by the Gnostics were jettisoned. Chadwick noted that Tertullian "shows how fear of Gnostic myths about transmigration played a large part in arousing fear of the pre-existence theory."[7] Indeed, after refuting Pythagorean and Platonic transmigration, Tertullian concludes triumphantly, "No tenet, indeed, under cover of any heresy has as yet burst upon us, embodying any such extravagant fiction as that the souls of human beings pass into the bodies of wild beasts" (which Plato had allowed in *Republic*, X):

> [B]ut yet we have deemed it necessary to attack and refute this conceit, as a consistent sequel to the preceding opinions,…in order that, by the demolition of the *metempsychosis* [transmigration of the soul] and *metensomatosis* [serial embodiment in different types of bodies] by the same blow, the ground might be cut away which has furnished no inconsiderable support to our heretics.[8]

Though Gnosticism had faded as a critical issue by the fourth century, the guilt by association persisted. To Tertullian and other opponents continuing to the present, preexistence—conceived as either Gnostic or Platonic in inspiration—is tainted by virtue of its unholy sources and smacks of transmigration besides.

To all of this crippling weight of baggage was added yet another powerful force, and that was the growing displacement of Plato by Aristotle in Christian thought. The long, drawn-out process led from the synthesis of Neo-Platonism and Christianity by Origen, to its most influential synthesis with Augustine himself, and then to a reformulated Aristotelian synthesis effected by Aquinas. But even before

Augustine, there were signs the pendulum had begun to swing. With the relative decline in prestige of the major philosophical authority espousing preexistence, Plato, and the ascendancy of the commanding authority of the Middle Ages, Aristotle, who clearly denied the independent existence of a human soul, the doctrine's fate was virtually sealed. One proof of the shifting philosophical dominance and its repercussions is already found in Gregory of Nyssa (c. 335–394). An earlier father, Methodius of Olympus (d. c. 311), had attacked Origen's theory of preexistence, even though he was himself a Platonist. Gregory found Methodius's arguments unconvincing and easily dismissed them. Gregory produced his own refutation of preexistence by resorting to Aristotelian, rather than Platonic, argument, as shown in his work *De hominis opificio* (*The Formation of Man*). He holds, in language reminiscent of Aristotle's work on the soul, that the self is a union of body and soul. "I cannot," therefore, "be both posterior and anterior to myself," as preexistence would require.[9]

To refute Origen, however, was not always to vanquish preexistence. Cyril of Jerusalem, a fourth-century theologian, was adamant in embracing preexistence while emphatically rejecting its Origenist formulation: "I would have you know this, too, that before the soul enters this world, it has committed no sin; but though we arrive sinless, now we sin by choice."[10] Conceding not even the primordial sin described by Origen, Cyril could hardly hope to win support for his belief in a Christian universe that was becoming less concerned with defending God's justice and human freedom and more with developing doctrines of God's grace and human depravity. (Cyril is also unusual in addressing directly the question of souls and gender. "The soul is immortal," he writes. "All souls are alike, both of men and women; it is only the bodily parts which are different.")[11]

A final complication leading up to the doctrine's disfavor concerns evolving theories of creation. For early Christians, God created the world—exactly how or out of what was not a subject of intense philosophical inquiry. Creation *ex nihilo* has long been the standard Christian version. In the nineteenth century, J. P. Landis could confidently characterize the orthodox position as biblically self-evident:

> The Bible does teach that God is the Creator of matter, the material or substance, as well as the order, of the *kosmos*. Creation was the absolutely free act of God, unconditioned by any preexisting thing. Matter, with its properties and forms…; spirit, with its life and feeling,…these all had their origin in the creative word of God.[12]

In reality, however, the first generations of Christian scholars felt no such certainty about the Bible's position. Among those informed by classical philosophy, Justin Martyr's position was for a time the standard Christian line: "And we have been taught that He in the beginning did of His goodness, for man's sake, create all things out of unformed matter."[13] He found comfortable congruence between Platonic conceptions of creation and a reading of Genesis that emphasizes creation as a reordering of chaos. Before Plato, other pre-Socratic philosophers also believed in the eternal existence of the cosmos and spirit alike. Empedocles (c. 494–434 BC), for example, held that "there is no origination of anything that is mortal, nor yet any end in baneful death." They were "fools," he wrote, "who think that what was not comes into being."[14] Like preexistence itself, creation *ex materia* or *ex nihilo* was in those days of doctrinal formation a disputed point. The biblical texts are ambiguous enough on the subject to allow for controversy, which still continues. What is clear, writes May, is that a characterization of creation *ex nihilo* as a doctrine that primitive Christianity found "ready-made in the Jewish tradition" and simply adopted or assumed for itself "can today no longer be sustained."[15] Most scholars would agree with David Winston: "no explicit theory of creation *ex nihilo* had ever been formulated either in Jewish or Greek tradition before Philo," and the case for Philo is ambiguous but unlikely.[16]

The implications of this doctrine for the survival of the concept of preexistence are obvious. In theory, God could create a world, a soul, and a body out of nothing, and as long as the soul is created prior to the body, we have both preexistence and creation *ex nihilo*. However, any cosmology that muddled the question of God's supremely majestic creative power by intimating that he used materials ready to hand—eternally existent or otherwise—fell into disfavor as the doctrine of creation *ex nihilo* gained ascendancy. There is something elegantly simple and theologically potent about conjuring the universe out of the vacuum of absolute nothingness. And any anthropology that situates the human soul anterior to those opening scenes of cosmic creation could be seen as imputing grandeur to the human at the expense of the absolute supremacy of the divine. That was clearly a possibility with the creation as described in *Timaeus*. As Platonism underwent its process of Christianizing (and Judaizing), a major shift in emphasis was to replace the primacy of ideas with the centrality of God. In part, this was effected by transforming the Platonic *eidoi*, or forms, into ideas that reside in the mind of God. At the same time, as the world formation described in *Timaeus* becomes the creative act of a Creator God, the idea of creation itself becomes profoundly theologized. In other words, the role and status of this Creator undergoes a reconstruction to make it fully consistent with a God conformable to Christian or Judaic conceptions. One consequence is that the philosophical problem of transcendence (how can a transcendent God effect a physical creation?) becomes the moral problem of distance (how does a sovereign God maintain the Creator-creature divide as inviolate?). And so we find a version epitomized by the immensely influential Hebraist, Menasseh ben Israel, in which Plato's *Timaeus* foreshadows a

Judeo-Christian God concerned to maintain essential distinctions. God's expression "let *us* make man," he writes, is a clear indication that God is here invoking the assistance of "secondary causes" of creation (as in Plato, he notes), because in the logic of this Creator God, "I have yet to make an animated creature with a nature approaching to an equality with immortals, yet, if made directly by me, it would be entirely divine, therefore let the body be furnished by you, and I will give you the other portion, which is the soul."[17]

Such fine-tuning of the doctrine of creation may distance God sufficiently from his creatures to alleviate the persistent concern we have seen that the soul not partake too much of divinity, but it does nothing to address the criticism that God is a mere craftsman on a cosmic scale. Christian Gnostics especially found it offensive that the supreme deity would be no more than a manipulator of existent materials. May postulates that it may have been the second-century Gnostic Marcion who first realized that a God who has the benefit of working with already existing, albeit unformed, matter "excludes the idea of the almightiness of the creator." And, assuming as he (like all Gnostics) did the inherent evil of matter, Marcion argued that any world created from it, even by God, would necessarily be evil as well. His position therefore revealed yet another danger arising from the theory of creation *ex materia*: "A God who uses this material cannot be the true God."[18] He is no better than a craftsman limited by his imperfect resources. That is why it may be largely in reaction to the Platonic conception of the world's formation that the Christian doctrine of creation *ex nihilo* emerges.[19]

A countertheory to Plato is already under development at the hands of Marcion's contemporary, the Christian Gnostic Basilides. He rejects the standard, Platonic conception of world formation out of already existing material precisely because "it is anthropomorphic and limits the omnipotence of God. God is not to be subject to the preconditions which apply to an earthly artist or craftsman." May calls this critique by Basilides "the earliest clearly discernable explicit contradiction in the history of Christian theology of the philosophical model of the formation of the world." It arises equally from his dissatisfaction with anthropomorphic models of divine activity and from a more far-reaching conceptualization of God's absolute omnipotence and transcendence. "The Gnostic supreme God produces in a simply wonderful way, corresponding to his boundless might."[20]

Though he was the first, Basilides was not the most influential thinker in the development of this doctrine. Theologians like Tatian (d. c. 185) and Theophilus of Antioch (d. c. 185) set creation *ex nihilo* on a firmer footing, but the doctrine received decisive formulation from Irenaeus (c. 125–200 CE), one of the earliest of the church fathers. A disciple of Polycarp, who was himself a disciple of John the Beloved, Irenaeus protested against those Gnostics who

do not believe that God (being powerful, and rich in all resources) created matter itself....For, to attribute the substance of created things to
the power and will of Him who is God of all, is worthy both of credit
and acceptance....While men, indeed, cannot make anything out of
nothing, but only out of matter already existing, yet God is in this point
pre-eminently superior to men, that He Himself called into being the substance of His creation, when previously it had no existence.[21]

Still, it would be 1215 before the Catholic Church officially affirmed the doctrine of
creation *ex nihilo* at the Fourth Lateran Council.

At the end of the fourth century, creation *ex materia* is in retreat, the Gnostics
are under sanction of death in the Roman Empire, Christianity is ascendant over
Platonism, but the question of preexistence is still the subject of widespread dis-
agreement. As Henri Irénée Marrou writes, it was "the typical question discussed at
the time."[22] Some influential writers and teachers continued to carry the banner of
Origen, often in modified form. One of the most prominent in this regard is Evagrius
Ponticus (345–399). He was a disciple of the Cappadocian father and important
theologian of the Trinity Gregory of Nazianzus (329–389). Gregory's position on
Origenism is confused. He advocated apokatastasis, suggesting that all would eventually be saved, and intimated, as we saw earlier, a view of Christ that hinted at pre-
mortal existence and varying degrees of spiritual progress there. Later writers like
Henry More would see him as an advocate of human preexistence, though some of
Gregory's writings seem to condemn it unambiguously: "I fear lest some monstrous
reasoning may come in," he wrote, "as of the soul having lived elsewhere, and then
having been bound to this body, and that it is from that other life that some receive
the gift of prophecy, and others are condemned, namely, those who lived badly."
(Still, Gregory hints that preexistence is not all that unreasonable as a hypothesis for
addressing the enigma that "a Jeremias is sanctified, and others are estranged, from
the womb." However, such speculation is "unsafe for us to play with.")[23]

The picture is complicated by the fact that his famous student and archdea-
con Evagrius vigorously embraced a doctrine of preexistence. Like Origen, Evagrius
argued that intelligences (*nous*) originally existed in God's presence among other
rational beings. For Evagrius, they were pure spirit, rather than being clothed in
a heavenly body. They fell to the plane of material existence, where the intelligences
developed into souls (which remain immaterial).[24] (That progression he describes,
originating with an "intelligence," may suggest why Gregory denied the preexistence of the soul, per se.) It is Evagrius's expansion and promotion of Origen's
theories, more than their original formulation in Origen, that will elicit such fierce
opposition in the Origenist crises.[25]

Another contemporary was Didymus the Blind (c. 313–398), revered in his era
as the greatest Christian scholar in Alexandria.[26] A confirmed follower of Origen,

Didymus believed that souls preexisted in heaven and descended into mortality either through an "inclination and desire for fellowship with bodies," or in order to assist other souls.[27] He turned this belief in preexistence to novel use. Not only does he allegorize the Fall of Adam and his clothing in skins as a metaphor for the soul's fall from heaven (as had Philo and Origen), but he rescues Job from the charge of faintheartedness. When he curses the day of his birth, writes Didymus, Job is merely lamenting those evils that precipitated his soul's descent into the world as "a painful day and worthy of a curse."[28]

Didymus also relies upon the rather Gnostic argument that, if rational existence arose out of material life, that would entail that "evil is prior to virtue." To avert this dilemma, one must invoke a pre-mortal spiritual existence. "And if it be conceded that the soul lived at no time apart from material life," he adds, "reality would have begun from evil."[29] What is most significant in regard to the teachings of Didymus, coming as they do at this juncture in theological history, is that they met with little or no resistance. According to the records of his teaching, Richard Layton remarks, his promotion of the theory of preexistence "does not seem to have raised significant concern for the students, and Didymus does not perceive a pressing need to defend the orthodoxy of his teaching."[30]

Into this maelstrom of competing doctrines and rampant speculation, Augustine enters the controversies over preexistence in a state of indecision and apparent ignorance of how the winds are blowing. Arnobius had described a similar condition of flux and uncertainty, his own speculations notwithstanding. In fact, in spite of Arnobius's own reservations, he had tacitly inclined to the idea that souls were either "sent forth from [God], or [had] fallen from Him" into "the darkness of this body."[31] Still, he had registered the lack of a larger consensus, and his own uncertainty, in the face of these questions:

> By what sire have [souls] been begotten, and how have they been produced?...We, too, admit that we are ignorant of this, do not know it; and we hold that, to know so great a matter, is not only beyond the reach of our weakness and frailty, but *beyond that* also of all the powers which are in the world....We do not say...from what causes and beginnings they have sprung. But what crime is it either to be ignorant of anything, or to confess quite openly that you do not know that of which you are ignorant?[32]

Augustine emulates both the language and the uncertainty of Arnobius in his own statement of the late fourth-century status quo:

> There are four views about souls: (1) they come into being by propagation [traducianism]; (2) they are created individually for each person who is born [creationism]; (3) they already exist somewhere and are sent by God into the bodies of those who are born ["sent" preexistence]; (4) they sink

Along with Paul, Augustine was one of the primary shapers of Christian thought in the church's first millennium. He initially believed that preexistence offered the best account of the soul's origins, though his later position was ambiguous. *Saint Augustine*, by Sandro Botticelli, c. 1480; Scala/Art Resource, New York.

into bodies by their own choice ["fallen" preexistence]. It would be rash to affirm any of these. For the Catholic commentators on Scripture have not solved or shed light on this obscure and perplexing question; or if they have, I have not yet come across any such writing.[33]

At one of the major crossroads for the development of the Christian tradition, then, not one but two theories of preexistence are still in play, as they had been for Arnobius a century earlier. These two may reflect the two New Testament formulations of beings cast out of heaven ("God did not spare the angels when they sinned, but cast them into hell"; 2 Pet. 2:4) and beings that seemingly chose to depart ("angels who did not keep their own position, but left their proper dwelling"; Jude 1:6). In any case, there are in Augustine's day growing signs of doubt that these two views can be harmoniously reconciled with an emerging orthodoxy. A case in point is a contemporary of Augustine, Synesius of Cyrene (c. 373–c. 414), trained as a philosopher in the Alexandrine school of Neo-Platonism. As such, he fully embraced the cosmology and human anthropology involving the One as source and origin, gradient emanations through layers of being, and the fall of the soul and its anticipated return to its divine origin. Asked to serve as bishop of Ptolomais (a Greek city of Libya), he agrees, but issues a letter, ostensibly written to his brother, in which he makes clear his reservations. He expresses concerns about his inability to embody the "sanctity of such a priesthood" and about his attachment to diverse pursuits. But all of these are as nothing in the face of his weightiest disqualification: he holds fast to unorthodox principles which can never be shaken. Foremost in the group, he writes, is that he will never be able to persuade himself "that the soul is of more recent origin than the body."[34] And on this point, he insists, he must be free to differ. Neither creationism nor traducianism accord to the soul the preexistence so firmly entrenched in the Neo-Platonism to which he is devoted.

One must not read too much into this accommodation, which he required and obtained, for several factors weigh here. First, the question was far from a formal resolution. It is probably an oversimplification to argue, as did a nineteenth-century divine, that "Platonism was now the received philosophy of the Church: and the necessity of arguing against the pre-existence of the soul was not so imperatively felt."[35] But Augustine's muted opposition had not emerged yet, and it is possible that holding one of the most respected lineages in the Roman world, with the additional appeal that his learning added to his aristocracy, Synesius was appointed for the prestige rather than the theological rigor he brought to the position.[36] Even so, by advertising his faith in preexistence on the eve of his appointment as bishop, he could not help but impede the retreat in which Augustine was about to halfheartedly acquiesce. And in this resistance, Synesius was not alone. Yet another contemporary, Nemesius, who, like Synesius, was a bishop (in Syria), similarly sided with

Origen in professing the doctrine of preexistence. He argued along Platonic lines in his treatise *On Human Nature* (*De natura hominis*). And he also found both creationism and traducianism to have problems that were simply insuperable.[37] Such flexibility as was evident in Synesius's appointment, however, was soon to be constrained by a number of pressing controversies unfolding at this time in the Christian church, which touched on matters of essential human identity and human nature, humankind's role in and responsibility for sin, God's justice, and the meaning and scope of grace. All of these and more are contingent on the way the soul is conceived to originate. And, as Augustine suggested, the scriptures are in this regard an insufficient guide, and the church's teaching was unsettled.

Augustine, at the time he wrote *On Free Choice of the Will* (around 395), was aware of the difficulties embodied in both creationism and traducianism. He quite clearly favored the fourth possibility he enumerated above—a fall from preexistence. Option 3 posits explicitly the preexistence of the soul as well, but option 4 adds individual moral agency to the brute temporal fact of spiritual preexistence. The point is important, since it starkly reveals the recurrent moral anguish for which the preexistence doctrine offered psychological balm. Augustine tells us that he is particularly concerned in this treatise to defend God's justice. And it is manifestly the case that the human condition as we experience it is characterized by both ignorance and a limited capacity for good. The conclusion seems inescapable that these circumstances constitute a punishment and, accordingly, must follow upon some sin of ours, else God the Creator of both humans and their world is perverse. In spite of his protestations earlier that God's righteousness is never in question, Augustine cannot resist the appeal of a theory that solves the question of God's all-too-apparent injustice:

> But if, instead, souls that have been created elsewhere are not sent by the Lord God, but come to inhabit bodies by their own choice, it is quite easy to see that the ignorance and difficulty that result from their own wills are in no way to be blamed on their Creator since he is without fault even if he himself sends souls to dwell in bodies.[38]

This is the recurrent appeal of preexistence: it gives to God's apparent capriciousness in assigning human lots a foundation in justice. The solution was also Origen's, of course, but Augustine knows little of this background (he did not read Greek, for one thing). Augustine is led to the cusp of embracing this spiritual anthropology, which he finds so appealing, if only he can find authorization for his heart's tendency:

> We must believe what is past, and what is yet to come, as far as is sufficient for our journey toward eternal things....As for...both body and soul

we…can have no knowledge of these things unless we experience them. Therefore, if by divine authority we are told anything about such creatures, whether past or future, we ought to believe it without hesitation.[39]

Augustine leaves his discussion of the soul's origin with a clear willingness to countenance the range of theories he has outlined. "I don't mean to imply that I forbid anyone who can to investigate…the origin of the soul," he writes, whether they are propagated, created individually, or sent or fallen from heaven. "It is," he asserts, "permissible to consider and discuss these matters."[40] And he does continue to consider and discuss these matters. It is impossible not to, as he continues to wrestle with questions that keep impinging on the subject of the soul's origin and moral status.

A few years earlier, c. 386–387, Augustine had openly embraced Plato's argument for preexistence in *Soliloquies*, wherein he attributed moral discernment to some kind of memory. "For the discernment which refuses to accept a false suggestion is a kind of memory." He likens it to "remembering and reviving a truth." In an analogy especially pertinent to the dramatic structure of his *Confessions*, he writes, "we may meet a man and have to ask where we made his acquaintance. When he reminds us, the whole thing suddenly comes back to memory as if a light had been kindled."[41]

It is often suggested that, in *Retractions*, written toward the end of his life, Augustine repudiates the Platonic doctrine of recollection and its related preexistence. In reality, his repudiation there is narrowly focused. In reviewing *Soliloquies*, he condemns not the passage cited above but one following, in which he originally held that those learned in the liberal arts draw their knowledge "out of oblivion." Plato's example of the slave boy proficient in math, he now argues, knows what he knows because the light of reason is combined with "suitable questioning." It bears noting that Augustine lets stand the argument cited, wherein rekindled knowledge of a person suggests a prior familiarity.[42]

It is apparent that, in Augustine's early career, he felt free to explore the four theories about the soul's origin then current. In addition to *Soliloquies* and the treatise *On Free Choice of the Will*, he raises the question in two other works produced a few years after his conversion. In *Two Books on Genesis against the Manichees*, Augustine fashions a kind of allegory out of the creation narrative. According to his version of the Hebrew Bible, "God made heaven and earth, and all the green of the field before it was upon the earth." "Hence," he interprets, "the green of the field means the spiritual and invisible creature.…Then the addition, 'before they were upon the earth,' means: before the soul sinned. For soiled by earthly desires it is correctly said to have come to be upon the earth."[43] About the same time, Augustine began work on *De Genesi ad litteram* (*The Literal Meaning of Genesis*), which he never completed. Here, Augustine follows Jewish tradition in reasoning that the soul, together with the angels, must have been created during the six days when all things were made. "Even before heaven and earth," he writes, "there was a creature that passed through time by incorporeal movements, and we rightly understand that time existed along with that creature just as in the soul that has become used to corporeal motions through the senses of the body."[44]

Initiating the account of his life as far back as he can trace it in *Confessions* (397–398), sometimes called the first autobiography in the West, Augustine finds the simple starting point of physical birth perhaps too easy. "Where was I before I was in the womb?" he asks, but gives up the question as insoluble. It is, he seems to decide, beyond the power of scripture, introspection, or religion to answer. And yet he cannot leave the question alone. "Tell me, I beg,…whether my infancy followed upon some earlier age of my life that had passed away before it. Was the time I spent in my mother's womb such another age?…And before that again, O God of my joy? Was I anywhere? Was I anyone?" If God, he goes on to reason, is infinitely good and beautiful, yet Augustine was "conceived in iniquity," then "where, my God, where," he pleads to know, "or when was I, Your servant, innocent? But I pass now from that time."[45] Yet the question presses upon him insistently and suggestively, in a subsequent reflection on human happiness. "Happiness is known to all," he reasons, "for if they could be asked with one voice whether they wish for happiness, there is no doubt whatever that they would all answer yes. And this could not be unless the thing itself…lay somehow in their memory." Then, making the observation personal, he asks, "But where and when had I any experience of happiness, that I should remember it and love it and long for it?"[46]

Aside from the general question of happiness, the more particular hunger for God is central to Augustine's self-understanding. Augustine asks how he could love a being whom he had never known and finds the answer in the misty chambers of deepest memory:

> I shall mount beyond this power of my nature, still rising by degrees toward Him who made me. And so I come to the fields and vast palaces of memory.…When I turn to memory, I ask it to bring forth what I want: and some things are produced immediately, some take longer as if they had to be brought out from some more secret place of storage.[47]

He goes on to reason that, as a general rule, "if the image of a thing is imprinted on the memory, the thing itself must first have been present, for the image to be able to be imprinted. Thus I remember Carthage and such other places as I have been in."[48] And so it is with the woman who lost a groat. "She would not have found it if she had not remembered it. For when it was found, how should she have known whether it was what she sought…? It is always thus when we seek and find anything we have lost."[49]

The implications for Augustine's own life trajectory are obvious, as the search for God, the allure of a familiar happiness, and the palaces of memory converge. "How then do I seek You, O Lord? For in seeking You, my God, it is happiness that I am seeking....Where have [humans] seen it that they should love it? Obviously we have [this memory of happiness] in some way, but I do not know how." Still, he insists, "somehow or other they have come to know it....I strive to know whether or not this knowledge is in the memory, for if it is then we have at some past time been happy—whether individually, or in that man who committed the first sin."[50] A notion of original memory centered in Adam makes neither more nor less sense than the concept of original sin, he seems to be saying. In both cases, prior existence or participation of some sort, rather than mere heredity, must be involved. Still, Augustine inclines to a more personal solution than any possible Adamic explanation.

A decade or so later, he writes *De peccatorum meritis et remissione* (*On Merit and Forgiveness*), in which he grapples with the fate of unbaptized children who die. There, he floats again the hypothesis of pre-mortal sinning. And at the end of chapter 1, he rehearses three possible origins of the soul: derivation from parents (traducianism), individual creation (creationism), and, third, not Origen's version of a fall, but the possibility that souls are "divinely sent" into mortality, which is the virtually forgotten "sent" hypothesis of his work on souls.[51]

While he is wrestling to resolve the problem, Augustine asks the erudite and influential Jerome for clarification on the subject, but receives no response. As Augustine continues to work through and around the dilemma, the doctrinal situation becomes more conflicted and urgent with the controversial teachings of the British monk Pelagius. Alarmed at the direction of contemporary teachings on the Fall of Adam, inherited guilt, and infant baptism, Pelagius became a powerful advocate of freedom of the will, along with his disciple Caelestius. Consequently, they raise powerful challenges to the doctrine of inherited depravity and unmerited guilt. This development precipitates a major shift in the whole development of Christian theology, which Pelikan characterizes this way: the classical Christian doctrine of sin embodies what Reinhold Niebuhr calls the "seemingly absurd position that man sins inevitably and by a fateful necessity but that he is nevertheless to be held responsible" for those inevitable, fated sins. For the first four centuries, the church "leaned noticeably to one side of the dilemma, namely, the side of free will and accountability rather than the side of inevitability and original sin." With the rise of Pelagianism and its critique of sin's inevitability, Christian orthodoxy had to turn for the first time to defend that horn of the dilemma—the doctrine of humans' sinful nature, an apparently unmerited and unavoidable universal condemnation. And Augustine recognizes that the church is facing a new challenge in this regard. "Before this [Pelagian] heresy arose," he writes, "they did not have the necessity to deal with this question, so difficult of solution."[52] In this new context, affirming the necessity for grace because of human depravity will become a more urgent imperative than affirming the justice of God in light of human free will.

The shifting terms of this defense of Christian anthropology had direct implications for the origin of the soul, and so it is no coincidence that this becomes a decisive moment in the history of preexistence. Until now for Augustine, and for Jerome until recently, all four possibilities for the soul's origin were viable options. The Pelagian crisis changes all that. One point of departure for the radical critique launched by the Pelagians against human depravity and fatedness is the doctrine of creationism, which is the origin of the soul in God's creative act at the time of human conception, so favored by the period's theologians. As the Pelagians reason, if God created each human soul individually long after Adam, then the doctrine of inherited spiritual depravity is inconsistent with a pure and perfect God. Seeing the extreme views to which creationism led the Pelagians would have been yet another reason for Augustine to steer clear of that theory of the soul's origins. Still, he has to find a way to settle these unresolved tensions between freedom and inherited guilt, creationism, traducianism, and preexistence. Then, with the fall of the Roman Empire in 410, Pelagius and Caelestius flee with other refugees to Augustine's home turf of North Africa. Augustine scholar Robert O'Connell describes the result:

> It is Caelestius who mounts an attack against the African Church's understanding of infant baptism; it could not be before the "remission" of any sin, since infants are sinless. Caelestius bases his argument on the creationist hypothesis of the soul's origin: it is an insult to their Creator to contend that, fresh from the creative hand of God, unborn souls can be sinful. The African theology of the matter was understandable, of course, since they were all following Tertullian in his erroneous espousal of the traducianist hypothesis; but, Caelestius implies, the creationist wisdom of the more intellectual Eastern Churches will soon dispel that error.[53]

What this means is that one hypothesis for the soul's origin, traducianism, is already on its way out. Jerome vigorously opposes it, and it will soon come to be largely exiled to the Eastern church. (Pope Anastasius II condemns the theory in his epistle to the Gallican bishops in 498.)[54] Caelestius favors creationism but for reasons that were potentially devastating to Christian doctrines of sin and grace. A fresh act of creation for each and every human soul legitimately raises the question, how then is a nonphysical attribute like guilt or sin or depravity inherited? They aren't, answer the Pelagians simply. Neither creationism nor the traducianism it displaced can easily satisfy the criticism Caelestius implicitly raises, that a soul that has never known agency cannot be morally culpable. That leaves some form of preexistence as the most viable option on the table. Augustine by this point dismisses one version, the Neo-Platonic, not so much for the reason Tertullian (and, later, ben Israel) did, for its breach of sacred distance, but for reasons of logical implausibility. The Neo-Platonic view holds the human soul to be "a detached fragment of the divine substance." But the soul cannot be part of God, or it would have to be not just inherently immortal, but also immutable and incorruptible. In such a case, it could neither fall nor progress, but would be eternally static. ("That which is changeable in any way, for any reason, or in any part, is not unchangeable by its nature," reasons Augustine. "However, it is sin to believe that God is anything but completely and truly unchangeable. Therefore, the soul is not a part of God.")[55] That still leaves some form of preexistence viable, especially if it entails a role for the human will. That advantage will turn out to be an essential ingredient that keeps alive, generations in the future, an otherwise soon to be discredited theory of human preexistence. But in the present circumstance, it is the right emphasis at the wrong time. Because as Pelagius and his disciples demonstrated, the celebration of free will is too easily developed into the position that humans are in principle capable of living lives of uncompromising virtue and remaining altogether free of sin. Having no sin, they would have no need of Christ or his grace. Christ's redemptive role was thereby diminished or denied outright. What the Pelagians did, in simplest terms, was to celebrate human freedom and autonomy at the expense of inevitable and original sin but, more disturbingly, at the expense of Christ himself and his whole redemptive mission. Redressing this potentially catastrophic heresy became Augustine's central concern for the remainder of his life. The Pelagian crisis revealed that freedom of the will was a disruptive doctrine, one that must be addressed and contained; to simply ignore its danger was to capitulate to the likes of Pelagius. It was imperative to develop a spiritual anthropology that made room for accountability, while validating the necessity for grace. It is likely that Augustine saw room to maneuver here. Given his dilemma, he may have sensed it was possible to reject Origen's particular theories, while still finding a way to rescue human choice by recourse to preexistence.

Writing to Marcellinus in 412, Augustine refers again to the four theories of the soul he had outlined in his book on the will, indicating he is no closer to a verdict. In fact, he insists, he had deliberately written on the subject "in so cautious a way as to endorse none of those four opinions or arguments about the origin of the soul. Against them I do not defend myself because I am correct to hesitate on this question." The "obscurity of this darkest question," he continues, simply does not admit of a clear solution.[56]

That Augustine sees the Pelagian heresy as impinging directly on his options is clear in a letter he writes to Bishop Optatus of Milevis in 420. But here, we see that, even backed into a corner, he could be coy:

> You, my brother, ask me to decide for you whether men's souls as made by the Creator come like their bodies by generation from Adam, or whether like his soul they are made without generation and separately for each individual. For in one way or the other we both admit that they are God's handiwork. Suffer me then in turn to ask you a question. Can a soul derive original sin from a source from which it is not itself derived? For unless we are to fall into the detestable heresy of Pelagius, we must both of us allow that all souls do derive original sin from Adam. And if you cannot answer my question, pray give me leave to confess my ignorance alike of your question and of my own. But if you already know what I ask, teach me and then I will teach you what you wish to know. Pray do not be displeased with me for taking this line, for though I have given you no positive answer to your question, I have shown you how you ought to put it. When once you are clear about that, you may be quite positive where you have been doubtful. This much I have thought it right to write to your holiness seeing that you are so sure that the transmission of souls is a doctrine to be rejected.[57]

Defending any doctrine associated with Origen, however, was becoming increasingly difficult by the last decades of the fourth century and the beginning of the fifth—the very years in which Augustine is trying to resolve the question of the soul's origins, negotiate the competing demands of grace and free will, and counter the Pelagian threat. Origen was not without his critics in his own lifetime, but opposition became more organized and pronounced as time went on. In the early fourth century, Methodius had made a virtual career out of refuting many of Origen's teachings. Now, the first so-called Origenist crisis fully erupted in Palestine when enthusiasm for Origen among a group of monks led to vehement reactions and denunciations. One major tenet of Origen's thought, subordinationism (the belief that Christ was created by and therefore is subordinate to the Father), had been decisively vanquished with the triumph of the views of Athanasius over Arius at the Councils of Nicea and Constantinople. Now, toward the end of the fourth century, controversy grew beyond Origen's views on the Trinity and preexistence to encompass issues as diverse as human sexuality, the ascetic life, resurrection, and his allegorical method of interpretation. In many cases, the disputed views were more accurately attributed to disciples and interpreters like Evagrius Ponticus than to Origen's actual teachings. "The charge of Origenism," writes one authority on this episode, "proved sufficiently malleable to serve as a reflex for changing religious concerns."[58]

The opposition gathered strength with the efforts of Epiphanius of Salamis, a zealous heresy hunter, to have John, the bishop of Jerusalem, condemn a series of Origenist teachings in 394. Among others, he criticizes Origen's concept of a pre-mortal fall into bodies for its implicit denigration of human reproduction.[59] Jerome and Rufinus, both translators of Origen's works, became embroiled in the controversy on opposing sides. Jerome, who had been reticent when Augustine queried him on the subject of preexistence and had formerly embraced Origen's teachings (calling him "the greatest teacher since the apostles"), measured the shifting winds and lashed out vigorously, distancing himself from Origen and condemning Rufinus. Rufinus, who had been a friend of Jerome, felt betrayed, and each wrote searing apologias pointing fingers at the other. Rufinus's task was made the easier by virtue of Jerome's many published works, which affirmed Origen's teachings on preexistence and which Rufinus now quoted from extensively. "You say that in this world, along with the other inhabitants, that is the angels, there were also souls," Rufinus says, paraphrasing from Jerome's biblical commentaries. "You say that these souls," Rufinus continues in quoting him, "who in a former age had been inhabitants of heaven, now dwell here, on this earth, and that not without reference to certain acts which they had committed while they lived there." It is a theory that Jerome apparently at one time found especially amenable to ideas of divine justice. Else, asks Rufinus, why had Jerome repeated Origen's argument that it would be impossible to reconcile the disparate conditions of human life with the justice of God, "unless there are some antecedent causes for which each individual soul had its lot assigned according to its merits"?[60] Rufinus himself adamantly insists, "there are no writings of mine in which there is any error to be corrected," adroitly managing to avoid either renouncing or endorsing Origenist preexistence.[61]

Jerome responds heatedly with several salvos of his own. Not writing in entirely good faith, Jerome lamely explains away what had quite clearly been pronouncements in support of preexistence. He acknowledges that he has "erred at times," but asserts he was in good company. In Rufinus's parody of his retraction, Jerome implicates Clement of Alexandria, Clement of Rome, Gregory of Pontus, Gregory of Nazianzus, and Didymus as similarly upholding the teachings of Origen on human preexistence and other now-disputed doctrines.[62] In reality, Jerome had been more coy, saying, "I must not mention their names lest I should be supposed to defend Origen not by his own merits but by the errors of others."[63] As late as 410 or 412, Jerome writes to the bishop Marcellinus, "I well remember your little problem about the [origin] of the soul; although I ought not to call it little, seeing that it is one of the greatest with which the church has to deal." Jerome then summarizes the theories of which he is aware, naming five instead of Augustine's four. He lists first the theory of preexistence that he associates with Pythagoras, Plato, and Origen. Second is the soul as part of the divine essence, which he ties to the Sto-ics, Manichees, and Priscillianists. Third, he names the Talmudic teaching of spirits reserved in a treasury. Fourth and fifth, he lists creationism and traducianism. He finds only the Talmudic doctrine foolish and unworthy of consideration. His own opinion, he says, he has given elsewhere, in his *Apology against Rufinus*, written in 402. But in that treatise, he had condemned metempsychosis and the belief associ-ated with Origen that human souls are lapsed angels. He had not definitively ruled out preexistence nor any of the other theories.[64]

Finally, Theophilus, the bishop of Alexandria, convokes a synod in Alexandria in 400 and persuades Pope Anastasius (fl. 398–402) to sign a letter condemning not Origen, but the teachings of his disciple Evagrius Ponticus. In the same year, Theo-philus reports to Jerome that he has cleansed Egypt of the Origenist monks.[65] By now, the debates have come to the ears of Augustine. He will adopt a position against Origen, but it would be a mistake to assume that this marks a decisive turn on his part against the doctrine of preexistence. Philip Schaff is just one example of a capa-ble scholar who is too precipitous in gauging the evidence: "Augustine emphatically rejects the doctrine of pre-existence," he writes, citing *The City of God*, XI.23.[66] But in this late work, Augustine only condemns Origen's theory of the reason behind the world's creation; he condemns neither Origen's theory of preexistence in particular nor pre-mortal existence in general.[67] In spite of general assumptions that Augustine moved beyond his flirtation with preexistence in his later years, the evidence sug-gests that Augustine was unwilling fully to relinquish the best hope for reconciling guilt, accountability, and God's justice. As more than one scholar has noted, it is clear that "Augustine's early works presuppose the…doctrine and he was never definitely to deny it."[68] Nevertheless, a cumulative burden is weighing upon the doctrine, and at this point even Augustine's neutrality will prove decisive.

It is the Pelagian threat that tips the scales in this regard. Augustine, who had labored assiduously to defend the freedom of the will, now feels at last that it is nec-essary to capitulate to make way for grace. Indeed, in his *Retractions*, written at the close of his life, he apologizes for his earlier stalwart defense of free will, explaining that he wrote the treatise of that name in response to the Manichees, not against the Pelagians, who did not yet exist. He concedes that he has had to make adjustments to his theology. "I, indeed, labored in defense of the free choice of the human will; but," he says tellingly (and "with a shudder," writes O'Connell), "the grace of God conquered."[69] Even so, he insists that, while fighting the battle to vindicate free will, he was never "completely silent on the subject of grace, which the Pelagians in their abominable impiety are trying to take away altogether." In the earlier context, he felt perfectly safe in arguing that "evil deeds…would not be punished justly if they were not performed voluntarily." That, of course, was to insinuate a powerful argu-ment for preexistence but also to play into the hands of Pelagius. But now, "these new Pelagian heretics...claim that the choice of the will is so free that they leave no room for God's grace, which they claim is given in accordance with our merits."[70] The schismatic controversy, in other words, has forced him to choose rather than reconcile sides. He had already laid the groundwork for his shift in emphasis when he wrote to Simplician in 396 or 397 that even our will is apparently predisposed by God in one direction or another. "No man is to think that he has received grace because he has done good works. Rather he could not have done good works unless he had received grace through faith." As for guilt, since we all descend from Adam, we all deserve punishment for his offense. "To Adam the entire human race traces the origin of its sin against God. Sinful humanity must pay a debt of punishment to the supreme divine justice. Whether that debt is exacted or remitted there is no unrighteousness Some are fortunate enough to have it remitted."

So where is the justice in an election that has nothing to do with merit, and in a punishment that has nothing to do with choice? Augustine replies, "Let us believe that this belongs to a certain hidden equity that cannot be searched out by any human standard of measurement....He decides who are not to be offered mercy by a standard of equity which is most secret and far removed from human powers of understanding....Only let us believe if we cannot grasp it."[71]

What this means is that, even if Augustine will vacillate or equivocate till the end of his life on the question of human preexistence, the primary impetus behind the doctrine's Christian survival has been obviated. It is not for us, Augustine suggests, to use reason to salvage God's honor. Free will is not worth defending if such defense compromises God's ability to choose whom, how, or when he will, and relegates grace to the peripheries of salvational history. God's apparent injustice must be subsumed by human capitulation to the mysterious workings of the divine. So our perplexity in the absence of any theodicy becomes a sign both of our abject humility and of God's radically other sovereignty. The powerful engine that persistently urged a resolution of the problem of God's justice has run out of gas. Human agency, so essential to human culpability, is no longer the desperately asserted foundation of a Christian anthropology that it was, now that God's justice has resolved itself out of the orbit of human understanding and apologias. It would be too much to generalize O'Connell's judgment to the whole history of Christendom, but in the case of God's justice, at least, the point is clear; reason must yield to faith. Of course, this had been urged and perhaps foreshadowed all along by Tertullian, who had written simply that the desire for knowledge must "give place to faith....To know nothing in opposition to the rule [of faith] is to know all things."[72] The aftermath of the Augustinian episode is, in the case of preexistence at least, a sacrifice of dogged rational inquiry for mystery and plain dictate. At the same time, the powerful undercurrent that persists in Augustine's own studied ambiguity is a tacit signal that the problem is far from resolved.

In resisting an open endorsement of preexistence, Augustine finds that traducianism at least offers a more viable account of original sin than the creationist alternative, and he eventually gestures in that direction. After all, that doctrine has the virtue of at least providing the appearance of a logic behind shared, inherited guilt. In Peter Martyr's elegantly simple formulation, "originall sinne is by generation traduced by the parentes unto us."[73] Augustine wrestled to make the doctrine morally as well as biologically sensible in one of his later works, *De civitate dei* (*The City of God*):

> Man, however, depraved by his own free will, and justly condemned, produced depraved and condemned children. For we all were in that one man, since we all were that one man, who fell into sin through the woman who was made from him before they sinned. The particular form in which we were to live as individuals had not yet been created and distributed to us; but the seminal nature from which we were to be propagated already existed.[74]

While it does not explicitly invoke traducianism, the statement effectively comports with the view that the soul is propagated in a continuous line from Adam to the present. At any rate, a fallen "nature" that clearly transcends simple physicality is passed down, which includes not only predispositions, but an already condemned self. At the same time, the passage clearly entails some kind of preexistence, but shifts promiscuously among the conceptual, ideal, and actual existences of premortal humankind. Bald assertion ("we all were in that one man") is undercut by qualification (the particular bodily form wasn't yet "distributed to us") and concluded by quasi-scientific demonstration ("the seminal nature from which we were to be propagated already existed"). This is why Edward Beecher will rightly insist that Augustine senses that he can only provide a legitimate basis for the logic of original sin by designating it a "forfeiture previous to birth." And "this is, indeed, a kind of pre-existence....He spoke of men as if they pre-existed, enjoyed their rights, and forfeited them; and this language reacted through his imagination on his feelings, and gave him relief."[75]

O'Connell agrees that Augustine's solution is really a subtle reprise of preexistence, which hinges on his use of the peculiar expression *propria vita*, or proper life. Tracking this concept through Augustine's letters to Boniface, the *De meritis*, the *De Genesi*, and elsewhere, O'Connell finds that Augustine imputes to the human soul an earlier existence, but one in which we were not truly distinct from Adam, as he had hinted in *Confessions*. Therefore, we avoid the Origenist problem of premortal individual falls, participate somehow in Adam's guilt, and remedy the problem of will and justice alike. Thus, he argues, Augustine never really repudiated his belief in human beings as "contemplative souls, plunged into the misery to which the painful 'mortality' of our present bodies clearly attests."[76] The theory had the additional benefit of allowing Augustine to feel that his version of preexistence had avoided Tertullian's materialist-tainted traducianism, which he considered *dementia*.[77] If Augustine had a "final view" of the origins of the human soul, it may well be this compromise, according to which "'we' all sinned in Adam's sinning, not as our 'proper' selves, but in a 'common' life we lived in that Archetypal Man."[78] A radically transmogrified preexistence saves the day, and Augustine successfully threads the theological needle. Certainly, one may well complain, as Augustine's interpreter in this complicated but ingenious solution admits, that "it seems doubtful whether Augustine's is any longer a theory of the 'origin of the soul' in the conventional sense supposed by both parties in the controversy." Or whether, we could add, the doctrine is preexistence in any meaningful sense.

Beecher's subtle imputation of a convenient self-consolation is more than an ad hominem criticism. His point is that, in a case where the theological stakes are so high, the difference between comforting rhetorical resolutions and authentic truth claims with salvific efficacy is no small matter:

> If the mode of forfeiture which he alleged, and upon which his whole defense of God turned, had been possible and real, then there would have been a place for the element of justice in his system. But, as there was no real pre-existence and no real action, it was not possible, and of course was not real.... He admitted and insisted upon the very highest standard of judgment, when setting forth the principles of honor and right,...and then, in fact, resorted to a mere verbal evasion of them, by a shadowy and unreal theory of the preexistence and action of the millions of the race in Adam, thousands of years before they were born.
>
> Yet, shadowy and baseless as is this theory, upon it for centuries the doctrine of the Western church, as to original sin, and also all the doctrines which grow out of it, were made to rest.[79]

Having abandoned his quest for theodicy and having found another paradigm to do the work of explaining original sin, Augustine even finds that his excursus on memory, so suggestive of preexistence, can succumb to alternative explanations. As he writes in *De trinitate*:

> The mind remembers the Lord its God. For...He is whole everywhere, and on that account it loves, moves, and has its being in Him, and, therefore, it can remember Him. Not because it recollects that it had known Him in Adam, or anywhere else before the life of this body.

But then Augustine immediately makes clear that what he has just denied is something akin to Platonic recollection, not Platonic preexistence itself. "For [the mind] remembers nothing at all of these things, and whatever there is of this has been blotted out by forgetfulness."[80]

Certainly, neither the logic nor the poetry is as compelling as his ruminations in *Confessions*, where he thought one could only so love a God and a happy life that one had known before. That Augustine may through such maneuvers have technically distanced himself from the Platonic/Origenist line is beside the point. The problem remains, and any solution must take the same essential form. It must, as Augustine did, "show how the fall of the *persona* (and not only man's soul) must in some way be considered as referring to a historical fall on account of which our *condition humaine* is penal." That is why, almost inevitably, even in Augustine's "un-platonic view of the relationship of Adam and man, something of the strength and appeal of the Platonic scheme can be felt."[81] Schaff concurs that, in effect, Augustine's concept of original sin is no true alternative to preexistence. It simply disguises it as "a generic pre-existence and apostasy of all men in Adam," occurring as "a transcendental act of freedom, lying beyond our temporal consciousness."[82] For the thousand years and more spanning St. Paul to Thomas Aquinas, no figure would have the formative influence on Christian theology that Augustine had. And his tacit abandonment of preexistence as a viable possibility probably sealed its fate, though it would take another century for a formal edict to make the condemnation formal and churchwide.

Augustine's eventual refuge in a reconstituted version of preexistence foreshadows a long legacy of eruptions that traducianism and creationism will prove unable to forestall. It is in this sense that we will see many instances of a reconstituted version of preexistence that will perform the cultural work of the original myth while avoiding the problems of embracing it literally.

After Augustine

A few decades after Augustine, the first official denunciations and anathemas directed at preexistence begin to appear. In the mid-fifth century, Leo the Great writes at least two letters of censure. To Turribius, the bishop of Astorga, he writes in response to the rise of the Priscillianists, a Gnostic-inspired group of extreme ascetics:

> They are reported as asserting that souls which are placed in men's bodies have previously been without body and have sinned in their heavenly habitation.... This blasphemous fable they have woven for themselves out of many persons' errors.[83]

To another bishop, Julian, he is more emphatic in a letter of 449:

> And hence that which was deservedly condemned in Origen must be punished in Eutyches also, unless he prefers to give up his opinion, viz., the assertion that souls have had not only a life but also different actions before they were inserted in men's bodies.[84]

Over the next decades, the star of Plato wanes in concert with the doctrine of preexistence in any formulation. So the end of the fifth century sees what one scholar calls "the first Christian work to challenge long-accepted Platonic assumptions about the eternal existence of the spiritual and material worlds." *Theophrastus* by Aeneas of Gaza also attacked the preexistence of souls in particular.[85] In that work, Aeneas responded to the arguments then current in support of the doctrine, implied by the queries "If we deny the preexistence of souls, how is it possible for the wicked to prosper and for the righteous ones to live in dire circumstances? How can one accept the fact that people are born blind or that some die immediately after they are born, while others reach a very old age?"[86]

It is in the next century, however, that the power of the emperor and of the church councils are arrayed against the doctrine. The second Origenist crisis, as it was called, was far more lasting and decisive in its consequences than the first. By the sixth century, according to one account, some of Origen's followers inferred from his writings—and those of certain disciples—that the human soul was originally and could be again on a par with Christ. "If the Apostles and Martyrs at the present time work miracles, and are already so highly honoured, unless they shall be equal with Christ in the restitution of things, in what respect is there a restitution for them?" one of them was reported to teach.[87] Dubbed Isochristoi (equal to Christ), their position could be seen as a logical development of certain earlier church teachings. In the fourth century, Gregory of Nazianzus and Basil of Caesarea had reported Origen as saying, "Now we know there is a Person, Who is the image of the invisible God, and it is His image which is called the image of the Son of God; and we think that this image is the human soul which the Son of God assumed, and which for its merit became the image of the image of God."[88] The implication here is that Christ at some past time was possessed of the same species of soul that is common to humans and rose from the ranks to the supernal heights of deity. Origen's particular theory aside, the same extrapolating logic which may have inferred human preexistence from Christ's preexistence in the early Christian church could with equal logic infer the possibility of human apotheosis along the model of Christ's. (In the seventeenth century, an Anglican impatiently dismissed such persisting rationales for preexistence, writing, "we may as well prove we were all born of Virgin-Mothers because he was."[89] Yet another interesting variation on the theme will appear when the eighteenth-century polymath Joseph Priestly complains that the logic actually worked the other way around: "Perhaps the greatest disservice that the introduction of philosophy did to Christianity was, that, in consequence of the general doctrine of the pre-existence of all human souls, the soul of Christ was, of course, supposed to have had a pre-existent state.")[90]

These Origenists were opposed by a more moderate group of Origenists called the Protoktistoi (first-createds), who believed that Christ was the firstborn among a host of souls, and they were accused by their enemies of turning the Trinity into a tetrad through their own unique Christology.[91] What began as an in-house feud seems to have led to the sense that the problem was not in the variety of Origenism being taught, but with the source of the whole galaxy of Origenist teachings—Origen himself. That, at least, is the account recorded by the sixth-century historian Evagrius Scholasticus, who describes God as having providentially "arranged everything to advantage so that the profanities might be driven out from both sides."[92]

Appeals for a resolution went out to the emperor, who at that time was Justinian. The timing was not propitious for Origenism, preexistence, or any doctrine marked by pagan influence or parallels. In his first year as emperor, 527, Justinian outlawed the Manichaeans and the pagans and instituted the death penalty for lapsed Christians. His next move was to abolish the academy in Athens, a bastion of Neo-Platonism. He was proactive both in combating these perceived enemies of Christendom and in shaping and defending orthodoxy, even authoring a number of theological treatises. Willing to impose his views of right doctrine by fiat, he wrote to his patriarch that "the two greatest gifts which God in His infinite goodness has granted to me are the *Sacerdotium* [ecclesiastical hierarchy] and the *Imperium* [secular hierarchy]," and "the true divine teachings…are the first among our preoccupations."[93] Of course, discerning just what constituted "true divine teachings" was as often a function of politics as of inspiration. One of Justinian's trusted advisors at this time was Theodore Askidas, who was favorably disposed toward Origen. However, pressure mounted on Justinian in 539, when the Roman legate Pelagius denounced Origenism and urged the emperor to take action. So, when he was asked to resolve the growing conflicts surrounding Origen's teachings, it is no surprise that he ended by condemning the whole movement, writing in 543 *Liber adversus Origenem*, appending ten anathemas, and calling a local synod to confirm them.

The first of these condemnations went straight to the heart of Origen's doctrine: "Whoever says or thinks that human souls pre-existed,…but that, satiated with the vision of God, they had turned to evil,…and had been condemned to punishment in bodies, shall be anathema." And the ninth condemnation fell on those who say or think "that the punishment of demons and of impious men is only temporary, and will one day have an end, and that a restoration [apokatastasis] will take place."[94]

The synod passed the petition for censure in 544, and in 551, Justinian issued an edict, the primary purpose of which was to revisit the doctrine of Christ's nature, supposedly settled at the Council of Chalcedon in 451. As part of his edict, however, he specifically condemned the doctrine of preexistence, without mentioning Origen by name. In words reminiscent of Gregory of Nyssa's (whom he quotes to other purposes in the edict), Justinian held that "man is not soul apart from body, nor body apart from soul, but he was created from 'non-being' and brought into existence as body and soul."[95] Justinian next assembled the Fifth Ecumenical Council, which convened at Constantinople in 553. The main purpose of this synod was to condemn the "Three Chapters," referring to three groups of doctrines not directly related to Origen but arising from other controversies. Still, it seems that Justinian used the occasion to confirm the anathemas against Origen. The accuracy of the records of the Fifth Ecumenical Council is still disputed. Origen's name appears in the eleventh anathema (of fourteen issued) as one to be condemned along with a group of six other heretics. Some scholars think that his name was a later insertion by his enemies, but others insist, "there seems no possible reason to doubt...that Origen was condemned by name in the Eleventh Canon of this council."[96] An additional controversy concerns a set of fifteen more anathemas often attached to the records of the council. Schaff suspected that this Fifth Synod never went so far as to authorize these additional anathemas (which were not discovered until the seventeenth century), which targeted Origen's teachings without mentioning his name.[97] Harnack, on the other hand, believed there to be no real doubt that the Fifth Council in fact "condemned Origen, as Justinian desired," using the fifteen anathemas as the basis.[98] Most recently, Jaroslav Pelikan's authoritative account of the council omits without comment the fifteen anathemas.

Although Origen's name was not actually attached to any of the fifteen, the language leaves no doubt that his views as expressed in *On First Principles* are the target. The first anathema attacked the same two doctrines that featured prominently in Justinian's list: "If anyone asserts the fabulous pre-existence of souls, and shall assert the monstrous restoration [apokatastasis] that follows from it, let him be anathema." Following the pattern in Justinian's work, this list of condemnations similarly rounds out the anathemas with a second, emphatic repudiation of this apokatastasis: "If anyone shall say that the life of spirits shall be like to the life which was in the beginning while as yet the spirits had not come down or fallen, so that the end and the beginning shall be alike, and that the end shall be the true measure of the beginning: let him be anathema."[99]

Used in an eschatological sense (as in Matt. 17:11 or Acts 3:21), the term suggests a return to circumstances or conditions that prevailed at creation or at another early time period. As we have seen, it developed in the thought of some of the church fathers into a doctrine that portended the restoration of the human soul to its previous state. For Origen, this entailed a return to the spiritual heights from which one fell out of preexistence into mortality and was often read as including Satan in the universal rehabilitation. For some, like Gregory of Nyssa, it simply meant a return to the original perfection embodied in the paradisiacal Adam and Eve.[100] Clearly, the council is here reflecting the widespread habit of taking Origen's reading of apokatastasis to imply a heavenly preexistence to which humanity will universally be restored.

While these events are unfolding in the Eastern Empire, Theodoric is ruling the Western Roman Empire. His principal advisor and senior government official is the philosopher Boethius, a dedicated classicist. A champion of Platonism, he wrote one of the most influential works of the Middle Ages, *The Consolation of Philosophy*. It was produced largely as a balm to himself, sentenced as he was to die as an unjustly accused traitor to Theodoric. (He would be executed in 525.) While imprisoned, he wrote this work in the form of a dialogue between himself and Lady Philosophy, a messenger who appears to offer chastisement and a way out of his self-pity. In imagery reminiscent of *Timaeus*, his guide promises to show him the way back "home." In one of the neatest Christian/Platonic syntheses, Lady Philosophy conjures the memory of "the heights of heaven," "the stars' own home," with its "awful light" where "the King of Kings [holds] His sway, and guides the reins of the universe." Confronted with that image, Boethius is directed that he must either acquiesce to despair as an "exile from the light" or follow instead the path that his "memory seeks to recall" and recognize that "[t]his is my home, hence was I derived, here shall I stay my course."[101]

Preexistence of the soul is not a major theme in this work; it is, rather, a premise. But it is prominently employed in this instance precisely because of its power to appeal to the emotions, provide an ample perspective in light of which suffering can recede to its proper dimensions, and galvanize the human spirit to positive action that is kindled by actual memory rather than a more nebulous hope. Significantly, in this seminal text of the Christian Middle Ages, it is not Christianity, but Platonism, that provides the healing balm. As Lady Philosophy says, she evokes Boethius's origin and primal home in order to "give wings to your mind, by which it shall raise itself aloft: so shall disquiet be driven away, and you may return safe to your home by my guidance."[102] Preexistence is here the philosophical trope by which consolation is effected.

A little later, in far away Northumbria, the Venerable Bede records an attractive element of the Christian faith to which King Edwin of Northumbria (584–633) was being proselytized in 627 CE. As the king vacillated in indecision, a counselor advised him:

> Your Majesty, when we compare the present life of man on earth with that time of which we have no knowledge, it seems to me like the swift flight of a single sparrow through the banqueting-hall where you are sitting at dinner on a winter's day with your thanes and counselors. In the midst there is a comforting fire to warm the hall; outside, the storms of winter rain or snow are raging. This sparrow flies swiftly in through one door of the hall, and out through another. While he is inside, he is safe from the winter storms; but after a few moments of comfort, he vanishes from

sight into the wintry world from which he came. Even so, man appears on earth for a little while; but of what went before this life or of what follows, we know nothing. Therefore, if this new teaching has brought any more certain knowledge, it seems only right that we should follow it.[103]

Edwin apparently found the argument convincing; he renounced idolatry and accepted baptism. It is not clear if, on this occasion, Edwin found that his conversion to Christianity satisfied his desire to know more of those realms both preceding and following mortal life. But it is possible, coming as it did just a few years before the doctrine of preexistence was anathematized by Justinian.

Subsequent to the general church council that Emperor Justinian convened, succeeding emperors, councils, and writers routinely reaffirmed the condemnation of Origen. Emperor Heraclius reiterated the condemnation of Origen and his followers Didymus and Evagrius Ponticus in his statement of faith (*The Ecthesis*) in 638. So did the Sixth Ecumenical Council of 680–681; the Seventh Ecumenical Council in 787 likewise condemned as blasphemy the "mythical speculations" of that trio.[104] St. John of Damascus (c. 676–749) could write in reference to a man once esteemed as the greatest father of the church that "the body and the soul were formed at the same time—not one before and the other afterwards, as the ravings of Origen would have it."[105] Similarly, the ninth-century scholar (and chief author of the Great Schism) Photius of Constantinople could dismissively refer to "the nonsense of Origen, on the 'pre-existence of souls.'"[106] So, a few centuries removed from the death of the most influential father next to Augustine, it was possible to dismiss Origen as a madman. Even as conservative a critic as Harnack, who noted that "orthodox theology has never, in any of its confessions, ventured beyond the circle which the mind of Origen first measured out," wondered if, having "expunged his heresies...it has put better or more tenable [doctrines] in their place."[107]

Sporadic outbursts reminiscent of Plato's—or Origen's—theory of preexistence will erupt occasionally in these years. Olympiodorus (presumably, the Neo-Platonist; 495–570), for example, will argue, rather originally, that infants both smile and cry in their sleep, and ask, "can this any otherwise happen than through the soul agitating the circulations of their animal nature in conformity with passions it has experienced before birth into the body?"[108] But such effusions seem more quaint gestures of nostalgia than serious philosophizing. As Gerald Bostock writes, "it is hard to believe that the case against pre-existence can be closed by the theological timidity of the sixth century."[109] But closed it was—though not irredeemably.

6

Middle Ages to the Renaissance

When the last soul has descended and the *Guf* is empty, the first infant
to be born without a soul, born dead as such an infant must be, will
herald the death of the world and so is called the final sign. Then all of
the sparrows will grow silent, and the world, as we know it, will end.

—Jewish myth[1]

Rabbinical Varieties

While Christians debated, theologized, and anathematized over
preexistence, Jewish speculation on the idea proceeded without
impediment. In the centuries after Philo, rabbinic formulations imputed
to a number of specific entities existence prior to the physical world:
the Torah and the throne of God were actually created; the creation
of the patriarchs, Israel, the temple, and the name of the Messiah was
contemplated.[2] According to another version, seven entities were created
before the world: the Torah, the throne of glory, the temple, the name of
the Messiah, along with repentance, the garden of Eden, and Gehenna.[3]
Human souls also make frequent appearance in both Mishnah (redaction
into written form of the oral law) and midrashim (commentary on the
Hebrew Bible), dating from about 200 CE onward. In his conception
of preexistence, Plato had been clear and emphatic in his dualism: "our
souls also existed apart from the body before they took on human form,
and had intelligence."[4] They existed, in other words, as entities possessing

independent being and self-awareness. As the idea of preexistence is formulated in these Jewish texts, such independence and capacity for volition are similarly indicated.

Though the doctrine of preexistence among the early Jews is evident across a wide spectrum of texts, such prevalence is striking, given some strongly worded counsel against this subject of speculation. The *Bereshith Rabbah* (Creation or Genesis Rabbah) is a classical midrashic Jewish text, dating from the sixth century and perhaps drawing on older materials. It states, in no uncertain terms, "It is forbidden to inquire what existed before creation, as Moses distinctly tells us (Deut. 4:32): 'Ask not of the days that are past which were before thee, since the day God created man upon earth.' Thus the scope of inquiry is limited to the time *since* the Creation."[5] One ingenious rationale for this position is based on the first letter of the Torah, *beth*:

> To the question, Why does the story of creation begin with the letter *beth* [the second letter, instead of the first letter, *aleph*], the *Talmud Yerushalmi Chagigah* 2:1 answers: "just as the letter *beth* is closed on all sides and open only in front, similarly you are not permitted to inquire what is before or what is behind, but only from the actual time of creation."[6]

If the scenes before creation are closed to speculation, those before mortality are not. And so it is, ironically, that the seventeenth-century Jewish scholar Menasseh ben Israel cites that same *Bereshith Rabbah* (III) as holding that human souls existed before embodiment, not just as ideas in the mind of God, but as entities with whom He actually consulted before creation, in order to make sure He did not clothe them with matter against their will.[7] Some midrashim detail this specific scenario prior to creation in explicating one of the riddles of Genesis. And it is in this connection that the divine assembly that features so prominently in Mesopotamian texts, and that intrudes so persistently in Hebrew Bible contexts, appears again in a way that explicitly positions human souls as participants in those heavenly councils. The Hebrews may have been monotheists, but the first chapter of Genesis complicates that belief structure by introducing, if not a divine assembly, then a problematic plural pronoun. The text in question is 1:26: "Let us make man in our image." Christians have seen in that wording everything from foreshadowings of the Trinity to a simple case of the "royal we." But a series of midrashic interpretations takes the grammar at face value in addressing the question, with whom did God consult? The same *Midrash Rabbah* that warned against inquiring beyond the veil of creation invokes a passage in Chronicles to find a surprising answer:

> R. Joshua of Sihknin said in R. Levi's name: He took counsel with the souls of the righteous, as it is written, "[And the records are ancient]. These

were the potters and those that dwell at Netaim and Gederah; they dwelt there in the king's service (1 Chron. 4:[22–]23). These were the potters [*yotzerim*, lit. 'makers' or 'formers']." They are so termed on account of the verse, "The Lord formed [*va-yitzer*] man from the dust of the earth" (Gen. 2:7). "And those that dwell at Netaim" corresponds to "And the Lord God planted a garden in Eden, in the East" (verse 8)...." "They dwelt in the king's service" means that the souls of the righteous dwelt there with the supreme King of Kings, the Holy One, blessed be He, with whom He took counsel, and created the world.[8]

According to this commentary, the council of souls "assisted in planting and some helped create the borders of the sea, as it is said, *Who set the sand as a boundary to the sea* (Jer. 5:22). Nor does God make any important decision without consulting the Council of Souls."[9] Howard Schwartz notes that it is not even specified that these righteous souls were created by God, "but only called together by God before He created the universe."[10]

This is not the only text in which the heavenly assembly of earlier ages recurs in this period with the clear ingredient of pre-mortal humans. Another midrash also singles out human preexistence as a necessary postulate following from Genesis 2:1–2, wherein the heaven and earth "and all the host of them" are pronounced created by the end of the sixth day. More specifically, the midrash indicates, "all the souls that existed from the time of Adam the first man until the end of time, were all created during the six days of Creation. And all of them were in the Garden of Eden, and all of them were present at the giving of the Torah [on Sinai]."[11] A number of sources indicate that these pre-mortal spirits are kept safe in a treasury, or cage (*guf*). The Syriac *Apocalypse of Baruch* was authored by Jews in the first century CE. In this work, responding to Baruch's prayers that the travails of Judah may end and God's righteous purposes triumph, the Lord responds that an important population has escaped Baruch's consideration:

> For as thou hast not forgotten the people who now are and those who have passed away, so I remember those who are appointed to come. Because when Adam sinned and death was decreed against those who should be born, then the multitude of those who should be born was numbered, and for that number a place was prepared where the living might dwell and the dead might be guarded. Before therefore the number aforesaid is fulfilled, the creature will not live again.[12]

This same theme of the heavenly treasury of the souls of men appears throughout rabbinic literature. The Talmud describes Arabot, last of the seven heavens, as holding "the spirits and the souls which are yet to be born, for it is written: 'For the spirit that enwrappeth itself is from Me, and the souls which I have made.'"[13] Other passages confirm that not "before all the souls in *Guf* will have been disposed of" will the Son of David come.[14] "All the souls which existed from Adam onward," wrote Menasseh ben Israel, citing the *Tanhuma*, "and which will exist until the end of the world, all these were created in the six days of creation, and they were all in the garden of Eden." And, he adds, they were all present at Sinai and participated in the making of the covenant. This last assertion he found attested by the verse in Deuteronomy 29:14, "I make this covenant to those who are standing here, and with those who are not here with us today."[15]

This theme of pre-mortal participation in important events and decisions makes it difficult to reckon such existence as merely "ideal." One midrash, *Tanhuma Pekude*, describes human incarnation as a step that the soul demonstrates reluctance to undergo—and understandably, given the physiological details. At the time of a woman's conception, the text relates:

> The Holy One, Blessed is He, immediately motions to the angel appointed over the spirits and says to him, "Bring Me the spirit of So-and-so."...Thereupon, the angel goes and brings that spirit before the Holy One, Blessed is He, and when the spirit arrives, it immediately bows and prostrates itself....Then, the Holy One, Blessed is He, says to the spirit, "Enter the droplet [of sperm] that is in the hand of So-and so." The spirit opens its mouth and says before Him, "Master of the World! The world I have been living in from the time I was created is sufficient for me. Why do You wish to put me into this putrid droplet, for I am holy and pure, and shaped from the form of Your glory." Thereupon, the Holy One, Blessed is He, says to the soul, "The world I am putting you into is better for you than the one you have been living in, and at the time I created you, I created you specifically for this droplet." Then the Holy One, Blessed is He, immediately inserts it there against its will. And after that the angel inserts the spirit into the mother's womb.[16]

No wonder that, in this version of pre-mortality, God finds it necessary to then assign two angels to guard the womb, lest the soul make its escape from its new domicile.

Later Medieval Period

We saw in the earliest Christian and Semitic traditions a primordial cosmos populated by variegated beings in fluid hierarchies. In Origen's conception, for instance, God, angels, demons, and human souls all mingle in the preexistent realms and in the present. The Gnostic *Gospel of Judas* refers to a universe peopled by 72 luminaries, who produce another 360 luminaries, and 12 aeons associated with another 12 luminaries, together with a great host of angels and myriad virgin spirits—and "the multitude of these immortals is called the cosmos."[17] Aristotle's universe was more simple, ranging from an unmoved mover through the intermediary of numerous intellectual substances, which are responsible for the movement of heavenly bodies.[18] Most Christian theology eliminates humans from that celestial real estate, but they will weave in and out of various cosmologies over the next centuries. The presence of angels, on the other hand, being so well attested biblically, will endure, and most orders of beings are subsumed into this one category.

In the Middle Ages, two groups of heavenly beings, intelligences and angels, predominate in theological and philosophical speculations about the heavenly world. Intelligence, or *nous*, it will be remembered, was the term both for the second hypostasis in Neo-Platonism and for what Origen held to be the individuated pre-mortal essence of humans. In the sixth century, the most influential theologian of the era, Pseudo-Dionysius, accepted on patristic authority the arranging of angels into several distinct types and orders. He develops an elaborate hierarchy of what he calls intelligences, which he takes to be synonymous with the Christian angels. In his work, the myriad supramundane entities resolve themselves into three hierarchies of three orders each: seraphim, cherubim, thrones; dominations, virtues, powers; principalities, archangels, angels.[19] Still, as Stephen Bemrose writes, certain differences between intelligences and angels meant that it was not possible in the minds of many thinkers to completely effect that conflation or assimilation. Christian angels, for one thing, were generally considered to be immortal but were "the object of an act of creation in time." They differ in this essential from intelligences, who were thought by Aristotle and others to be eternal.[20]

In the eleventh century, the great scholar Avicenna (who, though Islamic, was profoundly influential in the development of Scholasticism and, indeed, Western philosophy generally) similarly speculated on the inhabitants of heaven, believing that the class of angels encompassed two distinct beings: intelligences and souls. The first represent pure intellectuality, are wholly immaterial, and hence are incapable of influencing matter. Souls, on the other hand, act upon the heavens, imparting to them, for example, their circular motion. Meanwhile, another eleventh-century philosopher, Michael Psellos (c. 1018–1080), was busy cataloging the other side of the heavenly hierarchy. A Christian Neo-Platonist, his *De operatione daemonum* classified the various ranks of demons. (Henry More in the seventeenth century would rely on this work to adumbrate "the six sorts of sprights" in his own catalog of the cosmos.)[21]

The thirteenth century saw a resurgence of the Aristotelian emphasis on intelligences with works like *Liber de intelligentiis*, and writers speculated on their nature and role in the celestial workings. Still, opinion continued to be divided as to whether sphere-moving intelligences could be reconciled with the angels of Christendom. Francis Bacon and Aquinas said yes. Peter John Olivi feared that the strategy would invite pantheism, and Albert Magnus insisted, "angels are not to be equated with the Intelligences of the philosophers."[22] Some centuries later, when Milton used epic poetry to solidify a canonical view of the pre-mortal heavens, the heavenly hosts were uniformly designated as angels, with humans (and their souls) created in the aftermath of celestial war. But even then, some revisionists saw Milton's work as a conflating of categories that obscured the true variety of heavenly beings and humanity's pre-mortal involvement there.

While the councils had definitively declared against the doctrine of preexistence and the fathers for the most part banished traducianism, apparently not every subsequent theologian was convinced. Anselm of Canterbury (1033–1109) was the greatest Christian philosopher of his age, sometimes credited as the founder of Scholasticism. We have no record of his views on preexistence, except for a suggestive anecdote indicating that he thought the question was still an open one. His biographer Eadmer described a scene on Palm Sunday, when Anselm's death seemed imminent and friends had gathered around his bed. One of them said that it looked like the archbishop would be celebrating Easter with God. Anselm replied, "[I]f his will is set on this, I shall gladly obey his will. However, if he would prefer me to remain among you, at least until I can settle a question about the origin of the soul, which I am turning over in my mind, I should welcome this with gratitude, for I do not know whether anyone will solve it when I am dead."[23]

Increasingly, however, opponents of preexistence felt emboldened to represent creationism as the official dogma of the church. That was what Peter Lombard did in *Sentences* (c. 1150). Aquinas, in *Summa Theologica* (1265–1274), invoked the preexistence rationales of both Origen and Augustine in order to refute them and to declare the truth of creationism.[24] Meanwhile, the proscriptions of the church councils notwithstanding, and in spite of Justinian's suppression of paganism and the Platonic academy, Plato's *Timaeus* continued to exert its influence into the high Middle Ages. It was in these years more common, however, for preexistence to appear as poetic trope or mystical imagery than as rationally defended theology. One vehicle for this survival is the *Cosmographia; or, De Mundi Universitate Libri Duo sive Megacosmos et Microcosmos* of Bernard Silvester, written in the middle of the twelfth century. Bernard fashioned a myth of a worldly creation instigated by Nature's complaint about the disorder prevailing among the primal matter of the universe. God's providence, personified as Noys, oversees the organization of a stable material form to be united with the world soul, which emanates from the heavens. Book 2 recounts the creation of man, aided by the goddess Urania. In this account, man's soul derives from the world soul, with the addition of virtue;

his body comes from preexistent matter.[25] Urania then describes some of the sights—and the travails—that the human soul will encounter on its journey into and time spent in mortality. This is, in fact, her prime responsibility: "to look after the education of the soul as it descends to earth" and "to acquaint the soul with its celestial origin."[26] Noys even describes the pathetic scene in heaven of "countless souls weeping because they soon will have to descend from that splendor into these glooms."[27]

Similar imagery is found in the great mystic and contemporary of Bernard, Hildegard von Bingen. In her *Liber Scivias* is to be found one of the most remarkable illustrations ever rendered on the subject of preexistence and incarnation. A squarish object hovers in the heavens, representing the "Supernal Creator," "flaming, as it were, with many eyes" and filled with fiery globes. From this celestial repository of globes, representing human souls or spirits, a funnel channels one downward and into the womb of a recumbent woman. After the woman has conceived, this *"fiery globe which has no human lineaments possesses the heart of that form*, that is, the soul, burning with a fire of profound knowledge,... [and] gives strength to the heart and rules the whole body." The soul, however, does not take well to its new abode. Hildegard describes the lament of the soul upon finding itself marooned in a prison or "tabernacle" of corruption and its insistent claim to a nobler heritage:

> A pilgrim, where am I? In the shadow of death....I should have been a companion of the angels, for I am a living breath, which God placed in dry mud; thus I should have known and felt God. But alas! When my tabernacle saw that it could turn its eyes it turned its attention toward the North; ach, ach! and there I was captured and robbed of my sight and the joy of knowledge, and my garment all torn. And so, driven from my inheritance, I was led into a strange place without beauty or honor, and there subjected to the worst slavery.

She hears the laments of other globes, likewise oppressed by the devil's whirlwinds, but sees as well a globe that has broken free of its bonds and is led away by "certain spirits." If it is one who has overcome the devil's wiles through faith in Christ, then it will be "brought back by Him" and "gain the joys of celestial inheritance."[28]

A few centuries later, the first English book of female authorship appeared: Julian of Norwich's *Showings*. In 1373, this woman from Norfolk, England, suffered a severe illness. At a moment when death seemed imminent, she experienced a sudden vision of the passion of Christ, followed over the next day by several others. She soon produced a short account of her visions and, after lengthy reflections upon them over subsequent years, wrote a much fuller version that included, along with accounts of these many revelations or "showings," explications of their allegorical significance. Her historic role in giving us one of the first female voices on record in

xxx ௐ erba di ad hommes.ᵹ̃ duunꝰ p̃ceptꝰ obedias̃ ·ꝝ malũ abicientes.bonũ m amoꝛe
dei fideliter perficiant.   xxxi· De fide catholica. xxxii· ௐ erba ysaiᶾ ·

The medieval mystic Hildegard described the souls of humans descending as fiery globes
into mortal wombs and their grief over exchanging their noble inheritance "for a strange
place without beauty or honor." Illustration from *Liber Scivias* (*Codex Rupertsberg*, 12th
century), by Hildegard von Bingen; Erich Lessing/Art Resource, New York.

the English tradition, together with the depth and range of her visionary experience
and the intricate and theologically sophisticated readings she provides—all combine to make Julian one of the most significant figures in the tradition of Christian
mysticism.

One of her most famous passages is the vision recounted in her fourteenth
revelation. In this showing, she sees a lord regally attired and sitting on a throne,

accompanied by a servant who "stondyth before his lorde, reverently redy to do his lordes wylle." What happens next is briefly and simply narrated, but rich and portentous in theological significance, as her lengthy interpretation will show:

> The lorde lokyth upon his servaunt full lovely and sweetly and meekly. He sendyth hym in to a certeyne place to do his wyll. The servaunt nott onely he goyth, but sodenly he stertyth and rynnyth in grett hast for love to do his lordes wille. And anon he fallyth in a slade [valley or ditch] and takyth ful grett sorow. And than he gronyth and monyth and wallowyth and wryeth, but he may nott ryse nor helpe hym selfe by no manner of weye.[29]

That the allegorical reading will involve a fall and some kind of redemption or act of grace appears self-evident. But several details push the narrative and its interpretation in unexpected directions. It is, first of all, noteworthy that the servant is in a setting removed from and apparently preceding the mortal sphere. The fall "in a slade" is later cast more emphatically as a fall "from lyfe to deth in to the slade of this wrechyd worlde." One reading of the servant is, of course, to see him as Christ—and that is one variant Julian gives us. But that is not the primary meaning, as is evident from the initial scene of the fall, after which Julian records that she attended carefully to the vision to see what blame or retribution should befall the servant. To her surprise, "verily there was none seen, for oonly hys good wyll and his grett desyer was cause of his fallyng." In fact, the lord explains that, since the servant undertook his task out of love and "good wylle," he deserves by right to be compensated for his pain and suffering, his fear and anxiety, to an extent "above that he shulde have be yf he had nott fallen." The surprise only makes sense in a context where Adam's Fall, not Christ's condescension, is the subject. And as Julian confirms, "The servaunt that stode before hym, I understode that he is shewed for Adam." It is surprising enough that she sees Adam here as worthy of honor rather than reproach for his Fall. But then the third level of meaning takes us into a different theological realm altogether: "that is to sey, oone man was shewed that tyme and his fallyng to make there by to be understonde how God beholdyth alle manne and his fallyng."[30]

The fall into mortality, one in which Adam is typical but not unique and in which no blame inheres, evokes the kind of Platonic fall we have seen before, the theory Augustine referred to as "sent" preexistence. And indeed, Julian proceeds to confirm the Neo-Platonic bent of her theology in the chapters that immediately follow the allegory of the fallen servant.[31] For in the same revelation, she affirms that "the dwelling of the blessyd soule of Crist is full high in the glorious Godhede." But she is also given to understand that "where the blessyd soule of Crist is, there is the substance of alle the soules that shall be savyd by Crist." In fact, and here her

Neo-Platonic affinities are clearest, "I sawe no difference between God and oure substance, but as it were all God." So, it is also here that she flirts on the peripheries of heresy. For in 1053, Pope Leo IX declared the soul to be "not a part of God, but...created from nothing."[32] In probable recognition of this injunction against blasphemy, Julian then clarifies, "And yett my understanding toke that oure substance is in God, that is to sey, that God is God and oure substance is a creature in God." So God is unmade, while the human soul is made in a first stage of creation by which it is and remains a part of God but not identical to God. Later, she will add that, it being God's intention to make humankind, he appointed the task to "his owne Son, the Second Person. And when he woulde, by full accorde of alle the Trynyte, he made us alle at onys." The making "all at once" again evokes the creation account of *Timaeus*, as well as rabbinical versions, in which all the souls of humans are made in a primordial act of creation. "And in oure making," she continues, "he knytt us and onyd [united] us to hym selfe, by which oonyng [uniting] we be kept as clene and as noble as we were made."[33]

Now it is clearer how in her allegory the good and faithful servant, in falling, deserves not censure or punishment but a compensation as rich or richer than the goodly state and condition he risked in going forth. For while the purpose of the fall is not clear, Adam as prototype—and the human race in like fashion—descended to earth out of good will and great desire, forsaking a noble heritage and dwelling with and in Christ himself.

And that is a going forth into mortality in which Christ's incarnation mirrors and typifies Adam's and all humankind's: "And ferthere more I saw that the Seconde person, which is oure Moder substauncyally, the same derewurthy Person is now become oure Moder sensuall, for we be doubell of God's making, that is to sey, substaunciall and sensuall." In other words, Christ is the "mother" or engenderer of our dual nature, both the soul's essence[34] and the body's corporeal nature. "Oure substaunce is the hyer perty, which we have in our Fader God almighty. And the Seconde Person of the Trynyte is oure Moder in kynd in oure substauncyall making in whom we be groundyd and rootyd." As for Christ himself, "he is oure Moder of mercy in oure sensualyte takyng." He begets us spiritually, in other words, through taking upon himself our physical form and suffering accordingly. His atonement, therefore, depends upon his assuming that very same nature with which he endowed our preexisting souls.[35]

The idea of preexistence has persisted through the Middle Ages, until now, sporadically and unsystematically. By Julian of Norwich's lifetime, however, the theme of preexistence has received new impetus from developments that have been slowly simmering since Jewish antiquity in a tradition exempt from the strictures of Christian orthodoxy and that now flower in magnificent fashion in twelfth-century Provence, though its roots are far older.

Kabbalah

Virtually every major religion has a mystical strand, and Judaism is no exception. Mystical varieties of Judaism emerged in the early centuries of the Common Era, and the Talmud itself contains scattered hints and references to a tradition of mysticism (*torat ha-sod*) that was divided into two parts—referred to as the Act or Account of Creation and the Account of the Chariot (referring to Elijah's ascent into heaven). According to tradition, much of this esoteric knowledge was transmitted orally going back to the prophets, patriarchs, or even, according to the orthodox, Eden. From the diaspora on, knowledge of Kabbalah became hidden from the uninitiated and accessible to only a privileged few, who must be qualified, among other ways, through marriage and scholarship in the Talmud.

Kabbalistic texts pertaining to the creation inform B'reshit mysticism, whereas literature related to Elijah's vision of the divine chariot constitutes Merkabah mysticism. An example of the latter, *3 Enoch*, purports to relate the journey of Rabbi Ishmael into heaven, under the tutelage of the archangel Metraton. Produced probably in the fifth or sixth century, it incorporates Jewish traditions that originated in Palestine in the early Christian era.[36] In Rabbi Ishmael's version, there is the heavenly court we have seen before. And, as often happens, that motif is found alongside a version of preexistent souls. Metraton offers to show Ishmael both the righteous souls who have returned from their mortal lives and the souls of those who have not yet been "created" as mortals:

> Come and I will show you the souls of the righteous who have already been created and have returned, and the souls of the righteous who have not yet been created. He bore me up with him, and, taking me by his hand, he led me to the throne of glory and showed me those souls which have already been created and have returned, flying above the throne of glory in the presence of the Holy One, blessed be He. Then I went and expounded this verse, and found with regard to the text "The spirit shall clothe itself in my presence, and the souls which I have made" [Isa. 57:16], that "the spirit shall clothe itself in my presence" refers to the souls of the righteous which have already been created in the storehouse of beings and have returned to the presence of God; and "the souls which I have made" refers to the souls of the righteous which have not yet been created in the storehouse.[37]

As the editor glosses the unusual language here, the context makes clear that the "souls which have not been created" in the storehouse means those "which are to be put in to bodies yet to be created." Their actual preexistence is beyond doubt in this conception ("the preexistence of the soul is implied throughout this chapter," he notes). In accounts such as these, it seems unwarranted to insist that Jewish conceptions of preexistence pertain to ideas in the mind of God alone. The entirety of *3 Enoch* brims with celestial beings, and Enoch is continually being shuttled from "place" to "place" to see them. R. H. Charles concurs: "these souls were conceived as actually living beings."[38]

The mystical cosmology of Kabbalah and the goal of theurgy, or mystical union with the divine, are the particular context in which Kabbalistic notions of the soul need to be viewed. Beginning with the earliest Kabbalistic texts, the *sefirot* are taught as a scheme of manifestations or aspects of the divine personality. They represent the means by which the ultimate reality of God, Ein Sof, who is himself unknowable and outside categories, becomes knowable and accessible to the created order of things, including humans. Unlike some other philosophies of antiquity, therefore, Kabbalah emphasizes from its inception the desirability and possibility of an actual relationship with the divine. This is one form that theurgy takes, a systematic process, usually associated with ritual or magic, by which a human ascends through progressive stages into communion with, association with, or the condition of the gods or the divine. Generally, the integration is conceived as a *re*integration, a "coming home." Or, as a sixteenth-century Kabbalist put it, "the process is like a revolving wheel, first descending then ascending."[39] This pattern is seen in Greek, Jewish, and mystical varieties of theurgy as well. In the *Hermetica*, for example, the same process, which goes from preexistent souls to eventual theosis, is sketched: "All the souls…come from the one soul of the all….the dry-land souls change into winged things; the aerial into humans; and human beings, changing into demons, possess the beginning of immortality, and so then they enter the troop of gods….And this is soul's most perfect glory."[40] Therefore, just as the *sefirot* reflect a kind of chain of descent from the pure being of Ein Sof to the materiality of creation, they become, "from below to above,…a ladder of ascent back to the One."[41] As for the human soul, it is itself born of the union of two of the *sefirot*, Tif'eret and Shekhinah, "and the mystical journey begins with the awareness of this spiritual fact of life."[42]

The Kabbalistic tradition received its major modern impetus in the thirteenth century in Spain and southern France. A principal figure in the movement was the Spanish Jew Moses de León. Learned in both medieval philosophy and the literature of mysticism, de León produced in succession a number of important works with a mystical bent. In 1290, he wrote *Sefer ha-Mishqal*, in which he treats specifically the origin and destiny of the human soul. In important contradistinction to Platonic and Origenist conceptions, Kabbalists like Moses de León saw the soul's descent as progress rather than punishment or degradation:

> [T]he purpose of the human soul entering this body is to display her powers and actions in this world, for she needs an instrument. By descending

to this world, she increases the flow of her power to guide the human being through the world. Thereby she perfects herself above and below, attaining a higher state by being fulfilled in all her dimensions. If she is not fulfilled both above and below, she is not complete. Before descending to this world, the soul is emanated from the mystery of the highest level. While in this world, she is completed and fulfilled by this lower world....At first, before descending to this world, the soul is imperfect; she is lacking something. By descending to this world, she is perfected in every dimension.[43]

A distinct feature of this conception of incarnation is the refusal to see it as a fall into mortality, but rather as an actual ascent and an asset in the journey toward perfection. The notion of the body as complementing the soul stands in stark opposition to earlier traditions that saw physicality as a burden or prison to be lamented and overcome or transcended. We are clearly far removed here from Plotinus's shame at the very fact of his bodily self. Adolphe Frank finds here a crucial distinction from the Greek-inspired versions of preexistence:

[The binding of the spiritual and mortal elements in a] temporary union is not considered a misfortune. Unlike Origenes and the gnostic school life is not looked upon as a downfall or exile, but as a means for education and a beneficial trial. According to the Kabbalists, it is necessary for the soul...to contemplate the spectacle offered by creation, in order to attain self-consciousness and consciousness of its origin.[44]

Toward the end of the thirteenth century, Moses de León began to circulate texts that he said were based on the teachings of Rabbi Shim'on, a famous teacher of the second century. The immense work that resulted, attributed by some to de León himself,[45] was taken by Kabbalists as authentically ancient and was held to restore the true knowledge of humankind's nature and relationship to the divine, lost since the garden of Eden. The *Zohar*, as this central work of Kabbalah is called, is loosely structured as a wide-ranging, multigeneric commentary on the five books of Moses. In the *Zohar*, humanity's pre-mortal existence is clearly presented as an allegorical reading of the patriarch Abram's call from Ur into Canaan. Interpreting Genesis 12:1–4, the commentary reads:

Rabbi Jacob son of Idi said
"All soul-breaths of the righteous
have been carved from the bedrock of the Throne of Glory
to guide the body like a father guiding his son.
For without the soul-breath, the body could not conduct itself,
would not be aware of the Will,
could not actualize the Will of its Creator...."

> When the Blessed Holy One sends her from the place of holiness
> He blesses her with seven blessings,
> as it is written:
> "YHVH said to Abram,"
> this is the soul-breath
> who is *av*, "a father" to teach the body
> and *ram*, "high" above him
> for she has come from a high and lofty place.
> What does He say to her?
> "Go forth from your land, your place of birth,
> your dwelling, your place of bliss."
>
> "And from your father's house"
> Rabbi Jacob said, "this is the mirror that shines."
> "To the land that I will show you"
> means to such and such a body, a holy body, an upright body....
>
> "Abram went forth as YHVH had directed him."
> Blessed with these seven blessings,
> Abram, the soul-breath went forth,
> father to the body and high from the place of the highest.
> "As YHVH had directed him"
> to enter the body that she had been commanded to guide and train.[46]

A similar picture emerges from the *Zohar*'s treatment of the birth of Moses, as recorded in Exodus 2:1–2. In this story, Gabriel appears as the angelic guide who ushers souls into their appointed bodies:

> When the body of a righteous hero is born in this world
> the Blessed Holy One summons Gabriel
> who carries the soul-breath from the Garden
> and brings her down to his body, born into this world.
> Gabriel is appointed guardian of the soul-breath.[47]

A similar account is found in the Jewish Talmud (Niddah 30b), from which a Hasidic tradition developed that gives a delightful etiology of a universal facial feature:

> There is a legend in the Hasidic tradition which says that when a baby is conceived an angel accompanies the soul into the womb. And in the blood-thumping shelter of the mother, angel and soul speak of the life to come and decide together on the purpose of this incarnation. What is this soul coming to contribute? Who will help support this purpose? What challenges will be faced? Where comes love? There is, of course, a catch to

all this thoughtful planning. Just as the birth pangs begin, when the soul must fully enter the baby-self and the angel return to heaven, the angel reaches out and presses its finger against the baby's lip. We still have this mark, an indentation that runs sweetly from upper lip to nose. The philtrum is the angel's last gift. "Hush," it whispers to the stirring child, "now you must forget."[48]

An earlier, less romanticized version describes the angelic gesture in rather different terms. At the time of birth, the *Tanhuma Pekude* relates, "the soul is reluctant to leave her place. Then the angel fillips the babe on the nose, extinguishes the light at his head, and brings him forth into the world against his will. Immediately the child forgets all his soul has seen and learnt, and he comes into the world crying."[49]

It is likely that some earlier version of this tale was known to the second-century Gnostic Theodotus, who is quoted as writing:

[A]n ancient said that the embryo is a living thing; for that the soul entering into the womb after it has been … introduced by one of the angels who preside over generation, and who know the time for conception, moves the woman to intercourse; and that, on the seed being deposited, the spirit, which is in the seed, is, so to speak, appropriated, and is thus assumed into conjunction in the process of formation. He cited as a proof to all, how, when the angels give glad tidings to the barren, they introduce souls before conception. And in the Gospel "the babe leapt" [Luke 1:44] as a living thing.[50]

One description of the angel's role in the process of birth, recounted by the Kabbalist Menasseh ben Israel, explains the significance of the extinguished light:

[T]here burns a candle above the head of the unborn children, but as soon as the child has been born, an angel extinguishes the light. [ben Israel] sees as the meaning of this story, that before birth, the souls of men are very wise, and provided with knowledge of all things, but they are deprived of this knowledge when they are brought into a body. Still, their knowledge is not lost.[51]

Not only do human souls preexist their bodies, but their form too is different, according to the *Zohar*. "A human being is only called Adam when male and female are as one," says the *Zohar*. And a commentator explains, "According to the Midrash, Adam was created as a male-female entity and was then split into two. Similarly, the divine realm is androgynous, comprising *Tif'eret* and *Shekhinah*. From the union of this divine couple, all souls are born, and these souls too, in their original nature, are androgynous."[52] Another fragment adds more detail:

> Every soul and every spirit, before coming into this world, is composed of a male and a female united in one being. In descending to earth, these two halves separate and go to animate different bodies. At the time of marriage, the Holy One, blessed be He, Who knows all the souls and all the spirits, unites them as before, and they become again one single body and one single soul....If he is pure and acts godly, he will enjoy a union which resembles completely the one that preceded birth.[53]

And so we have come back full circle to the prelapsarian union mythologized by Aristophanes.

Skirting as they did the strictures of Christian orthodoxy, the *Zohar* and Kabbalistic traditions preserved, even as they developed in richly imaginative new ways, the ideas about preexistence that had migrated to the peripheries of Christian intellectual culture. In the following centuries, against a historical backdrop of condescension or worse toward all things Jewish, a number of enlightened and syncretistic thinkers would mine these traditions for the pearls they felt their Christian peers had dropped along the way.

Traditions kept alive through Kabbalistic and hermetic literature were nurtured and assimilated widely among seventeenth-century Christian mystics, poets, and divines. By this time, the orthodoxy of the Roman church had been shattered for almost a century. The hurly-burly of religious innovation, spurred by printing, unprecedented access to the scriptures, and a growing spirit of reform and free inquiry, led to an array of new heterodoxies—and many of them borrowed copiously from esoteric traditions. A preeminent figure in this regard was Jacob Boehme (1575–1624), a shoemaker of Görlitz. A pious Lutheran, versed in hermetic lore, Rosicrucian thought, and other esoteric writings, he was also given to mystical visions from his early youth. Boehme produced in 1612 the first of a steady stream of works, which almost immediately landed him in prison, made him a subject of both enthusiastic patronage and charges of heresy, and led to a life of exile from his birthplace.

His writings are diverse, often opaque, steeped in arcane lore, and resistant to simple outline or summary. While, in some ways, his religious thought—even on a topic like the human soul—could be safely conventional and straightforward, at other times he was self-contradicting and almost impenetrable. For example, in 1620, he wrote *Forty Questions of the Soul*. Question 10 tackles the nexus of the theological dilemma of the soul's origins head on: "Whether [the soul] is *ex traduce* and propagated after a human bodily manner? or every time new created and breathed in from God?" Expressing shock at the "proud blindness" of the question, he gives an emphatically proper Lutheran response: "The soul is not every time new created and breathed in, but is propagated after a human manner, as a branch groweth out of a tree, or, as I may better render it, as a man setteth or soweth corn or seed, and so a spirit and body groweth out of it."[54]

That, however, is a catechistical response that completely misrepresents the real complexity with which he treats this subject. For he had already expended a full hundred pages on the seemingly identical question, "whence proceeded the Soul Originally at the beginning of the World?" to a very different end. And even there, he informs the reader that comprehension of his views on this subject will be impossible, without first having read and digested his previous works, *The Three Principles of the Divine Essence* (1612) and *The Threefold Life of Man* (1620), which laid out his doctrine of the creation, the soul, and the fall of Lucifer. A principal influence on Boehme that goes a long way to explaining his competing anthropologies of the human soul is Neo-Platonism. With Plotinus and Porphyry, too, as we saw, the human soul is preexistent and exists dualistically, being incarnate upon birth even while remaining resident in the divine realm. Something similar seems to be the case with Boehme. He writes:

> Man is a similitude of God. Although it be just so in the eternal being, yet that is both without beginning and without end; and my writing is only to this end, that man might learn to know what he is, what he was in the beginning, how he was a very glorious eternal holy man, that should never have known the gate of the cruel birth in the eternity, if he had not suffered himself to lust after it through the infection of the devil, and had not eaten of that fruit which was forbidden him.[55]

The problem of a collective fall already makes spiritual anthropology a confusing affair, as we saw in Augustine. Whether Boehme intends this "man in the beginning" to be Adam or all humans, in a garden or a heaven, to be taken literally or figuratively, is not clear. And his subsequent development of the theme does little to resolve some of the uncertainties. Elsewhere, for example, he writes:

> [T]he soul is an eye in the eternal abyss, a similitude of eternity...and resembleth God the Father in his Person, as to the eternal nature....For the Word of the Lord [fashioned] the soul, by the eternal *Fiat* in the eternal will of the Father, in the centre of the eternal nature, and opened it with the Holy Ghost, or blew it up as a fire, which lay hid[den] in the eternity, and wherein all forms of the eternal nature stood from eternity....Yet that thing hath not been substantial, but essential, and hath been known in the Principle, in the flash, where the fire ariseth; but the shadow of it hath, from eternity in a figurative image, figured itself in the desiring will of God and hath stood before the Ternary of God.[56]

Speaking with only slightly greater clarity, he writes, "Though we speak of the creation of the world, as if we had been present, and had seen it, none ought to marvel at it, nor hold it for impossible. For the spirit that is in us, which one man inherits from another, that we breathed out of the eternity into *Adam*, that same spirit hath seen it all."[57] Finally, he explicitly embraces the contradiction he has by now expressed. The soul "is a new child, and yet not a new one either; the stock is from eternity, but the branches grow out of the stock."[58] Ultimately, he has settled on a Neo-Platonized traducianism.

It is not, in any case, with Boehme's writings on the human soul itself that he has registered his greatest impact on either philosophy in general or the idea of preexistence in particular. The concept for which Boehme is most remembered is the *Ungrund*, which is usually but inadequately translated "abyss." The *Ungrund* does not represent an actual state temporally antecedent to existence, but is how Boehme conceives of the infinite, undetermined potentiality which is the necessary ground of freedom itself. Although the concept cannot be equated with Platonic preexistence, it functions in a similar way and informs a host of nineteenth-century philosophical and theological explorations of preexistence, so it is worth establishing a basic understanding of the highly nebulous idea.

Boehme was influenced by hermeticists, Paracelsus, Kabbalists, and Plotinus— all of whom addressed the question of the universe's unfolding out of an original unitary existence. Boehme characterized creation as a dialectical process of differentiation emerging from God's "original undifferentiated non-being" and moving toward full self-awareness. The *Ungrund*, as his greatest explicator Nicholas Berdyaev writes, answers the questions "how it is possible to make the transition from God to the world"? and "from eternity to time"? But, more significantly for modern treatments of a doctrine of preexistence, the *Ungrund* "answers the need of Boehme to penetrate the mystery of freedom."[59] And freedom is the theological problem of problems, insofar as it holds the key to agency, sin, accountability, and, in Boehme's scheme, human dignity and personal redemption:

> The mysterious teaching of Boehme about the *Ungrund*, about the abyss, without foundation, dark and irrational, prior to being, is an attempt to provide an answer to the basic question of all questions, the question concerning the origin of the world and of the arising of evil. The whole teaching of Boehme about the *Ungrund* is so interwoven with the teaching concerning freedom, that it is impossible to separate them, for this is all part and parcel of the same teaching. And I am inclined to interpret the *Ungrund*, as a primordial…freedom, indeterminate even by God.[60]

In the hands of eighteenth- and nineteenth-century philosophers, Boehme's *Ungrund* and human preexistence will be developed as interconnected solutions to the problem of ultimate freedom.

7

Cambridge Platonists and the Miltonic Heritage

There must be a supply of soules for men to be bourne, either by new creating, or by assuming them already created, as out of a...Repository, or some Stowage of souls; or soules must be traduced by propagation, as bodies are.

—Richard Montagu[1]

The Cambridge Platonists

Boehme is one of a breed of thinkers who represent an especially rich, chaotic cross-fertilization of ideas and discourses across time and culture. A powerful tool in bursting the strictures of religious orthodoxy and cultural chauvinism was the principle we saw earlier of *prisca theologia*, which had been invoked by Augustine and other church fathers. This idea of a subtle, unified thread of divine truth extending from ancient times to the present, a tradition of mostly esoteric and largely lost wisdom, became a full-blown program under the great Renaissance scholar Marsilio Ficino. The most celebrated instance of this principle was his championing of the *Corpus Hermeticum*, that body of texts of supposed ancient Egyptian provenance, which Ficino translated into Latin and popularized in the late fifteenth century. Ficino was also profoundly admiring of the works of Plato, seconding Augustine's assessment that he "shone with a glory so illustrious that he entirely

eclipsed all the others."² Even so, Ficino assigned the *Hermetica* both chronological and qualitative priority over Plato and translated that body of work before
turning to the philosopher. Giordano Bruno, who went further in his admiration
than Ficino, believed that the religion taught by these Egyptians did not merely
anticipate the true gospel but was "the only true religion, which both Judaism and
Christianity had corrupted."³ Such impolitic enthusiasm led, in the case of his
embrace of metempsychosis in particular, to the heresy charges that culminated in
his execution at the stake in 1600.

In the political and religious turmoil of the English Civil War, Puritanism,
with its fierce Calvinist conceptions of human depravity and suspicions of secular
learning, triumphed over more Arminian strains of theology. Cambridge became
a center of theological resistance to those developments, and several Anglicans there
worked to blend the heritage of Plato and Plotinus, the humanism of Ficino, and
the *imitatio Christi* into a more expansive and ethically oriented Christianity. This
group of clergymen/philosophers became known as the Cambridge Platonists.
Though lacking the impact of their contemporaries Hobbes and Locke, these individuals nonetheless exerted profound influence on the era and into the Enlightenment and beyond. The roots of Cambridge Platonism are generally traced to an
exchange of letters debating the proper relationship of reason to faith in Christian
devotional life, which unfolded between Anthony Tuckney, master of Emmanuel,
and Benjamin Whichcote, provost of King's College, Cambridge. Whichcote had
expressed some, for the time, unconventional religious views in a series of discourses delivered at Trinity Church in 1636. Tuckney grew alarmed at what he saw
as a dangerous subordination of faith to the intellect and launched an epistolary
critique to that effect.

Ever since Paul had called the "wisdom of this world...foolishness with God"
(1 Cor. 3:19), and Anselm claimed to believe *in order* to understand (*credo ut intel-
ligam*),⁴ Christianity had negotiated the twin poles of rationalism and fideism,
wholesale reliance upon or wholesale suspension of reason in matters of faith. In
the era of the Cambridge Platonists, the balance was rather unequal. In 1560, the
Scotch Confession of Faith asserted that both reason and will were so impaired
by the Fall that apart from the light of Christ, "we are so dead, so blind, and so
perverse" that we cannot even "see the licht [*sic*] when it shines." And in 1577, the
Lutheran Formula of Concord had concurred, declaring that "in spiritual matters
man's understanding and reason are blind and that he understands nothing by his
own powers."⁵ The Cambridge Platonists could be said to respond to the dilemma
by denying the dichotomy at the center of the dispute. As C. A. Patrides writes,
"All that the Cambridge Platonists ever uttered reverts in the end to Whichcote's
refusal to oppose the spiritual to the rational, the supernatural to the natural,
Grace to Nature."⁶

Tuckney launched an exchange with Whichcote precipitated by the latter's championing of reason in matters religious. "It hath much grieved me," he wrote respectfully but imploringly in 1651, that "I have seldom hear'd you preach; but that something hath bin delivered by you, and that so authoritatively, and with the big words, sometimes of 'divinest reason,' and sometimes of 'more than mathematical demonstration.'"[7] Whichcote responded, firmly defending his belief in "natural light, or the use of reason," as a principle that in no way does "prejudice to saving grace by idolizing natural ingenuity."[8] Whichcote's affirmation of saving grace as a nonnegotiable principle of Christian devotion was sincere. But if his defense of reason was not itself heretical, his celebration of this "candle of the Lord" would lead in directions that were clearly far from orthodox.

A central influence on this group of thinkers was Origen, whose ideas had been recuperated and celebrated by the great Renaissance humanist Pico della Mirandola and the Florentine Neo-Platonists. Origen's rehabilitation, temporary though it was, began with the interest shown in his work by Pico, who was arrested in 1487 on heresy charges for championing the anathematized father in two of his published works. But a few years later, Pope Alexander VI ordered Pico released, and the way was cleared to continue the process of Origen's rehabilitation in earnest. Pico's enthusiasm was reinforced by the publication of a number of editions of Origen's writings, culminating in 1512 with his complete works in a Latin edition.[9] Furthering the work of Pico and the legacy he revived became a project of these Cambridge men (and at least one woman), who hoped to critique and reorient a substantial portion of the seventeenth-century Christian theological inheritance. It is hardly an exaggeration to say, as Patrides does, that the Cambridge Platonists boldly rejected "the entire Western theological tradition from St Augustine through the medieval schoolmen to the classic Protestantism of Luther, Calvin, and their variegated followers in the seventeenth century."[10] They found their heroes instead in the Greek fathers, especially in the man Henry More called "that Miracle of the Christian World"—Origen.[11]

More (1614–1687), who was completely unabashed in his embrace of Platonic preexistence, was suspicious of ancients and moderns alike who claimed extracanonical inspiration in matters spiritual. "Enthusiasts" were a special breed of dangerous heretics against whom he was at pains to defend, but he clearly excepted Plato and Plotinus as a "diviner sort of Philosophers," whose "enravished Souls" received "more than ordinary sensible visits of the divine Love and Beauty."[12] Others, like Benjamin Whichcote, the group's "Plato," didn't appeal to heavenly dispensations for the Greeks, believing they had ample access to "Natural Light."[13]

In their repudiation of a vast array of post-Augustinian developments, the Cambridge Platonists managed to reconstitute conceptions of human nature and destiny in ways that were daring, exuberant, and, in many cases, emphatically

Henrici Mori Cantabrigienfis S. S. T. D. Effigies. Æ. Æ. 61.

Most prominent of the Cambridge Platonists, Henry More wrote extensively in poetry and prose to incorporate Platonic and Origenist teachings on preexistence into English thought. *Henry More*, by William Faithorne, etching and line engraving, 1675, National Portrait Gallery, London.

heretical. It was only natural that such reformulations would extend to human origins as well. Central to their reconceived spiritual anthropology was the idea of "natural light," and it led in some very new directions. Bucking the trend of Puritan self-loathing, Whichcote found humankind to be "the Masterpiece of God's workmanship," "fit for Attendance upon God, and [to] converse with the Angels."[14] Pico had taken the celebration of the human spirit to its loftiest Renaissance formulation in *Oration on the Dignity of Man*. "The intimate of the gods," Pico calls humans, "the interval between fixed eternity and fleeting time" and deserving "the highest admiration." Humanity is, Pico insists in language clearly evocative of Origen and Plotinus alike, "to be envied not only by brutes but even by the stars and by minds beyond this world…a matter past faith and a wondrous one." The essence of humans, for Pico, is their mutability and infinite potential. Fulfilling his most sublime destiny, he wrote, man would be "unaware of the body and confined to the inner reaches of the mind,…neither an earthly nor a heavenly being; he is a more reverend divinity vested with human flesh."[15] These seeds of divinity were rooted in a god-like capacity to reason.

Inspired especially by the mystical ascent found in Plotinus and Neo-Platonism generally, Whichcote's colleagues developed this spiritualized faculty of reason into "a Power or Facultie of the Soul, whereby either from her Innate Ideas or Common Notions, or else from the assurance of her own Senses, or upon the Relation or Tradition of another, she unravels a further clew of Knowledge, enlarging her sphere of Intellectual light."[16]

Beginning with the germ of this natural light and following in the track of Neo-Platonism and Pico's exuberant humanism, Whichcote maps out the same course of intellectual ascent, raising humans "to more Noble and Generous Apprehensions,"[17] tending ever toward union with the divine. Celebrating such a trajectory, Cambridge Platonism inevitably culminates in a recuperation of the Hellenic idea of deification. The philosopher Ernst Cassirer considered the "central motif" of this group of English thinkers to be the self-determination of the soul.[18] In itself, that could mean no more than a semi-Pelagian resistance to the soul's total depravity and need for prevenient grace, or a humanist-inspired belief that individuals can exercise reason and virtue so as to guide their own spiritual destinies heavenward. The Cambridge Platonists, however, resurrected the notion suggested by Plato, elaborated by Plotinus, suggested by Peter, and seconded by many church fathers, that humanity's capacity for self-determination extends even to the potential to participate in the divine nature. Aharon Lichtenstein goes so far as to call deification the idea that governs Henry More's "whole ethical and theological thought."[19] It may be true, as one scholar writes, that as a rule in the early Christian era, "deification language is most often used metaphorically."[20] But the concept acquired especially powerful purchase in this generation of thinkers, who shunned orthodox constraints, and injected into Christian thought an unprecedented dose of exuberant humanism: "This indeed is such a θέωσις [theosis, or] Deification as is not transacted merely upon the Stage of *Fancy* by Arrogance and Presumption, but in the highest Powers of the Soul by a living and quickening Spirit of true Religion there uniting God and the Soul together in *the Unity of Affections, Will* and *End*," insisted the group's John Smith.[21]

Here, the heritage of the idea expressed in Mesopotamian poetry thousands of years earlier plays out once again. The kinship with divinity intimated in myths about the borrowed blood of the gods, with its courting of human presumption, is echoed in the prospect of divine union (or *reunion*, as we shall see) that is exhilarating yet not, these writers insist defensively, either arrogant or presumptuous. "Do not stumble at the use of *the Word* [deification]," writes Whichcote in a sermon devoted to the topic. "For, we have Authority for the use of it, Scripture. 2 Pet. 1.4. *Being made Partakers of the Divine Nature*; which is in effect our *Deification*."[22] And Ralph Cudworth cites Athanasius to the same effect: "God was therefore incarnated and made man, that he might Deifie us."[23] Humanity, these philosopher/theologians will assert time and again, is "deiform," borrowing the phrase from "Plato's school."[24]

To the Cambridge Platonists, then, deification and human preexistence were mutually reinforcing, if equally heretical, notions. (They appear in tandem in Pico as well, who in the same oration cited above, speaks of Job "who made his covenant with the God of life even before he entered into life.") For these seventeenth-century Platonists, preexistence in supernal realms was a powerful mythology to explain the inborn striving for transcendence that constitutes the religious vocation. And the possibility of theosis (deiformity or deification) is rendered less blasphemous and less inconceivable alike if styled as a return rather than as an unprecedented elevation. And from More's perspective, he has both scriptural warrant (2 Peter) and Platonic authority (he repeatedly cites Plato's counsel, "we ought to fly away from earth…to become like God") to pursue this ideal. Thus, in Lichtenstein's words:

> Deiformity [More] sees as "the true Life of Religion, which is the renewing of the Mind into the Image or Similitude of God." To return to its pristine purity, to attain a state of moral perfection and thus to resemble and reflect the glory of its Creator—this is the soul's task upon earth, "the perfecting of the Humane nature by participation of the divine."[25]

If the candle of the Lord, or natural light, was a starting point for this group's philosophy, fathoming its implications could lead back to primeval beginnings as well as to deified futures. These Platonists—and Henry More in particular—found support for their views on natural light in the work of the age's greatest philosopher, René Descartes, and his conception of innate ideas (to be dealt with more fully in chapter 8). Descartes, of course, was not about to employ the concept in order to rehabilitate Plato, but that is where the concept inevitably tended in the minds of More and his colleagues. Sterling P. Lamprecht writes in this regard, "Descartes wanted innate ideas as part of his equipment for insisting on the clarity and demonstrability of the new view of external nature, whereas the Cambridge Platonists wanted innate ideas…for defending their interpretation…of the spiritual realities defined in theological doctrines."[26] Lamprecht may have it backward. For it would seem that these Platonists posited "spiritual realities" like preexistence to explain what they took to be the self-evident fact of innate ideas, not the other way around. Like Descartes, they believed that the "*Idea* of a *Being absolutely and fully perfect*…is Naturall and Essentiall to the Soul of Man, and cannot be washt out nor conveigh'd away by any force or trick." But More goes further. It seems indisputable, he writes:

> [T]here is an active and *actuall Knowledge* in a man, of which these outward Objects are rather the re-minders than the first begetters or implanters. And when I say *actuall Knowledge*,…I understand thereby an active sagacity in the Soul, or quick recollection as it were.…The *Mind* of *man* [may be] jogg'd and awakened by the impulses of outward objects.

But those "out-ward senses doe no more teach us, [than] he that awakened the *Musician* to sing taught him his skill."[27] This sagacity he develops into his concept of "Divine Sagacity," which he elsewhere terms "a more inward, compendious, and comprehensive Presentation of Truth, ever antecedaneous to…Reason."[28]

More then proceeds to give an account of many of these actual ideas, the "naturall furniture of humane understanding," which precisely anticipate the table of categories that Kant will argue constitutes the inborn organizational principles of the mind, including cause and effect, whole and part, like and unlike, etc.[29] Nathanael Culverwel, in trying to account for human recognition of ideas and universals, similarly refers to "seeds of light…scatter'd in the Soul of Man…which fill it with a vigorous pregnancy, with a multiplying fruitfulnesse, so that it brings forth a numerous and sparkling posterity."[30] He insists that he is not embracing the Platonism his theory suggests (or Plato's "errour" that "the *Souls* of men were long extant before they were born"), but his reversion to the Platonic mythology affirms the difficulty of finding a different language adequate to do the work of Plato's myth, i.e., to explain how we can come to have knowledge of truths that precedes experience.[31] He tries Lord Herbert's comparison of the soul to a double window, one which looks upon the material world and the other upon the spiritual. But in the end, he reverts to Platonism in spite of himself. When the eye of the soul looks upon God, he writes, it apprehends "those *beamings out of eternal and universal Notions*, that flow from him, as the *Fountain of Lights*, where they have dwelt from *everlasting*," and he refers to human engagement with the material world as happening subsequent to the soul coming "down from the Mount" and putting on "the *veil* of *Sense*."[32] Finally, and somewhat disingenuously, Culverwel writes that, having presented both Platonic and creationist accounts of the soul's origin, he will not reveal which one he embraces himself. Even Gregory the Great, he adds, called it a question "which cannot be *determined* in this *Life*." But he cannot avoid saying as well that "the *generality* of the *Heathen*" think that every soul "was immediately *created* by *God* himself." " 'Tis enough for us," he says coyly, "that the *Spirit* of a *Man*, either by virtue of its *constant Creation*, or by virtue of its *first Creation*, is the *Candle of the Lord*,…the *shadow* of a *Deity*."[33]

Like Culverwel and More, the Oxford Anglican cleric Joseph Glanvill (1636–1680), a student of More, seemed to find inspiration from Descartes to combat empiricism on the way to explaining humankind's moral sense. In the context of his treatise on preexistence (which we will discuss below), innateness becomes just another word for preexistent knowledge. "We find our minds fraught with principles logical, moral, metaphysical, which could never owe their original to sense." And, as More notes on this passage, "To all sensitive [sensible] Objects the Soul is as *Abrasa Tabula*, but for *Moral* and *Intellectual* Principles, their Ideas or Notions are essential to the Soul."[34]

Whichcote, too, employs the language of Platonic recollection, as when he writes, "No sooner doth the Truth of God come to our soul's sight, but our soul knows her, as her first and old Acquaintance."[35] Similarly, Ralph Cudworth (1617–1688), More's contemporary and master of Christ's College, Cambridge, compared the soul in apprehending an idea to a person suddenly recognizing an old friend amid a sea of unfamiliar faces.[36]

The tendency of this group to fashion an epistemology in the language of Plato was so pronounced that Cudworth, like Culverwel, found it necessary to qualify his enthusiasm for the philosopher:

> Though all learning be not remembrance of what the soul once before actually understood, in a pre-existent state, as Plato somewhere would have it,…yet is all human teaching but maieutical [midwife-like],…the kindling of [the soul] from within; or helping it so as to excite and awaken, compare and compound, its own notions.[37]

Most of the group, in fact, stopped short of turning their use of Platonic language into a commitment to the actual doctrine of recollection or preexistence. Henry More was a notable exception.

The most prolific and influential of the Cambridge Platonists, More was initially more philosophically than theologically oriented, becoming one of Descartes's first enthusiastic advocates, an opponent of Hobbes, an influence on Newton's theological thought, and a principal mentor to the first published female philosopher of England, Anne Conway. He also, to his reputation's later detriment, believed in demons and witchcraft. He represented, in other words, the convergence of a traditional understanding of the spiritual universe with the dawning of a new scientific sensibility. Nowhere is that incongruous juxtaposition more evident than in what he puts forth as his two foundational principles for understanding the universe: "those two dazeling Paradoxes of the Motion of the Earth [Copernicanism] and the Præexistence of the Soul."[38]

In *Collected Philosophical Writings*, More indicates that he has already defended the idea in *Treatise on the Immortality of the Soul*, which he first published in 1659. But his beliefs in this regard actually preceded any formal philosophical treatment of the idea. They were forcefully and unambiguously, if poetically, rendered as early as 1647 in his collection *Philosophical Poems*, four years before Tuckney inaugurated the exchange with Whichcote that is generally taken to be the founding event in the formation of Cambridge Platonism. The poem that establishes the extent of More's Platonic indebtedness is boldly titled "On the Præexistency of the Soul." More prefaces his poem with only the slightest gesture of authorial distance. "I do not contend...that this opinion of the Præexistency of the Soul, is true," he avers, but insists it is "worthy the canvase and discussion of sober and considerate men," especially since it "hath been already judged of old, very sound and orthodox, by the wisest and most learned of preceding ages."[39]

More makes his source of inspiration clear in the proem's first lines, where he invokes "Aristo's son" to assist his muse:[40]

> I would sing the præexistency
> Of human souls and live once o'er again
> By recollection and quick memory
> All that is passed since first we all began.
> But all too shallow be my wits to scan
> So deep a point, and mind too dull to climb
> So dark a matter. But thou, O more than man!
> Aread, thou sacred soul of Plotin dear,
> Tell me what mortals are! Tell what of old we were!

And his guide, Plotinus, answers:

> A spark or ray of the Divinity,
> Clouded in earthly fogs, yclad in clay;
> A precious drop sunk from Æternity
> Spilt on the ground, or rather slunk away.
> For then we fell when we gan first t'assay
> By stealth, of our own selves something to [be],
> Uncentering ourselves from our one great stay,
> Which fondly we new liberty did ween,
> And from that prank right jolly wights our selves did deem. (I, III)

The aftermath of this fall, precipitated by proud self-assertion, is described in over a hundred stanzas that follow, beginning with a description of the various spheres through which the souls descend, acquiring the characteristics of fallen mortality along the way. A time of cleansing and sanctifying must follow, and if their purification is complete, nothing can impede their re-ascent. Some, however, too traumatized by death or attached to earthly things, will haunt the lower sphere as restless phantoms.

Given the fact that this is probably the longest poetic treatment ever published on preexistence (though the digressions on witches are extensive), it is no wonder that More incorporates most of the familiar motives and themes on the subject, while introducing new ones as well. The doctrine just "seems right to reason" and more rational than traducianism (which he likens to squeezing color from a rainbow). In addition, he writes in the most humorous if not most logically rigorous critique of that alternative, if the soul is physically transmitted through "humane sperm," then

> our soul can nothing be but bloud
> Or nerves or brains, or body modified.
> Whence it will follow that …
> Hard moldy cheese, dry nuts, when they have rid
> Due circuits through the heart, at last shall
> …look through our thin eyes
> And view the Close wherein the Cow did feed.
> Whence they were milk'd, grosse Pie-crust will grow wise,
> And pickled Cucumbers sans doubt Philosophize. (XC)

Following this point, he revives old arguments against creationism, asking, "why should [God] so soon contaminate / So unspotted beauties as mens spirits are / Flinging them naked into dunghills here? / Soyl them with guilt and foul contagion?" (XCII, 3–6). And finally, creationism impugns the dignity of deity and human alike, making God and every fornicator complicit in the generation of human souls in the foulest of circumstances. God is then the "ratifier" of acts that even fallen humans "oft wish undone" (XCIII, 9). As More later characterizes this point more colorfully, God must not be made to "bear a part amongst Pimps and Bawds, and pocky whores and Whoremasters, to rise out of his Seat for them, and by a free Act of Creation of a Soul, to set his seal of connivance to their Villanies."[41]

Preexistence not only provides the most satisfactory account of human origins, it has other explanatory power besides. Echoing the creation myth of George Herbert, who believed that God deprived man of "rest" so that "weariness May toss him to [His] breast," More speculates that our heavenly exile explains our alienated condition, our Augustinian yearning, wherein we are ever "groping after our own Centres near and proper substance" (V, 1–2). While he has already granted that we fell of our own impetuosity, this last thought leads him to consider if we were cast out by our "great Maker (like as mothers dear / ... from them do their children shove / That back again they may recoil more near) / Shoves of our soule a while, the more them to endear" (VII, 6–9). It seems just as likely, he speculates, that mortality is the basis for the soul's true freedom. Just as the Tree of Knowledge was the provocation that created the possibility of obedience along with the possibility of sin, so does God remove us from heaven and place us "'twixt the Deitie / And the created world, that thereupon / We may with a free resignation / Give up our selves to him deserves us best" (VIII, 3–6). Finally, this anthropology of the pure soul explains for More the innate sense of conscience. What Whichcote had called the "candle of the Lord," More styles here as the persistent spark of divinity, "like to a light fast lock'd in lanthorn dark, / Whereby, by night our wary steps we guide." Even through "slabby streets and dirty channels...some weaker rayes through the black top do glide" to bring us back home, "past the perill of the way" (CI, 1–7).

Ultimately, More concludes, the causes of a heavenly being descending "so low" into "earthly mire" are unfathomable (XCVIII, 1–2). But whether we are, in Augustine's options, exiles or volunteers, God's justice is vindicated more fully than in any conception of mortal life lacking such a prelude. Especially if, as is the case with More (and Origen), preexistence foreshadows postexistence and our status as displaced, "wandring tapers" (X) is temporary. Knowledge of this pattern to human existence is powerful in its capacity to console:

> If there admitted were
> A præxistency of souls entire,
> And due Returns in courses circular
> This course all difficulties with ease away would bear. (XCVIII, 9)

True enough, why mists should occlude memory is a mystery. Yet "who can call to mind / Where first he here saw sunne or felt the gentle wind?" (IC, 8–9).

More's hope that his poem would engender discussion by "sober and considerate men" was unexpectedly realized when he received a set of questions prompted by the poem, though they were sent not by a gentleman scholar but by Lady Anne Conway, one of the first women philosophers in the English tradition. More earlier had become a correspondent and mentor of Conway through a shared interest in Descartes. She read More's poem "Præexistency of the Soul," which he published in 1647, and wrote in 1652 asking a series of questions:

> *Upon the Reading of your* Poem *of the* Præ-existence of the Soul, *and serious thinking of it, I desir'd to be satisfied in Four Particulars, which are* these.
>
>   First, Whether God did create the *Matter* for the *Enjoyment of Souls,* since they *fell* by it?

Secondly, Whether the *Soul* could enjoy the *Matter* without being *Clothed* in Corporeity; and if it could not, how it can be the *Fall* of the *Soul* that makes it Assume a *Body*?

Thirdly, Upon supposition most of the *Souls fell*; Why did not *all* Assume *Bodies* together: And how *Adam* can be said to be the *first Man*, and all Men to *Fall* in *him*, since they *Fell* before: And how the *Souls* of *Beasts* and *Plants* came into *Bodies*?

Fourthly, How *Man* can be *Restor'd*, to what he *Fell* from; And why the *Devils* that *Fell*, cannot? Why *Christ's* Death should Extend more to *One* than to the *Other*?[42]

This appears to be something with little precedent or parallel in philosophy: a series of questions plumbing the logic of preexistence that are not merely rhetorical or tending toward dismissal. More and Conway would correspond for nearly three decades, and More's elaboration of these issues would unfold over the next several years.

More followed up his poetic treatment of preexistence with *On the Immortality of the Soul*. Here, he brings all of his philosophical guns to bear on the question of preexistence. Published in 1659, the work devotes two chapters to the subject. Although he is confident that there is not "the slightest collision or clashing" of this hypothesis with either scripture or the canon of faith, and though it was subscribed to by a catalog of religious and intellectual worthies past and present, still he recognizes that it is "an Opinion so wild and extravagant, that a wry mouth and a loud laughter (*the argument that every Fool is able to use*) is sufficient to silence it and dash it out of countenance." And so he proposes to address objections both common and unusual. Why can we not remember our pre-mortality? And how should we explain "the unconceivableness of the Approach and Entrance" of these souls into their bodies?[43]

More begins by rehearsing his objections to the alternatives. Traducianism, he argues, can't work because a spirit is indivisible by definition (at least, by his definition). Therefore, it could not derive from parental sources, like a branch from a trunk or shoot from a stem, as the name implies. Creationism, he opposes on two counts. The first is the familiar charge of injustice if a pure soul is immediately encumbered with a body and inherited condition so disproportionate to its innocence. And he repeats his criticism that touches on the indignity to God's majesty, if he is made complicit in every crime of "Whoredome, Adultery, Incest, nay Buggery itself, by supplying those foul coitions with new created Souls."[44]

A further argument for the inherent reasonableness of the hypothesis borrows as much from More's sublime rhetoric as from his rather creative logic: the age of the body, he reckons, is actually inexpressibly old. "Before it lighted into such a contexture as to prove the entire Body of any one person in the world," the matter of which the body consists "has been in places unimaginably distant, has filed, it may be, through the triangular passages of as many *Vortices* as we see Stars in a clear frosty night, and has shone once as bright as the Sun…insomuch that we eat, and drink, and cloath our selves with that which was once pure Light and Flame." (Modern astrophysics, interestingly, is here agreed. "We are made of material created and ejected into the Galaxy by the violence of earlier stars," writes one physicist. "The iron atoms in our blood carrying oxygen at this moment to our cells came largely from exploding white dwarf stars, while the oxygen itself came mainly from exploding supernovas…and most of the carbon…came from planetary nebulas, the death clouds of middle-size stars.")[45] More's inference would seem to be that one could hardly accord our paltry mortal shell a greater or more ancient legacy than the soul it houses. Both, it would seem, "do bear the same date with the Creation of the World."[46]

Then, he revisits one of the difficulties that Aristotle first raised and that Origen and the Neo-Platonists alike had tried to resolve: how can a perfect, unchangeable God create anything or otherwise effect change in the universe? Pre-mortal existence does not truly resolve the quandary, since creation here recedes into a distant past but does not disappear. Still, More finds preexistence an ingenious palliative to an insoluble problem, even as it makes God more benevolent than the God of orthodoxy:

> If it be *good* for the Souls of men to be at all, the *sooner* they are, the *better*. But we are most certain that the *Wisdome* and *Goodness* of God will doe that which is the *best*, and therefore if they can enjoy themselves before they come into these *Terrestrial* Bodies, (it being better for them to enjoy them [than] not,) they must *be* before they came into these Bodies.…For nothing hinders but that they may live *before* they come into the Body, as well as they may *after* their going out of it.[47]

More included this treatise in his 1662 *Philosophical Writings*, taking occasion in his "Preface General" to invoke in its support Plato, Aristotle, and Cicero, as well as church fathers Clement and Origen, "the Church of the Jewes" ("where no such Fooleries were mixed with it"), St. Basil, Gregory of Nazianzus, Synesius of Cyrene, the Latin fathers Arnobius and Prudentius, and, of course, Augustine.

Some of these are doubtful allies. Aristotle nourished no such sympathies; Cicero, in his assimilation of Platonism and Stoicism, did echo Plato's argument from recollection. He also found evidence in the universal affinity for music. As Augustine's contemporary Macrobius quoted him: "every soul in this world is allured by musical sounds…for the soul carries with it into the body a memory of the music which it knew in the sky."[48] Cicero was also reported to believe that "no origin of souls can be found on earth."[49] (The Stoics who influenced him had a conception of a world soul, in which humans participate, deriving largely from Plato.)[50] On the other hand, the cases of both Clement and Arnobius, as we saw, are ambiguous. Arnobius, for example, particularly refuted Plato's theory of recollection, arguing that, Plato notwithstanding, a person isolated from birth would manifest neither intellect nor awareness of anything not derived from the senses.[51] And Prudentius, a fifth-century poet, will also be cited by the nineteenth-century writer Friedrich Bruch as a proponent of preexistence, though all More can muster by way of evidence is a poem in which Prudentius refers to "this serviceable soul that had clearly been an exile and wanderer."[52]

More does more than just proof text using ancient sources, but brings allegorical reasoning to bear as well. In addition, unlike those who will invoke preexistence as an allegorical reading of the doctrine of original sin (by connecting human volition with the miseries of the human predicament), More argues that the two doctrines are compatible, since Adam was given, in his incarnation, a fresh start as it were and was therefore fully culpable for the sin he introduced. At the same time, More reads Romans 5:14, with its mention of Adam as prefiguring Christ, as requiring some version of preexistence to be rendered meaningful. (He is not the last to do so, as we shall see.) The logical inference he draws is that, if Adam prefigured Christ, then his task must have been similarly salvific. Being the first man in the flesh, it must unavoidably have been an earlier sin from which he was to rescue humankind. His commission was to "transmit that wholesome and Paradisiacal complexion of body to his Seed," thereby saving humanity "from the ill effects of that former lapse they had fallen into." Unfortunately, of course, Adam failed in his mission, and so we inherit something less than paradisiacal bodies.[53]

More's fullest prose exposition of the doctrine of preexistence comes to us some years later through the person of Bathynous, a character in his *Divine Dialogues* (1668). More had been refused an imprimatur for this work by the archbishop of Canterbury's licenser until he made clear that his assertion of preexistence was hypothetical rather than doctrinal.[54] His simple solution was to render the doctrine as a dream rather than as a character's speech or sermon. The context is a multiparty dialogue on the problem of Christian theodicy. The several participants try to convince themselves that "the state of the World may not be so bad as History or Melancholy may represent it," especially in regard to "that horrid Squalidity in the Usages of the barbarous Nations."[55] In other words, the principal cause of disturbance to these gentlemen is the spiritual blightedness of the pagans, which seems manifestly unjust. Philotheus proposes eleven solutions, ranging from the familiar to the novel. One explanation would see in non-Christian mythologies "symbols and parables" of the gospel—a veiled *prisca theologia*, in other words. The suggestion here is that saving truth is always available to the unenlightened heathen, if they but open their ears to God's whispers. Other theories offer rather less consolation, such as the theory that, however wretched we may be on this terrestrial globe, other realms "above this Earth and lower [are] well replenished with happy Souls or Spirits." More traditionally, Philotheus proposes that, "whatsoever evil mankind groans under, they have brought it on their own heads by their Disobedience and revolting from the First Good," "their" disobedience here apparently meaning "Adam's."[56]

No wonder, in light of these feeble attempts, that one listener complains that the proposed salves have "rather rankled the sore than healed it." It is only in this extremity that Philotheus resorts to his solution of last resort. So, per the censor's orders, More will cast this theory, which issues from the mouths of his characters, as "an *Hypothesis*." But such a hypothesis is, in the words of Hylobares, "a remedy indeed" to put the uneasy mind at rest regarding God's apparent injustice in countenancing sin and suffering. So powerful a remedy it is that, "though the Scene of things quite over the Earth were ten times worse," God's goodness would be vindicated.[57] In More's sly strategy, then, his proffered solution may be "hypothetical," but cast as it is in the context of the whole gamut of failed Christian theodicies, its consoling appeal in the face of the Job-like nightmare we call life is especially triumphant.

It is Bathynous, a "deep thinker," not the well-intentioned Philotheus, a "lover of God," who receives inspiration in the form of a dream to resolve the impasse. He recounts that an angelic messenger appeared to him, placed a benedictory hand on his head, and gave him the two keys of providence. The silver key unlocks a scroll that describes a Copernican universe. The gold key unlocks a scroll with twelve principles. Many of them were forgotten upon his waking, but what he remembers suffices to fully enlighten him: "All Intellectual Spirits that ever were, are, or ever shall be, sprung up with the Light, and rejoyced together before God in the morning of the Creation. In infinite Myriads of Free Agents which were the Framers of their own Fortunes, it had been a wonder if they had all of them taken the same Path." Hypothetical More's presentation of the doctrine may have been, and More speculated subject to the governing ecclesiastical powers. But his defense of the doctrine was nonetheless unequivocal.[58]

During these years, More's articulation of the theory of preexistence received a powerful stimulus through his growing interest in and familiarity with Jewish sources. In 1655, the renowned rabbi Menasseh ben Israel (1604–1657) visited England from Amsterdam. More arranged to meet him, to ask if he particularly and Jews in general believed in human preexistence. It was "the common opinion of the wiser men," the visiting Jew told More on that occasion "with great freedom and assurance," adding that "there was a constant tradition thereof."[59] Ben Israel, whose name we have already encountered, was one of the most learned and influential rabbis of his era and wrote extensively in defense of preexistence. He supported the doctrine on the basis of his reading of the Hebrew Bible, Jewish tradition, and Kabbalistic writings especially. From the *Zohar*, for example, he quoted Rabbi Johanan on the two domiciles of the soul, one for the unborn and one for the post-mortal. He considered, as a fundamental doctrine, all human souls to have been formed on the first day of creation, together with the light. This doctrine he elaborated in conjunction with Kabbalistic teachings about the ten superior lights, or *sefirot*, of which the souls are the third—just before the angels, who are fourth.[60]

More's case for preexistence was strengthened by his belief—and ben Israel's assurance—that it was part of the long-standing Jewish theological tradition. The Renaissance version of *prisca theologia*, plus its early forms among the church fathers, made it theologically safe—within limits—to find support or clarification for Christian doctrines in the writings of non-Christians. The Kabbalah was one such source. In particular, as one scholar writes, the Kabbalah offered "something of a permeable barrier between Christians and Jews, allowing for the circulation of ideas." On the one hand, "the belief that Christianity was implicit in the Jewish

Prominent rabbi, author, and printer Menasseh ben Israel elaborated Jewish ideas concerning human preexistence for a broader audience. *Menasseh ben Israel*, by Rembrandt Harmensz van Rijn, etching, 1636, National Portrait Gallery, London.

Kabbalah was the assumption of a long line of Jews who had converted for precisely that reason."[61] Alternatively, the view of the Kabbalah as an instance of *prisca theologia* legitimized the Christian appropriation of Jewish ideas—like preexistence—into a contemporary theological setting. Too great an affinity for it, however, could lead to charges of—and even imprisonment for—heresy and Judaizing.[62]

One reason that the Cambridge group in particular would be attracted to Kabbalistic tradition was its emphasis, like that of Neo-Platonism and hermeticism, on humanity's essential goodness and perfectibility and on mortality as paideutic or instructive rather than punitive. In regard to these sources, More's engagement with Conway on this subject would produce more fruitful repercussions than he could have anticipated. In the course of their friendship, he introduced to her the renowned physician and Kabbalist Francis Mercury van Helmont (1614–1699). Van Helmont and More's contemporary Christian Knorr von Rosenroth (1636–1689) celebrated Hebrew thought and language in a number of their works. Von Rosenroth believed that the purest fonts of the Christian tradition, the key to understanding God, creation, and the soul's origin and destiny, were to be found in the uncorrupted Kabbalah. He and van Helmont must have sensed a sympathetic mind across the channel. When van Helmont first came to visit More, in 1670, he brought from von Rosenroth a set of queries provoked by some of More's published works. Not surprisingly, given their shared interests, the first conversation they had was on the subject of the preexistence of souls.[63] More and these German Kabbalists became mutually influential, especially in regard to the question of the soul's origins. Von Rosenroth was so taken with More's theories that he translated portions of More's *Immortality of the Soul*. And it was after their meeting, and with More's assistance, that von Rosenroth compiled and published his *Kabbala Denudata*.[64]

This magisterial work is a Latin translation of much of the *Zohar* along with other Kabbalistic texts, published in 1677–1684. Even before the work's publication, von Rosenroth in particular was harshly criticized for his embrace of the doctrine of preexistence.[65] This version of Kabbalah was largely Lurianic, that is, deriving from the teachings of the sixteenth-century Jewish *zaddik* Isaac Luria. His mythology resonates with several parallels to Plotinus and Origen. Traces of the eternal God, who withdraws himself to give space for creation, are constituted into an image of the primordial man, Adam Kadmon. Further particles of divine light issue forth from him, but the vessels meant to contain them shatter, plummeting earthward. The purest sparks ascend heavenward, while others fall along with the material shards and are entombed as souls in physical bodies. The project of restoration (*tikkun*, which appears to be roughly analogous to apokatastasis) requires works of righteousness, so that the souls may be freed from their state of exile and re-ascend to the divine presence.

One distinct influence More derived from this work was biblical interpretation grounded in the threefold sense of literal, moral, and "Cabbalistical." This strategy avoided what he saw as the potentially faith-destroying pitfalls of reading Genesis strictly literally, even as it revealed Copernicanism and preexistence as the two keys to understanding true cosmology. Meanwhile, under the influence of van Helmont and others, Conway, like More himself, was developing an entire spiritual cosmology in which preexistence played a key part. Conway also came to be associated with leading Quaker George Keith and, along with van Helmont, they made preexistence "a central tenet in an animistic philosophy that postulated universal salvation" and "had more in common with the Lurianic Kabbalah than orthodox Christianity."[66] More stopped short of the wholesale embrace of Kabbalah that characterized Conway and her circle. Sympathetic as he was to that tradition, More grew distressed at Conway's wholesale embrace of Kabbalistic beliefs.[67]

The highly detailed cosmology that Conway developed incorporated Lurianic Kabbalah, Platonism, and her own original thought. She even composed a detailed theory of the incarnation of preexistent spirits, which was inspired more by classical reproductive theories than Kabbalah:

> The semen of a female creature [Galen's version of the woman's contribution to conception]...has a remarkable power of retention. In this semen, as in the body, the masculine semen, which is the spirit and image of the male, is received and retained together with the other spirits which are in the woman. And whatever spirit is strongest and has the strongest image or idea in the woman, whether male or female, or any other spirit received from outside of one or the other of them, that spirit predominates in the semen and forms a body as similar as possible to its image.[68]

Here is no orderly assignment of a spirit to its destined tabernacle, presided over by a supervising angel, but a natural struggle for self-realization in which the strongest spirit prevails.

The history of those pre-incarnate spirits Conway traces far beyond gestational strife to a distant past with decided echoes of Plato and Origen. Since God is eternal and unchangeable, she reasons, "it follows necessarily that creation results immediately, and without any interval of time, from the will to create." The spirits of all humans, like all creatures, "have existed for an infinite time from the beginning."[69] Spirits were pure "in their original state before they fell through their own wrongdoing." Indeed, some "remain for long periods of time without any of the crassness of body characteristic of visible things in this world," which is itself a consequence of that willful fall.[70] More optimistic than Plato in her assessment of human destiny, she is certain that one fall into sin is sufficient for any human to become acquainted with the pain of wickedness and to return to a path of virtue and sanctification.

That journey culminates not in simple restoration, but in a destiny even more glorious than the prelapsarian state:

> Every sin will have its own punishment and every creature will feel pain and chastisement, which will return that creature to the pristine state of goodness in which it was created and from which it can never fall again because, through its punishment, it has acquired a greater perfection and strength....Hence, one can infer that all God's creatures...must be changed and restored after a certain time to a condition which is not simply as good as that in which they were created, but better.[71]

More may have felt that Conway went too far in her embrace of Kabbalistic doctrines, but he was sympathetic enough to her work to provide a preface for the posthumous publication of her treatise in 1690.

Conway was not the only disciple whom More won to the cause of preexistence. One of his students took up the banner and published anonymously, without even the knowledge of his tutor, *A Letter of Resolution Concerning Origen and the Chief of His Opinions* in 1661. George Rust (c. 1628–1670), later Anglican bishop of Dromore, wrote the treatise as a way of clarifying and rehabilitating the Origenist contribution. The author's insistence that he neither knows nor cares much for orthodoxy (he was never "much awed by the word") is belied by the very anonymity of the voice he employs. Six dogmas are treated, including Origen's alleged Arianism, universalism, and other heterodoxies. But a third of the space is given over to his doctrines "that the Souls of men do præexist" and "that through their fault and negligence they appear here [as] inhabitants of the earth cloath'd with *terrestrial* bodies." Feigning an interest in fair representation only, Rust presents his case for "the reasonableness of this Opinion" of preexistence.[72]

Rust's apologia is largely an argument from definition. If spirit essence is inherently incorruptible and indivisible "either through age or violence," then that very nature makes the soul "capable of existing eternally *backward* as well as *forward*." And so:

> [We have here] an *Essence* capable of eternal existence: and since the powers and operations of life are not such things as can at pleasure be put on and off like loose-hanging *Adjuncts*,...so vital and active a substance as the Soul is, is as capable of acting according to her nature, and consequently of feeling and injoying the pleasure of her life and actions from eternal ages, as she is of bare existence throughout the long period of duration.

And then, following his mentor, he combines the Platonic concept of "ungrudgingness" with the argument from divine unchangeableness that we have seen elsewhere:

If you pitch upon the *Platonick* way, and assign the production of all things to that exuberant *fulness of life* in the Deity which through the blessed necessity and constraint of his most communicative nature emptied it self into all *possibilities* of *Being*, as into so many capable Receptacles, you must then pronounce her existence in a sense necessary, and after a sort coeternal with God.

Or, given God's supernal goodness, he continues, "ask your self, whether if the subject in question be capable of existing and enjoying some part of that infinite *goodness*, it be not evident from those Attributes that it will be made to exist." Then, forgetting his purpose of only objective representation of the case, he concludes that we must confess there to be no doubt as to the principle: "The Souls of men did exist and act before this present world was fitted for their habitation."[73]

One unique twist that Rust gives to his arguments for preexistence derives from his optimistic assessment of human potential, which is so typical of the Cambridge Platonists. All of us know individuals, he writes, in whom "appears so pure and Angelical an understanding, so firme and radicated [deeply rooted] a life of all holiness and sanctity, love and hearty benignity to all the world, of justice and purity, and whatever is truly divine." Contrasting such virtue with the utter depravity of "so many whole nations," which, he reminds us, are but "the Aggregate of single Souls born into the world in successive generations," it is clear that something has gone badly awry with humanity's self-realization. The inescapable conclusion: "all those wretched Souls had of old by their long *revolt* against God and the law of his righteous Kingdom highly deserved this Scourge." The irrational recalcitrance of those who refuse an early and true instruction in righteousness is further proof of a spirit already predisposed and therefore preshaped. Of course, Rust's analysis tends to exclude good Christians like himself from complicity in the pre-mortal rebellion. For, as good Christians suffer no present "scourge" or disadvantage, the implication is that they performed better in act 1 of their three-part play.[74]

Next, we hear some of the familiar arguments against the alternatives, such as the observation that soul creation is not a natural process like plant growth. It requires divine participation. Therefore, conception under sordid circumstances taints God as active accomplice. Finally, Rust follows More in reading Genesis as an allegory of the pre-mortal fall. The demotion of the "*æthereal* Angels" to the status of "*æthereal demons*" parallels the fall of "*aerial Genii*" into "*terrestrial men*."[75]

A second student to come under More's influence was Joseph Glanvill. He typified those Platonists, like Ficino earlier, who were fired with a passion that they were lighting upon truly inspired writings and felt charged with the responsibility to restore crucial truths to a Christianity that was inadequate to the task of self-justification without them. Rust had prefaced his meticulously argued *Letter* with a personal account of his own soul, upon which "several things lay so cross and scurvily" until he gave preexistence serious consideration. Then, everything began "to range itself in its right place and order,…and a lasting peace and calm…possessed me throughout." He has an earnest hope that his contemporaries will "joyfully receive Relief by the same means which ministered to my tranquility."[76] Similarly, Glanvill wrote to a friend, probably George Rust, that these "great & noble theoryes which our moderne origenians have enlightened the world with, have fired my desires to learne the whole hypothesis."[77] In this letter, he anxiously inquires whether shared origins with the highest orders of ethereal spirits mean that we are of like nature. In a related way, he hints at an anxiety that is remarkably absent from holders of Origen's views: are we *all* fallen spirits? More had hedged on this question, he notes. More had equated barbarous nations with fallen spirits and written that Adam's Fall had merely accelerated a process that would have naturally ensued without rebellion. Glanvill confronts it almost as obliquely. It would not be consistent with divine goodness, he notes, "to precipitate unblemisht spirits into a lower condition of life without their own fault or demerit." He wants to know how our fate will differ from the highest orders of ethereal spirits who did not fall; is not perfect immortality, perfect immortality? And what of those good souls who, according to Origen, descend to humankind out of love? Finally, Glanvill notes that the only alternative to seeing earth as a state of universal punishment is to view it as probation. He considers this possibility but finds it equally problematic. The first scenario is challenged by the lack of memory; punishment can have no value if it is disconnected from our consciousness of guilt. The second is challenged by circumstances such as infant mortality and disadvantaged "brutes." What kind of probation can accrue in such instances?

Glanvill apparently found his questions satisfactorily answered by Rust or by his own investigations. And in timely fashion at that, for the very next year he took up the cause of preexistence with his own substantial contribution, *Lux Orientalis; or, An Enquiry into the Opinion of the Eastern Sages Concerning the Præexistence of Souls*, which was published a year after Rust's book, in 1662. (It was repackaged with a follow-up essay by Rust in 1682, as *Two Choice and Useful Treatises.*) Glanvill, an Anglican clergyman educated at Oxford (unlike his Cambridge Platonist cohorts), prefaces his remarks with an apologia that is probably disingenuous (or surprisingly uninformed), claiming that, "as for the opinion of Preexistence,…it was never determined against by ours, nor any other Church, that I know of; and therefore I conceive is left as a matter of School Speculation, which without danger may be problematically argued on either hand."[78]

This substantial treatise reveals Glanvill to have been transformed in the space of months from a diligent student of preexistence into an ardent proponent. His book is the most bold and ambitious statement on the subject of his era. Unlike his predecessors, who couched their apologias in hypotheses, fictive dreams, and tentative language, Glanvill unabashedly presents his work as "a full proof, defence, and explication of *Præexistence*." Though he applauds Rust's contributions, he notes that Rust's essay was "confined to the reasons of *Origen*, and to the answering such objections as the *Fathers* used against him." The work he undertakes, on the other hand, he trumpets as the only book "extant in any language…that purposely, solely, and fully treats of *Præexistence*."[79] The book seems to have met with an enthusiastic reception. "It was so much valued by the more eager and curious searchers into the profoundest points of philosophy," said the publisher in explaining the second printing, "that there was given for it some four or five times the price for which it was first sold."[80]

Glanvill's obligatory critiques of creationism and traducianism reaffirm and expand upon the old objections. In the first case, God's participation in sinful intercourse, acting "by *explicite* and *immediate Will*," is inconceivable. And God's repeated acts of soul creation would clearly violate the biblical truth that God pronounced his creation complete on the sixth day. ("If all his works are rested from, then the creation of Souls…is rested from also," concurs More in a note.)[81] As for traducianism, if the parent is held to produce another soul out of nothing, we claim a power unique to that of God. It cannot be fashioned of bodily material, by definition. That leaves the parents' souls as source, but as the poet John Davies had urged a generation before, "tho' from Bodies she [Nature] can Bodies bring Yet could she never Souls from Souls traduce."[82] The soul being "indiscerpible," or indivisible, it is clearly not capable of imparting a fragment or seed out of itself. Even traducianism's alleged advantage in explaining original sin is a travesty. For the same logic that makes our souls "*particles* and *decerptions* [fragments] of our parents" would also make us guilty not just of Adam's sin, but "of all the sins that ever were committed by my *Progenitors* ever since *Adam*." Regarding this Adam, Glanvill finds in him a possible reply to his own earlier query regarding the descent of good souls into the world. Adam, he suggests, was perhaps one such soul, a "*Seraphic* and *untainted Spirit*," sent on a mission of mercy to provide suitable bodies for the fallen and to be an overseer and "*Steward* in the affairs of this *lower Family*."[83]

Glanvill also reprises More's argument from God's goodness and his accompanying capacity to realize any potential good. It is a blithely simple proposition:

> God being infinitely good, and that to his Creatures, and therefore doing always what is best for them, methinks it roundly follows that our souls lived and 'njoy'd themselves of old before they came into these bodies. For since they were capable of living, and that in a much better and happier state long before they descended into this region of death and misery; and

since that condition of life and self-enjoyment would have been better, than absolute non-being; may we not safely conclude from a due consideration of the divine goodness, that it was so?[84]

The reasons for the demise of preexistence are of interest to Glanvill as well. The doctrine lacks the sustaining weight of scripture, because the doctrine is too "*deep* and *mysterious*" to lay bare "to common and promiscuous *Auditories*." Then, as Aristotelianism comes to displace Platonism as the principal philosophical influence on Christian theology in the high Middle Ages, the major fonts for understanding the soul's origin dry up. "*Platonism* and the more *antient wisdom*, a branch of which, Præexistence, was, were almost quite *sunk* and *buried*."[85]

Predictably, these resurgent Origenists met with strong opposition. In fact, the prevalence and appeal of the idea in this period are indicated to some extent by the vehemence of the responses. Five years after Glanvill's sally, Edward Warren published in 1667 a treatise whose title declared unambiguously his position: *No Præexistence; or, A Brief Dissertation against the Hypothesis of Humane Souls, Living in a State Antecedaneous to This.*[86] Warren acknowledges the difficulty of the question that centuries of theological debate had done nothing to resolve. "The head of the slimy Nile is not so recondite and occult," he writes, "nor of half so difficult investigation, as the time of the Soul's immigration into being." Even so, Warren is distressed at the growing recourse in his age to preexistence as a solution. That is, he insists, no more than a "fable and Imposture" traveling "so confidently through the World, and every where vaunt[ing] itself for a genuine Truth." He attributes the idea's currency to "Platonist ranters," but the version he sets up to attack sounds more like Origen: "the Souls of men...existed long before in a divine and blessed state,...till at length cloyed with the Joyes of Heaven, they longed for corporeal pleasures." Subsequently, they "rioted on their luscious suavities" beyond the bounds of temperance, gave in to "immoderate ingurgitation of animal complacencies," until they were "struck...with a fatal dizziness [which] made them topple from their primaeval glory, into a lower and less happy station." Here below, they wander in search of coarser matter, suited to their polluted beings.[87]

Warren finds it imperative to address the elegantly simple argument that Glanvill, Rust, and More had invoked, namely, that God's infinite goodness could not accommodate a state in which human souls, for whom it is clearly best to exist, do not yet exist. His goodness and his omnipotence would have made it impossible to tolerate the unrealized existence of the human soul. Therefore, he must have created them before the physical creation ("the Souls of men, being capable of existence, long before they were vested with this gross corporeity; and it being best for them to have existed, long before that time; hence it inevitably follows, that they did so," in Warren's paraphrase). Warren resolves this problem by the argument that it is obvious that, because God does not, or does not immediately, actualize all potential good, "there is some thing in GOD, which in many cases restrains the activity of his Goodness, and suspends its efficiency of divers things, that otherwise might be done." This impediment, he continues, is God's will. So, rather begging the question, Warren concludes that God's will prevents him from the immediate and unfailing execution of all the good he could potentially do (God's "will…controls the exuberance of his Goodness"). The mere fact that God might have created souls to enjoy a primordial bliss is outweighed by the fact that God could, and apparently did, choose not to do so. A second argument that Warren addresses is the one deriving from justice. Only a preexistence in which humans chose and acted willfully could explain the apparent injustice of a world population blighted by "Atheism, or Polytheism, [or] Superstition." To this, Warren can only answer lamely that "God had no hand in stretching out that sable Cloud of ignorance." Not the most rigorous rebuttals these, and they are one indication of why ecclesiastical dictate rather than philosophical debate was more effective in silencing the theory.[88]

Meanwhile, poets of the era persisted in their iconoclastic anthropologies, Henry More being far from alone in his resort to versifying to explore and celebrate preexistence. An earlier poet, Edmund Spenser, was considered to be a literary father to More and others of his generation. Spenser's most memorable contribution to the poetry of preexistence is his "Garden of Adonis," a bucolic realm of Platonic splendor that serves as "the first seminarie / Of all things, that are borne to live and die," a kind of nursery of souls. The guardian of the place is

> Old Genius, the which a double nature has.
> He letteth in, he letteth out to wend,
> All that to come into the world desire;
> A thousand thousand naked babes attend
> About him day and night, which does require,
> That he with fleshly weedes would them attire:
> Such as him list, such as eternall fate
> Ordained hath, he clothes with sinfull mire,
> And sendeth forth to live in mortall state,
> Till they againe returne backe by the hinder gate.[89]

Preexistence seems to have been for Spenser no more than a poetic flirtation modeled on Platonic mythologies. The idea had more sustained development among some of More's contemporaries. Henry Vaughan (1621 or 1622–1695) was not of More's circle; in fact, the two were adversaries in their own pamphlet war. (More considered Vaughan to be "an enthusiast, a pantheist, and a materialist.")[90] But More's involvement in Platonism and Kabbalah was matched in Vaughan's case by familiarity with the *Hermetica*, where preexistence appears, as we have seen, as a frequent motif. Vaughan's brother Thomas would have been a major influence on him as well. Thomas was famous as an alchemist and seems to have also found in his esoteric sources the idea of preexistence. In the preface to his *Anthroposophia Theomagica*, he states, "I look on this life as the Progresse of an Essence Royall: the Soul but quits her court to see the countery. Heaven hath in it a Scene of Earth; and had she been contented with Ideas, she had not travelled beyond the map.... Her descent speaks her Original." Vaughan's comparison of the soul's descent into mortality to a royal progress is not just a poetic metaphor for the incarnation of a preexistent human; it is an audacious claim about that soul's prior dignity and elevated status. A few pages later, he adds, "Man had at the first, and so have all Souls before their intrance into the body, an explicit methodicall knowledge, but they are no sooner vesselled than that liberty is lost, and nothing remains but a vast confused knowledge of the creature." This is why he can write approvingly of the influential biblicist Arias Montanus (1527–1598), who called human birth "a little Incarnation."[91] Then, reverting to an image popular with the Platonists, Vaughan likens "the Soul of man, while she is in the body," to "a candle shut up in a lanthorn, or a fire that is almost stifled for want of aire." Elaborating the analogies, he likens spirits to the inhabitants of green fields, who, in their own country, "live perpetually amongst flowers in a spicy, odorous aire, but here below...mourn because of darkness and solitude, like people lockt up in a pest-house." Such origins explain the unsettled melancholy of earthly existence: "This is occasioned by [the soul's] vast and infinite capacity, which is satisfied with nothing but God, from whom at first she descended." And they explain the way of return: "He must be united to the Divine Light, from whence by disobedience he was separated....This Light descends, and is united to him, by the same means as his Soule was at first."[92]

Thomas Vaughan found corroboration for his beliefs in both Platonic and Kabbalistic texts, and Henry may have been largely introduced to the idea through Thomas. Like his brother, he wrote feelingly if not extensively on the subject. Henry's most famous effort, "The Retreat," was unambiguous in its Platonism:

> Happy those early days! when I
> Shin'd in my angel-infancy!
> Before I understood this place
> Appointed for my second race,
> Or taught my soul to fancy ought
> But a white, celestial thought.

Vaughan transforms the vague spiritual restlessness described by Herbert, who profoundly influenced him, into a more focused nostalgia:

...looking back—at that short space—
[I] could see a glimpse of His bright face;
...And in those weaker glories spy
Some shadows of eternity; ...
O how I long to travel back
And tread again that ancient track!
That I might once more reach that plain,
Where first I left my glorious train;
From whence th' enlighten'd spirit sees
That shady City of palm-trees....
Some men a forward motion love,
But I by backward steps would move;
And when this dust falls to the urn,
In that state I came, return.

In a lesser-known poem, "Corruption," Vaughan affirms the same principle:

Sure, it was so. Man in those early days
Was not all stone and earth:
He shin'd a little, and by those weak rays,
Had some glimpse of his birth.
He saw heaven o'er his head, and knew from whence
He came, condemned hither....
Things here were strange unto him.

In this vague mythology of pre-mortality, the Fall of Adam is conflated with the fall of spirits, and memories of Eden are a trope for heaven longing:

that act,
That fell him, foil'd them all;
He drew the curse upon the world, and crack'd
The whole frame with his fall.
This made him long for home, as loth to stay
With murmurers and foes;
He sigh'd for Eden, and would often say
"Ah! what bright days were those!"

Platonic mythologies may be promiscuously assimilated to purely fictive creations like poetry, and it is hard to know where poetic invention ends and theological earnestness begins. But Henry Vaughan also wrote in a more studied, Platonic fashion of the preexistence theme:

[I]t is an observation of some *spirits*, that *the night is the mother of thought.*
And I shall adde, that those thoughts are *Stars*, the *Scintillations* and

lightnings of the soul struggling with *darknesse*. This *Antipathy* in her is *radical*, for being descended from the *house of light*, she hates a contrary *principle*, and being at that time a prisoner in some measure to an enemy, she becomes pensive and full of thoughts.

Less ponderously, but with equal classical indebtedness, he quotes the Stoic emperor Hadrian, who considered his soul, "my pleasant soul and witty, [t]he guest and consort of my body."[93]

Thomas Traherne (1637–1674), though not one of the Cambridge Platonists either, belongs with them by sentiment if not university setting. Like the later Romantics, he gloried in childhood, but went beyond William Wordsworth's vague intimations of preexistence by vividly imagining incarnation as a moment of rapturous awakening from a prior state of being. No fall into mortality, this descent, but a glorious new beginning, which he heralds with titles like "The Salutation" and "Wonder." In the former poem, he beautifully evokes the first moments of self-contemplation, while clearly marking the body as the new acquisition of that soul which is the true seat of identity:

> These little limbs,
> These eyes and hands which here I find,
> These rosy cheeks wherewith my life begins,
> Where have ye been? Behind
> What curtain were ye from me hid so long?
> Where was, in what abyss, my speaking tongue....
> New burnished joys!...
> Long time before I in my mother's womb was born,
> A God preparing did this glorious store,
> The world, for me adorn.
> Into this Eden so divine and fair,
> So wide and bright, I come His son and heir.
> A stranger here.[94]

And in the latter, he develops further this theme of birth as transition:

> How like an angel came I down!
> How bright are all things here!
> When first among His works I did appear
> Oh, how their glory me did crown!
> The world resembled His eternity,
> In which my soul did walk;
> And everything that I did see
> Did with me talk.[95]

In "The Preparative," he imagines, or fancies he recollects, his awakening in the womb to his new incarnation:

> Before my tongue or cheeks were to me shown,
>> Before I knew my hands were mine,
> Or that my sinews did my members join,
>> When neither nostril, foot, nor ear,
> As yet was seen or felt, or did appear;
>> I was within
> A house I knew not, newly clothed with Skin.
>
> Then was my soul my only all to me,
>> A living endless eye,
>> Far wider than the sky,
> Whose power, and act, and essence was to see;
>> I was an inward sphere of light, …
> A naked, simple, pure Intelligence.[96]

Out of the womb and into the world, Traherne imagines, again as Wordsworth will, a link to pre-mortal realms that persists into early childhood. One may detect echoes here of Psalm 139, which we discussed earlier, with its celebration of the embryo's "frame,…made in secret, intricately woven in the depths of the earth." Mary Sidney Herbert wove a metrical paraphrase of that psalm, combining the same interest in embryology with a confused if evocative exploration of the soul's prior state. Her version, which circulated in manuscript in this era, reads in part:

> Each inmost piece in me is thine:
> while yet I in my mother dwelt,
> all that me cladd
> from thee I hadd.
> thou in my frame hast strangely dealt:
> needes in my praise thy workes must shine
> so inly them my thoughts have felt.
>
> Thou, how my back was beam-wise laid,
> and raftring of my ribs dost know;
> know'st ev'ry point
> Of bone and joint,
> how to this whole these partes did grow,
> in brave embrodry faire araid,
> though wrought in shopp both dark and low.
>
> Nay fashonles, ere forme I toke,
> thy all and more beholding ey

> my shaplesse shape
> Could not escape:
> all these, with tymes appointed by,
> ere one had beeing, in the booke
> of thy foresight, enrol'd did ly.[97]

Traherne traces the soul's incarnation even further in "Dumbness," an interpretation of prelinguistic infancy as a time when the soul, still in contact with divinity, builds up its immunities to the world of sin. After birth, "the gate of souls was closed," and he dwells for a while alone, "within a world of light,…Where I did feel strange thoughts, and secrets see / That were, or seemed, only revealed to me." Not the womb, but speechless isolation, creates "A fort, impregnable to any sin," allowing him to register those first communications with the divine, which will serve throughout his life to "whisper if I will but hear, / And penetrate the heart if not the ear."[98]

The theology of this parish priest was unorthodox: not only did he allude to preexistence, but he was also sympathetic to some of the Pelagian heresies, rejecting original sin and having great faith in the potential of humans to live unspotted by sin. Once again, we see the twinning of preexistence and heretically excessive humanism. We saw that, when Augustine turned to confront the Pelagian heresy over twelve centuries earlier, one casualty of the battle was Augustine's open support of preexistence. It is not that Pelagius promoted the particular unorthodoxy of preexistence, but that—as Tertullian recognized to his horror and the Cambridge Platonists to their delight—an emphasis on human preexistence comports quite comfortably with a celebration of humanity's primal purity, inherited innocence, and divine potential. And so it is that preexistence, human innocence, a revisionist reading of Adam's Fall, and, arguably, an intemperate praise of the human soul are inseparably interconnected and interwoven throughout the poetry of Traherne.

He propounds these theological interconnections directly in two poems, "Eden" and "Innocence." In the first, he quite pointedly differentiates his personal path from Adam's. Not in self-congratulation, but in honest recollection, he finds that his childhood inclinations mirrored Adam's original innocence, rather than his later guilt:

> …Simplicity
> Was my protection when I first was born.…
>   The first effects of love
> My first enjoyments upon earth did prove,
>
> And were so great, and so divine, so pure,
>   So fair and sweet,
>   So true, when I did meet
> Them here at first, they did my soul allure
>   And drew away my infant feet

> Quite from the works of men, that I might see
> The glorious wonders of the Deity.[99]

As if to brook no misunderstanding, he returns to the theme in "Innocence," again likening his childhood self to the Adam of paradise retained and even more emphatically denying the hold of Adam's sin upon his soul:

> But that which most I wonder at, which most
> I did esteem my bliss, which most I boast
> And ever shall enjoy, is that within
>   I felt no stain nor spot of sin.
>
>   No darkness then did overshade,
> But all within was pure and bright,
> No guilt did crush nor fear invade,
> But all my soul was full of light.
>
> A joyful sense and purity
> Is all I can remember....
>
>   I was an Adam there,
> A little Adam in a sphere
>
> Of joys! ...
>
> An antepast of heaven sure!
>   I on the earth did reign;
> Within, without me, all was pure.[100]

Traherne does not envision the self as encumbered in any way by Adam's error. He exults, in the immodestly titled "My Spirit," in a self that is "simple like the Deity," "its own...sphere / Not shut up here, but everywhere," and he breaks into a psalm of self-praise:

> O joy! O wonder and delight!
> O sacred mystery!
> My soul a spirit infinite!
> An image of the Deity!
>   A pure, substantial light! ...
> To its Creator 'tis so near
>   In love and excellence,
>   In life and sense,
> In greatness, worth and nature.[101]

Tertullian's worst fears fully realized, one might say.

Milton and His Imitators

The Cambridge Platonists found in poetry an effective medium for their celebration of human innocence, potential, and pre-mortal origins. While their poetry was both lyrically splendid and philosophically resonant, this century saw the career of an English poet whose work would eclipse them all and whose supreme poetic accomplishment would become the most influential version of pre-mortal events in the language. The year after Boehme's death in 1624, a young John Milton matriculated at Christ's College, Cambridge, with the intention of preparing for the priesthood. While a student, he turned instead to the writing of poetry. He would go on to publish, in 1667, *Paradise Lost*, justly considered one of the greatest Christian epics ever penned, doing for his literary tradition what Dante had done in Italian. Milton's own aims in the work were hugely ambitious, perhaps presumptuous, aspiring as he did "to justify the ways of God to man." His work forever enshrined Satan as a tragic figure and the prototype of the Romantic rebel hero. It also gave fame to the lowly apple as the fruit of paradise (unnamed as it is in the actual account in Genesis).

The prelude to the Fall of Adam and Eve that Milton narrates is the equally tragic fall of Lucifer the Bearer of Light, who becomes in the process Satan, the eternal adversary. His tragic loss of heaven entails the defeat in celestial warfare of myriad hosts who become forever after known as the fallen angels. Biblical foundations for the myth are sparse: the revelator records that he saw in vision the dragon, whose "tail swept down a third of the stars of heaven and threw them to the earth" (Rev. 12:4). Luke's Jesus remarks simply, "I watched Satan fall from heaven like a flash of lightning" (Luke 10:18); the prophetic voice of Isaiah, referring most immediately to the king of Babylon, laments:

> How you are fallen from heaven, O Day Star, son of Dawn! ["Lucifer," in the KJV] How you are cut down to the ground, you who laid the nations low! You said in your heart, "I will ascend to heaven; I will raise my throne above the stars of God; I will sit on the mount of assembly on the heights of Zaphon; I will ascend to the tops of the clouds, I will make myself like the Most High." But you are brought down to Sheol, to the depths of the Pit. (Isa. 14:12–15)

From these and a few other slender threads, Milton wove the ten (later, made into twelve) books of *Paradise Lost*, most of which are set in a time before Adam is formed of the clay.

In Milton's version, those angelic hosts are a distinctly heavenly race and humans a species that God creates expressly to compensate for their defection and expulsion. It is possible, however, to see Milton's work as bifurcating a story about one pre-mortal population's apostasy and earthly punishment into a story of two races. Such, at least, is the reading of various successors to his version, which attempt to set to rights his error. In 1714, an anonymous author, perhaps Abel Evans, published "Pre-Existence: A Poem, in Imitation of Milton."[102] "In imitation" turns out to be more a matter of "in correction." The poem depicts a scene in heaven after the defeat of the rebellious angels and their dispatch to hell. Not all dissenters, in this version, meet the fate of the eternally damned. For upon returning to heaven, the victorious hosts find there a suppliant throng of repentant rebels, "troops less stubborn, less involv'd / In crime and ruin." These plead so persuasively for clemency that God softens. Eventually, he decrees, they may again "emerge to light," but only after a penance described in terms so harsh as to certainly deter any future rebellion. They shall expiate their crimes upon "a dusty ball" even then taking shape, "deform'd all o'er with woods, whose shaggy tops / Inclose eternal mists, and deadly damps…choke the light," creating conditions of "continual pains" amid unremitting "scenes of horror."[103]

   With questionable mercy, God imposes, by way of preparation for their descent, long drafts of the river Lethe. The resultant human condition, for humans they shall all become, is one that dulls the shock of such a cataclysmic decline in fortune, but at the same time torments the soul, Tantalus-like, with reason and memory that feed but cannot satisfy an inarticulate longing for home. They must drink, therefore,

> till forms within,
> And all the great ideas fade and die:
> For if vast thought should play about a mind
> Inclos'd in flesh, and dragging cumbrous life,
> Flutt'ring and beating in the mournful cage,
> It soon would break its gates and wing away:
> 'Tis therefore my decree, the soul return
> Naked from off this beach, and perfect blank,
> To visit the new world; and strait to feel
> Itself, in crude consistence closely shut,
> The dreadful monument of just revenge;
> Immur'd by heaven's own hand, and plac'd erect
> On fleeting matter, all imprison'd round
> With walls of clay.[104]

Though humans' entombment in flesh and situation in a fallen world entail myriad forms of suffering, the physical travails pale alongside the existential horror of a fettered spirit displaced from heaven:

> Here Judgment, blinded by delusive Sense,
> Contracted through the cranny of an eye,
> Shoots up faint languid beams, to that dark seat,

> Wherein the soul, bereav'd of native fire,
> Sits intricate, in misty clouds obscur'd,
> Ev'n from itself conceal'd....
>   ...Now, he tries
> With all his might to raise some weighty thought,
> Of me, of fate, or of th' eternal round,
> Which but recoils to crush the labouring mind.
> High are his reasonings, but the feeble clue
> Of fleeting images he draws in vain....
> Reason is now no more...th' expiring flame
> Is choak'd in fumes.[105]

It is possible that the author has in mind an ancient rationale for the memory wash of Lethe. His work is clearly influenced by the strains of Neo-Platonism so pronounced in this era, and he may have been familiar as well with Gnostic sources, including the second-century Basilides, who espoused the preexistence of the soul. Basilides also posited a merciful motive behind the human forgetfulness of preexistence, though he left out the unsettling shards of memory:

> According to Basilides, beings perish when they attempt to transgress the boundaries of their nature. The purpose of the forgetfulness is to prevent naturally inferior beings from striving for a station beyond their nature, and to avoid the suffering attendant upon such improper striving.[106]

More specifically, as another scholar writes, Basilides anticipated a day, after those Christians capable of transformation and elevation to the transcendent realms have left the earth, when "forgetfulness will descend so that the creation will no longer be aware of the transcendent realm from which by nature it is excluded, and all spiritual striving will cease."[107] We here see the continuity—with variations—of the preoccupation first expressed in Babylonian texts, which equated forgetfulness of preexistence with a prudent safeguard—of the gods against unwanted competition, or of humans against a recognition of past glories too painful to bear in the present circumstance. For Evans, the fate of the fallen hovers uncertainly between compassion and torment, like an amnesiac who feels but cannot articulate his loss of happiness.

This Milton imitator has God say something that does little to resolve the ambiguity. In introducing the doom, including the forgetfulness, these rebellious spirits will face, God explains:

> all must have their manes [spirits] first below,
> So stands th' eternal fate, but smoother yours
> Than what lost angels feel; nor can our reign,
> Without just dooms, the peace of heav'n secure;

> For forms celestial new erect in glory
> Would totter, dazzled with the heights of power,
> Did not the nerves of justice fix their sight.[108]

Another eighteenth-century author agrees: "we had been inexpressibly more miserable, if we had retained the memory of our former Glory, and past Actions."[109]

Some critics of preexistence saw forgetfulness of such a prior state to be prima facie evidence of its falsity. But, in these examples, we find not only preexistence, but the veil of forgetfulness that divides eternity in twain has its own powerful justifications. In the Miltonic poem, the horrors of incarnation find a consoling counterweight in the promise of apokatastasis. God concludes his description of the earthly prison with the decree that, though "long shall seem the dreary road, and melancholy dark," it shall only last "till all in death / Shall vanish, and the prisoner, now enlarg'd, / Regains the flaming borders of the sky."[110] And so we are back to Origen's Christian appropriation of Plato. Only in this case, we have as well the borrowed authority of the most important Christian poet writing in the English tradition. The poem's Miltonic resemblances, its comfortable fit into his epic of pre-mortal combat, its familiar evocation of a sovereign God, warrior hosts, and fallen angels make the connection among those latter figures and mortal humans seem natural and even orthodox. Though the picture it paints of mortality is bleak almost without precedent, making life a prolonged purgatory and even the most virtuous of humans one-time malefactors, it has the virtue of providing, as we have seen elsewhere, both an etiology for human fallenness that satisfies justice and an explanation of human yearning for the infinite that evokes both hope and melancholy.

What Milton stops just shy of doing, this successor performs fully. And that is to make the war in heaven, for which there is solid if cryptic scriptural foundation, the basis for the pre-mortal fall asserted by Origen. It is an important step, reading as it does pre- and extra-Christian traditions of conflict in the heavenly spheres as shadowy counterparts to Christian allusions to the fall of Lucifer and of his myriad angelic followers. Modern theosophists fault Milton for not connecting the dots. "Milton," asserts a spokesperson for one such group, "in common with all save isolated groups of Hermeticists in Europe, lost the signal knowledge that the fallen angels, the rebel hosts, the armies of Satan-Lucifer were, collectively, man himself, and that the fiery lake into which they were hurled was just our good earth!"[111]

A century after Milton, a would-be historian of Masonry took a similar position. Laurence Dermott described a project he undertook to go beyond conventional histories of his brotherhood in order "to trace Masonry not only to Adam in his sylvan Lodge in Paradise, but to give some Account of the Craft even before the Creation." In other words, he is going to trace the origin of Masonry to its foundations in pre-mortality. He completed a volume, he tells us, in which he described what he refers to euphemistically as the heavenly "Transactions of the first Grand Lodge, particularly the excluding of the unruly Members." That story, he notes, was already recounted by Milton in *Paradise Lost*.[112] Dermott completed his project only to learn, through a humbling dream/vision, that his history is "not worth notice." He awakens and, in a story anticipating millions of future schoolboy excuses, finds that his dog is eating the completed manuscript. Dermott decides that the dog has treated his work in the way that it deserves. He writes a defense of the society instead, leaving us with no more than his tantalizing reference to the preexistence of Masonry and its unruly members—unless, per his allusion, one reads Milton's epic as a sufficient, though veiled, version.

Milton was certainly conversant with Origen and his story of preexistent apostasy, quoting him in his pamphlets. As Harry Robins writes, many of Milton's heresies are traceable to Origen; they both came to the Bible with similar minds.[113] Milton, however, though never one to shrink from heartfelt heresy (he was committed to creation *ex materia* and a defense of polygamy, among other theological idiosyncrasies), explicitly rejected preexistence because he believed that humans' creation in God's image recounted in Genesis 1:26 necessarily entailed the creation at that time and place of what most likens us to God—our souls. That fact "precludes us from attributing pre-existence to the soul which was then formed,—a groundless notion sometimes entertained."[114] Nevertheless, John Milton was not averse to employing the notion when it suited his poetic purposes. In *Comus*, for example, a pastoral play he called a masque, Milton pays subtle but unmistakable poetic tribute to Plato's conception of pre-mortality, with his references to "the prison'd soul" and his lament:

> The soul grows clotted by contagion,
> Imbodies and imbrutes, till she quite lose
> The divine property of her first being.
> Such are those thick and gloomy shadows damp,
> Oft seen in Charnel vaults and Sepulchers,
> Lingering and sitting by a new-made grave,
> As loath to leave the body that it lov'd,
> And link't itself by carnal sensualty
> To a degenerate and degraded state.[115]

If Milton resisted developing the motif with real intent, Abel Evans (or whoever the author was of the poem cited earlier) did not hesitate to repair the connection Milton had missed (or obscured) and identify the rebellious hosts with preexistent mortals. By making human beings part of the conflict, rather than the aftermath, such writers endowed Origen's account of humanity's pre-mortal fall with concreteness and vividness. A few years after the poetic imitation of *Paradise Lost*, another author with decidedly Miltonic overtones, too coy to reveal himself (to avoid obliging himself to defend his speculations, he tells us), published *A Miscellaneous Metaphysical Essay; or, An Hypothesis Concerning the Formation and Generation of Spiritual and Material Beings, . . . to Which Is Added Some Thoughts . . . upon Pre-existence*. It is often attributed to Richard Cosway.[116] The author intends his inquiry to be "consistent with Reason and Revelation," but he speculates rather freely, relying upon neither Plato nor scripture. An interesting twist he gives to the theory is his conjecture that "our Souls have existed from the first Formation of Beings, and may have been, or conscious, or dormant, until this time."[117] The dormancy theory had also been cited by Andrew Michael Ramsay just two decades earlier and attributed to Hebrew belief. The lesser spirits who fell and were banished from heaven, the *ischim*, were "suffered to fall into a kind of lethargy or fatal insensibility," which condition ends only with their insertion into a mortal body.[118]

The anonymous author holds that humans are currently in a "State of Imprisonment and Probation here," relying in part on "the Cabalistic Account, of the *Mosaic* Creation, the Formation of *Adam*, and Fall of Mankind" (via Henry More). So we have here a reading of Genesis 1–3 as an allegory for events that transpired before mortal life began. In this version of an earlier universe, "a perfect Harmony subsisted through all the Orders and Degrees of social Beings, from the highest Seraph, to the lowest Order." Through a fall into self-love, however, "Discord and Confusion took place in Society; the Harmony of the Universe was broke; the divine Laws of Society were unhinged; and by the experimental Knowledge of Evil, was the first Disobedience of the divine Laws made known." The form this rebellion took sounds, once again, like a reworking of Milton's epic vision:

> Some of the several Orders thinking of themselves more highly than they ought, . . . enter[ed] into private Cabals to scale the Heavens as it were, and take the Place of superior Orders by Force. . . . But this Rebellion of the angelic Orders was defeated by the Messiah at the Head of the obedient angelic Host; and the disobedient, lapsed, *angelic, and human Orders of Spirits*, were hurled down from the Powers and Enjoyments they had in the Heavens.[119] (my emphasis)

In this version, Christ's role as redeemer is preserved, though given new context and meaning:

> The Soul of the Messiah, after his Exaltation, and being made Prince and General of the obedient angelic Host, and after having conquered the rebellious Angels, and expell'd them from the aethereal Regions, and impell'd them into the Abysses, . . . knowing that many different Orders of

Being were concerned in the Lapse and Rebellion,…he offered himself as Mediator and Intercessor with the Almighty Being,…upon Condition that God the Father would allow them to become conscious, and would place them in a State of Probation.

And so, it was under those conditions that Christ submitted to his own descent into mortality to "atone for all such who had been inadvertently drawn in; and even for all those who had opposed his Exaltation."[120] Thus, pre-mortal, not postcreation, events are what he takes to be "meant in Scripture by the Fall of *Adam*, and the Reconciliation made by our Blessed Redeemer," much as the mystic Julian of Norwich had centuries earlier.

This tradition of reading the fall of the angels as involving mortals in their preexistent state persisted into the nineteenth century in the form of at least one full-length treatise on the subject. Here again, an anonymous author expounded the thesis that "man had some material link of connexion with the *fallen angels* [amounting to] identity."[121] This author, self-identified as "a layman," relies principally upon his reading of Genesis as indicating an ethic of individual accountability for evil, thus suggesting a race of "individual pre-existing rather than merely derivative sinners."[122]

The reality of a universal condemnation is clear from the story of the Fall. But as he reasons, "If newly created, it must be admitted that God creates a new and pure soul for the inscrutable and inexplicable purpose of animating a *corrupt* body, fallen under his own derivative curse and condemnation the instant it is born into the world.…[But] if the soul so embodied had evil pre-existence, the main question is at once solved." For God would certainly "not create *bad* spirits *as such*, nor would he punish such for obeying the nature he had given them." And since, he continues, it would make little sense to bring "pre-existing *good* spirits" into a cursed and condemned existence, the spirits of humankind must of necessity be spirits that were originally good but fell. Given that no other fallen spirits have been revealed to us, "there seems to be a very high degree of probability, if not moral certainty," that the rebellious angels are "the identical spirits who, embodied as men, are upon trial in this world for their contrition for, and repentance of, all evil committed by them."[123]

This layman finds additional and novel corroboration for his theory on other grounds, such as Paul's view that willful sinning *after* possessing truth is most offensive to God (Heb. 10:26) and the greater likelihood of Christ's supernal sacrifice to reclaim fallen angels of glory than to redeem poor, unworthy humans. This is because, first, the angels' merit was greater and thus "more likely to account for the sacrifice of the Saviour"; and second, as a fait accompli, their fall necessitated a redemption, whereas it makes little sense to believe that God would foreordain his

Son to such an immense sacrifice for a race not yet created, because his foresight would have led him to avoid a creation so costly to humans and Savior alike. It is, in sum, "far more probable, as well as reverential, to consider that so transcendent a sacrifice was to be made to *redeem an astounding evil that had already occurred, and was then existing*, in regard to the fallen angels." Finally, our author finds evidence of Adam's pre-mortal existence in God's dealings with him; based as they are on threats rather than love, they suggest familiarity with Adam's prior unrighteous tendencies.[124]

Indeed, many elements of the Genesis account lend themselves nicely to an allegorical reading of the Fall as referring to a pre-mortal era. As the "impartial inquirer" had earlier written, following Philo and Origen, God's act of "driving *Adam* and *Eve* out of Paradise, and giving them Coats of Skins to hide their Nakedness, was no more than the confining of lapsed Mankind to these our earthly Bodies, or taking Flesh upon us, and confining us to this Globe; And the hiding of our Nakedness, was the concealing of our former State from us." In his view, much of our preexistent state was one of dormancy, which is suggested by the deep sleep that precedes Adam's awakening.[125]

The entirety of the creation narrative need not be read allegorically to be read as giving an account of spiritual creation. Chapter 2 of Genesis has always posed something of a conundrum, giving as it does a second, and slightly different, version of the creation story. Contemporary biblical scholarship simply treats it as another creation narrative of different authorship, pasted sequentially after Genesis 1 rather than incorporated or synthesized with it. But verse 5 suggests a different possibility, with its reference to "every plant of the field before it was in the earth, and every herb of the field before it grew." Likewise, its pointed statement that "there was not a man to till the ground," coming as it does after the creation of man already given in the earlier account, can be taken to mean that we are now going to hear an account of the spiritual creation of human and creature alike. This is how the "inquirer" (following "cabalistic Interpretation") reads the biblical text, taking Moses to say in verse 5, "this account I have given you is not only a plain History of the Planting and Peopling of this Globe, but it is also an Account of the Generations of the Universe, antecedent to the present State of this Globe."[126]

The author finds additional support for preexistence not in esoteric lore or theological antecedents, but in contemporary science and discoveries made by the recently developed microscope in particular:

> [I]t is probable we have been in [a dormant state], from the Creation until our Birth....When we consider the Soul in the *Fœtus*, before the Birth, that it is a living Spirit, capable of Thought, Consciousness, and Reflection; and yet at that time has none, nor perhaps any Perception;...when

we consider, that this vivifying Spirit, or Principle, has had a Being, and was self-moving at the Time of Conception, as well as afterwards, when it comes to the Birth; and since, by the Improvement of Glasses [microscopes], we now see that these spiritual and seminal Forms are in the Seed of the Male before Coition and Conception; we have great Reason to believe, that all the Souls of Men...have been created from the Beginning, and perhaps long before the *Mosaic* Creation.[127]

At this point, the author argues the superiority of this conception of the soul's origins over against the orthodox, combining sympathy for an overworked God with points made by the Cambridge Platonists: "Or can we suppose our great God so far concurring with adulterous and incestuous Pollutions, as to exert his Almighty Power daily, and inject a Soul into the *Fœtus* form'd by their Act of Coition?" Furthermore, it seems especially perverse to implant an innocent human soul in a fetus that is shortly to die in stillbirth, leaving the soul devoid of human life but an inheritor of original sin, reaping thereby none of the advantages but all of the harm consequent upon mortality. He then takes on traducianism, arguing that the microscope has been misguidedly invoked in that theory's defense. "That our Souls were all originally in the first *Adam*," he writes, sounds too much like those materialists, who upon discovering "so many Souls or Animalcules...thrown off in each Act of Copulation" believe "that there are Souls within Souls, looking backwards as far as Thought can reach."[128]

Invoking a microscope in discussions of the soul's origin may seem a stretch, but applying the tools of science to the investigation of mind and soul had a long history, going back at least to the gynecological investigations of Aristotle and Galen. More recently, no less a thinker than Descartes, in trying to solve the problem of dualism, had zeroed in on the pineal gland as the locus of mind-body interaction (in both *Treatise on Man* and *The Passions of the Soul*). Anatomy was not illogically wrapped up with investigations of the mind and the soul, when the substantial reality of both was beyond question. It was inevitable that this new tool would be employed in addressing those questions where science and theology intersected. The twin developments of the telescope and the microscope were so interrelated that it is hard to know which occurred first,[129] but together they profoundly transformed and accelerated the course of modern scientific investigation. In the case of the microscope, after astounding the world with the discovery of teeming life beyond the threshold of unaided vision, scientists like Antonie van Leeuwenhoek turned their attention to the question of how life originated. That some life could begin by spontaneous generation had been asserted by Aristotle, and the idea persisted for over two millennia. The Italian Francesco Redi was the first to conduct an experiment with hermetically sealed rotting meat, to demonstrate that maggots did not spontaneously generate, in 1668. Then, Leeuwenhoek's discovery of insects' sexual organs (including the testicle of a flea) and even spermatozoa in minuscule creatures served as more evidence that the theory of spontaneous generation was not necessary to explain the origins of smallest life.[130]

A further biological puzzle to early scientists had been the need to account, in theories of embryonic formation, for the orderly development of such a complex being. Church writers like Augustine had long ago proposed that the future animal was at least partially physically anticipated in the semen of the father. In a version of materialistic preexistence analogous to traducianism, then, as Edward Ruestow writes, "Church fathers had also proposed that a seed-like beginning for every creature that would ever appear had been created in the original Creation."[131] As one authority put it, each fetus existed even before conception as "an entire Animal, furnished with all its proper Instruments for Life, Motion, and Procreation, and also the Fluids whereby it is nourished, though indeed so small, that no Power of human Imagination seems capable of being extended to."[132] Among other virtues, the theory had the benefit of adding an element of scientific plausibility to the concept of original sin, since all human beings would have been present in the body of Adam (or Eve, depending on whether the animalculists or ovists were writing) and therefore were physically if not willfully party to the first sin. As Augustine wrote, "if only one soul was created, and all human souls are descended from it, who can say that he did not sin when Adam sinned?"[133]

The seventeenth-century rationalist priest Nicolas Malebranche became an ardent advocate of that idea, sometimes referred to as "encapsulated preexistence." "The first females were created," he wrote, "with the subsequent individuals of their own species within them," in a manner that included "all the bodies of men...which will be born until the consummation of time."[134] The animalculists, more inclined to credit male priority in matters procreative, believed that all generations of humans were Chinese-boxed in the sperm of Adam rather than the eggs of Eve. As a poet of the age summarized, "Thus ADAM's Loins contained his large Posterity, / All People that have been, and all that e'er shall be."[135] The general idea caught on among numerous intellectuals, Leibniz included.

It is not so ironic, then, that the "impartial inquirer" finds the microscope a relevant tool for approaching the question of the soul's origin. What is surprising is that he finds it supportive of preexistence, rather than of the traducianism it seemed to imply. The "spiritual and seminal forms" to which he refers (doubtless, the human spermatozoa revealed first in Leeuwenhoek's microscope) do not reveal endless generations of mini-humans, as suggested in Malebranche's theory. (Seeds ended up providing better evidence of his encapsulated preexistence than did spermatozoa.) But they do, by their very motility, betoken a living principle, a mysterious version of human preembodiment, that accorded well with a theory of preexistent humans, clearly endowed with existence, if not consciousness. They added evidence to what he believed both scripture and reason affirmed, "that our Souls have had a Being long before our Appearance on this Stage of Life; that we have had our Being since the first Creation of all Things."[136]

Other, familiar arguments round out his defense of preexistence. The Fall of Adam makes more sense as an allegory than as a literal history of human sin. In light of preexistence, it makes perfect sense for the Holy Writ to call us

> strangers seeking our Way home to our native Country. But had we never been Inhabitants of that heavenly Paradise before the *Mosaic* Creation; or if our Souls were only created at or after Conception here, or even at the Formation of *Adam*, we had not Pretensions to call the aethereal Regions our Home, or be said to return to it.

Finally, he reminds readers that, if a case is to be made against preexistence, it needs stronger foundations than the problem of human forgetting. For clearly, "our Saviour's Soul, which we allow pre-existed, forgot many of his Transactions, and his Knowledge of Things before, or he could not, from his Birth, be said to increase in Knowledge."[137]

The heterodoxy of the Cambridge Platonists left little lasting impact on the course of theological developments. And the microscope, far from buttressing the case for preexistence, helped to usher in the very scientific revolution that would relegate learned disquisitions on subjects like the nature and origins of the soul to realms far removed from the laboratory. But the subject had not yet been exiled from philosophy, and in the seventeenth and eighteenth centuries, preexistence appears repeatedly in the efforts of Descartes, Locke, and Leibniz to revisit and improve upon the Platonic inheritance.

8

The Cartesian Aftermath

There are objections to the doctrine of pre-existence. But it seems to have been invented with a good intention, to save the honor of the Deity, which was thought to be injured by the supposition of his bringing creatures into the world to be miserable, without any previous misbehavior of theirs to deserve it.

—Benjamin Franklin[1]

American Renaissance man Benjamin Franklin reserved judgment about the reality of a human preexistence. If other thinkers had been as sanguine as he about the human condition and earthly circumstances, theodicy would seldom have emerged as a concern, and a major impetus behind preexistence would have been lacking. "Upon the whole," he wrote, "I am much disposed to like the world as I find it, and to doubt my own judgment as to what would mend it. I see so much wisdom, as to what I understand of its creation and government, that I suspect equal wisdom may be in what I do not understand." He was therefore quite content to resist the "impertinence" of inquiring into those regions "where [God] has thought fit to draw a veil."[2] Franklin's theological indifference to the question of preexistence to some extent typified a century that would see little of the religiously motivated inquiry into the soul's origins that had marked the preceding generations. Literary treatments and philosophical speculations, on the other hand, were still to be found.

In 1727, the Scottish writer Andrew Michael Ramsay published a fictional piece on the travels of Cyrus, prince of Persia. Montesquieu's *Persian Letters* (1721) had earlier provided a combination of exoticism and cross-cultural encounter in order to defamiliarize and comment upon Western politics, culture, and religion. In that case, two Persians leave the seraglio in order to visit Paris, from where they share observations on Western manners and mores with Persian friends. Ramsay altered the formula to make his Persian describe instead the "religion, manners, and politics" of a largely non-Western itinerary, all in the service of promulgating his version of the "ancient theology." As Ramsay indicates in his preface, he aims to show that "all nations had originally the same fundamental principles" flowing from "the same source." According to the Asians, Chaldeans, and Hebrews:

> [E]verything proceeds from God, and ought to flow back to him again. . . . Each man is a ray separated from its source, strayed into a corner of disordered nature, tossed about by the tumultuous wind of passion, transported from climate to climate by restless desires, purified by all the misfortunes it meets with, till it becomes like a subtle vapor reascending to the superior regions from whence it fell.[3]

Though the formulation sounds like simplified Neo-Platonism, Cyrus attributes these ideas to Persian religion and the teachings of the Egyptian Hermes, but gives the doctrine of preexistence in particular its most extensive coverage in his section on Pythagoras. Even there, his sources are largely undigested Platonist and Neo-Platonist, invoking as he does an age of "perfect innocence," when "the soul was not then imprisoned in a mortal body, as it is now; it was united to a luminous, heavenly, ethereal body." In that highest place, the souls beheld "truth, justice and wisdom in their source; it was there that with the eyes of the pure spirit they contemplated the first Essence." Through negligence and loving pleasure, more than order, the spirits fell, and "the wings of the soul were clipt; its subtle vehicle was broken; [and] the spirits were thrown down into their mortal bodies."[4] In the Hebrew version that he recounts, "two sorts of spirits lost their happiness by their disloyalty; the one, called *cherubim*, were of a superior order, and are now infernal spirits; the other, called *ischim*, were of a less perfect nature; [they] are the souls which actually inhabit mortal bodies."[5]

Though the vehicle is fiction, Ramsay clearly values the philosophical power of the idea. It has, his Cyrus tells another character, "removed all my difficulties about the origin of evil, by proving the freedom of intelligent natures; [the doctrine] shuts the mouth of impiety, by [its] sublime ideas concerning the pre-existence of souls, their voluntary fall, and their total restoration."[6] Ramsay's book was phenomenally popular and was one of the principal conduits affording Western readers exposure to Eastern religious ideas in the eighteenth century. It was published in

French, but was instantly translated into English and went through more than twenty-five British and American editions over the next century; there were also translations into German, Italian, Russian, and Spanish.[7] The Eastern garb in which Ramsay clothes his topic foreshadows the trajectory that preexistence will increasingly take in the West. Rather than try to resuscitate it as an improperly discarded Western theological idea, proponents will more and more associate it with the wisdom of the Orient. The strategy had the advantage of exploiting the eighteenth- and nineteenth-century exoticism that colored cultural production from chinoiserie to Ingres's paintings to Brighton's Royal Pavilion. At the same time, philosophers were pushing the idea of preexistence in new directions, without simply reinstating the Platonisms of the past.

Descartes and Innate Ideas

The seventeenth century had seen the fortunes of preexistence rise through the enthusiastic advocacy of the Cambridge Platonists, similarly inclined poets, and widespread interest in Kabbalistic lore. At the same time, the doctrine had been weaving in and out of the century's philosophical debates, bearing witness to the important intellectual work the paradigm accomplishes and to the emergence of surrogates in a more secular and less mythologically inclined environment. The same years that witnessed the rise of the Cambridge Platonists also saw the birth of the revolutionary "method" of René Descartes (1596–1650), who established philosophy on modern, rationalistic foundations. As we saw, Henry More and some of his colleagues perceived in Cartesian innate ideas a thinly veiled version of Plato's theory of preexistence and recollection. The Stoics, Greek philosophers of the Hellenistic era, had recognized, along with Plato, that humans are capable of recognizing certain fundamental realities or truths outside of themselves. This capacity they attributed to *koinai ennoiai* (common notions) or *physikai prolepseis* (natural preconceptions) imprinted in the minds of all humans.

For Descartes, ideas could only be of three types: they are derived from an external source, they are invented by the self, or they must be innate to the human mind. Hearing sound or feeling heat, in his examples, involve sensations that clearly proceed "from certain things that exist outside of me." Examples of the second category are "sirens, hippogryphs, and the like, [which] are formed out of my own mind." More complicated is the third category, such as the idea "of a Being supremely perfect— that is of God." Through a number of arguments (there must be as much reality in the cause as in the effect, that which is perfect cannot proceed from imperfection, and "there is manifestly more reality in infinite substance than in finite"), he concludes that the idea of God cannot have originated with him ("there is another being which exists, or which is the cause of this idea"). All that remains is for Descartes to determine the manner in which he has acquired this idea. "In some way," God put it there, he concludes. Accordingly, the idea of God "is innate in me, just as the idea of myself is innate in me."[8] Descartes found it easy to slip casually over the manner by which such innate ideas come to be part of the human mind. "In some way," he had been content to say. Plato, it would seem, was still in the wings.

John Locke (1632–1704) was the most famous critic of innate ideas. He takes up the debate at the precise point of Descartes's "in some way." He introduces his magisterial *Essay Concerning Human Understanding* by promising that "our first inquiry then shall be, how [ideas] come into the mind," and he immediately makes a coy reference to Descartes's position, which he recognizes as a surrogate for Platonic theories. "It is an established Opinion amongst some Men," he writes, "that there are in the Understanding certain *innate Principles*; some primary Notions,…Characters, as it were, stamped upon the Mind of Man; which the Soul receives in its very first Being, and brings into the World with it."[9] Locke is correct in his implicit dig that suggests, whatever their differing philosophical garbs, preexistent souls and innate ideas amount to the same thing: a theoretically imprecise and therefore dubious construct that resolves a philosophical difficulty. Locke discounts the necessity for such measures both by denying that universal assent to certain principles points to any "constant impressions which the souls of men receive in their first beings" and by arguing that children and idiots appear oblivious to such impressions. "If therefore children and idiots have souls, have minds, with those impressions upon them, *they* must unavoidably perceive them, and necessarily know and assent to these truths; which since they do not, it is evident that there are no such impressions."[10]

Having dispensed with arguments in favor of innate ideas, Locke addresses more directly the Platonic idea of preexistent souls in a discussion concerning "Identity and Diversity," wherein he asks:

> Whether the same immaterial Being, being conscious of the Actions of its past Duration, may be wholly stripp'd of all the consciousness of its past Existence, and lose it again beyond the power of ever retrieving again: And so as it were beginning a new Account from a new period, have a consciousness that *cannot* reach beyond this new State. All those who hold pre-existence are evidently of this Mind, since they allow the soul to have no remaining consciousness of what it did in that pre-existent State.…[But] personal identity, reaching no further than consciousness reaches, a pre-existent Spirit…must needs make different Persons.[11]

In other words, for his purposes, the Platonic doctrine of preexistence is neither true nor false: it is simply irrelevant to human concerns, since for him, human memory and not spiritual subsistence is the determining factor in human identity. Augustine, in spite of his attractions to the idea, had conceded essentially the same fault in the theory, though in more poetic form than Locke: "There is no harm done to someone sailing to Rome if he has forgotten the port from which he set out, as long as he remembers where he is headed. And he is no better off for remembering his port of origin if his mistaken ideas about where Rome is cause him to run aground on the rocks."[12]

Locke's contemporary, the German philosopher Gottfried Leibniz (1646–1716), tried to defend innate ideas against Locke's attack, but without embracing the exact form of Platonism it often involved. What results is yet another variation on the theme of preexistence, almost in spite of himself. "Nothing can be taught us of which we have not already in our minds the idea," Leibniz affirms in his discussion of Plato's theory. He continues, "Plato has excellently brought out [this idea] in his doctrine of reminiscence, a doctrine which contains a great deal of truth, provided that it is properly understood and purged of the error of pre-existence."[13] Yet, like Descartes, he replaces the literal preexistence of the soul with a doctrine that performs the identical work through means which he tries to differentiate from Plato without actually articulating them. Referring to *Meno*'s example of recollection, Leibniz agrees that Plato's demonstration with the slave boy "shows that the soul virtually knows those things, and needs only to be reminded (animadverted) to recognize the truths." The soul, then, does indeed possess "at least the idea upon which those truths depend. We may say even that it possesses those truths, if we consider them as the relations of the ideas."[14]

As he elsewhere writes more emphatically, it is possible that "the soul in itself is entirely empty, as the tablets upon which as yet nothing has been written (*tabula rasa*) according to Aristotle, and the author of the *Essay* [Locke], and [that] all that is traced thereon comes solely from the senses and from experience," but he considers it more likely—and conformable to scripture—that

> the soul contains originally the principles of many ideas and doctrines
> which external objects merely call up on occasion, as I believe with Plato,
> and even with the schoolmen, and with all those who interpret in this way
> the passage of St. Paul (Rom. 2:15) where he states that the law of God is
> written in the heart.[15]

Leibniz's language here explains why one philosopher can refer to him as "the last great representative of Platonic reminiscence."[16] Plato's *anamnesis* is logically and philosophically inseparable from Platonic preexistence, in spite of Leibniz's fruitless efforts to sever this link (as when he applauds the doctrine of reminiscence, "provided that one does not conceive of the soul as having already known and thought at some other time what it learns and thinks now").[17]

It was a delicate tightrope Leibniz was walking. As an intellectual in the age of Newton, he resisted embracing Plato's mythological fantasies literally. On the other hand, the alternatives were also problematic; the implications of Locke's position

German philosopher Leibniz struggled to find alternatives to Platonic preexistence, but his theories tended to replicate the idea in different language. *Portrait of Gottfried Wilhelm von Leibniz*, Foto Marburg/Art Resource, New York.

in particular were especially troubling. The problem is that Locke's theory of the mind as a tabula rasa does more than deny the inheritance of spiritual memories. It has the potential to dissolve the very seat of identity because Locke's theory makes not just memory and imagination but even the intellect a product of sense experience.[18] If intellect and therefore understanding, including self-understanding, are both contingent upon and constructed within the realm of sense experience, they cannot be already given, or innate; identity as a fixed substratum disappears. Locke defines the personal self in this way:

> Identity consists … [in] a thinking intelligent being, that has reason and reflection, and can consider itself as itself, as the same thinking being, in different times and places; which it does only by that consciousness which is inseparable from thinking … and as far as this consciousness can be extended backwards to any past action or thought, so far [it] reaches the identity of that person.[19]

In other words, personal identity "is nothing other than the traces of the different moments of perception of myself that memory retains."[20] We find ourselves here most of the way down the road that David Hume will take to its disturbing end: "we are never intimately conscious of anything but a particular perception; man is a bundle or collection of different perceptions which succeed one another with an inconceivable rapidity and are in perpetual flux and movement."[21] A human being as a chain of ephemeral perceptions, a self dissolved into a transient chain of mental processes, would not have struck many people as a particularly appealing alternative to Platonic fancies of pre-mortal spirits.

The stable self that Leibniz wants to maintain requires some fixed substratum that extends beyond or prior to the temporality and vicissitudes of experiential data received through the senses and stored as memory. If identity is merely a function of senses, memory, and states of consciousness, then the soul is little more than an illusion. Preexistence is not the only guarantee of an immortal soul or even a stable identity; at the same time, preexistent or innate ideas that have their being prior to and independently of sense experience are good evidence that some reliable core identity serves as their repository, and that identity we can associate with a soul. That is one reason that Leibniz wished to retain the viability of innate ideas if not their Platonic formulation.

An ingenious but convoluted argument in support of innate ideas emerged out of Leibniz's theory of monads. Monads, as Leibniz conceived them, are the fundamental, irreducible, and eternal constituents of the universe, analogous to, but not materially or spatially substantial like, atoms. Though monads are usually conceived of as infinitesimal, important exceptions exist: each human soul, for instance, constitutes a monad.[22] The entire past, present, and future features of every monad are always already present in it, and they maintain full autonomy and independence throughout existence, even to the point that none of them ever truly interact with anything else. For Leibniz, the apparent interactions and mutual influences that pervade the world of lived reality are an illusion; an omniscient God anticipated the infinite complexity of a diverse world and fully synchronized every element—every monad—therein, endowing creation with a preestablished harmony. (The theory is a clever if dubious solution to the intractable mind-body problem. There is no need to find a mechanism for the interaction of two ontologically disparate orders of things if both simply operate independently but in perfect sync.) And it was on this basis that Locke could be refuted. In his *Nouveaux Essais*, Leibniz has Philalethes, representing Locke, insist that all knowledge can be acquired "without the aid of any innate impression," to which Theophilus, representing Leibniz, replies:

> You know, Philalethes, that I have been for a long time of another opinion; that I have always held, as I still hold, to the innate idea of God, which Descartes maintained, and as a consequence to the other innate ideas which cannot come to us from the senses. Now, I go still farther in conformity to the new system, and I believe even that all the thoughts and acts of our soul come from its own depths, with no possibility of their being given to it by the senses.[23]

The soul's ideas are not derived from a prior state in Plato's sense, but rather fit into a preordained harmonious system that encompasses all of creation and that smoothes the interworkings of Cartesian dualism while rendering Locke's empiricist bases for knowledge unnecessary and even impossible. The basis for this grand scheme of Leibniz is couched in terms of a conceptual preexistence, which oddly combines theology with probability theory. Leibniz's universe sounds like Boehme's *Ungrund* or the undifferentiated One of Plotinus—a realm of unfathomable, unrealized potentiality waiting for self-realization. The reality that bursts forth into actuality is the one that triumphs in a process like the mathematical evaluation of hypothetical scenarios. As Roy Sorensen explains:

> In 1678 Leibniz was the first to define probability as the ratio of favorable cases to the total number of equally possible cases....He has the objective sense of "probably" in mind when explaining which possibilities succeed at becoming actual. Many possibilities are not co-possible. The possibility that conflicts with the fewest other possibilities becomes actual....This objective picture of possibilities requires a limbo where nonexistent entities battle to enter the realm of existence[24].

The problem, as Sorensen asks, is: "how can nonexistent things do anything?"

Leibniz found the solution by shifting from the logic of temporality to the timeless mind of God: "Possibilities start out as God's thoughts. These thoughts are complete plans for a universe. Each of these possible worlds is a consistent and complete way that things could be....Those backed by better reasons have a stronger tendency to become actualized by God." All of this entails a kind of double-speak, of course, since the theory requires "a limbo where nonexistent entities battle to enter the realm of existence."[25] No wonder that one scholar goes so far as to claim that Leibniz "drove the implications of pre-existence to their most radical metaphysical and theological formulation. Indeed, in many ways pre-existence was the centerpiece of his metaphysics."[26]

There is another function that preexistence serves, which emerges in the context of Leibniz's *Theodicy*. In that work, he addresses a foremost "difficulty," as he styles it, of reconciling the light of nature and the light of revelation. The difficulty is that "freedom is deemed necessary, in order that man may be deemed guilty and open to punishment." But such a freedom, he feels, is difficult to square with a God who is both omnipotent and omniscient. It is not that foreknowledge in itself entails determinism; rather, foreknowledge must have its foundation "in the nature of things, and this foundation, making the truth *predeterminate*, will prevent it from being contingent and free." In other words, whatever conditions allow God to predict the future would also determine that future. The logical unfolding of those conditions and their consequences, not God's knowledge, is the real threat to the principle of freedom. However, human choice complicates things, since "a simple contingent and free act has nothing in itself to yield a principle of certainty." Freedom, in other words, requires action unconditioned by external laws or causes. On what basis, then, can God foresee a future that incorporates human freedom? The full resolution of the problem is, he admits, "long and wearisome," but Leibniz finds a convenient solution: "I resort to my principle of an infinitude of possible worlds, represented in the region of eternal verities, that is, in the object of the divine intelligence, where all conditional futurities must be comprised." So, even if the future depends upon "free actions of reasonable creatures entirely independent of the decrees of God and of external causes, there would still be a means of foreseeing them; for God would see them as they are in the region of the possibles, before he decrees to admit them into existence."[27]

In the foregoing regard, Leibniz combines his principle of sufficient reason—that only those things exist for which there is a sufficient reason for them to exist—with the mathematics of probability and a conception very close to the ideal preexistence of early Judaism. In the latter regard especially, the similarity is manifest when he writes, "Man is himself the source of his evils: just as he is, he was in the divine idea. God, prompted by essential reasons of wisdom, decreed that he should pass into existence just as he is."[28] Exceedingly curious logic, this, that makes humanity's very existence an idea in the mind of God and yet an idea that has its own moral accountability. In order to salvage free will in the face of God's foreknowledge, Leibniz has to imagine an individual who is pre-mortal and only ideally existent yet responsible for his own inclinations and choices and therefore self-determining; at the same time, his entire being, to avoid the Platonic model, must be seen as no more than a potentiality yet to be summoned into existence. In Leibniz's philosophical language, extratemporal existence is not really existence: human "essence" is indicated by the divine understanding; human "existence" waits upon the divine will.[29]

It is hard to see how Plato's straightforward mythic conception is improved by Leibniz's comparable metaphysical dualism, with its superadded dose of logical obfuscation. If nothing else, Leibniz's protean application of Plato's idea, which eventuates in a new mysticism, reveals how powerfully appealing Plato's basic framework continued to be in a philosophical climate trying to preserve intact human freedom and God's justice against mounting obstacles.

Yet another way in which Leibniz circles back to Plato's template takes him through the thickets of biology rather than metaphysics. It should be remembered in this regard that preexistence in the age of Leibniz also had reference to a theory of embryology according to which fetuses are not created individually by the act of sexual procreation but simply unfold out of a germ that was already complete and developed, though unimaginably small, and existing from the first creation. Leibniz

wedded Plato's attribution of a preexistent dimension to the human soul—a powerful conception to explain certain forms of human knowledge or mental acquirements
with which we seem to be born—to a biological conception of the human body as
emerging, preformed, out of a chain of successive transmissions. For Leibniz, the
assimilation of these two views could not be accomplished to a more triumphant
end: the vindication of his pet principle of preestablished harmony in a manner that
is as scientifically validated as it is theologically sound:

> [T]he formation of organic animate bodies appears explicable in the order
> of nature only when one assumes a *preformation* already organic....Con-
> sidering that so admirable an order and rules so general are established
> in regard to animals, it does not appear reasonable that man should be
> completely excluded from that order, and that everything in relation to
> his soul should come about in him by miracle. Besides I have pointed
> out repeatedly that it is of the essence of God's wisdom that all should be
> harmonious in his works, and that nature should be parallel with grace.
> It is thus my belief that those souls which one day shall be human souls,
> like those of other species, have been in the seed, and in the progenitors,
> as far back as Adam, and have consequently existed since the beginning
> of things, always in a kind of organic body....This doctrine is also suf-
> ficiently confirmed by the microscope observations of M. Leeuwenhoek
> and other good observers.[30]

In *Monadology*, Leibniz reaffirms his glib optimism that scientific knowledge
has triumphed where metaphysical speculation about questions relating to preexistence has failed: "Philosophers have been very embarrassed hitherto in their attempts
to account for the origin of...souls. Today, however, exact researches on plants,
insects, and animals have come to establish the fact that natural organic bodies
are not spontaneously produced," and "it has been conjectured indeed...that not
only is the organic body already existent before conception, but even that there
is a soul in this body."[31] Unlike Plato's soul, however, which was unencumbered
by the body and therefore had more direct access to timeless truths in a realm of
absolutes, Leibniz imagines the preexistent soul to have not yet acquired the faculty
of reason itself. "It also for divers reasons appears likely to me," he writes (based on
microscope observations or not, he does not say), "that they existed then as sentient
or animal souls only, endowed with perception and feeling, and devoid of reason.
Further I believe that they remained in this state up to the time of the generation of
the man to whom they were to belong, but that then they received reason."[32]

After the death of Leibniz in 1716, the baton of preexistence was not immediately picked up by major figures in the Western philosophical tradition. It may
have been the years of relative silence, curiosities like Ramsay's *Cyrus* aside, that

led the English philosopher Abraham Tucker (1705–1774) to assert confidently that the doctrine of preexistence was by his day so "universally exploded" that he needn't waste time refuting it. Nevertheless, in 1763, writing under the name Edward Search, he did just that. And in so doing, he inadvertently accomplished three things. He only highlighted the deficiencies of orthodox theodicies that failed to do what preexistence accomplished. He refuted preexistence itself so ineptly that he could only cast suspicion on his side of the question. And by expending so much energy in the effort, he bore witness, as events were soon to show, that his dismissal of the doctrine's vitality was overly confident.

In hypothesizing the origins of preexistence as a doctrine, Tucker supposes that "the ancient Mythologists" (by which he presumably means Plato) were misled by a simplistic understanding of justice. Their attempt to link pre-mortal wrongs to present suffering was born, he posits, of their plain inability "to understand it consistent with goodness that any one should suffer for the failings of another." However, anyone expecting a reasoned defense of the logic of original sin or the catastrophic suffering of the innocent as occurred in the recent Lisbon earthquake of 1755 would be disappointed. For the fact "that pain and misery were brought into the world…by the fall of Adam" is "a very orthodox tenet." And that is the end of it.[33]

As for the merits of preexistence as a doctrine, he seems to feel it will run into trouble if applied to brute creatures. He breaks off this argument, however, with, for him, the more decisive proof: "every old woman knows the soul of the child was created at the very instant when the mother first felt herself quick." And finally, he is confident that even if we could demonstrate preexistence "ever so clearly" (perhaps it is not so exploded after all), being out of the range of present memory as it apparently is, it could not in any case be relevant to our own moral lives and is therefore perfectly liable to "exclamation or ridicule."[34] (Tertullian also had found preexistence to be vulnerable on the memory issue: if it is as divine as Plato makes it out to be, he wrote, "I cannot allow that the soul is capable of a failure of memory.")[35]

Tucker's obituary for preexistence turned out to be entirely premature; the generations succeeding his own were not at all disposed to dismiss the doctrine of ante-mortal existence as in any way ridiculous. Quite the contrary. The theologian Johann Friedrich Bruch (1792–1874) watched anxiously as Germany witnessed a virtual renaissance of the idea of preexistence, which had been flowering in his country for a few generations. In 1859, he published an entire volume on the history of *Teachings on the Preexistence* (*Die Lehre von der Präexistenz*).[36] Tracing the idea from Pythagoras to its demise under the edict of Justinian, he nonetheless saw it reemerge, to his consternation, "in new form" in the writings of an array of eighteenth- and nineteenth-century German philosophers and theologians. He named Friedrich Schelling, Wilhelm Benecke, Julius Müller, Friedrich Rückert,

Johann August Ernesti, and Immanuel Hermann Fichte. However, he found it remarkable that it was "the most sober of all philosophers of the early modern era," Immanuel Kant himself, who was responsible for resurrecting a doctrine that, at the close of the eighteenth century, was almost "totally and forever forgotten." It was at that very moment that Kant (1724–1804) put forward a theory that, as Bruch correctly perceived, rewrote Christian theodicy, propounded a new etiology of evil, and defended human freedom by recourse to the theory of Plato, disguised in new language. New language notwithstanding, Kant appealed to the doctrine with enough energy that he was interpreted by others as having "dogmatically taught...the preexistence...of the soul."[37]

The problem of freedom, Kant reasons, is that insofar as we are phenomenal beings, that is, beings of space and time, we are subject to the chain of causality that conditions and determines all sensory existence:

> [What this means is that] at every point of time I am still always subject
> to the necessity of being determined to action by *what is not under my
> control*, and the series of events—which is infinite *a parte priori* [receding

Germany's influential thinker, Kant, with his concept of noumenal humans, maintained the philosophical power and utility of preexistence but shifted the concept from a sphere before, to a sphere outside, the temporal continuum. *Immanuel Kant*, lithograph after a painting by Gottfried Doeppler, 1791, Bildarchiv Preussischer Kulturbesitz/Art Resource, New York.

backward] and which I can always continue only according to an already predetermined order—would nowhere start on its own [but] would be a steady chain of nature, and therefore my causality would never be freedom.[38]

He begins, in other words, with Aristotle's premise that only that which is cause of itself is free (*Metaphysics*, I.2). Always already implicated in a chain of causality, human beings are not free. As moral agents, however, we recognize within ourselves a call to duty and the ability to observe a moral law. We recognize that we commit actions we could have chosen not to and neglect others where we might have acted rightly. Kant explains the only conditions under which this felt freedom can be more than mere illusion:

> [T]he same subject, who on the other hand, is also conscious of himself as a thing in itself, also considers his existence *insofar as it does not fall under the conditions of time*, and considers himself as determinable only by laws that he on his own gives to himself through reason; and in this existence of his there is for him nothing antecedent to the determination of his will, but every action…, even the entire sequence of his existence as a being of sense—is…never to be viewed as a determining basis of his causality as a *noumenon*.[39]

What he is saying is that all humans recognize a dimension to the self (the noumenal self) that is not subject to or determined by external conditions or the events of the temporal order of things. In this capacity as a noumenal human, we feel our will to be authentic and unconditioned, i.e., free. As he puts it in another work, "as a rational being and hence belonging to the intelligible world, can man never think of the causality of his own will except under the idea of freedom: for independence from the determining causes of the world of sense…is freedom."[40] We have one existence, in other words, as entities in a universe of sense, wherein we are subject to the laws of nature. This is existence as a phenomenal human. We also, however, have existence as intelligence inhabiting the realm of understanding; this is existence as a noumenal human. In the latter case, "when he thinks of himself as intelligence endowed with a will,…he puts himself into determining grounds of a different kind from the kind when he perceives himself as a phenomenon in the world of sense….Now he soon realizes that both can—and indeed must—hold true at the same time."[41]

Hence, humans lead an extraordinary double life, including one as phenomenon, within which we remain subject to and inseparable from time, space, and the laws of causality. But as noumena, we are outside of time, space, and causality. And that is where we find the freedom that we intuit through our moral sense. Unlike the idea of preexistence in a temporal sense, Kant sees preexistence rather as an existence outside of—and hence not subject to—time, an existence which lies outside the realm of experience. Nevertheless, according to Kant, it is the precondition for our existence as phenomenal beings subject to experience.

Kant follows an essentially parallel line of argument in his treatise *Religion within the Limits of Reason*, which is primarily an inquiry into the genesis of evil. To attribute good or evil to an individual, he begins, is to impute "an ultimate ground" to that person on the basis of which she lives a moral or immoral life. This ground is innate but cannot be attributable to nature, or it would not be subject to moral valuations of good or evil. It cannot just be a biological or genetic inheritance but must rather be attributable to one's own choice. But since, he reasons, as an ultimate ground it cannot be reflected in mere experience (rather, it must precede and condition experience), it must be conceived as present already at birth. And so we arrive at the same conclusions as above:

> To have a good or an evil disposition as an inborn natural constitution does not here mean that it has not been acquired by the man who harbors it, that he is not author of it, but rather, that it has not been acquired in time....Yet this disposition itself must have been adopted by free choice, for otherwise it could not be imputed.[42]

One can see why Bruch saw Kant as simply retreading the path of Plato and Origen, but without the language of myth or religion. Quibbles about "before time" or "outside of time" aside, Kant holds that human beings, in some realm not of this earth or time, freely made choices that condition the nature they inherit upon birth in this world. The next step Kant takes, in searching out the etiology of evil, leads to territory even more nebulous. To say of a person that she is either good or evil by nature, he reasons, cannot be a statement about that individual alone. For to speak of a nature is to speak of what is general rather than what is particular. The attribution, therefore, "holds for the race." At the same time, since in plumbing the origins of humanity's corrupt nature, we are looking for that first freely chosen defiance of the moral law, it only makes sense to regard the primal action "as though the individual had fallen into it directly from a state of innocence."[43] If all of this sounds remarkably consistent with the mythology of Genesis, it should. Kant readily acknowledges that his analysis "agrees well with that manner of presentation which the scriptures use, whereby the origin of evil in the human race is depicted as having a [temporal] beginning." The only difference is that, based on the analysis of human freedom and therefore of moral culpability that Kant has already undertaken, he dismisses as fruitless any inquiry into the primal choice of evil that looks for it in time ("we cannot inquire into the temporal origin of this deed, but solely into its rational origin").[44] Since Kant traces the Fall to noumenal (or intelligible) man, it belongs to an impenetrable realm which is outside time itself. Kant nevertheless finds in the contemplation of that primal state inspiration and language worthy of any Neo-Platonist lamenting the fall from glory:

> Yet there is one thing in our soul which we cannot cease from regarding with the highest wonder, when we view it properly, and for which admiration is not only legitimate but even exalting, and that is the original moral predisposition itself in us. What is it in us (we can ask ourselves) whereby we, beings ever dependent upon nature through so many needs, are at the same time raised so far above these needs by the idea of an original predisposition (in us) that we count them all as nothing, and ourselves as unworthy of existence, if we cater to their satisfaction.... The very incomprehensibility of this predisposition, which announces a divine origin, acts perforce upon the spirit even to the point of exaltation.[45]

We have arrived at a remarkable point. Over two millennia removed from Plato and 1,500 years from Origen, the father of critical philosophy, Immanuel Kant, finds the myth of a primal fall predating even Adam to be an indispensable ingredient in any account of evil's existence and the individual's self-conception. This, in spite of the fact that he called the Christian reading of Adam's Fall "the most inept...of all the explanations of the spread and propagation of this evil."[46] The wonder is only compounded when a more recent scholar writes that Nietzsche, Heidegger, and Wittgenstein similarly find themselves unsuccessful in escaping such a paradigm. The Fall of Adam, Stephen Mulhall remarks, is "an expression of the enigmatic fact that sinful acts presuppose sinfulness, and sinfulness presupposes sinful acts." The representation of this conundrum is hard to improve. For while those three modern philosophers reject the biblical account, each, in the end, "recreates his own myth of the fall."[47]

There is another way in which Kantian philosophy replicates the intellectual work of Plato. One of the greatest revolutions in modern intellectual history (a "Copernican revolution," in his own words) began when this great German thinker set out to resolve one of the primary tensions of Enlightenment philosophy. On the question of how the human mind acquires knowledge, two different schools had different answers. The rationalists insisted that reason is the source of all knowledge. Specifically, Descartes and his followers argued that truth is deducible from a priori concepts (ideas that are universal and necessarily true). Empiricists, on the other hand, emphasized the origins of all human knowledge in experience. In Locke's famous formulation, the mind is a blank slate on which sensory experience inscribes the constituents of all knowledge.

Kant found both approaches flawed. As David Hume had pointed out earlier, reason is a powerful instrument for detecting relations among ideas, but in the final analysis can tell us nothing about how those ideas relate to the real world. And in any case, Kant could not accept that humans are born with ideas already present in their minds, as rationalists did. On the other hand, Kant also recognized the limitations of the empirical approach to knowledge. Relying upon our sensations of the actual world, we can never be certain of anything beyond just that—our own mental states produced by sensory experience. Neither have we sure grounds for moving beyond particular truths to universal claims.

In simplest terms, his solution to the problem involved a synthesis of the rationalist and empiricist positions. "Thoughts without content are empty, intuitions without concepts are blind.... The understanding is not capable of intuiting anything [with intuition understood as sensory experience], and the senses are not capable of thinking anything. Only from their unification can cognition arise."[48] His innovative insight, however, was in his recognition of a particular kind of knowledge that is not attributable to either rationalist or empiricist bases. His predecessors had accepted a distinction made by Leibniz between two kinds of judgments, or logical statements, that the mind can make. The first is analytic a priori judgments. In an analytic judgment, the claim about the subject of a sentence is implicit in the definition itself (the predicate is contained in the subject, in Kant's language). So to say, in Kant's example, that all bodies are extended is to make a claim that is verifiable by recourse to nothing more than the concepts contained in the statement itself. Or we could say, a rose is a flower. If we know the definitions of "body" and "extension," or "rose" and "flower," we have sufficient information to verify the truth of the statement. Such statements that are true by definition are also true a priori, that is, are necessarily and universally true and, as such, are independent of empirical verification. The other kind of statement is a synthetic a posteriori judgment. "Synthetic" suggests that the statement brings together two ideas not necessarily related by definition (the predicate is not contained in the subject). All bodies have weight, in Kant's example. We know a body, by definition, must occupy space, but nothing in the definition tells us that it must have weight. Similarly, a rose must be a flower (that would be analytic), but it need not be red or yellow; "that rose is yellow" would be a synthetic statement. And synthetic statements, because they are not necessarily and universally true by definition, rely upon experience for confirmation and are therefore a posteriori.

Some philosophers believed that these two forms of judgment comprised the limits of human knowledge. And recognizing those limits constituted what one scholar calls "the collapse of confidence" precipitated in large part by Hume.[49] Outside of matters of experienced fact and matters of necessary relations between ideas, he reasoned, we have no certainty. And since no inductive reasoning or generalizing could rest on certainty, matters of fact could only be, at best, particular. And relating ideas to ideas could tell us nothing about the real world.

Kant recognized that a third type of judgment is possible, one that is trust-worthy and utterly valid but does not rely upon either particular experience, like synthetic a posteriori judgments, or logical rules, like analytic a priori judgments.[50] We may confidently assert judgments of this third type, a priori synthetic judgments, Kant insisted, without relying upon either experience or the laws of reason. As an example, he cited the proposition that every effect has a cause. Kant argued that several statements in mathematics, physics, and ethics are of this sort. We can make these kinds of judgments, he reasoned, because the mind is hardwired in a certain way. It comes equipped with categories that allow us to interpret experience, organize sensation, and make sense out of the world. A principle like causality, in the example he cited, is recognized by the mind—and employed by the mind—as a universal and necessarily valid construct, but it is one which we do not derive from either reason or experience.

Kant would go on to enumerate and elucidate a number of these mental concepts, some of which relate to knowledge that comes through the senses and some of which relate to knowledge that comes through rational thought. Space and time, for Kant, are examples of such organizing features of the mind. These "a priori intuitions" are not themselves sensations but are like a mental grid on which sensations become intelligible and meaningful. In his language, space is itself "a necessary condition of all the relations within which objects can be intuited as outside us." We cannot posit its objective existence, but from a subjective, human standpoint, "through space alone is it possible for things to be outer objects for us."[51] In analogous fashion, what Kant calls "forms of judgment," like causality, plurality, and others, are not ideas but the matrix against which concepts can be related and made into ideas. They therefore make possible knowledge, insofar as they constitute the conditions under which sensory data are constituted into objects of thought.

Even as Kant effects a synthesis of rationalist and empiricist ideas, then, he powerfully argues that any complete account of how human knowledge is acquired must be able to explain how we know more than reason and experience alone can account for. The paradigm that results, a scheme involving Kantian categories of the mind, transforms Plato's theory of residual forms and dim recollections of preexistence into an array of innate, organizing mental categories that impose order on the world of experience and thus structure reality in ways that allow us to make sense of it. The enthusiasm that Henry More and his fellow Platonists showered upon Descartes was based on their view of innate ideas as a philosophical residue of Platonic preexistence. That Kant's paradigm similarly points back to the intellectual work of Platonic recollection is suggested by the fact that one of these forms of judgment specified by Kant is "equality"—the very concept which Plato points to in *Phaedo* as an instance of a universal which we intuitively recognize and which therefore points to pre-mortal origins.[52]

Though Kant's theory of categories of mind functions as a conceptual equivalent of preexistence, he addressed the literal preexistence of spirits with startling directness in other contexts. Kant seems to have been the first to find an incongruity between the triviality, banality, and utter contingency of circumstances attendant upon much of human procreation and a concept of the product thereby engendered as something majestic, touched with divinity, and endowed with immortality:

> The contingency of conception, which in humans as well as in irrational creatures depends upon opportunity, but besides this also on nourishment, on [self-control], on its moods and caprices, even on vices, presents a great difficulty for the opinion of the eternal duration of a creature whose life has first begun under circumstances so trivial.

Or, as he will conclude with gentle understatement: "It certainly seems questionable to expect such a powerful effect from such inconsequential causes." Like J. M. E. McTaggart, who will follow him, Kant finds such a doctrine of unidirectional eternity less than philosophically compelling, but not without remedy. And here he circles back to an unabashed and quasi-Platonic solution:

> Against this, however, you could propose a transcendental hypothesis: that all life is really only intelligible, not subject to temporal alterations at all, and has neither begun at birth nor will be ended through death; that this life is nothing but a mere appearance, i.e., a sensible representation of the purely spiritual life, and that entire world of the senses is a mere image, which hovers before our present kind of cognition and, like a dream, has no objective reality in itself; that if we could intuit the things and ourselves as they are we would see ourselves in a world of spiritual natures with which our only true community had not begun with birth nor would cease with bodily death.[53]

The philosophical idealism of Kant will be embraced and developed by the subsequent generation of German philosophers. With such august intellectuals invoking the ghosts of preexistence, it seems inevitable that the theological tradition that had abandoned the idea would find new grounds to resurrect it.

9

Philosophy and Theology, 1800–1900

It appeared that the theory of a pre-earthly existence of the human soul had been totally and forever forgotten; after all, Catholicism had rejected it and it had been discarded by the Protestants....However, the question emerged again in the modern era, albeit in a different form and the theory found capable apologists among the most eminent philosophers and theologians.

—Johann Friedrich Bruch[1]

Kant had going for him, at least in most of his system building, a rigorous method and a foundation in logic. Friedrich Schelling (1775–1854), however, Bruch dismissed as a fantastical theosophist. Indeed, to today's ears, Schelling's philosophy sounds irredeemably abstract and mystical. Part of the explanation is that Schelling was influenced by and freely incorporated ideas from Boehme and other mystics, the Neo-Platonists, and the Gnostics. But his foundation was solidly Kantian. As one scholar puts it, "among the problems that Schelling faced in seeking to work out a systematic philosophy of mythology, by far the most difficult concerned the ontology of human and divine freedom in their respective relations to thought and temporality. Included in this set of issues...[was] the possibility of a genuinely free will."[2] And so he naturally found Kant to be a useful point of departure:

> It was, indeed, Idealism which first raised the doctrine of free-
> dom into that realm in which it alone can be understood. In

consequence of it the intelligible essence of everything, and particularly of man, is outside of all causal connections as it is outside or beyond all time.[3]

What Schelling is saying here is that Kantian idealists had already argued the impossibility of escaping causality if one confined oneself to temporality. Freedom must be sought in a realm anterior to or outside of time:

> In original creation,…man is an undetermined entity (which may be mythologically presented as a condition antecedent to this life, a state of innocence and initial bliss). He alone can determine himself. But this determination cannot occur in time; it occurs outside of time altogether and hence it coincides with the first creation even though as an act differentiated from it. Man, even though born in time, is nonetheless a creation of creation's beginning.[4]

Schelling's ideas concerning the intelligible existence of humanity outside of time, defined by an original evil deed, are similar to Kant's. Both, however, move us little beyond the mythologies of the Platonists. And those mythologies have going for them at least a temporal logic consistent with human experience. Recourse to occurrences outside of time, on the other hand, escapes the fanciful poetic scenarios but only by linguistic equivocation and dubious metaphysics. For in Schelling as in Kant, actual events attributable to individual souls transpire in a noumenal or atemporal realm, as is clear when Schelling turns not to originary freedom, but to originary evil. We are, as a consequence, little removed from Origen's conception, though it is shrouded in the language of German idealism and Boehmian mysticism:

> This common judgment of a tendency to do evil,…as being a free deed, points to an act and thus to a life before this life.…Therefore man, who here appears as fixed and determined, took on a specific form in first creation and is born as that which he is from eternity, since this primal act determined even the nature and condition of his corporealization.…As man acts here so he has acted since eternity and already in the beginning of creation.[5]

Schelling's argument relies in part upon something akin to mystical intuition, as a means of corroborating his account of the human soul. "Though this idea [of an existence that does not precede life but is outside and independent of life] may seem beyond the grasp of common ways of thought," he writes, "there is in every man a feeling which is in accord with it, as if each man felt that he had been what he is from all eternity, and had in no sense only come to be so in time."[6]

Several other Germans of this era made a defense of preexistence, but they lacked the stature and influence of Kant or Schelling. The most fully developed theory in this regard was probably that of Immanuel Hermann von Fichte (1797–1879). A figure of some standing in his own day, he was subsequently overshadowed by his more famous father and is best known today only as the editor of the latter's works. His philosophical focus was the personality of God, which he termed "concrete theism," and his principal writings were *Ethics* and *Anthropology*. In the latter work, he fully exploits the idealist emphasis on the suprasensible to develop a theory of soul as the eternal reality that precedes and underlies the self. Rather than seeing this preexistent soul (which he also calls a "form principle") as being subjected to incarnation as punishment or exile, in his view, the soul actually forms its own body through mechanisms or agencies, which Fichte leaves unexplained:

> That other entity, the outer manifestation of this form principle, [is] shaped by continuous metabolism: let us call it "corporality" from now on; it is truly not enduring and not whole; it is the mere effect or copy of that inner bodily nature that throws it into the changing world of matter in somewhat the same way a magnetic force puts together, out of metal filing dust, a seemingly dense body that is then blown away in all directions when the uniting force is withdrawn.[7]

This soul is, for Fichte, more than primal material out of which personhood is formed, and it is more than an animating principle. "The intellect, the ability to create ideas, that which forms a person, the principle of what gives him his distinct individuality is no product of the creative act.... His personality is that which existed before mortal life, that which distances itself from the influence of the parents." As for the origins of that soul, Fichte emphasizes the direct creation by God of individual spirits, which collectively come to constitute "a system, a world, a spiritual universe."[8]

With anthropologies such as these, German idealism slides into mystical religion even as its minor players slip into oblivion. For a time, however, the idea of preexistence finds fertile soil among theologians appreciative of philosophy's recent attention to the suprasensible and among American prophets and churchmen working under native inspiration and social impulses.

Theological Renewal

Wilhelm Benecke (1776–1837) came to religious studies late in life, after a prosperous career in business and having produced the standard work in the field of maritime commerce. Materially prosperous, tragedy intervened to rob him of both his wife and child. The agony of personal loss combined with the intellectual incomprehensibility of human suffering to plunge him into a spiritual crisis. It was at this point in his life that a mysterious mentor appeared, under whose tutelage he emerged from despair in a story that has the ring of legend. A man with "an apostolic appearance and bearing," whom Benecke by chance encountered, led him to "the fountain of all solace," in large measure by bringing him "to look upon this life as a short period placed between a former and a future existence." Benecke found that this doctrine "at once furnished him with a key for the solution of all his religious and philosophical doubts."[9] He kept his personal understanding of this sublime theodicy to himself, through years of exile from Hamburg during the Napoleonic Wars and during his wanderings abroad.

Returning eventually to Heidelberg, a seat of German philosophical and theological training, he took up religious studies and made the book of Romans his special focus. Paul Johnson has remarked:

> [N]o one has ever fully understood Romans. No one can remain undisturbed by it, either. It is the most thought-provoking of all the Christian documents. It has a habit of forcing men to reconsider their whole understanding of religion....It has been used again and again to demolish and reconstruct systems of theology.

He instances the upheavals it occasioned from Augustine and Luther through Schweitzer, Bultmann, and Barth.[10] Benecke seems in this regard to have been no exception. Distinguishing his approach, however, was a major difference: he believed that preexistence was an important key with which to tackle the theologically difficult epistle, and he produced in 1831 *An Exposition of St. Paul's Epistle to the Romans*.

Benecke's account of his conversion to the idea of preexistence by a man of "apostolic appearance" may leave us in some doubt as to the precise origins of his conception. In his introduction, he provides an apologia that may be an explanation of how he derived the notion, or it may be an after-the-fact rationalization. In either case, he adds new layers to the intellectual work the doctrine performs. The existence of God and a spiritual world, Benecke reasons, renders the idea of revelation necessary if there is to be any communion at all between the two realms, since our powers of reason and sensation are insufficient to penetrate beyond the visible world. What spiritual certainty we do attain cannot emerge in a vacuum; since such certainty outside the scope of operation of our own understanding finds "no analogies for it elsewhere," it must be the outgrowth of that which "we find ourselves endowed with on our entrance into the world, as a gift in the germ."[11] In other words, we somehow come to have a sense of certainty about certain suprasensible propositions that was not logically derived. If conviction about such truths takes root, or resonates, it can only be because like is responding to like. We must come already equipped, so to speak, with the language or background to make sense of these spiritual intimations. Preexistence, in this sense, represents the precondition for the very possibility of attaining spiritual knowledge in this life. It is not so much that spiritual intuitions are evidence of preexistent realms, as for the Romantics and Transcendentalists, but the other way around. Preexistence becomes the necessary premise for the validity of any spiritual intuitions we have in this life. It is the aspect of self and experience against which we can measure the reality of that which we experience suprasensually.

An admirer of Benecke's commentary, citing the surge in Pauline studies in the early 1850s, found it timely to have the work translated. It appeared in English in 1854, exactly in time to add to the fray over preexistence that Edward Beecher engendered a year earlier (though it was already being refuted by English speakers who could read the original German).[12] Even those opposed to its heterodoxies credited its author as "one of the finest theologians of our time" and the work as "one that has few peers among the more recent theological literature."[13] To a German theologian who protested certain of his "expositions," Benecke had replied in 1832 with a lengthy letter, which his publisher attached to the English edition of his commentary. The principal controversy centered on Benecke's reading of Romans 5:12, with its famous teaching that "sin came into the world through one man, and…death spread to all because all have sinned." The question is, in what sense are we to understand "all" to have sinned? This is the problem of the doctrine of original sin, for which this verse is generally considered foundational. Theological solutions to this dilemma have been enormously complex and varied, but we find two general types. They either strive to make humans participants in and thus co-agents with Adam, in order to salvage God's justice (as with Tertullian and Ambrose or, as we have seen, thinkers from Augustine to the animalculists). Or they deny that human categories of justice are applicable and simply affirm that Adam sinned and that all humans incur guilt and/or a sinful nature as a consequence. As theologian Charles Hodge insists uncompromisingly, "[T]here is a causal relation between the sin of Adam and the condemnation and sinfulness of his posterity. This contradicts the theory which refers the present sinfulness of men, not to the act of Adam, but to the voluntary act of each individual man."[14] (Significantly, Hodge uses this emphatic language in order expressly to refute preexistence. In so doing, he is acknowledging that, judged by a more rational standard of justice, preexistence does indeed offer a superior construct. But judgment on the basis of "voluntary acts" is *not* God's standard, he insists.)

Benecke sees a third way, which avoids recourse to a metaphysics of coparticipation and a wounded justice alike. His solution is to read the words "all have sinned" as a statement altogether distinct from the reference to Adam's sin and to take it at its plain meaning. "Sin came into the world through one man" refers to Adam in the Garden of Eden. "All have sinned," a grammatically distinct unit, refers to different agents in a different setting. The reading is clever and original, and it greatly simplifies the theological quandary but at a cost: preexistence slips back into the equation. "With reference to verses 12–14," he writes:

> I have to observe...that I am far from saying or thinking that in this passage, or in the Mosaic account of the Creation and the Fall, the Pre-existence is taught in express words. I only maintain that the Apostle's argument leads us quite naturally to assume it. "Death," says St. Paul, "is a consequence of sin, and *all* men are mortal, not because Adam sinned, but because *all* have sinned." But even from Adam to Moses, men who received no positive law, by transgressing which they might sin and become mortal, died notwithstanding, and must, therefore, have been sinners, since such only are mortal. Where, then, could they have transgressed a divine law, for they had none given them in their human existence? I put it to yourself and every unprejudiced thinker, whether, allowing the premises, any other answer can be given than that which I have drawn from them; namely, in an ante-human existence![15]

Benecke's reading of Romans attracted approving notice, but always with the qualification that his particular solution to the quandary of original sin was flawed. Such disapproval was notable primarily for revealing the recurrent tendency to dispatch the notion of preexistence upon grounds that are neither as compelling nor as logical as the disputant seems to believe. As one critic alleged:

> The interpretation of the passage [Rom. 5:12–21] proposed by Benecke needs but a brief notice, since it proves itself at once to be untenable. He supposes, with Origen, that every man has sinned by himself, not, however, in this world, but in a state of pre-existence. The Scripture, however, does not acknowledge any personal pre-existence, it teaches rather merely a pre-existent state of being in the Divine mind, since God beholds the future as the present.[16]

It is perhaps arguable that preexistence can at times be read as a form of divine foreknowledge. To say this is the plain meaning "taught" by the New Testament, or that such an interpretation in and of itself renders alternative readings "at once to be untenable" is of course not the case. In the very years that Benecke was working out his commentary on Romans, an American prophet was making waves far more disruptive to the religious world.

Joseph Smith

Adolf Harnack had suggested the theological threat that Greek-inspired preexistence or versions that posited the actual, independent existence of pre-mortal entities could pose to God's sovereignty. "The ennobling of created things by attributing to them a pre-existence is a secondary result," he insisted. "The primary idea is not to ennoble the creature, but to bring to light the wisdom and power of God."[17] It is clear that Harnack saw preexistence as originally arising in the Jewish past as a way to emphasize that God's omniscience and plenitude would entail not just the power to create at will at any future time, but the eternally present conception in his being of everything that ever could or would be created. If God is seen as the source of all things, not just in the sense that everything can trace its origins back to God, but in the sense that, being outside of time himself, all things exist in him in a simultaneous present, then any idea of matter or, a fortiori, intelligence or spirit coexisting eternally with him would threaten his sovereignty and divine preeminence as traditionally constructed. The fact that theories of preexistence and of theosis so often are mutually implicating and reinforcing adds to the theological instability they represent. Both of these theories are most explicitly developed in the case of Mormonism, with consequences that bear out the anxiety expressed by fathers and scholars from Tertullian to Harnack.

J. B. Turner summarized the heresy of Mormonism by derisively informing his reader, "Every Mormon is not only to be a god hereafter; he has, in his own belief, been a demigod from all eternity, or at least an angel heretofore....When you meet a full-blooded Mormon, you meet an angel that *was*, a Mormon that *is*, and a god that IS TO BE."[18] Turner was fairly unusual in making the views of the Latter-day Saints (LDS) of human origins and destiny the focus of his ridicule. Opponents generally found more than ample ammunition in Mormon conceptions of new scripture (the Book of Mormon), modern prophets (Joseph Smith), and the practice, already rumored in Turner's day, of plural marriage. Smith, a self-avowed prophet claiming divine authority for his calling, had presented his new scripture to the world in 1830, the same year he organized the new church in upstate New York, claiming it to be the restoration of the gospel and the gathering of modern-day Israel foretold in scripture. By 1833, the congregating of thousands of new converts at gathering sites in Ohio and, more especially, in Missouri was alarming old settlers, and Mormon talk of inheriting the land around there as God's chosen people, their missionary efforts among Native Americans, and their espousal of new revelations and charismatic gifts led to violence and the first of a series of expulsions that culminated in Smith's murder in 1844 and the migration of the Latter-day Saints to Utah a few years later.

Smith made a career of promulgating ideas that were outrageous affronts to Christian orthodoxies—and his radical critique of conventional notions of God's sovereignty like the one defended by Harnack was no exception. His heterodoxy included a throwback to the disputed creation *ex materia* of Justin Martyr and other fathers. Smith insisted toward the end of his life:

[Creation] does not mean to create out of nothing; it means to organize; the same as a man would organize materials and build a ship. Hence we infer that God had materials to organize the world out of chaos—chaotic matter, which is element, and in which dwells all the glory. Element had an existence from the time He had. The pure principles of element are principles which can never be destroyed; they may be organized and re-organized, but not destroyed. They had no beginning and can have no end.

If such language sounds like the extension of divine attributes to brute matter itself, the implicit destruction of God's monopoly on eternal existence is something Smith goes on to make perfectly explicit. "We say that God Himself is a self-existent God. Who told you so? It's correct enough, but how did it get into your heads? Who told you that man did not exist in like manner upon the same principle?...Intelligence is eternal and exists upon a self-existent principle."[19] Smith had first broached this topic years earlier, and when he did, the doctrine appeared, as it were, out of nowhere.[20]

Smith's major monument to his professed powers of revelation and translation was the Book of Mormon, a history of pre-Christian colonizers of the New World, the primary group of which descended from Israelites. The book gave his followers their appellation (first "Mormonites," then the more durable designation "Mormons") and has served for almost two centuries as the principal exhibit in the case both for and against Smith's prophetic claims. The Book of Mormon, however, while involving fantastic claims of Israelite civilizations in the Americas, gold plates, and angels, is relatively conventional in its Christian theology. Radical doctrinal innovation came gradually.

Months after producing the Book of Mormon, Smith was at work on what he termed a re-translation of the Bible, though it was more a redaction with corrections and interpolations. In what would be published later as the Book of Moses, he intimated a spiritual creation of humans that antedated the physical creation. "I made the world, and men before they were in the flesh," he had God say to Adam.[21] Given the problem of reconciling the creation of Adam recounted in Genesis 1 with the statement in Genesis 2 that there was not yet a man to till the ground (v. 5), some commentators had long seen the former narrative as an ideal creation, or a creation in the mind of God only. Smith may have seen his interpolation in just such a light. However, three years later, Smith suddenly and unceremoniously revealed a more emphatic affirmation of human preexistence, sandwiched almost surreptitiously in between a promise of theophany to all earnest seekers and a series of personal admonitions directed toward a handful of followers. Unlike most of the thinkers we have examined, Smith's theory of preexistence as a divinely revealed principle neither proceeded from a reasoned attempt at theodicy or inquiry into the soul's origin, nor was it followed by an apologia for its logical or theological merits. Only the slightest claim for its philosophical solidity is implied in this revelation, pronounced in 1833: "Man was also in the beginning with God. Intelligence, or the light of truth, was not created or made, neither indeed can be." And then a kind of subsequent gloss: "All truth is independent in that sphere in which God has placed it, to act for itself, as all intelligence also; otherwise there is no existence. Behold, here is the agency of man."[22]

What appears here as almost cryptic philosophical brevity with hermetic undertones is rendered more familiar when viewed in the context of contemporary discussions that likewise brought into dialogue notions of autonomy, agency, and preexistence. Theologian Julius Müller, as we will see, influenced by the German idealists, predicated God's eternal nature on his embodiment of absolute freedom; more striking, in connection with Smith's formulation, is Müller's claim that "Personal Beings alone have the source of their existence in free self-determination." He quotes Schelling as writing that "every thing actual, even nature, has its source in activity, life, and freedom," but "Personal beings alone have one ground of their existence in *their own act*" (emphasis in original).[23] Plato, of course, had similarly defined the soul as "motion capable of moving itself."[24]

In 1835, Smith claimed another burst of inspired revelation and produced writings attributed to the biblical patriarch Abraham. The first chapter begins as a more ample retelling of the story of Abraham's flight from Ur to Canaan, briefly sketched in Genesis 1:31–12:4. By the third chapter, however, we are far removed from the Old Testament stories that are the familiar stuff of Sunday school— but not at all removed from some of the Canaanite traditions and divine councils we have seen. In this account, Abraham, possessed of a Urim and Thummim, an ancient oracle associated with seership and mentioned in the Bible, receives a panoramic vision of occult cosmology. His visionary journey takes him through space, near the very abode of God, and through time, back into heavenly assemblies that antedate the world's creation. Here, for the first time, we see an unambiguous Mormon doctrine of fully individuated, pre-mortal humans:

> Now the Lord had shown unto me, Abraham, the intelligences that were organized before the world was; and among all these there were many of the great and noble ones. And God saw these souls that they were good, and he stood in the midst of them, and he said: These I will make my rulers, for he stood among those that were spirits, and he saw that they were good; and he said unto me: Abraham, thou art one of them; thou wast chosen before thou wast born.[25]

Several striking affinities with Semitic traditions are immediately apparent. The council scene in particular is consistent with a standard motif in Mesopotamian and Ugaritic literature, wherein a divine assembly convenes to consider a problem and a series of proposals is offered, often with the one making the proposal demanding all power and glory (as Marduk demands in the Babylonian creation narrative *Enuma Elish*).[26] In the present instance, God stands surrounded by a number of exalted figures, who are referred to as "rulers," as in the Gnostic texts we discussed above. (It is significant that Smith recasts the first verse of Genesis as "the Head God brought forth the Head Gods in the grand, head council.")[27] As was the case with the Mesopotamian texts, the council discusses the creation of a human world ("we will make an earth whereon these may dwell").[28] As in the accounts of Kings and Isaiah, God consults members of the assembly. Here, too, he asks, "Whom shall I send?" (compare "Who will [go]?" [1 Kings 22:20] and "Whom shall I send?" [Isa. 6:8]). Further similarities with antecedents only heighten the family resemblance. The challenge of a Marduk or the schism among the gods described in Nag Hammadi texts are paralleled in Smith's account by a pre-mortal Lucifer attempting to supplant God ("give me thine honor," he demands). Rebuffed, he departs in fury, creating a schism in the heavens ("the second was angry, and...many followed after him").[29] As later developed in Mormonism, this pre-mortal rupture in heaven's harmony becomes the war in heaven described in John's revelation. The role of pre-mortal humans in the conflict is explicit but reverses the fate of those depicted in the poem by Milton's imitator seen above: in Smith's epic account, the righteous partisans of Christ earn the reward of mortal embodiment and progression; those in league with Satan become the fallen angels doomed to nonphysicality.[30] Finally, when the creation of the world ensues in the next scene, the text produced by this New York farmer unabashedly refers to "the gods," who proceed to organize the earth out of preexistent materials.

Smith appears to be one of the few Christian thinkers to develop notions of preexistence that do not derive from or rely upon the standard Platonic precedents. The figure of Abraham, the term "intelligence" (which Smith never clearly defined),[31] and the divinatory method by which Smith produced the text suggest why scholars like John L. Brooke would see hermetic antecedents and "striking parallels between the Mormon concepts" and "the philosophical traditions of alchemy and Hermeticism, drawn from the ancient world and fused with Christianity in the Italian Renaissance."[32] Literary critic Harold Bloom has also noted the striking parallels between these writings of Smith and ancient Jewish mystical texts (especially the Kabbalistic writings), saying, "I can only attribute to his genius or daemon his uncanny recovery of elements in ancient Jewish theurgy."[33] "What is clear," Bloom continues, "is that Smith and his apostles restated what Moshe Idel, our great living scholar of Kabbalah, persuades me was the archaic or original Jewish religion."[34]

Smith did not publish his account until 1842 and then only in the Mormon newspaper *Times and Seasons* in serial form. In 1844, only weeks before his death,

Smith returned to some of these themes in the most radical sermon of his career, referred to since as the King Follett Discourse.[35] On that occasion, he remarked that he desired "to reason more on the spirit of man" and asserted that "intelligence is eternal and exists upon a self-existent principle. It is a spirit from age to age and there is no creation about it." That little indefinite article "a" before spirit is a crucial and contested item, for the question not clearly resolved in Smith's spiritual anthropology has to do with the relationship between the terms intelligence and spirit. One of the most influential LDS intellectuals, B. H. Roberts, held on the basis of that indefinite article that the two terms were synonymous; God did not fashion or beget "intelligence" into individual spirits.[36] Supporting this view is the fact that, from the Middle Ages through Shakespeare and Milton and into the nineteenth century, "intelligence" had the meaning of an incorporeal or spirit being. But such a view has not been persuasive to subsequent Mormon leaders, who understand Smith to have believed that God fashioned the eternal substance called intelligence into individual spirits, at which point they acquired the essential nature that still constitutes their core identity. It is in this sense that respected LDS theologian James Talmage called the human spirit "an organized intelligence,"[37] and that God can be referred to by Mormon thinkers like Orson Whitney as "the Begetter of [the human] spirit in the eternal worlds."[38] Mormon apostle Bruce R. McConkie, who wrote influentially on LDS doctrine but not with official sanction, declared that "we were born as the spirit children of God the Father. Through that birth process spirit element was organized into intelligent entities."[39] This would be a process that is essentially parallel to the one described by Evagrius Ponticus, who, as we saw, believed that humankind began as intelligences in the presence of God and then developed, or developed into, souls on their path into mortality. Certainly, Smith's claim that spirit, or intelligence, has existed eternally, rather than just pre-mortally, is unusual but not unique in the history of the idea of preexistence. George Rust also considered it likely that the soul existed "eternally *backward* as well as *forward*," and Anne Conway similarly held that human spirits "have existed for an infinite time."

Some overlap with Gnostic, Origenist, and Platonic formulations notwithstanding, the Mormon doctrine of preexistence is, in many regards, unique. Its origin certainly is, insofar as, unlike virtually all other versions, it did not arise out of Smith's engagement with any particular moral, theological, or philosophical dilemma. In that regard, it is as if Mormonism propounds the solution but isn't sure what the question is. (Ironically, Mormons reject the concept of original sin, thus eliminating what has historically been a primary impetus to the development of a doctrine of preexistence.) One feature of LDS preexistence not found elsewhere is a conception of familial organization that precedes mortality. Though largely unofficial folklore, the belief finds possible support in a dream vision attributed to Brigham Young. In his reverie, he visited the prophet Joseph Smith, who told him:

"Be sure to tell the people to keep the Spirit of the Lord; and if they will, they will find themselves just as they were organized by our Father in heaven, before they came into the world. Our Father in heaven organized the human family, but they are all disorganized and in great confusion." Joseph then showed me the pattern, how they were in the beginning. This I cannot describe.[40]

Another peculiarity of the LDS doctrine of pre-mortality is the insistence that, while spirit is not physical, it is material. "All spirit is matter, but it is more fine or pure, and can only be discerned by purer eyes," wrote Joseph Smith.[41] Glanvill used similar language in asking why it would be illogical to conceive of preexistent spirits as being in a "purer state of Life,…joyn'd only to such a refined body, which should have been suitable to its own perfection and purity."[42] His mentor Henry More had earlier been more emphatic in arguing, against Descartes, that if spirit were not extended, if it could not be located in space, then it could not exist. Exactly what purpose is served by sheathing a pure form of matter in an impure form is never explained in Mormon doctrine. And the criticism that Anne Conway leveled against More's conception seems pertinent to Mormonism as well:

But if they allege that body and spirit agree in certain attributes, such as extension, motion, and shape, with the result that spirit has extension and is able to reach from one place to another, and also change itself into whatever shape it pleases, in such cases it agrees with the body and the body with it.[43]

Why is the whole scheme, in other words, not redundant?

Doctrinally, the LDS teaching on preexistence was probably more significant for its implications about human potential than for its unique version of the spirit's ontology. As B. H. Roberts wrote in tones that surely flirt with the Pelagian heresy:

This doctrine [of preexistence] throws a wonderful light upon the being and nature of man. Notwithstanding the great influence of parentage and environment upon character, in the light of this doctrine, we may understand how it is that in spite of indifferent parentage and vicious environment some characters arise that are truly virtuous and great; and that purely by the strength of that intelligence and nobility to which their spirits had attained in the heavenly kingdom before they took bodies upon earth. Their grandeur of soul could not all be suppressed by environment in this life, however inauspicious for their development. As the sun struggles through clouds and mists that at times obscure his brightness, so these spirits, stirred by their innate nobility, breaking through all disadvantages attendant upon ignoble birth and iron fortune, rise to their native heights of true greatness.[44]

By positing a spirit so far removed in time and space from this world of sin and vice, humanity's core identity is emphatically constructed as inherently good. In polar opposition to traducianism, which sees spirit and body alike as conceived in and bearing the full heritage of a primeval sin, Smith uses the preexistence of the soul to emphasize the fact that "every spirit of man was innocent in the beginning."[45] Neither is incarnation a punishment for a pre-mortal fall, as it was for the Gnostics and Origen. On the contrary, those privileged to enter the world of mortality do so precisely because they successfully "kept their first estate" and are promised that, if they triumph in the second phase of their eternal development, then "they who keep their second estate shall have glory added upon their heads for ever and ever."[46] (The language evokes the epistle of Jude, with its reference to "the angels which kept not their first estate" and were cast down [1:6 KJV] as well as the language of Origen.)[47] In other words, the doctrine functions in Mormon thought as a powerful version of theodicy. Again, Roberts writes:

> If a wider survey be taken of mankind, and those advantages and disad-
> vantages under which whole generations, nations and races of men have
> lived be taken into account; if the fact of their pre-existence be considered
> in connection with that other fact that the spirits of men before coming to
> this earth were of unequal intelligence and of every degree of nobility; if
> it be remembered that in the pre-existent state all spirits had free agency,
> and that they there manifested all degrees of fidelity to truth and righ-
> teousness, from those were valiant for the right to those who were utterly
> untrue to it, and rebelled against God; if it be further remembered that
> doubtless in this earth-life these spirits are rewarded for their faithfulness
> and diligence in that pre-existent state—if all this, I say, be considered,
> much that has perplexed many noble minds in their effort to reconcile
> the varied circumstances under which men have lived with the justice and
> mercy of God, will disappear.[48]

Also implied by this history of the soul is the human proximity to divinity, which has alarmed guardians of orthodoxy throughout ecclesiastical history. A per-haps infelicitous word choice by Smith pointedly reveals the danger here. In that same King Follett sermon, he boldly asserts, "The mind of man—the intelligent part—is as immortal as, and coequal with, God Himself. I know that my testimony is true."[49] Subsequent editors have inserted "coeternal" for "coequal," as if the term were mistranscribed in the original or as if correcting for a nineteenth-century usage whose meaning was different or prone to misunderstanding. And indeed, the latter is probably the case. Etymologically speaking, as the *Oxford English Diction-ary* reveals, the Latin origin of "coequal" means literally "of equal age, companion in age." And going back to the seventeenth century, the term unambiguously meant "of the same age, coeval." Still, the historical slippage in meaning from "equally old" to "fully equal" dramatically validates the concerns traceable to the Christian fathers, that a conception of preexistent souls tends—perhaps inexorably—toward a blasphemous collapse of sacred distance between the human and the divine. And indeed, that collapse is explicitly rendered as a righteous aspiration in the culmination of Smith's sermon, wherein he urges his followers:

> You have got to learn how to make yourselves Gods in order to save yourselves and be kings and priests to God, the same as all Gods have done—by going from a small capacity to a great capacity, from a small degree to another, from grace to grace, until the resurrection *of the dead*, from exaltation to exaltation—till you are able to sit in everlasting burnings and everlasting power and glory as those who have gone before, sit enthroned.[50]

Though the King Follett Discourse was never canonized, this doctrine of theosis effectively was—by an LDS First Presidency pronouncement in 1925: "Man is the child of God, formed in the divine image and endowed with divine attributes, and even as the infant son of an earthly father and mother is capable in due time of becoming a man, so that undeveloped offspring of celestial parentage is capable, by experience through ages and aeons, of evolving into a God."[51]

Edward Beecher

In 1827, the same year that a young Joseph Smith began translating what he said were gold plates delivered to him by an angel, a similarly young countryman was receiving visions of another sort. Edward Beecher (1803–1895) was born into one of America's most reform-minded and theologically blue-blooded families: the son of Lyman Beecher, one of the major figures of the second Great Awakening, and the brother of the flamboyant preacher Henry Ward Beecher, the novelist Harriet Beecher Stowe, and the suffragist Isabella Beecher Hooker. Edward was an ordained minister, a Christian essayist and editor, and a cofounder, along with the soon-to-be-murdered Elijah Lovejoy, of the Illinois Antislavery Society. Though he was eclipsed in history by more celebrated family members, Stowe's biographers would insist that, great as were Lyman Beecher's intellectual powers, "he was no match" for Edward who, along with Harriet, was "a metaphysical Titan."[52]

Edward Beecher's life was consumed by a spiritual odyssey that was in part highly personal, in part a battle waged on behalf of his sister Catherine, and in part a missionary's zeal to solve the "great controversy" of his day. As his brother noted of him, Beecher's "struggle of the imprisoned spirit for reunion to its primeval source" was "agonizing."[53] Here already are the intimations of the resolution Beecher would

Edward Beecher

Scion of the most famous family in America, theologian Edward Beecher wrote the most extensive and widely read defense of preexistence in the concept's history.
19th century, Courtesy Harriet Beecher Stowe Center, Hartford, Connecticut.

find. To call God the source of the spirit is not necessarily to subscribe to the view of a pre-mortal state in his presence. Most Christians would assent to God as humanity's source, but in the sense of Creator, not original abode, finding "reunion" to be more metaphorical than literal. However, Beecher's quest for spiritual communion, which was launched by a family tragedy, would culminate well beyond metaphor.

His sister Catherine lost her unbelieving fiancé at sea in 1822, and the misfortune precipitated—or revealed—a deficiency in her own faith. The problem, she confided to Beecher, "originates in my views of the doctrine of original sin." The damnation of the unbeliever, her own ambiguous feelings of guilt, questions about blame and accountability and a merciful God—all threw her into spiritual turmoil. "Is there any satisfactory mode of explaining this doctrine?" she asked. According to Edward's biographer, her challenge became his lifelong quest.[54] His arduous spiritual formation took place against the backdrop of a collision between his father's impassioned defense of religious orthodoxy with its harsh Edwardsean Calvinism and the intellectual attractions of liberal progressivism and enlightened ideas about social justice.

By 1826, he had graduated from Yale as valedictorian; served as the headmaster at the Hartford Academy; led revival work with his famous father in Litchfield, Connecticut; briefly attended Andover Theological Seminary; taught divinity students as a tutor at Yale; and at the ripe age of twenty-two, had begun his first year as a pastor at Boston's prestigious Park Street Church. In the next months, the conflict prompted by his own deeply felt conversion experience and his intellectual revulsion at Christian orthodoxy heated up. His biographer/brother recorded his wrestling with God:

> Pain, sickness, and death come on the human race antecedent to the development of reason. Such a constitution resembles punishment applied in anticipation of a crime.... [Calling total depravity] voluntary seems like removing a difficulty by language only. In short, original, native, entire depravity is a hard doctrine to be explained.... The question is, is not the present system a malevolent one?...Evil exists. If it does prove malevolence in God we are lost, or else must love a partial being. We cannot analyze the thing.[55]

For centuries, Christian characterization of the human predicament had been essentially the same as Beecher's, but its acceptance was more blithe and unproblematic. As Augustine had put the case with curious logic and no hint of protest, "if another soul, not merely before it sins but at the very outset of its life, is placed under a punishment...it has a great good for which to thank its Creator, for the merest beginning of a soul is better than the most perfect material object."[56] He considered any complaint on the subject "slanderous"; some ask, he wrote, "if it was Adam and Eve who sinned, what did we poor wretches do? How do we deserve to be born in blindness of ignorance and the torture of difficulty?...My response is brief: let them be silent and stop murmuring."[57]

Beecher was in many ways typical of the progressive-minded intellectuals of the nineteenth century, who were no longer content to suffer in silence. In an age zealous for reform and proud of its enlightened sensibilities, he could no longer live with the cognitive dissonance, or what he called the all-too-obvious facts of human depravity and suffering coming into collision with fundamental notions of moral justice. But unlike the apostates entirely willing to forsake the religion of their youth and celebrate "God's funeral," to use Thomas Hardy's phrase, Beecher continued to seek a resolution. And when he found it, it came as a "virtual revelation"; after his figurative "groping in some vast cathedral, in the gloom of midnight, vainly striving to comprehend its parts and relations,...suddenly before the vast arched window of the nave a glorious sun had suddenly burst forth."[58] The resultant vision was a paradigm-shattering epiphany that Beecher wanted to share at once with his congregation and the world, but his cautious father urged restraint and so did friends.[59] Beecher kept the revelation to himself—for a quarter century. Then, he threw caution to the wind and issued a 400-page manifesto, the boldest and most detailed exposition of the doctrine of preexistence in religious history.

Beecher called his work *The Conflict of Ages; or, The Great Debate on the Moral Relations of God and Man.* The conflict to which Beecher referred was a schism that he felt had riven Christianity from its earliest days, causing "paralysis and division" for all of its subsequent history. "On the one side," he wrote, "have been the advocates of that system the peculiar characteristic of which is the doctrine of a supernatural regeneration rendered necessary by the native and original depravity of man." He traces this tradition to Paul's epistle to the Romans and associates it with Augustine, Calvin, and Puritan theology. On the other side, "in all ages, ever since the days of Celestius, Julian and Pelagius, there have been, in large numbers, men highly estimable for intelligence and benevolence...who have...opposed this system, as at war with the fundamental principles of honor and right."[60]

Beecher's invocation of Caelestius, Julian, and Pelagius, of course, is not exactly an appeal to orthodoxy, and on the face of it, the debate as he characterizes it hardly seems either balanced or of doubtful outcome. As a matter of history, the teachings of Pelagius and his disciple Caelestius were condemned as heretical by Emperor Honorius in 419. Julian was a bishop of Eclanum who embraced their cause. Principal among their heresies was their refusal to countenance the doctrine of original sin and humans' inheritance of either Adam's guilt or a reprobate nature. They also emphasized humankind's free will and inherent capacity voluntarily to turn to God without prevenient grace.

Beecher's point and the moral appeal of his argument are that, on the one hand, it is true that the institutional church definitively enshrined as religious dogma humanity's inherent guilt, sinfulness, and incapacity to move toward God independently of God's grace, severely restricting human agency. In that sense, the issue was officially decided. But in a more important sense, the question had obviously never been settled to general satisfaction. The history of Christianity has been a history of prolonged debates on free will and predestination, on the scope of salvation and the eventual fate of the reprobate, on reconciling God's justice with human dignity and personal accountability. The problem is given greater urgency by the spirit of Beecher's age; in an era consumed by progressive ideals and liberalism, manifest in a range of reform movements from the abolition of slavery to women's rights to penal reform, the theme of justice reverberates throughout and is a principal source of orthodoxy's fading appeal.

Beecher's radical take on the Great Conflict is that almost two millennia of efforts to reconcile faith and fairness, dogma and intellect, have failed. "To make new-created beings...with a preponderance toward evil, would be highly unjust and dishonorable in God," Beecher writes, and no sophistry or good intent has gotten around that intractable affront to reason and sensibility. And yet, the case is equally certain that the history of humanity reveals an unambiguous propensity for evil, i.e., a real depravity of nature. In other words, "the human race has come into a fallen and ruined state, even before action." And yet, as the prominent seventeenth-century Calvinist theologian Francis Turretin acknowledged, if there was in Adam "any inclination to sin by nature, then God would be the author of it, and so the sin itself chargeable upon God." How could the same not be true if propensity to sin is imputed to the human family as a whole? Beecher asks. Yet the penalty is imposed upon the entire human race. "Its infliction," protests Beecher, "is antecedent" to any violation of any law, insofar as "Men *begin to exist* out of communion with God."[61]

No "sophistry" can escape this contradiction, which plays out in both the Bible and human history. French philosopher Blaise Pascal (1623–1662) thought nothing could be "more contrary to the rules of *our wretched justice* than to damn eternally an infant, incapable of volition, for an offense…which was committed six thousand years before he was born," yet he embraced "this mystery,—the most incomprehensible of all." Theologian Peter Abelard (1079–1142), like countless others, agreed that the very behavior in which God freely indulged, treating his creatures "in whatever way God may wish to," would be "deemed the summit of injustice among men." All such attempts to make sense of these incontrovertibles are doomed to perpetual failure, Beecher argues, not because they are mysteries, but for the simple reason that a crucial piece of the puzzle has been lacking. To fashion "a firm and decided defense of the whole Christian system, it is essential that we no longer confine the mind to those limited views" circumscribed by orthodox belief but range into "other and more extended fields of thought."[62]

The extended fields Beecher has in mind he at last reveals. On the basis not of the personal vision he experienced two decades earlier, or what he refers to as "a direct and specific divine revelation in language," but relying rather upon a rational appraisal of the Christian system and its deficiencies, he proposes Christianity's error in its simplest terms: the fallacy "that men as they come into this world are new-created beings." The fate of this assumption, he writes hopefully, may parallel that of the earth-centered universe. With such an analogy, he both invokes the precedent of long-standing church-sponsored error and, like the philosopher Kant a century earlier, compares the paradigm shift he hopes to effect to a Copernican revolution. This revolution, which he modestly calls "the readjustment," entails the most fully detailed exposition and defense of the doctrine of preexistence of which we have record.[63]

The essential features of his theory were succinctly and fairly summarized by a critic who nevertheless admired the "strong and humane heart" behind it:

> God, in the beginning, created a race of spiritual beings. These he constituted free-agents, and dealt by them, in all things, justly and honorably. He gave them a nature essentially good, with well-balanced minds, and

constitutional faculties, tending powerfully to obedience and holiness. Every thing was favorable to their continued virtue and enjoyment. There were no devils in existence to lead them astray; no evil influences of any great magnitude to act upon them; no temptations which they were not easily able to resist and conquer....In this primal state of affairs, myriads of the race sinned and fell, and lost all just claims on God, forfeited their rights to his kind regard, and fell under his wrath and curse. Still, the Divine Being was inclined to mercy, and of His own sovereign will he fashioned this world as a *vast moral hospital*, in which he graciously allowed these fallen and guilty wretches their present state of probation, and gave them mortal bodies corresponding to their material condition....On this state of being, therefore, these fallen spirits enter, having brought all the elements of their present depravity along with them from this previous state.[64]

The merits of this theological readjustment are many, according to Beecher:

If, in a previous state of existence, God created all men with such constitutions, and placed them in such circumstances, as the laws of honor and of right demanded,—if, then, they revolted and corrupted themselves, and forfeited their rights,...then all conflict of the moving powers of Christianity can be at once and entirely removed.

Or, as he puts the case more succinctly, "by supposing the pre-existent sin and fall of man, the most radical views of human depravity can be harmonized with the highest views of the justice of God."[65]

Beecher's proposal not only relieves God of the charge of injustice (as premortal entities, we willfully engaged in "a course of sinning"), but it explains the human propensity toward evil and carnality (prior actions of the fallen spirits "leave in their minds that predisposition to sin which we...designate by the name sinful habit"). It has the additional merit of escaping Christianity's "constant and powerful tendency...to degrade the nature of free agency itself." Additionally, it provides a more morally appealing conception "of the original constitutions of all new-created beings, and of God's sincere good-will toward them, and sympathetic treatment of them," and, finally, "it presents the scriptural doctrine concerning a kingdom of fallen spirits in a light much more rational, intelligible, and impressive."[66]

Rational, intelligible, and impressive, his theory might have been. Still, Beecher did not underestimate the public's unwillingness to embrace his readjustment. "I am well aware," he writes, "that there is, in many most excellent persons, a disposition to revolt from this view," but he insists that historical prejudice rather than rational consideration is the cause. He then launches into an impassioned warning that unwillingness to recuperate this ancient truth amounts to complicity with a spiritual conspiracy against one of Christianity's most precious though untenable doctrines:

> If there is in fact a malignant spirit, of great and all-pervading power, intent on making a fixed and steady opposition to the progress of the cause of God,—and, if he well knows that there is one truth of relations so manifold, important and sublime, that on it depends, in great measure, the highest and most triumphant energy of the system of Christianity,— then beyond all doubt, he would...pervert and disgrace it. He would present it in false and odious combinations....He would fill the church and the ministry with a prejudgment against it,...so profound as to make its falsehood a foregone conclusion.[67]

Turning abruptly from supernaturalism to science, Beecher finds in the antiquity of the earth itself not the challenge to biblical literalism that so distressed his contemporary John Ruskin ("If only the Geologists would let me alone I could do very well, but those dreadful hammers! I hear the clink of them at the end of every cadence of the Bible verses!" Ruskin had lamented just two years earlier.)[68] Rather, Beecher finds the prehistoric eons of the earth's existence to be evidence presumptive that other kingdoms were then being built. "Are we to suppose that in all of these past ages there were no intelligent beings in existence?...The existence of some of the angels from the beginning of the creation, and the creation of other intelligent spirits from that time onward, in other parts of the Creator's kingdom,...are in the highest degree reasonable and probable."[69]

In spite of Beecher's enthusiasm for the basic doctrine he promulgates, he acknowledges that the theory is not brimming with detail: "I do not mean that we can historically retrace and set forth the actual course of events in God's dealings with new-created beings." But it resolves the fundamental problem of theodicy, even as it endows life with new significance. "It discloses the true end of this world as a moral hospital, a moral hospital of the universe, [containing] the diseased of past ages, the fallen of all preceding generations of creatures...and makes life, from beginning to end, a constant system of education for eternity."[70]

Beecher's book landed like a bombshell in the theological world of midcentury America. His was not the first attempt to introduce the doctrine into nineteenth-century orthodoxy, and Beecher might have learned from other recent forays. Belated outrage erupted in the Presbyterian *Christian Observer* in 1840 when readers learned that their own Dr. Ashbel Green (1762–1848), a minister and past president of Princeton University, had propounded in an 1825 issue of the *Christian Advocate*, which he published, a defense of preexistence. "The safest and MOST RATIONAL" version of the soul's origin, he had argued, is "to suppose that ALL souls were created at the beginning of the world; that they remain in a *quiescent* state *till* the bodies which they are to inhabit are formed."[71] "We know not whether to smile or frown," minister and author George Duffield had responded in print in 1832. The editor of the *Observer* was less restrained: this is a "monstrous hypothesis," he remarked. "Most monstrous speculation, unscriptural, anti-scriptural, and absurd," fumed a reader.[72]

Still, the response engendered by Beecher's publication was greater by several magnitudes. Almost twenty years after its publication, controversy still raged, with one journal noting in 1870 that "the amount of material already printed, in the form of reviews, criticisms, replies, &c., would form several volumes of the size of the book itself. Its publication must constitute an era in the world's thought."[73] Another reviewer was equally effusive in describing the book's impact:

> Dr. Beecher's "Conflict of Ages" has been honored with a remarkable degree of attention. It has been reviewed and re-reviewed in Newspapers, Magazine Articles, Courses of Lectures, and in book-form. It has furnished a good deal of employment, and given rise to quite a little body of literature. It seems to have come down on pulpit and religious press like rain upon mown grass, as showers that water the earth in time of drought. The crop has been abundant.[74]

"The problem proposed for discussion," agreed the *Baptist Christian Review*, "is the most difficult and momentous that can engage the human mind."[75] Most telling of all, perhaps, was the opinion of the prominent Washington antislavery paper the *National Era*, which announced:

> *The Conflict of Ages!* An impression has already been produced by this masterly treatise, the most profound, wide reaching, and permanent. It is perfectly manifest to all competent observers, that we are upon the eve of a theological discussion, the most comprehensive, radical, and portentous, the world has ever seen. To this discussion this book leads the way, with a momentum irresistible....It contains the seeds of the thinkings and debatings of the next hundred years. The work has caused a great commotion among the D.D.'s in our land. It merits their attention. It has reached its *fifth* edition in the brief space of *three months*! A success unprecedented in Theological Publications![76]

"All those who have Theological doubts and difficulties should examine the solution this work affords," the paper earnestly suggested. Other contemporaries were just as enthusiastic. "This book gives to orthodoxy the severest blow it ever had," wrote the influential Universalist editor Thomas Whitmore in the *Trumpet*.[77] Beecher seems not to have misrepresented the case when he claimed, seven stormy years after publication, that "no defense has been made against my argument, but both the New York *Evangelist* and the *Congregationalist* virtually concede its correctness." Not that objections weren't raised, but they did not amount to rebuttal. "A dream," "inconclusive," "no proof" were the gist of typical responses.[78] Half a century later, his less-than-objective descendants could casually refer to his book as "so influential in determining the current of religious thought in America."[79] Even allowing for some rhetorical excess (and family bias), the quantity of similar pronouncements on the book's impact and notoriety suggests that we are dealing here with a major disruptive episode in American theological debate, which has silently passed out of historical consciousness. Theologians and public figures including Hosea Ballou, Moses Ballou, David N. Lord, Sylvanus Cobb, George Ellis, Henry Weller, Leonard Bacon, E. A. Park, Charles Hodge, Thomas Starr King, Henry James the elder, Oliver Wendell Holmes, James Freeman Clarke, and Ralph Waldo Emerson all took note.[80]

Beecher's book was not the idiosyncratic speculations of an eccentric at the theological margins, but the product of a mind at the heart of New England's intellectual religious culture. The philosophical precursors we have already reviewed appear to have laid an intellectual groundwork; the Unitarian flowering in his lifetime attests to the appeal of a more humanistic and innovative theology; and the effusive and prolonged critical response confirms its widespread impact. The seriousness with which Beecher's thesis was taken is also evident in the fact that not just a slew of long articles, but even books were issued by way of rejoinder. Moses Ballou responded as God's self-appointed champion, with *The Divine Character Vindicated: A Review of Some of the Principal Features of the Rev. Dr. E. Beecher's Recent Work*. Like virtually all of the other reviewers, Ballou was respectful of Beecher as "one who deservedly stands high in the ranks of New England orthodoxy." Beecher's effort, he acknowledged, was theologically informed, full of "candor and manliness," and "vital, fervid, and genial" in its expression. Also like so many reviewers, Ballou fully agreed that the theological conflict that Beecher undertook to resolve, between the human condition and principles of honor and right, was "the most momentous and important of any ever opened to the human mind, and its "oppressive moral problems…have hung like an incubus upon the church for centuries."[81] The desperation of Beecher's proposal, all seemed to agree, was hardly blameworthy in the face of what all agreed was a religious crisis in the West, compounded of what Ballou called "the present tide of atheistic speculation" and "religious indifference," precipitated in no small measure by the growing unease with Reformed theology in an age of liberal progressivism. The gravity of the crisis was typified by what Ballou saw as two proffered solutions: the repudiation of human depravity by the formidable William Ellery Channing, the foremost Unitarian preacher of the century, or the denial of eternal punishment by other liberals, like Randolph Foster.

Ballou's own prodigious response—itself a volume of over 400 pages—was commensurate with the effect he judged Beecher's defense of preexistence would have and was already having. The prestige of Beecher, his book's "adoption of an entire new ground of defense," its promise "to harmonize the conflicting doctrines" of evangelical religion, plus "the extravagance of the theory" brought to bear—all assured that Beecher's book was winning "a very general hearing" and commanding "a greater influence than almost any kindred publication of modern times." Ballou feared that it had "an attraction not found in similar works" and would continue to be "sought for and read by thousands."[82]

Ballou's book, of course, engendered its own reviews, one of which seemed rather more concerned about the force of Beecher's argument than it wished to let on. Like the Baptist reviewer, this one also acknowledged that Beecher "as well as others" found the problem of human suffering and God's justice to be a "painful conflict." But Beecher's proposed solution, this editorialist for the *Universalist Quarterly and General Review* insisted, was "so destitute of direct support, and so incredible in itself" that it "did not greatly need to be refuted at all." And he may have been right in arguing:

> [A]s respects any danger of its being generally accepted, there could be no urgent call for its refutation. Be it by the instigation of the Devil, as the Dr. appears to suppose, or be it by the force of common sense, as we are inclined to suppose, one thing is almost certain, namely, that people will not believe themselves to be ancient spirits, newly born into this world, from a pre-existent state of which they have no trace of remembrance nor hint of Revelation,—they will not believe all this, merely for the sake of clearing any theological system of its moral offences. They will sooner give up the system.[83]

Still, there was no denying the simultaneous appeal and consternation associated with the book's thesis. Even those who disavowed his conclusions felt that Beecher had shone a spotlight on a fatal defect in Christianity that could no longer be ignored:

> [T]he work lays bare, in the very core of our common Orthodoxy, that same intolerable conflict with the principles of Divine honor and righteousness, which had often been logically proved to exist, but which had been as often denied.... The peculiarity [of] Dr. Beecher's work...is that it comes to us in the character of a disclosure, in the character of testimony to a fact known, and grievously felt, and no longer endurable....Somehow, and somewhere, the Creed is at war with the Divine Perfections. So much may now be regarded as fact.[84]

By and large, the Universalists applauded this critique, as it provided an opening for them to extend the indictment of Christian justice to the problem of eternal damnation, which they considered to be a greater outrage to moral sensibility than was original sin. One reviewer, who was only too happy to quickly dissect Beecher's claims but exploit the remains, writes that Beecher bases his attempt to justify God's ways to humanity

> by our existing and falling in a pre-existent state. As all think he must fail in this object, many conclude his book is useless; but *mark*—though he fails in this object, he succeeds in proving conclusively, that the doctrine of eternal woe, as now held, cannot be vindicated on the principles of justice, and greatly dishonors God.... I rejoice that his book has appeared; for, to use a comparison, the Doctor has, with a giant hand, torn down the old house.[85]

Some began their reviews with marks of respect for Beecher's "considerable resources of erudition, logic, and language," but could not excuse his speculations, which made of the human race "the fragments of a demon army, long ago tried and lost." His theory lacking, as they saw it, any biblical sanction, they felt no compunction in dismissing the whole scheme: "The very idea of being an *old demon*, recreated, or rather reconstructed, and brought into this life for a second trial, strikes us as inexpressibly ludicrous, nay, we ought rather to say, intensely horrible." Even such wholesale dismissal, however, did not denigrate the problem Beecher was tackling. In the end, it was more respectable to relegate the Great Conflict back to the unsolvable: "Doubtless a great mystery is involved in the presence of sin among men, or in any part of the universe. But mystery is involved in all things.... Practically, then, the conflict is ended with all who believe the Bible as it is, and humanity as it is."[86]

The debates engendered by this, the most prolonged defense of preexistence in Christian history, might have continued much longer if not for developments that eclipsed media attentiveness to theological controversies. As Edward's brother Charles lamented, the whole issue was "in a measure soon forgotten in the excitement of the civil war."[87] A poignant coda to the Beecher episode is found in a note penned by a descendant upon the bequeathal of the "Life of Edward Beecher" manuscript biography to the Illinois College Library in 1950. John Beecher wrote on that occasion to President H. Gary Hudson:

> I am about to send on to you at last the manuscript *Life of Edward Beecher* by his brother Charles.... It is none too rich in human interest, perhaps, being concerned overwhelmingly with Edward's "spiritual" (theological) development and his belief in the pre-existence of the soul, an unfortunate excursion into the realms of heresy which apparently wrecked his career. Charles also subscribed to this doctrine and this explains his interest in

the subject of the biography. Edward Beecher apparently became obsessed with the idea in his later years and developed the delusion that he was born to be the "Copernicus of morals."[88]

Beecher had tried to resuscitate belief in preexistence at one of modern Christianity's most vulnerable moments. By the mid-nineteenth century, Calvinism, the faith of America's founders and of generations of New England intellectuals, was increasingly taken to be simply irrelevant. Oliver Wendell Holmes wrote of its abrupt demise, comparing it to a "one-hoss shay" that was "built in such a logical way." But by 1855, he wrote, "You see, of course, if you're not a dunce, / how it went to pieces all at once, / All at once, and nothing first / Just as bubbles do when they burst."[89] The irony here is that the family most responsible for its demise was Edward's own. According to the *Princeton Review* of 1857, blame for the decline of Calvinism was to be laid squarely at the feet of Lyman Beecher's children.[90] So, one could say, Edward was trying to avert a catastrophe that he ended up being complicit in accelerating.

Beecher's would be the last fully sustained effort to win theological legitimacy for pre-mortal existence in the American tradition. Still, the idea would continue to resurface on random ad hoc occasions. One of the most outstanding preachers of the generation after Beecher's bombshell (some thought him the greatest orator of the era) was Phillips Brooks (1835–1893). For many years a charismatic presence in the pulpit of Boston's Trinity Church, Brooks is today best known as the author of "O Little Town of Bethlehem." In one of his sermons, this Episcopal bishop of Massachusetts urged his listeners:

[F]ollow the human spirit in its development. It is possible for our imaginations even to picture the soul praying for life before it has begun to live. We all remember those verses from Pope's *Messiah* which are made into one of the hymns of our hymnal. The poet is singing of the kingdom of God that is to come, the new Jerusalem and its inhabitants:

> See a long race thy spacious courts adorn,
> See future sons and daughters yet unborn,
> In crowding ranks on every side arise
> Demanding life, impatient for the skies.

The cry of the unborn for life! That is the sound which fills the poet's vision. By and by comes God's answer to that prayer. The unborn come to the birth and life is given.[91]

While Brooks was not philosophically equipped to make a serious apologia for his doctrine, poetry was available and less threatening. And so he continued his argument:

When as in Pope's imaginative picture their spirits prayed for life, and when God gave them life, this was what God gave them. This poetry, this genius, the sublimeness was all wrapped up in that first gift of life when God said, "Let this man be."…All that was to open out of their being forever, all that they were to be on to the endless end, all this God gave them when He answered the prayer of their unborn spirits.[92]

Pope was, in the cited poem ("The Messiah: A Sacred Eclogue," 1712), imitating Virgil who, in his epic masterpiece the *Aeneid*, had similarly envisioned unborn spirits anxiously awaiting their moment in history when they could burst through the mists of pre-mortality. Aeneas's father, Anchises, spies in a lush valley of the underworld myriad "souls, till then confined there, who were bound for daylight in the upper world."[93] In both cases, the poet was probably using the trope to reinforce a sense of a great destiny unfolding under providential foreknowledge, rather than advocating preexistence itself. Elsewhere, however, Pope hinted at a preexistence from which we are, in the tradition of Basilides, mercifully mentally veiled. In his *Essay on Man*, Pope remarked, "Heav'n from all creatures hides the book of Fate, / All but the page prescribed, their present state, / …Or who could suffer being here below?" That the past as well as the future may be the object of deliberate obfuscation is suggested in his lines following, with their Platonic invocation of "the soul, uneasy and confined from home."[94]

It's not surprising, as his biographer noted, that Brooks read Origen and Philo and adored Plato (*Phaedo* was his favorite dialogue). "The body must be valued only for the protection and the education which the soul may gain by it," Brooks said in one sermon, which was named after a concept dear to the Cambridge Platonists.[95] Preexistence resonated not only in Brooks's sermons, but it filtered into his poetry in mini-allegories:

> [In his verse,] he speaks of the thoughts now springing up so abundantly in his mind, as if they were angelic intelligences descending from God, with whom they had pre-existed and held communion, coming down into the soul with God's blessing upon them. These thoughts he personifies, as carrying memories of the blessed life, and of the heavenly hymn; which, while they came to men in blessing, are themselves yearning for the joys they have left behind them, and so tempt men Godward, as they return to the source when[ce] they came.[96]

With a similar theme of homesickness, his contemporary the clergyman/writer George MacDonald would produce a long poetic cycle titled *Diary of an Old Soul*, which he inaugurated with a prayer that God would, "in thy gentleness and truth, Lead back thy old soul, by the path of pain."[97]

Julius Müller (1801–1878) was, along with Edward Beecher, the most prominent advocate of preexistence of his era. An influential theologian at the University of Halle in Prussia, he achieved his reputation largely through his two-volume
work *Die christliche Lehre von der Sünde*, which was published in 1839 and was
used as a textbook in many German universities. By 1868, it had gone through five
editions and was published in English as *The Christian Doctrine of Sin* in at least
two translations. One of those translators saw Müller's chief contribution to be
the rescue of Christianity from the determinism to which the philosophies of his
contemporaries Auguste Comte (1798–1857) and John Stuart Mill (1806–1873)
were tending, through positivism and the doctrine of invariability, respectively.[98]
"The great question of human liberty," he writes, "Müller argues out with a master
mind, and in the present work [*Christian Doctrine of Sin*] freedom is philosophically established." It is with perhaps some understatement that the translator ends
his introduction by curtly acknowledging that he is "not unaware … how much has

German theologian and professor Julius Müller found the preexistence of the soul to be the
only foundation on which a theory of sin and accountability could be logically based. 19th
century, Courtesy Martin Luther University of Halle-Wittenberg, Germany.

been said of the difficulties [that Müller's solution] presents." Like his contemporary Beecher, Müller was seen as a keen analyst of profound Christian dilemmas. One critic wrote that Müller, like Beecher, resorted to preexistence as an "*alleged necessity* as a means of reconciling other dogmas with the acknowledged attributes and character of God."[99] Also as with Beecher, Müller's cure was seen by many to be worse than the disease.

Freedom, once again, is here at the center of a discussion of the soul and its moral accountability. And this leads, once again, to the question of the soul's origins and first causes. Volume 1 of Müller's study seeks to determine the reality and nature of sin. It is at the beginning of volume 2 that he turns to the more philosophical problem of what makes sin possible to begin with. And that question becomes the preponderant problem of his analysis, since his immediate answer is freedom of the will. It is a problem because it does not take Müller long to conclude that the prerequisite for free will, or moral autonomy, is difficult to secure. That prerequisite is what he calls an opening for free action, "a spot in our present life wholly unconditioned by anything preceding it," which would function in the moral sphere like the fixed spot of Archimedes, from which the Greek boasted he could lever the world. Ideally, we would find a perfect "freedom *in aequilibrio*," a "moment when there is a perfect balance of opposite impulses," which would divide our lives in twain. Every preceding act would be seen as arising from indeterminate circumstances and so not fully attributable to our charge. Following this self-defining pivot, we would bear full accountability for the chain of causality that follows, because the inclinations to which we freely yielded in that Archimedean moment shape our subsequent character and, therefore, choices. Like Kant before him, Müller must concede that "we cannot hide from ourselves the fact that each successive moment is conditioned in some degree by that which has preceded it." Accordingly, every choice we make is shaped by all of the choices that went before. And the constant search for an unconditioned moment, this "constant reference to a past which contains in its bosom the germ of the present, sends us continually back from one stage to another." This is not, insists Müller, a quest to establish a merely hypothetical basis for agency, but is one to find that actual, unconditioned "freedom of the first decision," which would be the only adequate explanation possible for our very real consciousness of guilt.[100]

The slippery slope of endless regression takes Müller to a realization whose eureka moment of discovery he can only suggest by the majuscules with which he trumpets it:

The course of our inquiry compels us TO LOOK BEYOND THE REGION OF THE TEMPORAL IN ORDER TO FIND THE ORIGINAL SOURCE OF OUR FREEDOM....Human freedom must have its beginning in a sphere beyond the range of time, wherein alone pure and unconditioned self-determination is possible. In this region we must seek that power of original choice.

Some might suggest that the unconditioned moment exists, veiled by the mists of early mental development, somewhere in our childhood. Such an assumption, he writes, "is very venturesome" for two principal reasons: no one denies that a child is justifiably considered less, rather than more, morally accountable than an adult. It is illogical to impute to the weaker of the two stages the foundation for the entire edifice of human moral accountability. In addition, it offends our sense of fairness that God would relegate to the weakness of childhood, with its scant understanding of the stakes involved, "this most important decision as to the character of the moral life."[101]

Müller believes that he has argued his point from philosophical principle rather than religious intuition. Still, he is led inexorably to what he himself hinted were "expedients apparently far-fetched and even desperate"[102] in order to flesh out a conception of freedom that encompasses both human accountability and divine justice. The alternative, he suggests and as history might show, is to concede the field to determinism, as apologists desperate to save religion from Pelagianism at any cost were fully prepared to do.[103] If he felt it necessary, Müller suggests, he could invoke still other philosophical arguments for the conclusions he has reached. Instead, he merely footnotes his contemporary J. P. Romang's claim that "what originates in time perishes in time" as a self-evident axiom.[104] Still, once arrived at as a solution, pre-mortal existence appears to Müller as a paradigm with compelling power to solve the dilemma of free will and also to explain those aspects of the human condition that fall under the domain of otherwise indecipherable intuitions and sentiments:

> The conclusion to which we are thus driven reveals to us...the mystery of that inextinguishable melancholy and sadness, which lies hidden at the foundation of all human consciousness, being most profound in the noblest natures. The lower animals are light and joyous, content if their actual wants are supplied, secure and untroubled from without. But in the consciousness of man that dark cloud of moral evil casts its shadow even in his most joyous moments; and amid the sounds of heartiest joy there runs an unsilenced undertone of secret sadness....Personality alone possesses this original source of uneasiness and anguish, because its existence can be traced back beyond the confines of time.[105]

Only after establishing to his satisfaction the philosophical as well as intuitive appeal of preexistence does Müller add the weight of historical precedent, noting, "the idea of a self-decision of the will previous to the birth of the soul into this world...has been adopted by many."[106]

At least one Italian work of this era championed preexistence as well, in language that revealed more than a passing familiarity with the works of Origen and with a confidence that modern science offered persuasive support. In *Pre-existence and Future Existence; or, The Soul Created in the Image of God*, Andréa Pizzani claims:

> [L]earned modern writers have declared that progress is the law of creation....[The astronomer and secretary of the Royal Society] Sir John Herschel, in his discourse upon Natural History,[107] hints at a succession of life. It cannot be supposed that man is the last link in the chain which unites the creature to the Creator....Humanity may be supposed to be one of a series of beings, superior and inferior.

Herschel had indeed written that, "in whatever state of knowledge we may conceive man to be placed, his progress towards a yet higher state need never fear a check, but must continue till the last existence of society."[108] Pizzani thought that this view was consistent with his Origenist conception of what he called "final restoration and progression," finding in morality, rather than biology, the motive engine ("elevation is the consequence of virtue").[109] Preexistence is implicit in this scheme, he reckoned, since the "plurality of existences" necessary for spiritual evolution to reach its apotheosis required substantial progress leading up to our present status and into a glorious future. As the Darwinian paradigm continued to transform scientific thought, others would similarly find in preexistence an anthropology perfectly consistent with a view of progress that spans eons rather than lifetimes.

Perhaps the fullest development of this synthesis is to be found in an article written by Norman Pearson in 1886. Finding it illogical to assume a human existence that is "eternal at one end only" (as he says that most people, save the positivists, do), he sets out to examine three questions pertaining to the origins of the soul. "Does the soul spring into being for the first time with the birth of our physical body? Has it existed before such birth, either from eternity, or as an antenatal creation? Assuming its pre-existence, under what conditions has it existed?" He then lays out some scientific premises to guide him in his resolution of a question where religion and science overlap: whatever its origin, a soul must be considered to be "a constituent part of the universe." Second, "cosmic as well as mundane forces" may be at work in the universe, but "all development must be an orderly evolution of its subject-matter." Finally, force and matter must be preserved, with nothing added or lost, created or destroyed. For this last reason alone, the sudden eruption of a soul into the universe would violate the equation, even if the source of that soul is "extra-terrestrial energy," i.e., God. A soul, therefore, can only reasonably be considered "a product of some sort, not a new creation, seeing that the whole testimony of nature is against such a conclusion."

To subject its origins to scientific inquiry, however, requires treating the soul as "something in the nature of matter," or else it is in the realm of the unknowable. And here, Pearson is aided in his quest by recourse to the theories of the philosopher William Kingdon Clifford (1845–1879). Clifford posited mind as the one absolute reality, consisting of a substance called "mindstuff," divisible to the atomistic level and "in its nature material." As the primal element of all nature, mindstuff is everywhere present, but not everywhere sufficiently developed to constitute sentience or consciousness. Nevertheless, in accordance with the scientific laws of development, "as physical life mounts higher, soul-life follows in its train." Pearson's conclusion is therefore a triumph of science and religion alike, meshing in perfect synthesis: "If we are compelled to regard the soul as conforming like the rest of the universe to natural law, are we not entitled to presume...that its origin and growth must be referred to that great natural order of evolution which, so far as we can discern, is universal in its range?" He asserts, "[T]he evolutionist is constrained by the double claims of religion and science to reject any theory of the soul" which connects it to a miraculous creation at the time of birth. Rather, what he calls "orthodox evolutionism" leads inexorably to a concept of the soul as being previously formed as "a structural product of evolution."[110]

Like those of an earlier age who found the microscope to be an ally rather than an antidote to metaphysical speculations on the soul's origin, Pearson and Clifford represent a cadre of resourceful thinkers who found Darwin to be a new resource, rather than an enemy, in the quest to maintain the viability of preexistence in the presence of new scientific paradigms.

10

Romanticism and Transcendentalism, 1800–1900

the Soul ascends
Drawn towards her native firmament of heaven.
—William Wordsworth[1]

Romanticism

One of the richest and most compelling motifs in Romantic thought is the mystery and insatiability of human yearning. If any character can lay claim to embodying most of the manifold facets of Romantic heroism, it is surely Faust, whose titanic discontent overshadows all other attributes and absolves all other vices; the agonies of dissatisfaction catalyze Faust's life of undifferentiated striving and, in Johann Wolfgang von Goethe's version of the tale, culminate in God's own apology for his legacy of sin and selfishness. Faust's vindication and salvation are a clear affront to and subversion of a centuries-old morality tale. Vainglorious professors who transgress the bounds of orthodoxy to ascend Icarus-like to forbidden realms in pursuit of occult knowledge and power are supposed to end in hell. And they always did, until Goethe's iconoclastic heavenly intervention.

Faust's rehabilitation at the hands of the Romantics is but the most extreme response to a human predicament that has been almost universally acknowledged for centuries: the tragic and defining characterization of the mortal condition as an uneasy amalgam of the divine and the human, the infinite and the limited. And the consequent human disposition has been, logically enough, one of unease, discontent, and yearning for the undefined and indefinable. Faust's is the story of a failure to come to terms with the explosive tension at the heart of the human condition (or, in Goethe's case, a heroic failure to solve an impossible dilemma). It is the business of poets to explore the dimensions of tragic human predicaments. But while Goethe was busy plumbing the depths of Faust's soul agony and ultimately absolving him, other Romantic poets were exploring the possible bases for the cosmic contradictions that made him what he was in the first place. Such explorations of the roots of human restlessness and yearning led directly to hypotheses of preexistence.

Augustine, as we saw, was one of the most eloquent to articulate the human sense of homesickness and longing for an unknown object of desire. His masterpiece, *Confessions*, is the account of a man whose desperate quest for fulfillment takes him through a range of life experiences, from intellectual satisfactions to the fleshpots of Carthage to the heady mysteries of Manichaean religion. Ultimately, he finds that the gaping insufficiency of his self, the sense of incompleteness, alienation, and misdirected longing, takes him where God intended all along—back to him: "Let us now return to Thee, O Lord....We have no fear that there should be no place of return, merely because by our own act we fell from it: our absence does not cause our home to fall, which is Thy Eternity."[2] Augustine's quest becomes the paradigmatic journey of Everyman, a journey that is launched precisely because of the innate hunger and unease that humans, as spiritual beings, find in their earthly, and therefore temporary, foreign habitation.

One might object that the spiritual affinity for an indefinable infinite is a yearning for the divine author of the self, not for some preexistent abode of that self. Certainly, a theology that sees God as the source of all existence, the human soul included, could with reason interpret human yearning for the infinite as a desire to return to the source, i.e., the moment of our creation by and origin in God. It seems at least equally reasonable, however, to read "longing" and "homesickness" and "yearning" in the plain sense of a desire for an abode or condition that we have known before. That much seems logical to Augustine, who wonders in *Confessions* how we can seek for that which we have not already known.

In the age of Shakespeare, the great poet George Herbert created his own poetic etiology of human yearning and aspiration toward the ineffable:

> When God at first made man,
> Having a glasse of blessings standing by;
> Let us (said he) poure on him all we can:
> Let the world's riches, which dispersed lie,
> Contract into a span.

So strength first made a way;
Then beautie flow'd, then wisdome, honour, pleasure:
When almost all was out, God made a stay,
Perceiving that alone of all his treasure
Rest in the bottome lay.

For if I should (said he)
Bestow this jewell also on my creature,
He would adore my gifts in stead of me,
And rest in nature, not the God of Nature:
So both should losers be.

Yet let him keep the rest,
But keep them with repining restlesnesse:
Let him be rich and wearie, that at least,
If goodnesse lead him not, yet wearinesse
May tosse him to my breast.[3]

What Augustine depicted through autobiography, Herbert represents mythically and poetically. Reworking Genesis into his own creation story, Herbert imagines God deliberately omitting from the human constitution a sense of contentment, which accounts for the relentless restlessness of which the human heart is possessed.

Situated both ideologically and historically between the religious paradigm of Augustine and Herbert, on the one hand, and the later secular model of Freud, on the other, the Romantics struggled to develop their own account of human identity and spiritual anthropology, one that will account for human yearning for transcendence and nostalgia for an eternity from which we are exiles without succumbing to the religiosity of the former nor the secular psychologizing of the latter. And in this endeavor, they find assistance in the timely arrival on the scene of a congenial philosopher.

Plato Rediscovered

It is somewhat astonishing, given the unparalleled respect accorded to the "divine Plato" from his day to the present, that no English translation of his complete works existed until the nineteenth century. The first to produce one was Thomas Taylor (1758–1835), in 1804.[4] That fact alone explains in great measure Abraham Tucker's premature 1763 obituary of the doctrine of preexistence, as well as its powerful resurgence in Taylor's lifetime. Taylor was not just a translator but an impassioned disciple and promulgator of Plato's views. His self-proclaimed task was to establish the deserved preeminence of Plato, celebrate the "dignity and sublimity" in this source "of all that ennobles man," and show that other systems are erroneous to the degree they oppose Plato's views. At Taylor's hands, Plato becomes the founder of a "theology," one that Taylor unapologetically finds utterly incompatible with inconveniences like the Christian Trinity. Indeed, he is unforgiving in his criticism of Neo-Platonists like Ficino, Pico, and Henry More—"pseudo-Platonists," he calls them, "who, in order to combine Christianity with the doctrines of Plato, rejected some of his most important tenets, and perverted others, and thus corrupted one of these systems, and afforded no real benefit to the other."[5] If it is true that the Enlightenment naturalized Plato in its hostility to all supernaturalism, religious and otherwise, then Taylor recasts him as a mystic without the Christian trappings.[6] And as events would prove, the age was only too ready to explore—or rediscover— alternative mythologies to the Christian one.

The principal mythology that Taylor championed was Plato's "account of the human soul, that most important Platonic dogma." This account includes both a preexistent origin and a supernal destiny:

> Through our flight from divinity, and the defluction [dropping off] of those wings which elevate us on high, we fell into this mortal abode....The soul, while an inhabitant of earth, is in a fallen condition, an apostate from deity, an exile from the orb of light....Our apostacy [sic] from our better natures is only to be healed by a flight from hence.[7]

Taylor's principal object is to awaken his readership "from the sleep of sense,...and gain a glimpse of this most weighty truth, that there is another world, of which this is nothing more than a most obscure resemblance, and another life, of which this is but the flying mockery." What lies in store is likewise hard to reconcile with orthodox Christianity: "When the soul therefore has recovered her pristine perfection...she governs the world in conjunction with the gods. And this is indeed the most beautiful end of her labours....This is the most perfect fruit of philosophy to familiarize and lead her back to things truly beautiful."[8]

Taylor was tremendously influential in leading a number of his contemporaries to these things "truly beautiful." He was known and respected by William Godwin, Samuel Rogers, Henry Crabb Robinson, Leigh Hunt, Thomas Love Peacock, Percy Shelley, and probably William Wordsworth, Samuel Taylor Coleridge, and John Keats as well. And the spiritual father of them all, William Blake, was likely at his friend John Flaxman's house in the 1780s when Taylor gave a series of twelve lectures on Plato's philosophy, perhaps laying the groundwork for Blake's embrace of spiritual realms and preexistent abodes.[9]

Blake

> About his path and about his bed, around his ears and under his eyes,
> an infinite play of spiritual life seethed and swarmed or shone and sang.

Spirits imprisoned in the husk and shell of earth consoled or menaced him. Every leaf bore a growth of angels; the pulse of every minute sounded as the falling foot of God; under the rank raiment of weeds, in the dripping down of thistles, strange faces frowned and white hair fluttered.[10]

Of all the English Romantics, William Blake was the most unabashedly mystical and the most unapologetic in his embrace of Platonic preexistence. His Platonism, however, was clearly qualified, for Blake's most emphatic heresy was the utter repudiation of Platonic-Christian dualism. Blake was positively insistent that the subordination of the body to the spirit, the association of sexuality with evil, and the equation of bodily pleasure with sin were doctrines straight from hell. But elsewhere, Plato's influence combined in Blake with a mystical strain of Swedenborgianism to produce Romanticism's strongest advocate for preexistence. "I am more famed in Heaven for my works than I could well concieve [sic]," he wrote. "In my Brain are studies & Chambers fill'd with books & pictures of old, which I wrote & painted in ages of Eternity before my mortal life; & these works are the delight & Study of Archangels."[11] His deep friendship with the sculptor Flaxman provoked intimations of a bond that preceded birth. "You, O Dear Flaxman, are a Sublime Archangel, My Friend & Companion from Eternity; in the Divine bosom is our Dwelling place. I look back into the regions of Reminiscence & behold our ancient days before this Earth appear'd in its vegetated mortality to my mortal vegetated Eyes."[12]

Blake was profoundly influenced, early on, by the great Swedish mystic Emanuel Swedenborg (1688–1772), who wrote prolifically of his frequent visitations to and from the spirit world. Swedenborg alternately affirmed and rejected human preexistence. "The first man, and those born at first, have not been led by any other than the Lord alone…also before man was born, in the same manner as after man was born; for man…existed similarly before his nativity as [he existed] afterwards," he wrote in *Spiritual Diary* (1747–1765). In his last work, written in 1771, he reversed his position, relegating the belief "that human souls created at the beginning of the world enter into bodies and become men" to "the fables of the ancients."[13] His position is complicated by the fact that he asserted the existence of both a corporeal, natural soul formed through mortal experience and a spiritual, celestial soul formed by the Lord.[14] Blake eventually moved well beyond Swedenborg, who he came to feel was too tame in his unorthodoxies. Blake found more lasting influence in the same strain of Kabbalistic mysticism so popular with Henry More's circle, Lurianism. These esoteric influences, with their mythologies of preexistent humanity, pervade a number of Blake's obscure, difficult works, including *Jerusalem*, *The Book of Urizen*, and others. However, his most accessible and direct treatment of preexistence is *The Book of Thel*, produced in 1789. This dramatic poem narrates the plight of a forlorn spirit/shepherdess of that name, a daughter of "Mne Seraphim," who lives in the vales of Har on the far side of the river Adona (which evokes Spenser's pre-mortal garden of Adonis). With poignant lyricism and biblical cadences, she laments the transience of life and her own insubstantiality. "Thel is like a wat'ry bow, and like a parting cloud, / Life a reflection in a glass, like shadows in the water, / like dreams of infants, like a smile upon an infant's face." Offered consolation by Lily of the Valley, who blithely and unselfishly accepts the cycles of life and death, Thel persists in her self-pity. She next addresses Cloud, who similarly manifests a humble submission to transience as a prelude to eternity and reminds the spirit: "Everything that lives / Lives not alone, nor for itself." Still unsatisfied, Thel at last confronts Clod of Clay and the infant Worm, powerful emblems of the dual nature of corporeality with its twin dimensions of substantiality and corruptibility. Clay offers the unembodied Thel the opportunity to enter the realm of mortality, with the rare option of returning as well to her pre-mortal home.

Entering into the "land of sorrows & of tears," Thel finds herself standing before her own grave, where a "voice of sorrow" and experience recites a terrifying litany of questions:

> Why cannot the Ear be closed to its own destruction?
> Or the glist'ning Eye to the poison of a smile?
> Why are Eyelids stor'd with arrows ready drawn,

Romantic visionary William Blake found his own preternatural talents to be proof that his soul had been schooled in a world before mortality, and he based a major poem on the concept. William Blake, by John Linnell; HIP/Art Resource, New York. Title page to *The Book of Thel*, c. 1789, hand-colored relief etching by William Blake. Reproduced by permission of the Huntington Library, San Marino, California.

> Where a thousand fighting men in ambush lie?
> Or an Eye of gifts & graces, show'ring fruits and coined gold?
> Why a Tongue impress'd with honey from every wind?
> Why an Ear a whirlpool fierce to draw creations in?
> Why a Nostril wide inhaling terror, trembling & affright?
> Why a tender curb upon the youthful burning boy?
> Why a little curtain of flesh on the bed of our desire?[15]

In stark contrast to the safety and insularity of preexistent stasis, life is here depicted as unfiltered exposure to the onslaughts of an indifferent universe, which the bodily senses register and amplify indiscriminately. Like a raw nerve exposed to a maelstrom of sensations, mingling pleasure and pain, the good and the bad, Thel recoils with a shriek and flees back to the safety of Har.

Other than the hint that only a pre-mortal apprenticeship could explain his preternatural talent, Blake does not provide a rationale per se for preexistence. His Kabbalistic influences, his poetic preoccupation with the contrasting states of innocence and experience, and the specter Thel faces of incarnation as daunting prospect rather than fall from grace—all suggest that his conception of mortality is one of educative advancement rather than incarceration or fall. This view comports with the elegantly simple moral he states in one of his *Songs of Innocence*: "we are put on earth a little space, / That we may learn to bear the beams of love."[16]

Coleridge and Wordsworth

Literature would seem to be one place where, since the poet "nothing affirmeth," preexistence could serve as imaginative speculation or poetic topos whose fruitful possibilities threaten neither orthodoxy nor philosophical decorum. And indeed, with the "birth of the modern" represented by nineteenth-century Romanticism, preexistence experienced a remarkable fluorescence. The two dominant figures of early British Romanticism, however, Samuel Taylor Coleridge (1772–1834) and William Wordsworth (1770–1850), were both the age's most articulate, impassioned purveyors of the idea and, curiously, the most uncomfortable in being associated with it.

Coleridge's most famous pronouncement on pre-earth life is his sonnet to his son Hartley, which begins:

> Oft o'er my brain does that strange fancy roll
> Which makes the present (while the flash doth last)
> Seem a mere semblance of some unknown past,
> Mixed with such feelings, as perplex the soul
> Self-questioned in her sleep; and some have said

The greatest of the Romantic poets, Wordsworth and Coleridge, found the idea of preexistence personally compelling and poetically useful but publicly distanced themselves from the doctrine. *William Wordsworth*, by John Cochran, HIP/Art Resource, New York. *Samuel Taylor Coleridge*, by Peter Vandyke, Snark/Art Resource, New York.

> We liv'd, ere yet this robe of flesh we wore.
> O my sweet baby! When I reach my door,
> If heavy looks should tell me thou art dead,
> (As sometimes, through excess of hope, I fear)
> I think that I should struggle to believe
> Thou wert a spirit, to this nether sphere
> Sentenc'd for some more venial crime to grieve;
> Did'st scream, then spring to meet Heaven's quick reprieve
> While we wept idly o'er thy little bier![17]

One could impute his speculation about life as penance to his morbid and melancholic predisposition (he wrote, after all, poems called "Melancholy," "Dejection," and "Fears in Solitude" and a play titled *Remorse*). However, the notion is fully consistent with the trope of mortality-as-fall that most versions of preexistence entail. Where does Coleridge get this idea? He explicitly connects his sonnet to "Plato's doc[trine] of Preexistence" in a letter to his friend John Thelwall, but indicates a more personal origin when he adds, "if you never have had [intimations of preexistence] yourself, I cannot explain [them] to you." In an earlier letter to Thomas Poole, he referred to "almost all the followers of Fenelon" as believing that "*men* are degraded Intelligences, who had once all existed, at one time & together, in a paradisiacal or heavenly state." The link with François Fénelon is suspect, however; in addition to Plato, Coleridge would have found support for the idea in a heterodox thinker with mystical leanings whom he was reading at the time of Hartley's birth: Andrew Michael Ramsay, who expounded the doctrine of preexistence in *Travels of Cyrus*, as we saw above, and in another work published posthumously, *Philosophical Principles of Natural and Revealed Religion*.[18]

Coleridge's familiarity with the idea was shared by Wordsworth, who made it the basis of his great "Immortality Ode." One of Wordsworth's perennial preoccupations was adulthood's loss of the innocence and spirituality so unstudied and intrinsic in children. Like an Adam and Eve who only appreciate Eden from the perspective of having lost it, so we experience intimacy with the divine, he lamented, only through the retrospective gaze of fallen adults. He captured the paradox in a simple sonnet wherein he contrasted his own mature apprehension of the sublime with his child's oblivious immersion in it:

> Dear child! dear Girl! that walkest with me here,
> If thou appear untouched by solemn thought,
> Thy nature is not therefore less divine:
> Thou liest in Abraham's bosom all the year;
> And worshipp'st at the Temple's inner shrine,
> God being with thee when we know it not.[19]

It is in his "Immortality Ode," however, that he most fully explores the philosophical dimensions of the dilemma and proposes a paradigm to both explain the tragic sense of inevitable spiritual diminishment and find consolation for its inevitable progress. His simultaneous universalizing and secularizing of the biblical motif of the Fall are unmistakable from the poem's first lines:

> THERE was a time when meadow, grove, and stream,
> The earth, and every common sight,
> To me did seem
> Apparell'd in celestial light,
> The glory and the freshness of a dream.
> It is not now as it hath been of yore;—
> Turn wheresoe'er I may,
> By night or day,
> The things which I have seen I now can see no more.

In spite of all his attempts at self-elevation, despite the jollity and vivacity of the beautiful spring festival where he finds himself, he cannot shake the sense, read between the lines of nature's joyous script, of unequivocal loss:

> …there's a tree, of many, one,
> A single field which I have look'd upon,
> Both of them speak of something that is gone:
> The pansy at my feet
> Doth the same tale repeat:
> Whither is fled the visionary gleam?
> Where is it now, the glory and the dream?

These first stanzas, as one critic notes, were written "as a spontaneous, almost feverish exposition of a personal problem; he then broke off for at least two years before attempting to continue the poem and answer the problem." And then, with a condescension that accurately typifies 200 years of critical response, the scholar continues, "The answer, when it came,…was the vision of a maturer but arguably less inspired personality."[20]

The answer to which he refers, of course, is the only spiritual anthropology that, to Wordsworth's mind, makes sense out of the human condition, which is coming to be seen as indelibly tragic by his increasingly skeptical generation. One cannot peruse the poetry of the Romantics without being struck by the soul agony of an entire generation, drawn more than any other to the possibilities of the sublime, of transcendence, of the beautiful in nature and in humankind, but thwarted and oppressed at every turn by stultifying systems, rigid hierarchies, and inflexible orthodoxies. Thus, the common lament in the poets of the age: "Man is of dust," muses Wordsworth elsewhere, but "ethereal hopes are his." "Too, too contracted are these walls of flesh," he mourns, "for any passion of the soul that leads to ecstasy."[21] Lord Byron's Lucifer taunts the man Cain, because he is a creature of "high thought…[but he is] linked to a servile mass of matter."[22] Robert Browning describes the quintessentially tragic human plight more simply as the intersection of "infinite passion, and the pain / Of finite hearts that yearn."[23] And so they all conclude, with Wordsworth, that "unless above himself he can Erect himself, how poor a thing is man!"[24] Wordsworth makes sense of it all in an epiphany that, though at least two years in coming, breaks forth with sudden clarity:

> Our birth is but a sleep and a forgetting
> The soul that rises with us, our life's star
> Hath had elsewhere its setting, and cometh from afar
> Not in entire forgetfulness, and not in utter nakedness,
> But trailing clouds of glory do we come from God who is our home.

Most ironic, perhaps, is this unexpected turn, given the ode's title. For reversing the traditional poetic mode of Christian consolation, this meditation on immortality offers hope by reaching backward, rather than forward in time. Life becomes a journey away from, rather than toward, the light of promise:

> Heaven lies about us in our infancy!
> Shades of the prison-house begin to close
> Upon the growing Boy,
> But he beholds the light, and whence it flows,
> He sees it in his joy;
> The Youth, who daily farther from the east
> Must travel, still is Nature's priest,
> And by the vision splendid
> Is on his way attended;
> At length the Man perceives it die away,
> And fade into the light of common day.

Then, with the substitution of preexistence for original sin in place, the undeniability of the Fall is granted, even as it is rescued from theology, and the cult of childhood, which is traceable at least to Jean-Jacques Rousseau, receives a compelling rationale. The child of the poem is a "mighty prophet" and "seer," one "whose exterior semblance doth belie [his] soul's immensity" but not its antiquity, exhibiting as the child does clear and discernible evidence of his "heritage." The poem's consolation, then, is multifold. Socialization and distraction tend to make the child "forget those glories he hath known, / And that imperial palace whence he came." But the sense of unease in the world, the poignant yearnings and sense of loss exacerbated by those "shadowy recollections" of preexistence, simultaneously attest to a nobler heritage that is the core of human identity. At the same time, the tenuous faith in future life is sustained and even replaced by the more emphatic recollection of a former one:

> Our souls have sight of that immortal sea which brought us hither,
> Can in a moment travel thither,
> And see the children sport upon the shore,
> And hear the mighty waters rolling evermore.[25]

As is typical in this verse form, the greater Romantic lyric, the poem ends with the poet reconciled and serene in the affirmation which the revealed insight makes possible. Preexistence in this poem is not a mere ornament, digression, or casual speculation. It is philosophically and structurally the nucleus of the poem, the key to any power the poem has to console, explain, or move beyond the paralysis of the poet's tragic dilemma.

Seldom has a poem elicited such a dichotomous response. From its first publication to the present, critics have been simultaneously enraptured and (like the author himself) embarrassed by the poem. Scholars have long noted Wordsworth's discomfort with religious nonconformity, evidence of which multiplies in his advancing years and is reflected in numerous poetic revisions. Wordsworth's editors note that "he became increasingly self-conscious about how [his unortho-dox] beliefs might seem to the orthodox. The result is countless little fudgings, insertions of reassuring Christian reference[s]."[26] (This statement is perfectly borne out by Wordsworth's late redactions of his major philosophical poem *The Excursion*. The famous section on "the Ruined Cottage" originally had recourse to a triumphal humanism in order to save a failed Christian vision of consolation. By the 1850 version, it had acquired all of the familiar trappings of a dutifully conventional orthodoxy.)[27]

Poetic expression must never be simplistically equated with personal belief, but in this case the personal stakes kept erupting into the public comments of both of these Romantic poets, and there were clearly conflicted feelings behind them. Coleridge, for example, insists that "he has often experienced the feeling" he describes in the first four lines of his Hartley sonnet.[28] At the same time, however, after depicting the idea, affirming its purchase on him, and proselytizing Wordsworth, he almost petulantly repudiates the notion on his own and Wordsworth's (as well as Plato's) behalf:

> [Wordsworth's] ode was intended for such readers only as had been accus-
> tomed to watch the flux and reflux of their inmost nature, to venture at
> times into the twilight realms of consciousness and to feel a deep interest
> in the modes of inmost being, to which they know that the attributes of
> time and space are inapplicable and alien, but which can not be conveyed
> save in symbols of time and space. For such readers the sense is sufficiently
> plain, and they will be as little disposed to charge Mr. Wordsworth with
> believing the Platonic pre-existence in the ordinary interpretation of the
> words, as I am to believe, that Plato himself ever meant or taught it.[29]

Elsewhere, Coleridge backtracks enough that one scholar refers to his "apology for this notion," when he writes to his friend John Thelwall that he is too much a "Berkleian" to literally believe in "this descending, & incarcerated Soul" as anything more than a poetic device.[30]

Wordsworth's contradictory stance is even more stark. In advocating for the doctrine in his poem, he makes it into a cosmic paradigm in light of which human experience and the deepest yearnings and mysteries of the human heart find explication. The indelible wistfulness of advancing age, the luminescent purity of young children, the sense of estrangement and awkwardness with which we fill our mortal roles—all resolve themselves into logical correlates of a conception of pre-mortal lodgings in realms of glory and a subsequent, intervening veil of forgetfulness. The seriousness of intent of this philosophical inquiry into the human predicament, Wordsworth's personal commitment to sincerity as the paramount poetic virtue beyond any compromise, and the impassioned rhetorical intensity of the poem itself, referring to "a Presence which *is not to be put by*" and its consequent affirmation of an insight that now holds sacred status as "the fountain light of all our day" and "the master light of all our seeing"—surely, these considerations make of his spiritual anthropology more than a mere device of poetic convenience. Nevertheless, like Coleridge, Wordsworth's conservatism was ultimately sufficient to impel him to a formal disclaimer, but it took the form of Galileo's confession.

"I think it right to protest," he says in one of his conversations with Isabella Fenwick, "against a conclusion, which has given pains to some persons, that I meant to inculcate such a belief [in a prior state of existence]. It is far too shadowy a notion to be recommended to faith." Still, he considers with stubborn petulance, "let us bear in mind that, tho' the idea is not advanced in revelation, there is nothing there to contradict it, and the fall of Man presents an analogy in its favor." And going beyond Coleridge, Wordsworth not only affirms his personal responsiveness to the intimations of his poem's title but is confident in affirming their universal resonance: "To that dream-like vividness and splendor which invest objects of sight in childhood, every one, I believe, if he would look back, could bear testimony," and that is sufficient evidence, to him, that "the notion of pre-existence [has] sufficient foundation in humanity for authorizing me to make for my purpose the best use of it."[31] Echoes of Galileo's *eppur si muove*, in other words.

The discomfort that Coleridge and Wordsworth felt in being identified with belief in preexistence, their emotional sympathies notwithstanding, is mirrored in the numerous critics, then and now, who have felt impelled to assert that the poets never meant to be taken seriously in their flirtation with the idea. Perhaps they do protest too much. One scholar makes the case that "nineteenth- and twentieth-century literary criticism, at least when confronted with pre-existence, is as concerned with suppressing heterodoxy as the early Christian church was."[32] It is rather astonishing that the premier biographer of Wordsworth, in dealing with this poem, calls it his "greatest achievement in rhythm and cadence" yet, almost incomprehensibly, avoids completely any mention of its startling hypothesis, saying simply that it "reflect[s] Wordsworth's thinking about his life's work."[33]

The poem's soaring sublimity has even led to several attempts to perform it to music. One critic's comment on the musical failure only reinforces the paradox: "such words would beggar even the greatest music," wrote Martin Cooper, markedly distinguishing the words from the ideas those words convey.[34] Regarding the content of the poem, J. K. Mathison was one in an almost unending line of critics who have found it necessary to sniff, "we have no right to deprive the idea of its setting and treat it as if it were abstracted from a treatise which Wordsworth presented to a meeting of philosophers."[35]

Shelley

Percy Bysshe Shelley (1792–1822) was one of only a few Romantics to engage in real philosophical reflection on the subject of preexistence. He and Byron were both dismissed by establishment critics as members of the "Satanic school" of poetry and deserved their reputations for flouting traditional morality in provocative and conspicuous ways. But neither deserved his reputation for atheism. Hostile to institutionalized religion and its blithe indifference to social evils, both were nonetheless entirely agnostic on the subject of God and the immortality of the soul. Shelley's position outside conventional orthodoxies allowed him the liberty to approach the question of preexistence from an unconventional direction, just as Menasseh ben Israel, a contemporary of the Cambridge Platonists, had earlier. Ben Israel had reversed the usual equation by arguing not that immortality logically implied preexistence, but the opposite. Christians typically assume postexistence, so arguing from that belief to former existence makes sense. That argument had first been propounded by the Platonists, who argued that "nothing could be everlasting which had not always existed." (Augustine found the argument unconvincing and refuted the logic, though not necessarily the conclusion.)[36] Even the arch-skeptic David Hume found that the argument had appeal, holding that "reasoning from the common course of nature,…*what is incorruptible must also be ingenerable.* The soul, therefore, if immortal, existed before our birth." Then, he added slyly, "and if the former existence noways concerned us, neither will the latter."[37] But ben Israel was arguing with "Sadducees"—probably seventeenth-century Jews like Uriel da Costa, who were denying immortality and the resurrection. Ben Israel argued from the common Jewish embrace of preexistence to establish that souls can exist in a perfectly happy and blessed state without bodies. Logically, therefore, they can perfectly well exist after the dissolution of human bodies.[38] Shelley also thought that the beliefs were interdependent. Though, like most Romantics, a Platonist at heart (he would translate into English *Ion* and portions of *Phaedo*), he here resorts to his own line of reasoning, not even making use of the Christian or Platonic terminology of soul or spirit, but addressing instead the origin and duration of what he calls "the principle of life," or the "generative principle" that animates all plants and animals:

> Have we existed before birth? It is difficult to conceive the possibility of this.…It certainly *may be*; though it is sufficiently unphilosophical to allege the possibility of an opinion as a proof of its truth. Does [this soul, or "principle"] see, hear, feel, before its combination with those organs on which sensation depends? Does it reason, imagine, apprehend, without those ideas which sensation alone can communicate? If we have not existed before birth; if, at the period when the parts of our nature on

which thought and life depend, seem to be woven together, they *are* woven together; if there are no reasons to suppose that we have existed before that period at which our existence apparently commences, then there are no grounds for supposition that we shall continue to exist after our existence has apparently ceased. So far as thought and life [are] concerned, the same will take place with regard to us, individually considered, after death, as had place before our birth.[39]

Shelley was the most Platonic, even as he was the most emotionally excessive, of the major Romantics. A famous story recounted by his friend Thomas Jefferson Hogg reveals an exaggerated playfulness but also the beginnings of Shelley's abiding interest in preexistence:

> One Sunday we had been reading Plato together so diligently, that the usual hour of exercise passed away unperceived: we sallied forth hastily to take the air for half an hour before dinner. In the middle of Magdalen Bridge we met a woman with a child in her arms. Shelley was more attentive at that instant to our conduct in a life that was past, or to come, than to a decorous regulation of the present according to the established usages of society, in that fleeting moment of eternal duration styled the nineteenth century. With abrupt dexterity he caught hold of the child. The mother, who might well fear that it was about to be thrown over the parapet of the bridge into the sedgy waters below, held it fast by its long train. "Will your baby tell us anything about pre-existence, Madam?" he asked, in a piercing voice, and with a wistful look. The mother made no answer, but perceiving that Shelley's object was not murderous, but altogether harmless, she dismissed her apprehension, and relaxed her hold. "Will your baby tell us anything about pre-existence, Madam?" he repeated, with unabated earnestness. "He cannot speak, Sir," said the mother seriously. "Worse and worse," cried Shelley.

Then, Hogg adds, "Shelley sighed deeply as we walked on. 'How provokingly close are those new-born babes!...But it is nonetheless certain...that all knowledge is reminiscence.'"[40]

In his poetry, Shelley made frequent use of the motif of preexistence, but generally as a trope to intensify by contrast the melancholy of life or to etherealize erotic desire. In his unfinished "Prince Athanase" (1817), his Byronic hero is tormented by secret pains and world weariness. His friends deduce "that memories of an ante-mortal life / Made this, where now he dwelt, a penal hell."[41] Four years later, in *Epipsychidion*, his autobiographical love lyric, he repeats the allusion. Poetically serenading his beloved Emily, he invokes "a far Eden" to which they will flee,

"Beautiful as a wreck of Paradise." There, "every motion, odor, beam, and tone, / With that deep music is in unison, / Which is a soul within the soul … / Like echoes of an antenatal dream."[42] In those realms beyond and before time, he laments, his love should have found its first expression. But his Emily was "Too late Belovèd," the poet says:

> For in the fields of immortality
> My spirit should at first have worshipped thine,
> A divine presence in a place divine;
> Or should have moved beside it on this earth,
> A shadow of that substance, from its birth.[43]

Byron and Lermontov

Tarred with the same brush that branded Shelley an arch-apostate, Lord Byron (1788–1824) was in reality a doubter who found aspects of religious belief compelling, but wrestled with the philosophical and theological contradictions in at least two earnest tragedies, *Manfred* and the even darker *Cain*. In the latter, he provocatively presents a sympathetic portrait of humankind's first felon. Byron had a finely attuned ear for the cadences of biblical scripture and successfully evokes a dark, mythic version of the Edenic aftermath, devoid of Christian platitudes and consolations. Whether Byron was familiar with ascension narratives or not, he creates a fantastic version to rival Enoch's, except that it spans heaven, hell, and all between, and his guide is a Lucifer worthy of Milton.

When asked by Cain's wife where he dwells, the demon answers, "heaven and earth—and that / Which is not heaven nor earth, but peopled with / Those who once peopled or shall people both— / These are my realms!" Unlike the neatly divided realms beheld by Enoch, these worlds apparently hold an indiscriminate mix of the unborn and the dead. A scene later, Lucifer takes Cain on a tour of the cosmos, where he sees, compressed in different spheres, all of the layers of human history. This is no universe divided by Platonic levels of reality but an unremittingly physical terrain in which the forms of human existence co-reside on murky planets beyond human ken. "Where fly we?" Cain asks. "To the world of phantoms, which / Are beings past, and shadows still to come," Lucifer answers.[44]

One of Byron's admirers was the Russian poet and novelist Mikhail Lermontov (1814–1841). His highest form of praise was his rewriting of the Byronic hero in Russian terms (*A Hero of Our Time*) and his death in comparable Romantic fashion (Byron sickened and died fighting for Greek independence, Lermontov in a duel). A short poem by the Russian incorporates the motifs both of human longing for a primeval home and of an angel/porter of human souls:

An angel was flying through midnight's deep blue,
And softly he sang as he flew;
The moon, and the clouds, and the stars in a throng
All listened: in heavenly song.

He sang of the blessings of souls without sin
In the gardens of Paradise; hymns
To God the almighty he sang, and his praise
Was pure and completely unfeigned.

He carried toward earth, with its tears and its grief,
A soul just beginning its life;
And long, long thereafter the soul could still hear
The song he sang—wordless, but clear.

The soul languished long in its worldly attire,
Still knowing a wondrous desire;
And that heavenly music was never usurped
By the wearisome songs of the earth.[45]

Carlyle and Goethe

In much Romantic poetry, the allusions are too fleeting to suggest a serious philosophical basis for the idea of preexistence. Still, it resurfaces as a poetic trope with easy fluency in a number of writers, including Thomas Carlyle (1795–1881), who can casually refer to "Man himself, and his whole terrestrial Life" as "but an Emblem; a Clothing or visible Garment for that divine ME of his, cast hither, like a light-particle, down from Heaven."[46] Similarly, the greatest Romantic of all, Johann Wolfgang von Goethe (1749–1832), in his greatest work, *Faust*, had agonized:

Two souls, alas, are dwelling in my breast,
And either would be severed from its brother;
The one holds fast with joyous earthy lust
Onto the world of man with organs clinging;
The other soars impassioned from the dust,
To realms of lofty forebears winging.[47]

Those exalted ancestral realms (*Gefilden hoher Ahnen*) connote a distant past that anticipates future glory. In Goethe's personal view, a shadowy, pre-mortal existence is behind us, and theosis is the eventual destiny awaiting us subsequent to our return there. Borrowing from Leibniz the idea of the soul as a superior form of monad, Goethe said to Johannes Falk: "That Monades may be capable of a general historical retrospect, I will not dispute....The progress of a mona[d]...will elicit many things out of the dark bosom of its memory, which seem like divinations, though they be at bottom only dim recollections of some foregone state." Explaining the loss of memory, he ventured that "the former states or circumstances through which we...have passed, were too insignificant and mean, for much of it to have been, in the eyes of Nature, worthy to be remembered again." Then, sounding like Timaeus, who paired every human soul with a celestial body, he said of his contemporary the poet Christoph Martin Wieland:

> [I]f thousands of years hence I were to meet this same Wieland as...a star of the first magnitude, were to see him, [I would]...witness how he quickened and cheered every thing that approached him by his beautiful light....We can admit no other destination for monads, than, as blessed co-operating Powers, to share eternally in the immortal joy of gods. The work of creation is intrusted to them.

And then, carried away in his exuberant vision, Goethe cited Diderot's provocative version of theosis: "If there *is* not a God, yet, perhaps, there will be one."[48]

In that same *Faust*, Goethe had created the memorable character Homunculus ("little man" in Latin), an alchemical creation of Faust's aspiring protégé Wagner. Shielded in its glass vial, aspiring to actualization and autonomy, the precocious creature is surely one of the most original embodiments of the idea of human preexistence. Indeed, as a Goethe scholar writes, "most commentators accept the evidence of a reported remark by Goethe that Homunculus represents 'pure entelechy,' pure intellect or spirit in a state of pre-existence, before it has become 'darkened' or 'confined' by physical or temporal existence."[49] "I...aspire to come to be," Homunculus cries in his quest for corporeal form.[50]

Victorian Versions

As the century progressed into the Victorian era, poets showed, if anything, an even greater openness to nontraditional forms of spirituality, often Eastern influenced. One of these was Alfred, Lord Tennyson (1809–1892), who espoused a poetic version of Spiritualism that found in the idea of preexistence both a rationale for friendship that seems to transcend temporality and a consolation for its devastating and tragic interruptions (preexistence, for Tennyson and some of his contemporaries, could sometimes blur indiscriminately with metempsychosis):

> As when with downcast eyes we muse and brood,
> And ebb into a former life, or seem
> To lapse far back in a confused dream

> To states of mystical similitude,
> If one but speaks, or hems, or stirs his chair,
> Ever the wonder waxeth more and more,
> So that we say, "All this hath been before,
> All this hath been, I know not when or where;"
> So, friend, when first I look'd upon your face,
> Our thought gave answer, each to each, so true—
> Opposed mirrors each reflecting each—
> That, tho' I knew not in what time or place,
> Methought that I had often met with you,
> And either lived in either's heart and speech.[51]

Following the death of his sister, Tennyson revisited the subject. In "The Two Voices," he explicitly defends belief in a prior existence by comparing the intervening veil of forgetfulness to that subsequent to infancy:

> Or if thro' lower lives I came—
>
> …
>
> I might forget my weaker lot;
> For is not our first year forgot?
> The haunts of memory echo not.
>
> And men, whose reason long was blind,
> From cells of madness unconfined,
> Oft lose whole years of darker mind.
>
> Much more, if first I floated free,
> As naked essence, must I be
> Incompetent of memory.
>
> …
>
> Moreover, something is or seems
> That touches me with mystic gleams,
> Like glimpses of forgotten dreams—
>
> Of something felt, like something here;
> Of something done, I know not where;
> Such as no language may declare.[52]

The most traumatic loss that Tennyson suffered was the sudden death of his friend Arthur Henry Hallam in 1833. Tennyson belabored his grief over a period of seventeen years into a magnum opus that confronts and wrestles with the entire weight of nineteenth-century scientism and skepticism in his quest for personal confidence in the durability of human relationships. Originally titled "The Way of the Soul," his sprawling *In Memoriam* is more a desperate bid for faith than the calm and collected account of its capture. In one disputed passage,[53] pondering whether the departed will remember those people and experiences left behind, Tennyson considers the analogy with the living who remember, imperfectly, their own prior existence:

> But he forgets the days before
> God shut the doorways of his head.
> The days have vanish'd, tone and tint,
> And yet perhaps the hoarding sense
> Gives out at times—he knows not whence—
> A little flash, a mystic hint;
> And in the long harmonious years—
> If Death so taste Lethean springs—
> May some dim touch of earthly things
> Surprise thee ranging with thy peers.
> If such a dreamy touch should fall,
> O, turn thee round, resolve the doubt;
> My guardian angel will speak out
> In that high place, and tell thee all.[54]

Finally, Tennyson wrote near the end of his life a simple poem, which casts death as a return to primeval origins. Its lyrical symmetry balances the pre- and post- phases of human existence not as cyclical repetition, but as a straightforward journey "out of the boundless deep" that finds closure in the return home. Its privileged place in his canon—he requested that it be the final poem in all editions of his poetry—makes it a clear summation of his creed:

> Sunset and evening star,
> And one clear call for me!
> And may there be no moaning of the bar,
> When I put out to sea.
>
> But such a tide as moving seems asleep,
> Too full for sound and foam,
> When that which drew from out the boundless deep
> Turns again home.
>
> Twilight and evening bell,
> And after that the dark!
> And may there be no sadness of farewell,
> When I embark.

For though from out our bourne of Time and Place
The flood may bear me far,
I hope to see my Pilot face to face
When I have crossed the bar.[55]

Tennyson's contemporary Dante Gabriel Rossetti (1828–1882) gave the same motif a more erotic turn:

I have been here before,
But when or how I cannot tell:
I know the grass beyond the door,
The sweet keen smell,
The sighing sound, the lights around the shore.

You have been mine before,—
How long ago I may not know:
But just when at that swallow's soar
Your neck turned so,
Some veil did fall,—I knew it all of yore.[56]

By late Victorianism, the preexistence motif seemed almost de rigueur, with Robert Browning (1812–1889) making his contribution to the genre as well:

Earth changes, but thy soul and God stand sure:
What entered into thee,
That was, is, and shall be:
Time's wheel runs back or stops: Potter and clay endure.
He fixed thee 'mid this dance
Of plastic circumstance,
This Present, thou, forsooth, would fain arrest:
Machinery just meant
To give thy soul its bent,
Try thee and turn thee forth, sufficiently impressed.[57]

Even on those occasions when the theme appeared in traditions outside the German or Anglo-American, the roots could often be traced back to those conduits. Francisco Sellén (1838–1907) was a leading Cuban poet who spent time in Germany. He translated both German and British Romantics and produced a melancholy meditation on preexistence that appeared in English translation:

I have lived before. Where? That I cannot tell,
Nor how, nor when. Of those forgotten years
Only vague echoes from the darkness swell,
Bringing familiar murmurs to my ears....

My soul mounts upward into loftier spheres,
Where, beyond the boundaries of time and space,
I lived and loved before these earthly years
Chained me, an exile, in my present place.

I see, in fleeting rays of heavenly light,
The glory of a distant paradise;
Then all is overwhelmed by starless night,
My anxious questionings meet no replies.

Heavy my heart with memories of old;
My power to live and strive is overcast
By wild desire the mystery to unfold,
Which binds my present to that vanished past.

This is my heritage of sorrow now,
That veiled an unknown form which once I wore:
I cannot fathom when, nor where, nor how,
I only know that I have lived before.[58]

The American Scene

In the United States, as in England and to a limited extent Germany, preexistence was also finding fertile ground in the realm of poetical and philosophical speculation along with theological expression. These manifestations occurred at both the peripheries and at the heart of high culture. In midcentury, the same region that was rich in supernaturalistic enthusiasm and that gave rise to Mormonism, Millerism, and other religious movements also spawned an interest in spirit communication through rappers, those who entered trance states, and other mediums; this blossomed into the Spiritualist movement. A leading figure in this arena, sometimes called the John the Baptist of Spiritualism, was Andrew Jackson Davis (1826–1910), who attended lectures on animal magnetism in the 1840s and thereafter discovered clairvoyant powers in himself. Though preexistence did not figure prominently in American Spiritualism, Davis recorded in *Memoranda* a morning given over to "conversation with visitors concerning the doctrine of learned French Spiritualists who strenuously inculcate the 'eternal *past* individuality of every human being.'"[59] Assenting to the idea himself, Davis cited by way of support several of the Cambridge Platonists, as well as two titans of the recent Romantic age: Walter Scott (1771–1832) and Robert Southey (1774–1843). Southey, Wordsworth's predecessor as England's poet laureate, wrote of his belief in "progressive existence," opining that, at some point, "we shall recover the consciousness of some lower stages through which we have passed."[60] Scott's personal intuition of preexistence was more commented upon at the time. He famously recorded in his journal an experience that has some similarity to what would now be called déjà vu, but which conjured in his mind something rather more Platonic:

> I cannot, I am sure, tell if it is worth marking down, that yesterday, at dinner-time, I was strangely haunted by what I would call the sense of pre-existence—namely, a confused idea that nothing that passed was said for the first time....The sensation was so strong as to resemble a *mirage* in the desert, or a calenture on board of ship, when lakes are seen in the desert, and sylvan landscapes in the sea. It was distressing yesterday, and brought to my mind the fancies of Bishop Berkeley about an ideal world. There was a vile sense of want of reality in all I did and said.

He tried to dismiss the feeling as due to bad digestion or too much wine, and then confessed, "something of this insane feeling remains to-day."[61] Davis concluded his overview of the doctrine (he also cited Wordsworth and Tennyson) by suggesting that Spiritualism offers a more scientific explanation for the intuition of preexistence than do Plato and his successors: "It seems to me, whenever I hear or read any thing from the pre-existence philosophers, that they would obtain a more rational explanation of their 'evidences' by investigating the three forms of mediumship," which he had explicated in his own writings.[62]

Preexistence also found gifted expression by a southern writer best known for his poetry in support of the Confederate cause, who was known internationally in his prime. But both before and after the Civil War, Paul Hamilton Hayne (1830–1886) wrote poems of great emotional intensity on the subject of preexistence. In 1855, he published a sonnet of that title:

> If immortality be not a dream
> Wherefore should we never have known of yore
> Another life than ours, a mystic shore,
> Whose memory haunts as a shadowy beam
> Of pallid starlight haunts a clouded stream?

Regretting that our "weak lore" gives no such assurance, he senses nonetheless that "we rise to Heaven / by infinite gradations,...till the immaculate soul / Stands on the heights of Godhead pure and whole."[63]

He gave the subject longer treatment in another poem of the same title that, like Tennyson (who reportedly greatly admired Hayne), found interpersonal magnetism a spur to such thinking:

While sauntering through the crowded street,
Some half-remembered face I meet,

Albeit upon no mortal shore
That face, methinks, hath smiled before.

Lost in a gay and festal throng,
I tremble at some tender song—

Set to an air whose golden bars
I must have heard in other stars.
…

At sunset, as I calmly stand,
A stranger on an alien strand—

Familiar as my childhood's home
Seems the long stretch of wave and foam.
…

O swift, instinctive, startling gleams
Of deep soul-knowledge! not as *dreams*

For aye ye vaguely dawn and die,
But oft with lightning certainty

Pierce through the dark, oblivious brain,
To make old thoughts and memories plain—

Thoughts which perchance must travel back
Across the wild, bewildering track

Of countless æons; memories far,
High-reaching as yon pallid star,

Unknown, scarce seen, whose flickering grace
Faints on the outmost rings of space![64]

Transcendentalism

Beecher had found that even the liberality of Unitarianism was not generous enough to accommodate pre-mortality as a religious tenet. One exception was a group of contemporaries for whom the idea of preexistence became a virtual commonplace. Finding religious orthodoxy to be no hedge to exploring an idea so rich in potential, several young Unitarians, called "transcendentalists," organized themselves into a club in 1836. Their standing and influence was such that, almost a century later, a scholar would remark that these thinkers took "up a tradition which had never totally lapsed and which today is enjoying a genuine revival among philosophical scholars." Fantastical elements notwithstanding, this world view "has ever retained the respect of the philosophically minded," he added.[65] The doctrine found a comfortable home with these thinkers for many reasons. Their religious nonconformity continued and extended the revolt against Calvinist doctrines that we saw in a theologian like Beecher, who was developing his revelation into a book during these same years. Espousing the inherent dignity of humanity and aspiring to lives of virtue and self-realization, without the hindrance of dogma or the constraints and particularism of narrow Christian creeds, they naturally were open to radically new—or radically old[66]—ideas about human nature, origins, and the capacity to recognize truth. George Ripley, who would go on to found the utopian community Brook Farm, explained the connection between the movement's name and that last subject in particular:

> There is a class of persons who desire a reform in the prevailing philosophy
> of the day. These are called Transcendentalists, because they believe in an
> order of truths which transcends the sphere of the external senses. Their
> leading idea is the supremacy of mind over matter. Hence they maintain
> that the truth of religion does not depend on tradition, nor historical facts,
> but has an unerring witness in the soul. There is a light, they believe, which
> enlighteneth every man that cometh into the world; there is a faculty in
> all—the most degraded, the most ignorant, the most obscure—to perceive
> spiritual truth when presented.[67]

Platonism provided the movement with an explanation for this universal light, upon which Ralph Waldo Emerson (1803–1882), a commanding figure of the movement, had seized as early as 1830. "The soul is an emanation of the Divinity, a part of the soul of the world, a ray from the source of light. It comes from without into the human body, as into a temporary abode."[68] In Emerson's exploration of the soul's origins and destiny, he exploded Christian categories and assimilated Eastern influences along with Platonic. In his exuberant vision, he found little patience with orthodoxies, whether religious, philosophical, or cultural. He chided:

> We cannot part with our friends. We cannot let our angels go. We do not
> see that they only go out that archangels may come in. We are idolaters
> of the old. We do not believe in the riches of the soul, in its proper eter
> nity and omnipresence....But we sit and weep in vain. The voice of the
> Almighty saith, "Up and onward forevermore!"[69]

An expansive if somewhat mystical version of human prehistory, his concept of the historical human reads initially like a simple celebration of fellow feeling, of kinship felt across time and culture:

> The Greek had, it seems, the same fellow-beings as I. The sun and moon, water and fire, met his heart precisely as they meet mine. Then the vaunted distinction between Greek and English, between Classic and Romantic schools, seems superficial and pedantic. When a thought of Plato becomes a thought to me,—when a truth that fired the soul of Pindar fires mine, time is no more. When I feel that we two meet in a perception, that our two souls are tinged with the same hue, and do as it were run into one, why should I measure degrees of latitude, why should I count Egyptian years?...The advancing man discovers how...universal man wrote by [the poet's] pen a confession true for one and true for all. His own secret biography he finds in lines wonderfully intelligible to him, dotted down before he was born.[70]

The difference here is that Emerson imputes some real, heritable component to this connection with the past. He insists that there is, in the history of human evolution,

> the philosophical perception of identity through endless mutations of form....And what see I on any side but the transmigrations of Proteus....The transmigration of souls is no fable. I would it were; but men and women are only half human. Every animal of the barn-yard, the field and the forest, of the earth and of the waters that are under the earth, has contrived to get a footing and to leave the print of its features and form in some one or other of these upright, heaven-facing speakers....The universal nature, too strong for the petty nature of the bard, sits on his neck and writes through his hand.[71]

Eastern influence is especially in evidence as Emerson develops his own spiritual anthropology into a concept he referred to as the "Over-soul":

> What is the ground of this uneasiness of ours; of this old discontent? What is the universal sense of want and ignorance, but the fine innuendo by which the soul makes its enormous claim?...The philosophy of six thousand years has not searched the chambers and magazines of the soul. In its experiments there has always remained, in the last analysis, a residuum it could not resolve. Man is a stream whose source is hidden. Our being is descending into us from we know not whence.[72]

In this highly abstracted version of preexistence, Emerson's acute historical consciousness blurs with his profound intuition about an actual spiritual dimension to human personality that transcends time. In a more modern vein, Friedrich Nietzsche wrote in virtually identical terms of the burden of our own historicity, but saw in it a danger rather than a cause for celebration. This is because Nietzsche found a vivid historical consciousness to be a potential enemy of life and insisted that whatever transhistorical inheritance impinges upon our present may be and must be transcended. Even the paragons of cultural elitism, the Greeks, "faced a danger similar to that which faces us: the danger of being overwhelmed by what was past and foreign, of perishing through 'history.'"[73]

Nietzsche was skeptical of approaches to history like Emerson's, with their sentimental humanism and idolatry of the past. For the person whom Nietzsche calls the antiquarian, "the history of his city becomes...the history of himself; he reads its walls, its towered gate, its rules and regulations, its holidays, like an illuminated diary of his youth....Sometimes he even greets the soul of his nation across the long dark centuries of confusion as his own soul."[74]

Ultimately, human authenticity and real life, for Nietzsche, depend upon an escape from the burden of a history that is "universal," "objective," and mindlessly interiorized as a cultural inheritance. Lacking Kant's recourse to a noumenal world outside of history, Nietzsche relies instead upon a kind of forgetting in order to exert sovereignty over the contingencies of history. But this process is fraught with risk:

> For since we are the outcome of earlier generations, we are also the outcome of their aberrations, passions and errors, and indeed of their crimes; it is not possible wholly to free oneself from this chain. If we condemn these aberrations and regard ourselves as free of them, this does not alter the fact that we originate in them. The best we can do is to confront our inherited and hereditary nature with our knowledge, and through a new, stern discipline combat our inborn heritage and implant in ourselves a new habit, a new instinct, a second nature, so that our first nature withers away. It is an attempt to give oneself, as it were *a posteriori*, a past in which one would like to originate in opposition to that in which one did originate:—always a dangerous attempt because it is so hard to know the limit to denial of the past and because second natures are usually weaker than the first.[75]

To the extent that Nietzsche invokes a mythical preexistence, it has appeal only because it offers a model of freedom from, rather than the initiation of, a human past. It represents, in his language, the "unhistorical," the only "foundation upon which anything sound, healthy, and great, anything truly human, can grow."[76] This point is clearest in his image of the child in its Edenic innocence, before it becomes immersed in and subject to history:

Man...braces himself against the great and ever greater pressure of what
is past: it pushes him down or bends him sideways, it encumbers his steps
as a dark, invisible burden which he can sometimes appear to disown and
which in traffic with his fellow men he is only too glad to disown, so as to
excite their envy. That is why it affects him like a vision of a lost paradise to
see the herds grazing or, in closer proximity to him, a child which, having
as yet nothing of the past to shake off, plays in blissful blindness between
the hedges of past and future. Yet its play must be disturbed; all too soon
it will be called out of the state of forgetfulness.[77]

And so, like Müller's concept of preexistence, a perfect equilibrium found only outside of causality and so outside of time, Nietzsche's grounding of the genuinely
human corresponds to an "unhistorical...duration," in which one stands "on the
threshold of the moment,...balanced like a goddess of victory, without growing
dizzy and afraid." Any other version of preexistence, trailing clouds of glory or any
other discernible baggage, is a burden.

For Emerson, by contrast, as for Wordsworth, the human heritage we bring
into this world of "a presence which will not be put by" is no burden, but rather
the very source of that inspiration and authority that make those nearest the veil
"an eye among the blind," "best philosophers," "mighty prophets," and "seers blest."
Emerson's conception of preexistence, at times clearly influenced by Eastern philosophy, elsewhere appears in the atemporal mode of the German idealists:

The soul...abolishes time and space....A man is capable of abolishing
them both. The spirit sports with time,—

> Can crowd eternity into an hour,
> or stretch an hour to eternity,

We are often made to feel that there is another youth and age than that
which is measured from the year of our natural birth....The soul looketh
steadily forwards, creating a world before her, leaving worlds behind her.
She has no dates....The soul's advances are not made by gradation, such
as can be represented by motion in a straight line, but rather by ascension
of state, such as can be represented by metamorphosis.[78]

Oliver Wendell Holmes recognized in Emerson's ruminations a clear embrace
of preexistence and lamented Emerson's involvement in such ideas, which he associated with a curiously selected trilogy of names: Pierre Leroux, Edward Beecher,
and Brigham Young.[79] Leroux (1797–1891) was a political radical who was active in
the 1830s and 1840s and, along with Edgar Quinet (1803–1875), rejected orthodox
religious views but espoused "the preexistence of souls, life as a series of expiations,

[and] terrestrial progress as both social and spiritual."[80] Neither registered any significant impact. Holmes wished that Emerson's had been less. Impatient with all of this Romantic sentimentalism, he almost sounded homesick for the bracing realism of a more Calvinist outlook on childhood. "The cloud of glory which the babe brings with it into the world is a good set of instincts, which dispose it to accept moral and intellectual truths,—not the truths themselves. And too many children come into life trailing after them clouds which are anything but clouds of glory."[81] Emerson's fault, Holmes groused, was in taking "the lofty rhapsodies of [Wordsworth's] noble [Immortality] Ode as working truths" and inculcating them, along with his "gospel of intuition," in a coterie of young disciples, thereby opening "the door to extravagances of unbalanced minds."[82]

Unbalanced or no, Emerson's disciples and associates were listening. Frederic Hedge (1850–1890), who organized the Transcendentalist Club, wrote the first article describing the movement, and launched its journal the *Dial*, held that "our soul…is older than we are.…The eternal destination which faith ascribes to the soul presupposes an eternal origin." Not only, he wrote, does psychology "favor the presupposition of pre-existence," but "this was the theory of the most learned and acute of the Christian Fathers. Of all the theories respecting the origin of the soul it seems to me the most plausible and therefore the one most likely to throw light on the question of the life to come."[83] Following in the wake of Basilides, Milton imitators, and Pope, Hedge also found in forgetfulness a strength rather than a weakness of the theory: "A happy thing if the soul pre-existed, it is for us that we remember nothing of the former life. The memory of a past existence would be a drag on the present, engrossing our attention much to the prejudice of life's interests and claims."[84] At the same time, Hedge invoked the safety net of gentle humor on the subject, insisting that preexistence was "rather an exceptional than universal fact.…The greater portion of mankind, we submit, are much too green for any plausible assumption of a foregoing training in good or evil. This planet is not their missionary station, nor their Botany Bay, but their native soil."[85]

Cyrus Augustus Bartol (1813–1900), a Unitarian minister and member of the group, wrote:

> [D]oubtless the almanac or family register will tell us when we were born. But our soul is older than our organism. It precedes its clothing. It is the cause, not the consequence, of its material elements; else as materialists understand, it does not properly exist. Jesus asserted the truth of all men when he said: "Before Abraham was I am." Who can tell when he began?[86]

Indeed, the generally accepted preexistence of Christ was a precedent and model that Bartol invoked repeatedly and emphatically. When Jesus referred to his own pre-mortality, Bartol insisted, "he meant no pre-existence you do not share." And again, "Jesus pre-existed, we say. Why not everybody, if *he* was a man?"[87]

Amos Bronson Alcott (1799–1888), one of the more fervent of the transcendentalists (and the "most representative and picturesque," according to one scholar),[88] worked to keep the movement's flame alive till the eve of the twentieth century. Along with the Unitarian pastor and writer William Ellery Channing and under the influence of Coleridge, Alcott aspired to a new fusion of Christian and Platonic ideals. He ran a progressive, experimental school in Boston (the Temple), led a short-lived utopian community (the Fruitlands), lectured widely, and contributed regularly to the *Dial*. His contributions appeared under a section called "Orphic Sayings," celebrating the doctrine of preexistence as it was known in ancient religions. Alcott holds:

> To conceive a child's acquirements as originating in nature, dating from his birth into his body, seems an atheism that only a shallow metaphysical theology could entertain in a time of such marvelous natural knowledge as ours. "I shall never persuade myself," said Synesius, "to believe my soul to be of like age with my body." And yet we are wont to date our birth, as that of the babes we christen, from the body's advent,…as if time and space could chronicle the periods of the immortal mind, and mark its longevity by our chronometers.[89]

"The soul does not chronicle her age," he writes elsewhere, "yet a celestial light irradiates this obscurity of birth, and reveals her spiritual lineage. Ancestor of the world,…dateless, timeless. She is coeval with God."[90] In another of his "Orphic Sayings," he writes, "The insatiableness of her desires is an augury of the soul's eternity.…A never ending still beginning quest of the Godhead in her bosom; a perpetual effort to actualize her divinity in time.…She is quivered with heavenly desires: her quarry is above the stars; her arrows are snatched from the armory of heaven."[91]

Alcott's rhetorical excesses cannot obscure what he elsewhere states as a simple matter of fact: "As conception precedes birth, life quickens life, in like manner souls precede their assumption of the human form. I am before I find myself bodily."[92] Finding it unnecessary to complicate generalities with specifics, Alcott takes it as a given that, for "the ancient wise men…the soul, being a descendent [*sic*] of divinity, was taken to be the eldest of all things in the corporeal world.…Pre-existing before bodies it presided over and ruled these."[93] His emphasis is not on human purgatory, fall, or punishment, but on the gradual process of theosis rooted in celestial origins. "The body is," essentially, "an instrument for the soul," and "all heads are portraits, more or less exact, of the typical Godhead. But the features elude stiffening in the brittle clay."[94]

As has so often been the case, Alcott relied in the final analysis more on sentiment and intuition than on philosophical analysis to defend his views. If Augustine could find in the stirrings of godly love a motive for conversion and nostalgia
for pre-mortal proximity to the divine, Alcott found brotherly and romantic love
equally compelling arguments for the reality of prior existence:

> [A]s to our memory of what has happened here, we shall remember
> what and whom we have loved, and forget all else. We shall not wish to
> remember that which we do not love, but the memory of all that we have
> loved here we shall carry with us, as we brought with us from that other
> world the memory of that which we loved there. They who have loved one
> another here will know one another hereafter.[95]

Alcott's views won him more notoriety than influence among contemporary
philosophers, although there were exceptions. One of his most enthusiastic supporters was George Holmes Howison (1834–1916), a founder of American per-
sonalism and of the Department of Philosophy at the University of California at
Berkeley. In 1878, Alcott founded an innovative summer school called the Concord School of Philosophy, which attracted throngs of adult students, prominent
academics, and, as lecturers, a slate of aging transcendentalists that included William T. Harris, editor of the *Journal of Speculative Philosophy*, Channing, Hedge,
and sometimes Emerson himself. A frequent participant was prominent Platonist
Hiram K. Jones. Virtually every year of the school's duration (almost a decade),
Jones lectured on the doctrine of the soul's preexistence.[96] Such presentations were
not always without controversy. In the school's fourth year, Alcott's remarks on
preexistence "called forth a long and animated discussion upon immortality, in
which the Rev. Dr. R. A. Holland questioned the relations of immortality to preexistence." Alcott replied, "[S]ouls never came into time. The soul is a universal,
and cannot enter the particular. But the soul manifests itself in objects which are
in time....Human heredity gives *ex*-istence; but the *sub*-sistence of the soul was
with God from all eternity."[97]

In the final year of the school, Jones's lecture on preexistence again precipitated
a lively discussion. Nathaniel Hawthorne's sister-in-law, Elizabeth Palmer Peabody,
and professor of psychology Alexander Wilder defended Jones's position. The
Hegelian Harris, though he acknowledged Jones's erudition, parted ways with him
on the literalness of the Platonic scheme of things.[98] Peabody had earlier made her
own defense of the doctrine, arguing in 1882 that "our common ideals of justice,
love, and beauty, testify to, for they constitute, the preexistent man of Plato, and by
reason of them all children are more alike than they are different....But the individuality, the different *peculium* of each individual in each instance, also expresses
somewhat of God, their preexistence with the Father."[99] She invoked as support the

Italian philosopher Vincenzo Gioberti's (1801–1852) view that "the soul has seen God before embodiment." The child's birth, she insisted in Wordsworth's language, "need *not* be an absolute forgetting of 'the glories he has known and that imperial palace whence he came.'"[100]

In large measure, the appeal that these thinkers found in the idea of preexistence was nothing new. Fewer theological inhibitions in this era, rather than newfound intellectual work done by the doctrine, goes a long way to explain its popularity. At the same time, contemporaries showed special interest in two dimensions of preexistence. First, the concept was amenable to ideas then current about human progress and unboundedness. Although preexistence is not an essential prerequisite to the doctrine of theosis, we have seen the connection repeatedly. Human origins in a realm of purer spirit, early associations with divinity, and the inherent goodness and potential that such beginnings suggest (as opposed to the depravity and inherited sinfulness that the Christian Fall entails)—all mean that theosis frequently follows from a doctrine of pre-mortal existence. In these conceptions, human movement is like a spiral that returns us to our point of origin; our roots guide our return, but our potential has been more perfectly realized through the detour. Plotinus, admired in this generation, had captured the wedding of preexistence and theosis with elegant simplicity:

> Plato says the One is not outside anything, but is in company with all without their knowing. For they run away outside it, or rather outside themselves. They cannot then catch the one they have run away from, nor seek another when they have lost themselves. A child, certainly, who is outside himself in madness will not know his father; but he who has learnt to know himself will know from whence he comes.[101]

The transcendentalist Alcott similarly found that the theory of a pre-mortal fall logically implied a recuperation not just of heaven, but of divinity itself. "All unrest," he wrote, "is but the struggle of the soul to reassure herself of her inborn immortality; to recover her lost intuition of the same, by reason of her descent amidst the lusts and worship of the idols of flesh and sense. Her discomfort reveals her lapse from innocence; her loss of the divine presence and favor." But, by the same token, "every soul feels at times her own possibility of becoming a God; she cannot rest in the human, she aspires after the Godlike. This instinctive tendency is an authentic augury of its own fulfillment. Men shall become Gods. Every act of admiration, prayer, praise, worship, desire, hope, implies and predicts the future apotheosis of the soul."[102]

Such self-identification with the divine provides a compelling logic for linking preexistence and theosis; it also makes explicit the theological danger of blasphemous hubris that both represent. And Plotinus seems blithely oblivious to those hazards, as he continues rapturously down this road: the soul that comes to know itself brings "itself into accord with that which all souls ought to, and the souls of the gods always do; and it is by bringing themselves into accord with it that they are gods. For a god is what is linked to that center." And, "if then one sees that oneself has become this,…and if one goes on from oneself, as image to original, one has reached 'the end of the journey.'"[103]

In the nineteenth century, this master conception of human origins served for some thinkers, Alcott included, as a basis not for contesting, but for assimilating Darwinian science into a view of humankind that both privileges the role of the past in human identity and embraces the evolutionary impetus behind all life:

> No one can be indifferent to the matter of descent without missing the key for unlocking the mysteries of character.…Ancestral dispositions and traits are not safely ignored. Genealogies tell tales. And it is a significant fact of our times that the genesis of species, races, families, and individuals is receiving the attention of accomplished thinkers and careful observers. Thanks to the Darwins and their school,—whatever their pretensions to scientific certainty.[104]

Alcott's philosopher friend Harris saw in his views an account more in keeping with Proclus, Plotinus, and Origen than Darwin, insofar as agency rather than pro-gression was emphasized. He outlined the essential features of Alcott's theory:

a. The first Principle, or God, is a Person—a self-determining or creative, self-dirempting [sic] or self-dissecting.
b. He creates that which is most like Himself, hence self-determined or cre-ative beings. They differ from the Absolute Person only in degree; they are pure souls.
c. These pure souls may lapse or may not. They have the possibility of lapse, since they are free.
d. Those that lapse create thereby bodies for themselves.[105]

And indeed, to the question of whether life offers progression or recuperation, he answered "both": "There is an instinct or tendency of the mind upwards, which shows a natural endeavor *to recover and raise* ourselves from our present sensual and low condition into a state of higher order and purity" (my emphasis).[106] As he elaborated, "souls do not lapse in equal degrees…and it is conceivable that some preserve their integrity intact, never descending into matter and mortality":

> Perchance God shapes souls bodiless, pure minds,
> Lapsed souls shape those that fleshly be,
> Man's soul the horizon 'twixt both kinds,
> In whom we do the world's abridgement see.[107]

His most eloquent expression of progress as the recapture of a distant past was perhaps in his poetic tribute to Emerson, where he urged the reader:

> Recall the memories of man's ancient state,
> Ere to this lost orb had his form dropt down,
> Clothed in the cerements of his chosen fate;
> Oblivious here of heavenly glories flown,
> Lapsed from the high, the fair, the blest estate,
> Unknowing these, and by himself unknown.[108]

In criticizing Emerson's views, Holmes may have analyzed effectively a second great appeal that this doctrine of preexistence held for the transcendentalists. He chided:

> The gospel of intuition proved to be practically nothing more or less than this: a new manifesto of intellectual and spiritual independence....That the organ of the mind brings with it inherited aptitudes is a simple matter of observation. That it inherits truths is a different proposition. The eye does not bring landscapes into the world on its retina,—why should the brain bring thoughts? Poetry settles such questions very simply by saying it is so.

Not just any poetry, of course, but more to the point and, in this case, more effectively, poetry that asserts an authority that is unimpeachable, because, in Holmes's words, it is trusting to subjective intimations "without reference to any other authority." He was proclaiming "a gospel of intuition."[109] Holmes was probably right. Emerson himself said, "Transcendentalists are men who believe in themselves, in their own convictions, and rely upon them." They are "self-trusting" and "self-relying."[110] To trace one's own eternal origins to the realm of the divine is not only to invoke the aura of Platonic certitude and transcendent truth, it is to appeal to a self rendered more ancient and majestic than the merely self-sufficient construct of post-Enlightenment rationalism. This glorying in a newfound authority that is both within and outside the self was evident in the words of Cambridge Platonist Henry More, who shared similar views of preexistence:

> I shall commend to them that would successfully philosophize, the belief and endeavor after a certain principle more noble and inward than Reason itself, and without which Reason will falter, or at least reach but to mean and frivolous ends. I have a sense of something in me while I thus speak, which I must confess is of so retruse [concealed] a nature that I have no name for it, unless I should adventure to term it *Divine Sagacity*.[111]

It is, of course, the Christian concept of inspiration, or the voice of God, or the Holy Spirit, in new garb. More mystical and less sectarian, it combines the advantages of a prophetic voice with a more universal mandate.

In addition to the religious journals of the day and the later debates at the Concord School, the subject of preexistence spilled onto the pages of the popular press. An 1857 contributor to the nineteenth-century miscellany *Notes and Queries* traces the recent literary interest in the subject, quoting Scott's famous diary account and other contemporaries, such as the Victorian novelist Samuel Warren (1807–1877). "I am strongly disposed to think," Warren said in a public lecture, "that every person who has meditated upon the operations of his own mind, has occasionally, and suddenly, been startled with a notion that it possesses qualities and attributes of which he has *nowhere* seen an account." He quotes Edward Bulwer-Lytton to similar effect, discussing "that strange kind of inner and spiritual memory, which often recalls to us places and persons we have never seen before, and which Platonists would resolve to be the unquenched and struggling consciousness of a former life."

Even without the advantage of historical distance, the writer recognizes that there is something new in this nineteenth-century resurgence of the idea—or what he calls these "mysterious impressions"—of pre-mortal experience. After rehearsing several other testimonies and instances, including those of the recently departed Wordsworth and his contemporary Lord Lyndsay, the writer ponders a decidedly non-Platonic explanation for what he considers may be a pathology:

> Are there new diseases of the mind as of the body, the result of higher civilization, and artificial modes of life, inducing a greater delicacy and susceptibility of the nervous system? Or are we indebted to our more active and refined enquiry, and more accurate habits of mental analysis for making us acquainted with mental phenomena, which existed before unobserved and unrecorded?

And then he proffers what may well be the most novel demystification of preexistence yet offered, which he calls "the most plausible solution." According to this theory, propounded in 1844 by Dr. A. L. Wigan in his work *A New View of Insanity: The Duality of the Mind*, the two hemispheres of the brain are understood as two organs that generally act in concord, but when they do not, a miniscule time lag in the processing function of one creates the illusion of an experience or intuition being an echo, or recollection, of a far more distant time and place.[112] Nichols's essay engendered various replies, some affirming the reality of the concept, others arguing for "mysterious memory" as a better term. The magazine would return to the subject of preexistence sporadically over the next ten years.

In the final analysis, the measure of the idea's currency in the nineteenth century is best reflected in one of the most impressive theological compendiums of the age. At over 900 pages, William Alger's encyclopedic *The Destiny of the Soul: A Critical History of the Doctrine of a Future Life* was first published in 1860. By its tenth edition (1880), it included a 5,000-title bibliography by the Harvard librarian Ezra Abbot, a considerable fraction of which came under the headings "Origin of the Soul" and "Pre-Existence." Alger noted that "the subject of the derivation of the soul has been copiously discussed by hundreds of philosophers, physicians, and poets, from Vyasa to Des Cartes, from Galen to Ennemoser, from Orpheus to Henry More, from Aristotle to Frohschammer." But in recent years especially, he noted, German literature "has teemed with works treating of this question from various points of view."[113]

In his encyclopedic work, Alger found that preexistence was "most widely affirmed" in the past and in the present also was "not without able advocates among the scholars and thinkers." Two principal varieties existed, he noted. One asserted human incarnation as a step up from a lower sphere. Writing apparently under the newly cast shadows of Darwin and Spenser, Alger interpreted the theory as evolution poorly understood:

> [I]t is enough here to say that the most authoritative voices in science reject it, declaring that, although there is a development of progress in the plan of nature,...yet there is no advance from one type or race to another, no hint that the same individual ever crosses the guarded boundaries of genus from one rank and kingdom to another.[114]

The other theory, which Alger deemed more worthy of attention, was the possibility that mortality represents a descent of the soul "from an anterior life on high." And of this school, he wrote, there are three varieties. The first, which he traced to the Manichaeans, alleges that "spirits were embodied by a hostile violence and cunning, the force and fraud of the apostatized Devil." In his colorful depiction of the belief, "whenever by the procreative act the germ body is prepared, a fiend hies from hell, or an angel stoops from bliss, or a demon darts from his hovering in the air, to inhabit and rule his growing clay house for a term of earthly life."

The second holds that "the stable bliss, the uncontrasted peace and sameness, of the heavenly experience, at last wearies the people of Paradise, until they seek relief in a fall." (We can hear in these words an echo of Origen's discussion of souls that fall out of "satiety.") The third and more common theory sees life as a descent and punishment for sin freely committed. Rather than trace this version to Origen, Alger associates it with Plutarch, who believed that the human soul "has removed, not from Athens to Sardis, or from Corinth to Lemnos, but from heaven to earth; and here, ill at ease, and troubled in this new and strange place, she hangs her head like a decaying plant."[115]

Ultimately, Alger can do no better with these various traditions than to dismiss them all with a curt wave of his hand, since they are "absolutely destitute of scientific basis."[116] This may seem an odd refutation, since the discussion occurs in the context of a work whose subject is, after all, "the doctrine of a future life"—a subject with little more claim to the support of the empirical sciences than the prehistory of the soul. Somewhat surprisingly, other theologians and orthodox apologists criticized preexistence in similar terms, blithely unaware of the blatant irony of their position. The Reverend Moses Ballou, for example, who probably wrote the longest modern refutation of preexistence (*The Divine Character Vindicated*, 1854), complains that "reason and observation do not seem to lead to it, except remotely and indirectly....It may be true, and it may not be. Who knows, or can positively tell us? The theory cannot be reached 'with direct and tangible evidence either *pro* or *con*.'"[117]

In any case, Alger is at his most insightful when he perfectly captures not the scientific bases, but the affective appeal, that the doctrine has exerted over the ages, most especially in the heyday of Wordsworthian Romanticism and its American Transcendentalist counterpart:

> The fragmentary visions, broken snatches, mystic strains, incongruous thoughts, fading gleams, with which imperfect recollection comes laden from our childish years and our nightly dreams, are referred by self pleasing fancy to some earlier and nobler existence. We solve the mysteries of experience by calling them the veiled vestiges of a bright life departed, pathetic waifs drifted to these intellectual shores over the surge of feeling from the wrecked orb of an anterior existence. It gratifies our pride to think the soul "a star traveled stranger," a disguised prince, who has passingly alighted on this globe in his eternal wanderings. The gorgeous glimpses of truth and beauty here vouchsafed to genius, the wondrous strains of feeling that haunt the soul in tender hours, are feeble reminiscences of the prerogatives we enjoyed in those eons when we trod the planets that sail around the upper world of the gods.[118]

It is easy to see why the idea has persevered so doggedly. Even its most arduous critics, intent on demystifying its appeal, end up enamored of it instead.

11

Preexistence in the Modern Age

[Abram] Besicovitch and Harry Williams asked me what God was doing
before the Creation. I said: "Millions of words must have been written
on this; but he was doing Pure Mathematics and thought it would be a
pleasant change to do some Applied."

—J. E. Littlewood[1]

The twentieth century would see one last effort to resuscitate the idea of
preexistence on philosophical and theological bases. It was essentially the
Cambridge Platonists redux. In a presidential address to the American
Society of Church History, Canon Charles Raven, a professor of divinity
at the University of Cambridge, made a brash assault on the validity of
a theological tradition that developed in the absence of the foremost
defender of preexistence:

> The first adequate theology, still perhaps the noblest ever
> formulated, [was] the Logos theology of the Greek Apologists,
> which had its fullest expression in the Christian Platonism of
> Clement of Alexandria and Origen....It is one of the tragedies
> of history that the work of this brilliant succession of Christian
> thinkers was allowed not merely to come to an end, but to fall
> into neglect, oblivion, and condemnation. If we are to handle
> effectively the task of elucidating a Christian theology for the
> twentieth century, we must...return to the point at which
> Origen was removed.[2]

Berdyaev

The man leading the charge to rehabilitate Origen in the twentieth-century setting was Nicholas Alexandrovich Berdyaev (1874–1948). Like Plato, Origen had found that the justice of God was most logically established by recourse to a pre-mortal realm in which humanity's free will could play out. Only on such a foundation could the mortal condition be affirmed as a product of human choice. Preexistence sustains God's justice even as it grounds humans' freedom. This same logic was embraced by Berdyaev in his elaboration of a doctrine of preexistent, self-aware souls. "By their fall away from the preexistent state," he writes, "all beings endowed with freedom have themselves determined their place in the world of space and time."[3]

It is unlikely that Berdyaev, any more than Beecher, Henry More, or other crusaders for the cause of preexistence, ever posed a real threat to established orthodoxy.

The most important Russian philosopher of the twentieth century, Nicholas Berdyaev wrote in passionate defense of freedom and thought preexistence to be the only alternative to "the terrorist and servile doctrine of everlasting hell." Photo from Dorlys, Paris, n.d.

Just the same, he managed to set off alarm bells in some ecclesiastical circles that sound to the present day, through his work to rehabilitate the theology of Origen. Timothy Ware, Bishop Kallistos of Diokleia, a highly respected scholar of Eastern Orthodoxy, published two authoritative texts, *The Orthodox Church* and *The Orthodox Way*. One reviewer, however, protested that his orthodoxy relied upon dangerously unorthodox figures, two of whom are connected by one heretical doctrine in particular:

> Worse than all of this, however, and truly astonishing, is the fact that among the ostensibly Orthodox authors whom he cites in his book, His Grace includes Origen and Synesios of Cyrene. Origen was condemned as a heretic by the Fifth Ecumenical Synod for teaching the Platonic doctrine of the preexistence of souls....As for Synesios, although Consecrated Bishop of Pentapolis by Patriarch Theophilos of Alexandria, he...only agreed to be Consecrated on two conditions: "that he should be permitted to continue his marriage, and should not be forced to abandon his philosophical opinions regarding the preexistence of the soul."[4]

A Web site associated with the Orthodox Church similarly warns against "contemporary heresiarchs" who purvey such heresies as "'pre-existence of the soul' and other cabbalistic and occult-gnostic inventions."[5] As the most prominent modern philosopher to emerge from the Eastern Orthodox tradition and an unabashed defender of preexistence, Nicholas Berdyaev was undoubtedly a source of such consternation.

A heresiarch he may be considered by some, but no less a figure than Paul Tillich has referred to Berdyaev as "one of the outstanding and most representative religious thinkers" of the era.[6] Another scholar characterizes the position of this Christian existentialist as a "a modern, de-mythologized conception of metempsychosis in terms of a universal, shared history of which all persons are a part, regardless of their temporal specificity."[7] But one needn't find some appropriately modern conception of a "shared history" to explain Berdyaev's system. It is much more straightforward:

> If we refuse to accept the terrorist and servile doctrine of everlasting hell we ought to admit the pre-existence of souls in another sphere before their birth on earth....This means that reincarnation on one level cannot be admitted, since it contradicts the integral nature of personality, and the unchangeableness of the very idea of man....Leibniz rightly speaks not of metempsychosis but metamorphosis.[8]

Berdyaev's clear reference to "the pre-existence of souls...before their birth on earth" and to their capacity for choice and accountability reflects a doctrine that pertains to the pre-mortal individual literally and unambiguously. Just the same,

Berdyaev develops a theory of temporality that complicates the picture. "The doctrine of pre-existence is a profound one," he writes, "because it is based upon the memory of existential time." Existential time is distinct from cosmic and historical time, both of which are linear, impersonal, and chronologically ordered. Existential time, on the other hand, "depends upon intensity of experience, upon suffering and joy.... [It] is evidence of the fact that time is in man, and not man in time, and that time depends upon changes in man.... In existential time, which is akin to eternity, there is no distinction between the future and the past."[9]

What Berdyaev calls here "existential time" would seem to comport with what Boehme calls "still eternity." As one scholar explains:

> The records left us by mystics all suggest, and many state, that, in those moments when a saint sees no longer through a glass darkly, he feels that he is transcending time, that he is grasping in one instant a harmony which includes and reconciles all the conflicts of successive, transitory life.... Non-successive, still eternity, then, is not just an odd metaphysical fancy inherited by Christianity from Platonism, but it is grounded on a persistent and widespread psychological phenomenon.[10]

In this view, it is not because of any perceived waffling about the reality of pre-existence that it makes no sense, strictly speaking, to refer to our existence before historical time, any more than it makes sense to speak of time before the big bang.[11] In both cases, the birth of the cosmos is the coming into being of time itself and the precondition for any before and after. The human soul of each individual, however, most emphatically does not come into existence simultaneously with the created body, according to Berdyaev. That is why he writes that "the teaching of Origen is more acceptable than the traditional theological doctrine of the creation of the soul at the moment of conception, or of its coming into being in the process of birth by way of hereditary transmission."[12]

Berdyaev further follows Origen in locating the fall of humankind not in the garden of Eden, but in the transition from existential into historical time. And indeed, his logic would appear to suggest that the fate of an eternal soul cannot be circumscribed by an accident of history: "Man's existence in the setting of this world is but a moment of his spiritual journey. But his destiny is sunk deep in eternity and cannot depend solely upon this fallen time. The Fall of Man did not occur in this phenomenal world nor in this time. On the contrary, this phenomenal world and its time are a product of the Fall."[13] Or, as he puts it elsewhere with succinct eloquence: "Time is not the image of eternity (as in Plato, Plotinus), time is eternity which has collapsed in ruin."[14] In yet another work, Berdyaev writes simply, "[M]an is a fallen creature—an earthly being preserving memories of heaven and reflections of a heavenly light." In this life, the human may well appear to be a product of evolutionary progress, a "perfected animal." But any materialist conception of the human, he argues, misses the point that "man's dynamism springs from freedom and not from necessity." That is why, if one is to avoid an impoverished naturalism, "one must recognize the pre-existence of the soul. The soul is not a product of the generic process and is not created at the moment of conception, but is created by God in eternity, in the spiritual world. Only in that case can human personality be metaphysically independent."[15]

The language here is strikingly reminiscent of Boehme, who had replied to the question "whence proceeded the Soul Originally at the beginning of the World?" with the assertion that "all things are originally sprung and derived from eternity."[16] Berdyaev's indebtedness to the German mystic becomes even clearer as he develops his analysis of human freedom. Berdyaev has sometimes been called "the philosopher of freedom *par excellence*."[17] So it is no surprise that he finds that the kind of freedom preexistence makes possible outweighs the dangers to traditional constructions of God's sovereignty. This freedom he bases on the concept of the *Ungrund*, which we saw in Boehme. German philosophers from Franz von Baader to Hegel had developed and expanded Boehme's concept, and theologian Julius Müller had built his own case for human freedom—and, ultimately, human preexistence—on Schelling's appropriation of the idea, referring to the "'primary Basis,' or 'the Ungrounded,' of which nothing can be predicated save that it is 'predicateless.'"[18] Schelling's own formulation was unmistakably influenced by Boehme. "As there is nothing before or outside of God," he wrote, "he must contain within himself the ground of his existence. All philosophies say this, but they speak of this ground as a mere concept without making it something real and actual."[19] A historian of philosophy traces its further development by Berdyaev:

> Berdyaev says: "Out of the Divine Nothing, or of the *Ungrund*, the Holy Trinity, God the Creator is born." The creation of the world by God the Creator is a secondary act. "From this point of view it may be said that freedom is not created by God: it is rooted in the Nothing, in the *Ungrund* from all eternity…for both God and freedom are manifested out of the *Ungrund*. God the Creator cannot be responsible for freedom which gave rise to evil…." Hence it follows that God has no power over freedom which is not created by him: "God the Creator is all-powerful over being, over the created world, but He has no power over non-being, over the uncreated freedom." This freedom is prior to good and evil, it conditions the possibility of both good and evil. According to Berdyaev, the actions of a being possessing free will cannot be foreseen even by God, since they are entirely free.

If this sounds like God's infinitude must be diminished to make room for human freedom, that is precisely the case. N. O. Lossky continues:

> Berdyaev denies God's omnipotence and omniscience and maintains that He does not create the cosmic entities' will, which springs from the *Ungrund*, but merely helps that will to become good; he is led to that conclusion by his conviction that freedom cannot be created and that if it were, God would be responsible for cosmic evil. A theodicy would then be impossible, Berdyaev thinks.[20]

Here, we see yet one more time the fulfillment of the worst fears of the Mesopotamian gods, the justification of Augustine's fear that preoccupation with free will could work to the detriment of God's grace and humanity's dependence on it, and the vindication of those anathemas that saw an inexorable linkage in Origen (reflected later in the Cambridge Platonists) between preexistent glory and a dangerously boundless humanism.

If the demise of Calvinism was one casualty of modern liberalism with its progressive notions of justice and reasonableness, the West's dogged commitment to free will has likewise threatened the underpinnings of theism itself with an urgency that has never slackened. Early American theologian Jonathan Edwards, for example, thought he had reconciled absolute sovereignty with human free will by asserting that human beings were free in the only way that mattered, i.e., "their choices were thoroughly their own, not bound except by their *own* moral natures and inclinations."[21] That formulation, of course, only narrowed the focus of the problem. Because if God created all human beings, body and soul, then he created the basis of those "natures and inclinations." As modern philosopher Thomas Nagel puts it:

> It makes no sense to condemn oneself or anyone else for a quality which is not within the control of the will.... If one cannot be responsible for consequences of one's acts due to factors beyond one's control, or for antecedents of one's acts that are properties of temperaments not subject to one's will, or for the circumstances that pose one's moral choices, then how can one be responsible even for the stripped-down acts of the will itself, if *they* are the product of antecedent circumstances outside of the will's control? The area of genuine agency, and therefore of legitimate moral judgment, seems to shrink under this scrutiny to an extensionless point.[22]

Berdyaev was only one among scattered twentieth-century philosophers who found freedom increasingly difficult to defend without recourse to preexistence. John McTaggart Ellis McTaggart (1866–1925), a British philosopher famous, among other things, for useful theorizing about two kinds of time[23] (and also as an atheist proponent of immortality), has pointed out the seemingly obvious when he argues that, if God created our souls, he "could have prevented all sin by creating us with better natures and in more favorable surroundings....Hence we should not be responsible for our sins to God."[24] Edwards was fully aware of this problem but found comfort in its being universally acknowledged. "Every version of Christianity had the same problem. All Christians taught that there *is* sin in the world and that God created the world."[25] Aquinas had addressed this issue in *Summa Theologica*, recognizing the logical difficulty presented by his own acknowledgment, on the one hand, of God as "First Cause" and, on the other, of Aristotle's dictum that *only* that which is "cause of itself" is free.[26] God can be free, therefore, but nothing that derives from, exists outside, or follows upon that first cause can be. In other words, belief in God as the source of all being would seem to be fundamentally incompatible with human moral agency if human beings are his creatures. Besides, McTaggart argued, preexistence is at least as reasonable as future immortality. "[T]he belief in human pre-existence is a more probable doctrine than any other form of the belief in immortality." As he reasoned, "immortality would almost necessarily stand or

The Cambridge philosopher McTaggart held the paradoxical position of being both an atheist and a vigorous proponent of the soul's pre-mortal existence. *John McTaggart Ellis McTaggart*, by Walter Stoneman, bromide print, 1917, National Portrait Gallery, London.

fall with pre-existence," for it is difficult to see "how existence in some future time could be shown to be necessary in the case of any being whose existence in past time is admitted not to be necessary....Any demonstration of immortality is likely to show that each of us exists through all time—past as well as future."[27]

The twentieth-century Cambridge philosopher John Wisdom agreed with McTaggart when he found, from the premises that blame presupposes free will and that free will only exists if no cause of our action is to be found outside ourselves, "however far back we go," that only a belief in preexistence can reconcile the principle of free will and the belief that every event has a cause. "Pre-existence then follows from our considerations," he concludes, and "this pre-existence must have been world-long."[28] He hastens to add in a footnote, "It is hardly necessary to warn the reader that this sort of conclusion is unfashionable." Perhaps not so surprisingly, some philosophers have shown themselves quite willing to accept literally any alternative to such a scenario. Wisdom's argument, for instance, is critiqued by Helen M. Smith, who holds, apparently without irony, that "if judgments of blame imply pre-existence it goes to show, not that we have pre-existed, but that we are never justified in attributing blame."[29]

The debate over free will has taken new directions as a result of a spate of twentieth-century theorizing that purports to explain not only the brain, but consciousness in terms of strict materialism. Philosopher Daniel Dennett finds the problem to be a pressing one in a world where the self, being conceived in purely materialistic terms, would thus appear to be "a mere thread in the fabric of causation." How can we, in other words, be both an agent and an object in a world governed by deterministic laws of cause and effect?

> On the one hand, we have the image of the agent, the do-er, the locus and source of action rather than mere reaction. We think of ourselves as such agents. As [John] Rawls notes, "citizens think of themselves as *self-originating sources* of valid claims."...We want to be able to say of ourselves, as Harry Truman famously said, "the buck stops here." On the other hand we have the image of the physical human being as no more salient, really, than domino number 743 in a chain of a million dominoes. If we are mere conduits of causation, it seems, we cannot also be agents. (my emphasis)

Dennett goes on to cite philosopher Roderick Chisholm's formulation of the dilemma:

> If we are responsible...then we have a prerogative which some would attribute only to God: each of us, when we act, is a prime mover unmoved. In doing what we do, we cause certain events to happen, and nothing—or no one—causes us to cause those events to happen.[30]

And so we come again back to Aristotle's statement of the problem. We are prime movers or we are not free. Dennett is impatient with what he sees as a false either-or leading to these "obscure and panicky metaphysics,"[31] and he argues for the presence of "elbow room" for agency in spite of the deterministic tugging of the empirical universe. His recognition of the difficulty of the problem and the immensity of the stakes attests to its enduring relevance and intractability, his belabored attempt at a solution notwithstanding.

The entire problem of a first cause (along with Dennett's philosophical gymnastics) could be obviated, of course, by following Chisholm's logic to its inexorable conclusion, that is, positing multiple "unmoved movers" existing alongside God. But this would require both belief in a soul and a radical rejection of God as absolutely sovereign—that is, if sovereignty is understood in the terms found in the Westminster Confession, according to which "He is the alone fountain of all being." Reconstituting that idea of sovereignty provides one way of eliminating a temporal origin for human souls (thereby making of them unmoved movers) in order to solve the problem of human freedom. William James suggests the reasonableness as well as the difficulty of such a solution, noting:

> Theism, whenever it has erected itself into a systematic philosophy of the universe, has shown a reluctance to let God be anything less than All-in-All. In other words, philosophic theism has always shown a tendency to become pantheistic and monistic,...and this has been at variance with popular or practical theism, which latter has ever been more or less frankly pluralistic, not to say polytheistic, and shown itself perfectly well satisfied with a universe composed of many original principles, provided we [are] only allowed to believe that the divine principle remains supreme and that the others are subordinate.[32]

In other of his writings, as David Paulsen comments, James personally endorsed this metaphysical pluralism, apparently postulating freely acting agents as among the entities co-original with God.[33]

This avenue out of the impasse reveals in the doctrine of preexistence both a temptation and a danger. For clearly, creating a multiplicity of souls coexisting with God would be a theological sword to cut the philosophical Gordian knot of determinism. But to posit preexistent souls can be construed as an affront to God alone as eternal and a diminishing of the distance that separates Creator from creature. Fear of this slippery slope of a collapsing sacred distance is clearly evident in Eastern Orthodoxy. It is no coincidence that the modern church most hostile to "heresiarchs" preaching preexistence also emphatically "disassociates [it]self from all attempts to make a bridge between the infinite and the finite."[34] This concern is doubtless one of the primary factors in orthodox resistance to an idea that was increasingly recognized as incompatible with the creedal understanding of God as it emerged in the early Christian centuries (as well as with the God of Judaism). Berdyaev, as one of the most influential advocates of preexistence in twentieth-century philosophy, could there-fore be seen as sealing the fate of the doctrine, theologically, by laying bare not just its efficacy in solving the problem of free will but the theological cost as well.

Outside the realm of theological speculation and inspired by other motiva-tions than the rescue of moral agency from determinism, some philosophers have occasionally returned to assess the value and cogency of the doctrine of preexis-tence. The thought of our own dissolution—the simple fear of oblivion—probably impels humankind to seek faith in an afterlife. But on the face of it, it would seem no more intrinsically logical to assert a belief in a continuing, eternal existence after this life than to assume a prior, equally eternal existence before our present life. Some philosophers accordingly have followed in the wake of Hume, who found a unidirectional infinity illogical (as did Menasseh ben Israel and Shelley, as we saw). British educator Arthur Henry King recollected spending a few days with Bertrand Russell at the Swedish university where King was teaching. He recalled the philosopher asking "whether it was reasonable to suppose that something immor-tal could just suddenly begin in time."[35] A classical scholar wrote, "[I]n the thought of the preexistence and immortality of the soul lies an attempt at consistent think-ing, a groping for something like an eternal, imperishable Being."[36]

John Knox, Jr., has also argued that pre-mortal existence is even more rea-sonable than postexistence. What he designates "a rationally respectable case for individual pre-existence" relies upon Leibniz's principle of sufficient reason. Leib-niz argued that everything that is must have a reason for both its being and for its being what it is and not something else. Knox's argument is complicated, but holds essentially that the eruption into existence of subjective entities like self-conscious humans cannot be possible because no reason or explanation for self-identity is possible. Since we nonetheless exist, we must have always existed. Knox's argument is, he insists, free from reliance upon "support from either religion or from parapsy-chology." It relies rather upon particular notions of selfhood and identity, namely, that "first-person statements carry extra-scientific import." What he means by this is illustrated with the example of two rocks with identical qualities and spatiotem-poral coordinates, which are, for all practical purposes and in every sense of the word identical. But between oneself and a qualitatively identical twin, there will always remain, "at least to the person concerned,...an intelligible distinction":

Unlike, perhaps, the coming-to-be of a rock, the inception of a self-conscious being as the very one it is (and not some other one, even one just like it) does indeed make sense, and thus (should such an event take place within the temporal stream) demand an explanation. That explana-tion might have to be private; for perhaps no one but oneself would know what particular person one was or, therefore, would be in a position to explain why just that person had come into being. But if so, what would seem to follow is not that one's emergence into being would require no explanation, but instead that (my own view) no such explanation could possibly exist.[37]

Ironically, perhaps, Knox finds that one cannot argue along similar lines for the reasonableness of future immortality. Human preexistence, he finds, is logically necessary. Any guarantee against future annihilation of the self, on the other hand, is not. It is quite conceivable, for example, that persons have existed for all time through the sustaining influence of some superior power, whose abiding support is by no means necessary or assured.

Knox also appeals to reflection and introspection to make his argument. Like Wordsworth, who found pre-mortal intimations a "fountain light" of our day and the "master light" of our seeing, Plotinus found innate embers of memory to be the catalyst to our striving. Every soul that knows its history seeks to return to its divine source. In our present state, "since a part of us is held by the body, as if someone had his feet in water,…we lift ourselves up by the part which is not submerged."[38] Knox, on the other hand, merges transcendentalist spirituality with a gesture toward logical rigor. "I…have the intuition," he writes, "that I—this very self—might have been born of different parents, indeed as a different species of animal. And this intuition is very strong with me; I think it is sound. If it is, then that very fact may imply that my birth and my beginning are two different things."[39] Put more simply, he is saying that to be able to say without any sense of self-evident absurdity, "If I had been born…," is to implicitly recognize a self that is logically prior to any particular incarnation.

Perhaps the most unusual approach to the subject is the argument from aesthetics outlined by the influential religious scholar D. P. Walker. He has pointed out that the normative Christian conception of eternity—especially compared to the Platonic ideas we have already discussed—is "metaphysically unsatisfactory," exhibiting as it does "arbitrary and asymmetrical features." More specifically, he writes:

> [T]he Christians are perhaps at a real disadvantage in having two eternities [the heaven and the hell inhabited by human souls] which have a beginning but no end.…Why not an [eternity going backward] instead of [forward] (beings who have no beginning but an end)? or why not both? or why not a successive eternity with neither beginning nor end, as in the Neo-Platonic scheme? To anyone thinking in Platonic terms the *aeternitas a parte post* [eternity only going forward] would of course seem highly paradoxical; such a truncated, lop-sided eternity would be an absurdly inadequate image of the ideal, still eternity. This Christian scheme is, I suggest, untidy and inelegant.[40]

It would appear, in other words, that Walker is here conceding the aesthetic appeal of an eternity thus predicted on symmetry and harmony. Walker believes that a sense of this imbalance was a motive influencing the Cambridge Platonists of the seventeenth century. In his view, the major challenge is "to eliminate the *aeternitates a parte post*. With heaven this was usually done by asserting the pre-existence of the soul, i.e., by extending the *aevum* backwards to infinity."[41]

Returning to the argument from personal affinities first seen in Aristophanes and memorably developed by Tennyson, McTaggart finds that emotional bonds confirm logic:

> A still more striking instance is to be found in personal relations. Two people who have seen but little of each other are often drawn together by a force equal to that which could be generated by years of mutual trust and mutual assistance. The significance of this fact has been, I think, very much underrated. As a rule, the only case of it which is considered is the case—by no means the only one—when the attraction is between people of different sexes, and the inexplicability is then rather hastily explained as due to the irrationality of sexual desire.[42]

In the arena of philosophical debate over preexistence, however, the sword of logic could cut both ways. A philosopher relates one of Ludwig Wittgenstein's philosophical jokes:

> "…5, 1, 4, 1, 3—Done!" exclaims a haggard old man.
> "You look exhausted, what have you been doing?"
> *"Reciting the complete decimal expansion of π backwards."*

"A beginningless individual," the writer continues, "borders on contradiction. Yet philosophy itself may have begun by embracing this absurdity."[43] One could argue that a beginningless individual does not *border* on contradiction; the idea is flatly impossible. For, as the joke illustrates, if one can never proceed from the present through an infinite series of past moments and arrive at a terminus, then one could certainly never begin at that infinitely remote terminus and proceed to the present. The present, simply put, could never have arrived if one had to pass through an infinite number of days or years to get here.

Theosophy

While Berdyaev and McTaggart represent the philosophically inclined approach to a twentieth-century revival of preexistence, there was a more mystically oriented revival of the idea as well. Esotericist and scholar of ancient religion G. R. S. Mead notes that we have made no progress, in the millions of years of human existence, in fathoming either the secret of "whence we come" or the meaning of a human condition marked by pain, suffering, inequalities, and injustice. Given this situation, he insists, "we cannot afford to cast aside without a hearing any theory that attempts seriously to throw light on the darkness." He argues, "[T]he general hypothesis of pre-existence...does not, it is true, solve the fundamental problems, but it pushes back some of the initial difficulties." Its ethical appeal, he continues, is twofold: "It furnishes an ampler ground for the development of the soul than the cribbed, cabined, and confined area of one short earth life," and, more familiarly, positing a prior existence filled with moral choices and behaviors "permits us to entertain the notion of a law of moral causation" to explain our present circumstances, without offending "our innate sense of justice."[44]

He notes that, in "our own days we find those who...still hold to the idea of preexistence as the most hopeful hypothesis. Convinced of the fact of evolution, they reject the pessimistic doctrine of a fall, and regard the past of the soul optimistically as a scale of ascent."[45] The normally footnote-scrupulous Mead does not identify these contemporary "holders of the idea of preexistence." Presumably, he has in mind the Theosophical Society to which he belonged. In addition to his work as a scholar and translator of ancient texts, Mead was the personal secretary to Madame Helena P. Blavatsky and editor of the society's *Theosophical Review*.

The esoteric tradition rooted in Gnosticism and Neo-Platonism, with subsequent manifestations in the *Corpus Hermeticum* and Kabbalah, waned with the end of the Renaissance, though it found isolated reprises in Rosicrucianism, Freemasonry, and the mysticism of figures like Jacob Boehme and Emanuel Swedenborg. Its most syncretistic revival, however, would come in the form of the Theosophical Society formed by Madame Blavatsky in the late nineteenth century. Blavatsky was a Ukrainian who fled from her husband at the young age of seventeen, embarking on a series of world travels that took her into contact with virtually every secret society, occult doctrine, or esoteric practice of her day. She studied and absorbed elements of Freemasonry, Tibetan Buddhism, Coptic and Druze mystery cults, Persian Sufism, Ismaeli Gnosis, and a host of other traditions claiming access to higher knowledge or ancient wisdom. In the United States, she flirted briefly with Spiritualism, which was flourishing in the years after the Civil War, before forming an organization in 1875 with Henry Steel Olcott and others which they called the Theosophical Society. The group espoused three aims: (1) to promote the universal brotherhood of humanity; (2) to encourage the study of ancient and modern religions, philosophy, and science; and (3) to investigate the unexplained laws of nature and the psychic powers latent in humans.[46]

In 1877, Blavatsky published her first major work, *Isis Unveiled*, a compendium borrowing widely from non-Christian religions and setting out many of the movement's principal themes and preoccupations. In this ambitious attempt at something approaching a universal religious syncretism, she wove into her comprehensive overview a critical commentary on teachings from the Kabbalah, Hinduism, Paracelsus, mesmerism, hermeticism, Pythagoras, Proclus, Buddhism, Egyptian religion, Zoroaster, Gnosticism, and others. Her radicalism was in her refusal to privilege, as prior syncretists like Ficino and More had, the Christian mythos. She reversed the equation of *prisca theologia*, arguing that Judaism and Christianity were built upon the same mythologies as other systems, which could only be rightly understood by those versed in the keys of hidden knowledge. The earlier wisdom traditions are not derivative borrowings from Moses nor prophetic foreshadowings, but the purer fonts of divine truth. The Bible, by contrast, is but "the latest receptacle of this scheme of disfigured allegories."[47] (Also sure to further alienate mainstream Christians was her decision to name the society's official journal *Lucifer*.)

Theosophy and its New Age derivatives are today sometimes culturally marginalized, associated with the likes of Shirley MacLaine and West Coast, incense-filled bookstores. At its peak, however, the Theosophical Society appealed to a wide swath of the general public and to prominent intellectuals, based on its liberal-minded eclecticism, the vogue of Eastern religions, and an ostensibly scientific orientation. The Irish poet William Butler Yeats was a member of the society, as were Alfred Russel Wallace, Sir William Crookes, Thomas Edison, and crusader Annie Besant. Even Albert Einstein reportedly showed interest in Blavatsky's writings.

The single most significant influence of the society may have been the impetus it gave in America to Eastern religious thought, including the doctrine of preexistence. In her work on Isis, Blavatsky wrote that "both the human spirit and soul are preexistent. But, while the former exists as a distinct entity, an individualization, the soul exists as preexisting matter, an unscient [incapable of intellection] portion of an intelligent whole. Both were originally formed from the Eternal Ocean of Light."[48] She later elaborated in a virtual manifesto on the subject: "The doctrines of Theosophy are simply the faithful echoes of Antiquity. Man is a *Unity* only at his origin and at his end. All the Spirits, all the Souls, gods and demons emanate from and have for their root-principle the SOUL OF THE UNIVERSE—says Porphyry." Her version of this doctrine, she insisted, "was taught by Brahmins, Buddhists, Hebrews, Greeks, Egyptians and Chaldeans; by the postdiluvian heirs of the prediluvian Wisdom, by Pythagoras and Socrates, Clemens Alexandrinus, Synesius and Origen, the oldest Greek poets as much as the Gnostics."[49] The controversies associated with Blavatsky's career and her refusal to regard Christianity as having any kind of epistemological or moral primacy probably made her advocacy of preexistence more a detriment than an asset to the idea's credibility in the larger cultural landscape.

Twentieth-Century Literature

The dawn of the twentieth century saw the almost total eclipse of preexistence in Christianity (Berdyaev's advocacy of and Mormonism's undiminished adherence to the tenet excepted). Occasional eruptions of the idea do appear, as in Christian apologist G. K. Chesterton's lyrical excursus on the peculiar nature of what he calls "Christian optimism." While stopping shy of the term preexistence, Chesterton recaptures the logic and language alike of Augustine to intimate a common human memory of prelapsarian worlds. He finds an ironic cause for optimism in resigning himself to the universally shared consequences of Adam's sin; the feeling of unmistakable alienation and exile attests to a happier antecedent dimly remembered:

> The modern philosopher had told me again and again that I was in the right place, and I had still felt depressed even in acquiescence. But I had heard that I was in the *wrong* place, and my soul sang for joy, like a bird in spring. The knowledge found out and illuminated forgotten chambers in the dark house of infancy. I knew now why grass had always seemed to me as queer as the green beard of a giant, and why I could feel homesick at home.[50]

As the motif disappeared from religious discourse, so did it decline in artistic representation as well. Still, notable exceptions appeared sporadically and unsystematically. In one of the early twentieth century's greatest works of fiction, *Remembrance of Things Past*, Marcel Proust engages in a Platonic excursus in order to argue for a real, transcendent ground to the values that guide human life and aspiration:

> All that we can say is that everything is arranged in this life as though we entered it carrying the burden of obligations contracted in a former life; there is no reason inherent in the conditions of life on this earth that can make us consider ourselves obliged to do good, to be fastidious, to be polite even, nor make the talented artist consider himself obliged to begin over again a score of times a piece of work the admiration aroused by which will matter little to his body devoured by worms....All these obligations which have not their sanction in our present life seem to belong to a different world, founded upon kindness, scrupulosity, self-sacrifice, a world entirely different from this, which we leave in order to be born into this world, before perhaps returning to the other to live once again beneath the sway of those unknown laws which we have obeyed because we bore their precepts in our hearts.[51]

The theme is more developed in the six-act "fairy play" written by the Belgian Maurice Maeterlinck, *The Blue Bird* (1908). The story is a fantastical quest involving children, animals turned human, fairies, talking trees, and personified foodstuffs. Two impoverished peasant children, Myltyl and Tyltyl, are sent on a search for a bluebird by the fairy Bérylune. Given a special hat that "gives new light to dimmed eyes," they enter a world transformed into enchanted beauty and are accompanied by their (now-talking) dog and cat and other animated objects (like Bread and Light).[52]

First, they journey to the Land of Memory and visit their deceased grandparents and seven siblings. They visit the Palace of Night, with its fearful mysteries, and the Palace of Happiness, with its sham pleasures and authentic delights (like the little "Happiness of Running Barefoot in the Dew" and the great "Joy of Being Just," which are allegorical entities like talking Platonic forms). At last, guided by the benevolent Light, they pass through the graveyard and into the Kingdom of the Future, "where the children wait that are yet to be born." Interspersed with angels, throngs of children clad in long azure robes play, talk, sleep, cultivate fruit and flowers, and work at inventions. Light explains to Myltyl and Tyltyl that "it is from here that all the children come who are born upon our earth. Each awaits his day....When the fathers and mothers want children, the great doors...are opened and the little ones go down."[53]

Reminiscent of the rabbinic versions, there are "thirty thousand halls like this, all full of them....Enough to last to the end of the world!" In a delightful exchange, the pre-mortal children, as curious about what awaits them as are the travelers about these spirits, ask about birth, life in the world, poverty, mothers, and death. Love and kissing strike them as comical, though one enterprising spirit couple has already discovered both. And all spirits, the mortal children learn, "must take something with them to earth; [they] are not allowed to go from here empty-handed." In the biggest surprise of all, Tyltyl and Myltyl even meet a prospective sibling, though his stay will be brief. He will bring with him, he innocently remarks, scarlatina, whooping cough, and measles, when he arrives on Palm Sunday next year.[54]

Their conversation is interrupted by the opening of enormous portals and the announcement that the day's crop of the earth-bound must depart on the galley of the Dawn. One reluctant spirit must be pushed, but the general sentiment is eagerness—so much so that several would-be stowaways must be turned back. "It's always the same thing!...You can't deceive me!...It's not your turn!...Go back and wait til to-morrow....Nor you either; go in and return in ten years....A thirteenth shepherd?...There are only twelve wanted."[55] And so it goes for a harried, bearded man named Time. Humor mixes with pathos as the desperately resisting parted lovers are torn from each other's embrace and receive no consolation, no promise of being reunited in the land and life below. Here, in the Kingdom of the Future, the two peasant children find and secure a Blue Bird of Happiness for the third time. But upon their return, it, like the previous two specimens, changes color. It doesn't matter. The next morning, when their sickly neighbor child wants a bird for Christmas, Tyltyl gives her a dove he had captured before his adventures. And in her delight, she finds both healing and happiness.

William Wordsworth's "Immortality Ode" is the most celebrated treatment of preexistence in the Anglo-American tradition. Yet one of the most beloved American poets of the twentieth century went well beyond Wordsworth in the imagining of circumstances attendant upon humankind's descent from a world of spirits into mortality. Robert Frost describes a paradise from which valorous souls choose to answer the call to undergo "Trial by Existence." Written in a heroic mode reminiscent of Greek epic, the poem describes how "the angel hosts with freshness go, / And seek with laughter what to brave," soon finding that "from a cliff top is

With the possible exception of Wordsworth's "Immortality Ode," Frost wrote the modern era's most successful poetic treatment of pre-mortality, "Trial by Existence." *Robert Frost*, photo by Clara E. Sipprell, National Portrait Gallery, Smithsonian Institution/Art Resource, New York.

proclaimed / The gathering of the souls for birth, / The trial by existence named, / The obscuration upon earth." Two aspects of the scene dominate Frost's narration: the exemplary courage of the souls (though by no means all) who undertake earth life and the free will that conditions their going forth:

> The slant spirits trooping by
> In streams and cross- and counter-streams
> Can but give ear to that sweet cry
> For its suggestion of what dreams!
> And the more loitering are turned
> To view once more the sacrifice
> Of those who for some good discerned
> Will gladly give up paradise.

Plato's prophet is not named, but the preview by "lots and sample" is here accomplished just the same:

> And none are taken but who will,
> Having first heard the life read out
> That opens earthward, good and ill,
> Beyond the shadow of a doubt;
> And very beautifully God limns,
> And tenderly, life's little dream,
> But naught extenuates or dims.
> Setting the thing that is supreme.

Wordsworth also is gently invoked; Frost's bold spirit, "heroic in its nakedness," recalls the former's babe, who comes "not in utter nakedness." The lack of any "lasting memory at all clear" in Frost's souls suggests the vague "intimations of immortality" vouchsafed to Wordsworth's more sensitive hearts. The stark difference, however, is ultimately in the permeability of the veil that cuts us off from our anterior existence. Wordsworth celebrates those whisperings of the divine, the sparks of the sacred, which he detects in mortal life and which are both explained by and attest to a prior, greater proximity to God himself. For Frost, our utter obliviousness to our preexistence makes human mortality into a choice fraught with the most sublime moral courage. Indeed, when God pronounces the fate of those who leave the "morning light of heaven" to be denied the memory of having chosen to embrace an existence of unremitting earthly woe, among the assembled spirits "awe passes wonder then, / And a hush falls for all acclaim." Ultimately, then, even the consolations of Wordsworth's faint stirrings and obstinate questionings of the heart, which for him are proof of humanity's insatiable striving and Faustian dissatisfaction, are denied to Frost's more valiant souls, who suffer their fate like stolid

Stoics, oblivious to life's deeper meaning, consigned to simply suffer "in the pain that has but one close, / Bearing it crushed and mystified."[56]

More in the tradition of Traherne is the British poet Frances Cornford's (1886–1960) oft-anthologized poem on the subject, called simply "Preexistence":

I laid me down upon the shore
And dreamed a little space;
I heard the great waves break and roar;
The sun was on my face.

My idle hands and fingers brown
Played with the pebbles grey;
The waves came up, the waves went down,
Most thundering and gay.

The pebbles, they were smooth and round
And warm upon my hands,
Like little people I had found
Sitting among the sands.

The grains of sand so shining-small
Soft through my fingers ran;
The sun shone down upon it all,
And so my dream began:

How all of this had been before:
How ages far away
I lay on some forgotten shore
As here I lie today.

The waves came shining up the sands,
As here today they shine;
And in my pre-Pelagian hands
The sand was warm and fine.

I have forgotten whence I came,
Or what my home might be,
Or by what strange and savage name
I called that thundering sea.

I only know the sun shone down
As still it shines today,
And in my fingers long and brown
The little pebbles lay.[57]

What moves Cornford's poem beyond the possible reading of simple déjà vu is its evocation not of other incarnations, but of a supernal, Wordsworthian shore, its reference to lands that precede recorded history (pre-Pelagian), and its gesture toward origins, her true "home," rather than mere precedent.

The theme was more recently addressed, though with playful whimsy rather than heroic somberness, by the Polish Nobel laureate Wislawa Szymborska. Revisiting the scenario of Blake's *Thel*, she imagines the process of embodiment as a slightly mystifying and altogether distasteful proposition:

> If they did let us choose,
> we probably pondered long.
>
> The proposed bodies were uncomfortable
> and wore out hideously.
>
> Ways of
> satisfying hunger disgusted us,
> we were repelled
> by will-lessly inherited characteristics
> and the tyranny of glands.
> …
>
> The majority of specific fates
> we were offered for scrutiny
> we rejected
> with sadness and horror.
>
> Questions like the following came up:
> is it worth
> bearing in pain a dead child
> and why be a sailor
> who will not reach dry land.
> …
>
> Meanwhile a large number
> of shining stars
> had already gone dark and cold.
> Now was the time to decide.
> …
>
> The whole business
> needed to be reconsidered.

Weren't we offered a journey
from which we would return
assuredly and swiftly?

A sojourn beyond eternity
quite monotonous after all
and knowing no movement....

Anyway, our numbers were dwindling.
Those most impatient had disappeared somewhere.
They were first into the fire
—yes, that was clear.
They were just starting it
on a steep bank of a real river.

Some
were even returning.
But not in our direction.
And they seemed to be carrying a trophy.[58]

We find a poignant reference to the idea in the very first sentence of another Eastern European work, the autobiography of Vladimir Nabokov, where he finds simple intuition to be a sufficient grounding for his belief—though his bleak tone could be interpreted to undermine immortality as much as to suggest pre-mortality. "The cradle rocks above an abyss, and common sense tells us that our existence is but a brief crack of light between two eternities of darkness. Although the two are identical twins, man, as a rule, views the prenatal abyss with more calm than the one he is heading for."[59]

The early twentieth century also saw the theme of pre-mortality portrayed in scattered European literature and opera. In one of his less-known operas, Richard Strauss collaborated with poet Hugo von Hofmannsthal to produce *Die Frau ohne Schatten* (*The Woman without a Shadow*), first performed in Vienna in 1919. The fanciful tale involves the Empress, daughter of a spirit prince, who must find a shadow (a clear type for fertility or children) or she will return to the world of spirits and her husband will turn to stone. She finds an unhappy peasant wife, unwilling to have children, who agrees to deny fatherhood to her husband and to sell her own shadow to the Empress. Like Faust's blood, which congeals before he can sign the devil's contract, voices of the woman's unborn children magically, musically bewail their fate and beg their mother to give them life. But the wife hands over her shadow, and her enraged husband, who longs for progeny, raises his sword to kill the woman. At this moment, nature itself revolts at the mother's deed, and the earth opens to swallow them both. They find themselves separated in underground caverns, and the wife frantically but vainly tries to still the growing cries of her unborn children.

Eventually, the Empress renounces her nefarious scheme, and because of her willingness to sacrifice herself rather than the peasant couple's happiness, she is rewarded with her own shadow. The opera culminates in the joyous songs of the unborn. A few years earlier, the popular American writer Kathleen Norris had written with assertive confidence that "there's no responsibility like that of decreeing that young lives simply *shall not be*."[60] It is difficult to register the pathos of the cries in Strauss or the moral urgency of Norris aside from the premise of actually existent pre-mortal entities.

The theme of preexistence appears less commonly in later twentieth-century literature and drama. The playwright Sam Shepard (with Joseph Chaikin) deals with it in a brief radio play, *The War in Heaven*, which captures in a lyrical, disjointed monologue the disorientation of a fallen angel who finds himself embodied:

> I died
> the day I was born
> …
>
> I am here
> by mistake
>
> I'm not sure how it happened
>
> I crashed
> I know I crashed
> in these streets
> I came down
>
> I don't know what went wrong
>
> I was a part of something
> I remember being
> a member
> I was moving
> I had certain orders
> a mission.

He is alternately modeled on Origen's intelligences, as he remembers the ranks of principalities and dominions, "those above me and those below," and how he "crashed in a moment of doubt"; and on a wistful Lucifer, who remembers "a time when the light from my eyes was so powerful it would blind the sun" and then recoils at the nothing he has become. Haunted by intimations of something "ancient old old old before birth even," he finds, as Cicero did, his own healing, confirming balm in music:

> something
> something will clear
> sometimes music
> that will clear things
> away
> music
> that will clear
> the air

He concludes with brief pathos, "I am here by mistake."[61]

It is no mistake that leads the angel Damiel to forsake his wings for mortality in Wim Wenders's film masterpiece *Der Himmel über Berlin* (1987; *Wings of Desire*, 1988). Enticed by his love for Marion, a vulnerable, pretty trapeze artist, but equally by the allure of rubbing one's hands when cold, getting ink on one's fingers, and experiencing the vicissitudes of life and time, he chooses his fall. "Down from our lookout of the unborn!" he determines. "Observing...happens at eye level." Once embodied, Damiel is surprised to learn that many humans retain memories of their own pre-mortal, angelic pasts and are the more noble and compassionate as a result.

In its less-ponderous American remake (*City of Angels*, 1998), pre-mortality is little more than an innovative pretext for a falling-in-love complication. But for Wenders, the concept is both powerful allegory and possible prehistory. "The idea of angels becoming human is a much more universal process," he said in an interview:

> Perhaps all of us, at one time, made such a decision....In fact, there is quite another way in which the angelic metaphor can be realized: When Marion reflects upon her past life, it is apparent that she, too, has been living in a kind of preexistence, alive, but without real *Gemeinsamkeit* [community] and without real purpose. In that sense, her "birth" into the Technicolor existence of real life and that of Damiel occur simultaneously.[62]

Pop Culture and Parascience

A burgeoning industry, made possible by New Age eclecticism, incorporating Eastern religion especially, chronicles an array of spiritual contacts with pre-mortal spirits, generally in the context of mothers (but also fathers and siblings) being visited by future children in dreams and visions. Prebirth experiences, or PBEs as they are called in the literature, may have been an inevitable next step from NDEs, or near-death experiences, which generally chronicle contact with beings of light after clinical death. In any case, some PBEs arise out of death experiences, where the two realms of the preborn and the post-mortal intermingle. In others, however, the two realms are entirely distinct. Many investigators of prebirth experiences offer at least some scientific basis for their claims, often conducting them under the aegis of medical and academic—or quasi-academic—institutions. One such study, for example, carried out as part of a "graduate writing program at Maharishi University" in Fairfield, Iowa, surveyed "several mothers" about birth and prebirth experiences. On the basis of these interviews (and a smattering of ethnographic research), the authors present a table of 165 cultures and religions that report preconception experiences with spirit children, along with dozens of personal accounts. Typical is "Jennifer's" story:

> I had a beautiful, awe-inspiring vision. I saw the souls of twelve children who wanted to be born. They faced me standing in a semi-circle in a less earthly world with a lot of light. They had human form, but were angelic, ethereal....My attention was drawn to one who had a connection with me. He wanted to be ours. Within days, we conceived our second child.

Many of the interviewees go beyond descriptions of anticipatory intuitions to real encounters that they feel were clearly substantiated by subsequent events. "While I was pregnant with my second child, my third child's spirit visited me late one night....He circled around me a few times, and told me, 'We know each other. I love you and want to help you. I will be your son.'" The woman conceived shortly after the second child's birth and related, "I felt his presence throughout the pregnancy. And the instant he was born, I looked into his eyes and recognized the little spirit who had spoken to me months before."[63]

Another author collected dozens of stories from prospective mothers and fathers that similarly attest to their contact with their children before conception;[64] a third writer chronicled her own experience in this regard and added the stories of several others. One recorded a dream where she addressed her unborn child's concern about embodiment. She noted his anxiety for the smallness of the young form he would inhabit. "I told him it would be an adjustment, and I reassured him that it's okay to have a body, and that there would be many things he'd like about it....And though he was coming to me as a child, I knew his spirit was adult." True to the dream vision, a dangerously premature son was born to her shortly thereafter, but he soon prospered.

Men as well as women recount dream visions of their preexistent children. In one example, Roy Caldwell saw his recently killed friend conversing with a little girl about himself, his wife, and his home. The next day, his wife gave birth to a daughter who grew into a girl "with blond, curly, bouncy hair and shining, laughing, blue-green eyes; the same little girl I saw with my friend Lee as his spirit was leaving the earth and her spirit was preparing to come down."[65]

If the spirits of the preborn and the departed mingle freely, one would expect those who have near-death experiences to encounter the unborn from the perspective here imputed to Lee. And indeed, from this other end of the mortal continuum, adults and children alike who have reported NDEs describe a realm to which they are ushered by beings of light, where they recognize loved ones who have passed on, but some have also noted "babies waiting to be born." Others claim to have conversed there with spirits destined to become their own children. One mother gave a promise to one such spirit to "love him unconditionally as long as he needed me" and believed that she gave birth to him two years later.[66]

If such stories are easily dismissed as fanciful projections of anxious, expectant parents, they are nonetheless another cultural manifestation of the perseverance of pre-mortal existence as a powerful interpretive tool, which endows human relationships with the sacred aura of transcendent time lines and majestic beginnings. In harmony with Kant's remarks, such visionary windows into the origins of our own children compensate for the almost intolerable contingency and happenstance behind human conception.

12

Parallel Paradigms

A man may be an admirable poet without being an exact chronologer.
—John Dryden[1]

Confusing dates may be a minor poetic offense compared with inventing an entire human prehistory. Still, poets might be excused for an indulgence in that most extreme utopianism, the pastoral of all pastorals. For such is the motif of preexistence, devoted as it is to an Eden in which all humans have participated, where a universal humanity basked in God's eternal presence, and in which the entire race of Adam was unsullied by any taint of guilty sin or mortal decay.

The history of this remarkable idea, however, provides abundant evidence that more than poetic self-indulgence is behind its perseverance. It may be true that, in the West at least, the concept is not religiously viable in the institutional churches of the Christian mainstream. That is a fate which was set in stone when the Latin West prevailed over the church of Alexandria. As the writer Jorge Luis Borges commented in reference to his own Gnostic recreations, "Had Alexandria triumphed and not Rome, the extravagant and muddled stories that I have summarized here would be coherent, majestic, and perfectly ordinary."[2] Instead, the colorful, fluid, multitiered heavens of Origen were sidelined by the more staid theological universe that followed in the wake of Augustine. And philosophically, preexistence, like most questions of a religious or even metaphysical cast, is not today a common contender for academic discussion, in spite of the sporadic exceptions we have noted. Its persistence, however, in more popular forms, like the prebirth accounts we have seen, reaffirms the idea's enduring psychological and emotional attractions, which operate relatively independently of theological or philosophical merits.

The three modes of expression this volume has surveyed—poetry, religion, and philosophy—do not exhaust the pool of artists and truth seekers who have found in preexistence an appealing or even indispensable paradigm for performing significant cultural work. They represent, perhaps, the fields of human endeavor that have embraced the belief in its more literal aspects. But an array of parallel paradigms have emerged over the course of modern history—often consciously modeled on the myth of a preexistent past—in order to do comparable cultural work. Together, they attest to the important functions that preexistence has served and explain its historical resiliency.

In Plato's myth of pre-mortality, a model of ambiguous historical reality is employed in order to create a logically plausible explanation for what *is*. People *do* have intuitions of universals, for example, and Plato's story renders that fact comprehensible. The purpose of the paradigm, in other words, is explanatory. Similarly, attributing present inequities to pre-mortal behavior gives preexistence powerful consolatory power. Belief in pre-mortal choices and actions makes sense out of the gross discrepancies in circumstances and conditions into which we are born. In both instances, therefore, Plato is making the case that his story, or something of the kind, is likely to be true.

Other great thinkers have postulated human prehistories not so much to explain present social structures or epistemological dilemmas as to justify or advocate political systems. Political theorists of the seventeenth and eighteenth centuries, like Thomas Hobbes, John Locke, and Jean-Jacques Rousseau, created mythical first states for humankind as well. Not extending backward to any preexistent time, this first condition of the race, the famous "state of nature," nevertheless served in those thinkers and in others as a kind of mythical first estate, a hypothesis somewhere between pseudo-anthropology and mere thought experiment, which serves as a foil to humans as social animals situated in civilizations and presided over by governments. For Hobbes, such a condition entailed a perpetual war of every human against all and a life that was "solitary, poor, nasty, brutish, and short."[3] Locke disagreed, arguing that the state of nature was a state of perfect freedom, governed by the law of nature, which is reason. Rousseau, the eternal optimist when it comes to human nature, held that, in our original state, all were benevolent, childlike, and untainted until subjected to the corrupting influences of civilization.

Depending on the imagined natural condition of the first humans, one finds a persuasive argument for absolute monarchy (as a welcome respite from the chaos of the Hobbesian state of nature) or political liberalism founded on contractual relationships (as a trade-off of fragile, natural liberties for secure, conventional liberties in Locke and Rousseau). Those constructs have more the shape of secular versions of Eden than of life before incarnation. With the work of American philosopher John Rawls, the sense of a historical past disappears altogether, swallowed up in a thought experiment that explicitly predicates a hypothetical moment before human time. The problem that Rawls has posed for himself is not so far removed from that of Plato's *Republic*: how best to articulate a social contract that would characterize a truly just society. To do so, Rawls has recourse to what he calls the "original position":

> Thus we are to imagine that those who engage in social cooperation choose together, in one joint act, the principles which are to assign basic rights and duties and to determine the division of social benefits. Men are to decide in advance how they are to regulate their claims against one another and what is to be the foundation charter of their society....The original position is not, of course, thought of as an actual historical state of affairs, much less as a primitive condition of culture. It is understood as a purely hypothetical situation characterized so as to lead to a certain conception of justice....The principles of justice are chosen behind a veil of ignorance. This ensures that no one is advantaged or disadvantaged in the choice of principles by the outcome of natural chance or the contingency of social circumstances.[4]

This is a striking instance of invoking preexistence not to explain inequities, but to imagine them out of existence. Other philosophers we have discussed rely upon transmuted versions of preexistence to address problems of epistemology—explaining forms of knowledge that lived experience cannot. We already saw how Descartes's innate ideas and Kant's mental categories functioned in just such a way—and were recognized as such by critics like More and Bruch, respectively. In the sciences, preexistence similarly appears in reformulated though clearly recognizable ways.

We saw how Emerson celebrated and Nietzsche deplored the specter of "historical man." Each was, in different ways, reflecting an intuition of the shaping weight of a distant past, to which Darwin gave scientific foundations and concrete particulars. That Darwin actually saw his achievement as rewriting the whole panoply of Platonic formulations and philosophical obfuscation into a more respectable and modern scientific notation is clear in one simple remark recorded in his notebooks. Commenting on *Phaedo*, Plato's account of Socrates' death, he observed that Plato writes "that our '*necessary ideas*' arise from the preexistence of the soul, are not derivable from experience." And then he added, "read monkeys for preexistence." Thus, as one critic aptly characterizes the sea change that Darwin self-consciously ushered in, "metaphysics is instantly collapsed into biology."[5] But it wasn't Platonists or metaphysicians alone whom Darwin threatened to make endangered species. Darwin saw as well the implications for questions of human personality, psychology, and identity itself, though he feared to express them too openly. In another notebook, he wrote, "To avoid stating how far, I believe, in Materialism, say only that emotions, instincts, degrees of talent, which are hereditary are so because brain of child resemble[s] parent stock."[6]

Efforts by Darwin's contemporaries to avoid such a total collapse into materialism, to find instead a tenable marriage between science and immaterialism, continue to the present, though such proponents generally operate outside the scientific mainstream. Though the Darwinian implications for biblical creationism have largely stolen the show, some nineteenth-century writers were curiously concerned to salvage the very concept of preexistence that Darwin had so confidently exiled from contemporary debates. If the historical value of preexistence has been the array of cultural work the paradigm performs, one contribution associated with Plato's theory in particular is its response to the query, how do humans know things they shouldn't reasonably be expected to know? Not just Pythagorean proofs, but love at first sight, the sense of right and wrong, intuition of the sublime, or yearning for a heavenly home. William Walsh, a Victorian essayist, wrote to defend, in this brave new world,

> a different form of pre-existence which, is recognized by modern science. Our instincts, we are told, are all survivals from our ancestors, they register the accumulated and inherited experience of past generations.... If our feelings are reminiscences of the feelings of our forefathers, if we live over again their emotions, why may we not, when the mind is abnormally active and introspective, live over again some actual circumstance in one of our ancestor's lives, or reproduce the scene through which he passed?

He even found poetic support in a piece by Frederick Peterson, "Heredity":

> I meet upon the woodland ways
> At morn a lady fair:
> Adown her slender shoulders strays
> Her raven hair;
>
> And none who looks into her eyes
> Can fail to feel and know
> That in this conscious clay there lies
> Some soul aglow.
>
> But I, who meet her oft about
> The woods in morning song,
> I see behind her far stretch out
> A ghostly throng,—

A priest, a prince, a lord, a maid,
Faces of grief and sin,
A high-born lady and a jade,
     A harlequin,—

Two lines of ghosts in masquerade,
Who push her where they will,
As if it were the wind that swayed
     A daffodil.

She sings, she weeps, she smiles, she sighs,
Looks cruel, sweet, or base;
The features of her fathers rise
     And haunt her face.

As if it were the wind that swayed
Some stately daffodil,
Upon her face they masquerade
     And work their will.[7]

Of course, one could claim that, in this instance, poetry is the last refuge of the scientifically vanquished. Even if they are correct who proclaim that "ultimately, to be sure, memory is a series of molecular events,"[8] science has not yet managed, even to many scientists' satisfaction, to perform the cultural work of preexistence as effectively as myths and poems like Peterson's have done. As philosopher and psycholinguist Jerry Fodor remarks, a major problem persisting for scientific empiricists is to deal with "the traditional Rationalist observation that we apparently know more than our environment tells us."[9]

In the realm of psychology, Carl Jung found a comparable problem emerging with Freud's psychoanalytic method. Freud described his approach to the discipline as like that of "those discoverers whose good fortune it is to bring to the light of day after their long burial the priceless though mutilated relics of antiquity. I have restored what is missing,...like a conscientious archaeologist."[10] Later, Freud would emphasize the layering of history to be found in both fields, with the shared advantage that the scientist in both cases can perceive and therefore assess the multiple layers in their excavated, and therefore simultaneous, coexistence:

Now let us, by a flight of the imagination, suppose that Rome is not a human habitation but a psychical entity with a similarly long and copious past—an entity, that is to say, in which nothing that has once come into existence will have passed away and all the earlier phases of development continue to exist alongside the later one. This would mean that in Rome the palaces of the Caesars...would still be rising to their old height on the Palatine....In the place occupied by the Palazzo Caffarelli would once more stand—without the Palazzo having to be removed—the Temple of Jupiter Capitolinus; and this not only in its latest shape, as the Romans of the Empire saw it, but also in its earliest one, when it still showed Etruscan forms and was ornamented with terracotta antefixes.[11]

In this analogy, we see that part of the power of Freud's explanatory model is in his understanding of the perseverance of memory, his intuition of a kind of law of conservation of psychic energy. We don't just move through life like a ship through water, but we register each bump and bruise to our damaged ego and thwarted instincts and bury—or repress—unresolved conflicts deep within layers of consciousness. Jung would later characterize Freud's accomplishment by contrasting it with conventional approaches to such conundrums as hysteria and other neuroses: "To this problem medicine gives an excellent answer: 'The x in the calculation is the predisposition.' One is just 'predisposed' that way. But for Freud the problem was: what constitutes the predisposition?"[12] To discover those root causes requires not just assessing present imbalances or bodily or mental dysfunctions but digging deep into the mind and, therefore, backward in time.

So, like the political philosophers we have discussed, Sigmund Freud thus embarks on a program of reconstructing earliest beginnings, but he takes the individual psyche rather than human society as his subject. Not all of Freud's excavations begin with pathology. One of the most important and instructive of his theories follows upon his recognition of certain universals—or quasi-universals—in the human condition, which he is evaluating as a possible source of the religious predisposition of humankind. This particular discussion begins with language that immediately and strikingly parallels the whole Platonic schema by interrogating the basis for the sensation experienced by a friend, "which he himself is never without, which he finds confirmed by many others, and which he may suppose is present in millions of people. It is a feeling which he would like to call a sensation of 'eternity,' a feeling as of something limitless, unbounded—as it were, 'oceanic.'"[13] This is a carefully phrased adaptation of Augustine's question: how do we account for our primal longing for the eternal, the sublime, the transcendent?

Freud manages to resolve to his satisfaction the dilemma of these vague human intuitions of eternity, without recourse to either preexistent realms or to some kind of Kantian innate categories. He traces it, rather, to a stage of psychic development in early infancy:

> An infant at the breast does not as yet distinguish his ego from the external world as the source of the sensations flowing in upon him. He gradually learns to do so, in response to various promptings....In this way, then, the

ego detaches itself from the external world. Or, to put it more correctly, originally the ego includes everything, later it separates off an external world from itself. Our present ego-feeling is, therefore, only a shrunken residue of a much more inclusive—indeed, an all-embracing—feeling which corresponded to a more intimate bond between the ego and the world about it. If we may assume that there are many people in whose mental life this primary ego-feeling has persisted to a greater or less[er] degree, it would exist in them side by side with the narrower and more sharply demarcated ego-feeling of maturity, like a kind of counterpart to it. In that case, the ideational contents appropriate to it would be precisely those of limitlessness and of a bond with the universe—the same ideas with which my friend elucidated the "oceanic" feeling.[14]

Here, as elsewhere, Freud generally finds that his method produces satisfactory results—even if, as he acknowledges in the present case, "it is not easy to deal scientifically with feelings." His erstwhile admirer Jung, however, finds Freud's theories to be inadequate in the face of an array of human experiences that defies the reach of psychoanalysis. And so it is that, in a manner roughly analogous to the step taken by the German idealists, Carl Jung will push his search for causal origins further than Freud's ego formation, going beyond a merely temporal continuum and into the realm of timelessness. He does this through the elaboration of his two principal contributions to psychological theory: the archetype and the collective unconscious. Both ideas are so richly resonant with Platonic conceptions of preexistence that commentators routinely begin with such a comparison—explicitly or implicitly.

By 1916, Jung had already derived the essence of his theory in response to what he considered to be the deficiencies of Freud's system. Freud, criticized Jung, had tried to reduce all of the contents of the unconscious "to infantile tendencies and desires" that had been repressed.[15] One criticism Jung raised was that, if this were the case, then exposing those repressions would leave the unconscious to wither and die in purposelessness. But that never happens under analysis. Jung felt that some of the tendencies and desires to which Freud referred could indeed be explained as elements of the personality, relegated to the unconscious "by the educational process"—but only some of them. In addition to this layer of the unconscious, this layer "of a personal character" comprising past conscious thoughts that had been repressed, a thorough inventory of the unconscious would reveal much more, involving both darkest evil and "the noblest deeds and loftiest ideas imaginable."[16]

These other elements—and their origins—are revealed through a different version of psychoanalysis. For patients in analysis, Jung reasons, the process of healthy self-realization involves helping them to assimilate at the conscious level the contents of their personal unconsciousness. Jung's ideas make a critical shift as he goes on to argue that, in this process, other elements unrelated to one's personal history are revealed and released with dramatic repercussions. As he analyzes this move, he articulates a theory of the collective unconscious that can be seen as a radical, clinicalized reading of Plato. In some cases, as the analysand (the subject of therapy) uncovers and assimilates elements from the unconscious, the patient displays a peculiar "godlikeness," an increase of "self-confidence far surpassing the conscious optimism [of its possessor]....If...we dissect the notion of godlikeness, we find the term comprises...a certain psychic function having a *collective* character superordinate to the individual mentality."[17]

In other words, Jung traces these unconscious elements to a collective unconscious, a transpersonal repository of preexistent forms constituting the spiritual residue of humankind's entire evolutionary history and inherited in the psychic structure of every newly born individual. The transpersonal nature of this unconscious is Jung's explanation for "the remarkable analogies presented by the unconscious in the most remotely separated races and peoples."[18] In *Psychologie und Alchemie*, first published in 1944, Jung characterizes these archetypes as "inherent in the collective unconscious and thus beyond individual birth and death. The archetype is, so to speak, an 'eternal' presence, and the only question is whether it is perceived by the conscious mind or not."[19] Elsewhere, he describes archetypes as "primordial images," possessing an "archaic character" and "common to entire peoples or epochs,...times, and races," which arise entirely independently of environmental conditions or sense perceptions as a "precipitate" or "condensation of the living process." They thus possess "because of their universality and immense antiquity...a cosmic and suprahuman character."[20]

As in Plato, we find here a theory that attempts to explain how human beings can be possessed of deeply embedded forms of knowledge—motifs, themes, scenarios—that they have no apparent grounds for possessing. As Jung writes, they are "without known origin; and they reproduce themselves in any time or in any part of the world—even where transmission by direct descent or 'cross-fertilization' through migration must be ruled out."[21] Yet all persons are possessed of these images, which "are the most ancient and the most universal 'thought-forms' of humanity," even though in most people the "deposits" are dormant or only vaguely apprehended.[22] Transcending the reach of Freud's psychoanalytic method, this "collective layer comprises the pre-infantile period."[23] And human intuition of this a priori knowledge leads to a powerful identification with divinity (which manifests itself as striving for theosis in the Platonic heritage or for "godlikeness" and a source of possible dysfunction in Jung). Jung even compares these archetypal forms to "half-souls" (a Neo-Platonic expression used by Origen) that "lead their own independent life." If this sounds rather like a renaming of the aeons and spiritual beings who populate the "heavenly hierarchy" we have seen from the Gnostics through Dionysius the Areopagite, Jung expressly acknowledges just that.[24] What these and other predecessors called pre-mortal souls and spirit beings, Jung calls pre-infantile images, "dominants of the unconscious." Perhaps most tellingly for this book, Jung's defense of the paradigm in the final analysis is not its rationality or its scientific basis per se, but its simple power as an explanatory paradigm. As he says admiringly of his own thesis, it "explains the truly amazing phenomenon that certain motifs and myths and legends repeat themselves the world over in identical forms. It also explains why it is that our mental patients can reproduce exactly the same images and associations that are known to us from the old texts."[25] His theories were, in this regard, an extension of his personal intuition. "My life as I lived it," he wrote in his autobiography, "had often seemed to me like a story that has no beginning and no end. I had the feeling that I was a historical fragment, an excerpt for which the preceding and the succeeding text was missing."[26]

Jung's is the most famous, but far from the only version of a collective memory that connects us to, rather than positions us in, an earlier existence. Ay Warburg produced *Theory of Social Memory* in 1927, and Samuel Butler wrote *Unconscious Memory* even earlier (1880). In that work, Butler sought to explain what he called "the existence of a direct knowledge underivable from any sensual impression or from consciousness." A few years earlier, in a throwback to seventeenth-century ovists, he had argued that "the small, structureless, impregnate ovum from which we have each of us sprung, has a potential recollection of all that has happened to each one of its ancestors prior to the period at which any such ancestor has issued from the bodies of its progenitors."[27]

The effort to find a scientific basis for a memory that is, in Jung's vocabulary, "suprahuman," or transhistorical, finds more recent expression in a scientist who has gone further than most in attempting to give intellectual respectability to an area of research and explanatory paradigms usually relegated to the quasi-scientific netherworld of the paranormal. Rupert Sheldrake is clearly working outside the scientific mainstream. "The most controversial scientist on Earth," hypes one blurb.[28] He is also a product of Cambridge University and was a research fellow of the Royal Society and a former Frank Knox Fellow at Harvard. He lays out an impressive body of evidence for his radical theory of "morphic resonance," which is based on his belief in a kind of assimilated, rather than inherited, collective memory. His theory has foundations in the science of the 1920s, when three biologists independently proposed that the structural development of an organism (morphogenesis) is conditioned by fields rather than by material bases inherent in that organism. As developed by Sheldrake:

> [T]he idea of morphic resonance sheds new light on the phenomena [*sic*] of heredity, which can be seen to depend both on genes and on morphic fields inherited by morphic resonance. The form and behavior of organisms are not coded or programmed in the genes any more than the TV programs picked up by a TV set are coded or programmed in its transistors.[29]

This novel view of heredity and memory Sheldrake calls the theory of "causative formation," which "sees the inheritance of organic form—including the forms of molecules themselves—in terms of the inheritance of organizing fields that contain a kind of inbuilt memory." According to this point of view, "living organisms...inherit not only genes, but also habits of development and behavior from past members of their own species and also from the long series of ancestral species from which their species has arisen." What this means is that things like the structure of a fruit fly's legs and even the funnel-building habits of *Paralastor* wasps are determined by morphic fields rather than genetic inheritance. Creatures inherit the instincts of their species "through invisible influences, acting at a distance"—a distance that can be geographical as well as temporal. His reasoning is based partly on the fact that, while some instincts are inherited, some habits are clearly acquired by other mechanisms. And those habits cannot be heritable, since there is no way for them to modify the genetic code. And yet, such habits are seen to appear with no discernible mode of transmission or imitation.[30]

The best documented case of such an observable habit, transmitted without any discernible origin in either heredity or imitation, involves the blue tit of Great Britain. In 1921, these birds were first observed to pierce the caps of milk bottles to get at the contents. Once a few birds had acquired the habit, the practice accelerated rapidly, and it also erupted at regular intervals over the next several years. This, in spite of the fact that this species of bird does not travel more than a few miles from its breeding place. The phenomenon was also recorded in various countries on the European continent. The blue tit's behavior is but one example, not only of a habit determined by morphic resonance, but of the fact that such resonance is amplified by reiteration. In other words, not only can habits acquired by one animal "facilitate the acquisition of the same habits by other, similar animals, even in the absence of any known means of connection or communication," but the more frequently the habit is practiced, the speedier its acquisition by other organisms. As the title of his book indicates, Sheldrake finds, as Plato did, that "the presence of the past," however oblivious we may be to its influence, is the best explanation for our possession of knowledge, insights, and habits that admit of no other source.[31] His theory appears to be a working out of the striking assertion made by the Romantic author Thomas de Quincey, cited in a nineteenth-century discussion on the "Sense of Pre-Existence": "What else than a natural and mighty palimpsest is the human brain?...Everlasting layers of ideas, images, feelings, have fallen upon your brain softly as light. Each succession has seemed to bury all that went before. And yet, in reality, not one has been extinguished."[32]

A more scientifically mainstream author, Richard Dawkins, likewise invented his own vocabulary to account for the phenomenon of historical memory in a species. In *The Selfish Gene*, he coined the term "meme" to refer to a salient feature of culture that is transmitted across generations. He explains:

> [A meme is] a unit of cultural transmission....Examples of memes are tunes, ideas, catch-phrases, clothes fashions, ways of making pots or of building arches. Just as genes propagate themselves in the gene pool by leaping from body to body via sperm or eggs, so memes propagate themselves in the meme pool by leaping from brain to brain via a process which, in the broad sense, can be called imitation.[33]

Daniel Dennett was so enamored of the idea that he explored the possibility of a "science of memetics" and concluded that "whether or not the meme perspective can be turned into science, in its philosophical guise it has already done much more good than harm."[34] In any event, he sees a rigorously mechanical account of cultural transmission to be the best alternative to capitulation in the face of the perennial dilemma faced by Plato, Kant, Jung, Chomsky, and others who would resort to either myths or half-measures. Preexistence is clearly an unscientific solution. But the others may not really be so far ahead. Dennett deplores those who "concede that the mind is, after all, just the brain, which is a physical entity bound by all the laws of physics and chemistry, but insist that it nevertheless does its chores in ways that defy scientific analysis. This view has often been suggested by the linguist Noam Chomsky and enthusiastically defended by...Jerry Fodor...and Colin McGinn."[35] It may be more telling than it is ironic that the memetics touted by the scientific Dawkins and Dennett has not yet attained the influence of the Chomskyan linguistics being chided as unscientific.

Chomskyan linguistics is so manifestly Platonic in its evocation of an inherited knowledge base that both its founder and other scholars have noted the parallel. In the first chapter of *Language and the Problems of Knowledge*, Chomsky lays out his evidence for an innate language faculty:

> [It seems] that the child approaches the task of acquiring a language with a rich conceptual framework already in place and also with a rich system of assumptions about sound structure and the structure of more complex utterances. These constitute the parts of our knowledge that come "from the original hand of nature," in Hume's phrase. They constitute one part of the human biological endowment, to be awakened by experience and to be sharpened and enriched in the course of the child's interactions with the human and material world. In these terms we can approach a solution of Plato's problem, along lines not entirely unlike Plato's own, though "purged of the error of preexistence."[36]

Chomsky in this last sentence is quoting Leibniz, who, as we have seen, saw the need to incorporate innate ideas into any adequate theory of knowledge, but he wanted to do so on more respectable grounds than Greek myths of preexistent spirits. He was thus instrumental, in Chomsky's view, in furthering the development of a modern human psychology that "is a kind of Platonism without the preexistence." The result is a recognition of the *Meno* problem, but one that stops short of extending the search for epistemological origins beyond fuzzy philosophical or psychological terms. Leibniz thus substituted pseudo-scientific language for myth, without even attempting the real work of etiology—of accounting for an original source or mechanism of acquisition, which Plato's myth accomplished. What must be noticed in this regard, however, is that the dilemma thus unsolved becomes now a simple source of wonder. With Chomsky's views of innate linguistic knowledge (the universal grammar), as in his rendering of the basis of Cartesian linguistics, we arguably never move from myth to science, in other words, but only from mythification to mystification, from what moderns patronizingly dismiss as naïve to what they unblushingly embrace as magic.

> That the principles of language and natural logic are known unconsciously and that they are in large measure a precondition for language acquisition rather than a matter of "institution" or "training" is the general presupposition of Cartesian linguistics. When [Géraud de] Cordemoy, for example, considers language acquisition, he discusses the role of instruction and conditioning of a sort, but he also notices that much of what children know is acquired quite apart from any explicit instruction, and he concludes that language learning presupposes a possession of "la raison toute entière; car enfin cette manière d'apprendre à parler, est l'effet d'un si grand discernement, et d'une raison si parfaite, qu'il n'est pas possible d'en concevoir un plus merveilleux [a fully developed reason; because in the final analysis, learning to speak in this way is the consequence of such great judgment and perfect reason that it is impossible to imagine a more marvelous faculty]."[37]

Cognitive scientist Steven Pinker avoids what he sees as the needless mystification of the language problem by considering language to be an instinct and thereby subsuming it within evolutionary theory. He is baffled by the pointed resistance to such a move on the part of Chomsky and many of his opponents, who are agreed that "a uniquely human language instinct seems to be incompatible with the modern Darwinian theory of evolution." Pinker quotes Chomsky:

> It is perfectly safe to attribute this development [of innate mental structures] to "natural selection" so long as we realize that there is no substance to this assertion, that it amounts to nothing more than a belief that there is some naturalistic explanation for these phenomena.[38]

Chomsky's resistance may be construed as his recognition of a point illustrated so abundantly throughout the long history of the concept of preexistence: replacing mythic tropes with scientific nomenclature may not guarantee the intellectual or cultural progress such a move portends.

Yet another variation on inherited knowledge is the idea of what Darold Treffert has called "ancestral memory." A researcher of "Savant syndrome," Treffert grapples with the question of how people of marginal functional intelligence can demonstrate prodigious talent that defies any known explanation, like those "human calculators" who can compute primes, products, or calendrical facts at phenomenal speeds. William Blake felt that his genius was adequately accounted for by his long apprenticeship "in ages of Eternity before [his] mortal life." We see in Treffert, once again, an alternative explanation that resorts to only slightly more scientifically respectable language. He theorizes:

> [T]he talented savant can, with constant repetition and practice, create sufficient coding so that some unconscious algorithms develop (although he will have no understanding of them). However, in the prodigious savant, access to the rules of music or rules of mathematics, for example, is so extensive that some ancestral (inherited) memory must exist to account for that access. Such memory, in these individuals, is inherited separately from general intelligence.[39]

Ancestral memory, Treffert goes on to explain, though in terms more typical of nineteenth-century formulations than twenty-first-century cognitive science, is "composed of traits, skills, attributes and abilities that are inherited just as eye color, height, body build and many other physical characteristics are inherited. These are the various instincts and genetic unfoldings one sees in both animals and humans." He then quotes a 1940 scientific article that attempts in similar terms to account for the brilliance both of such savants and of musical geniuses like Mozart:

> In each of the foregoing cases, then, we have a peculiar example of the possession of an extraordinary congenital aptitude for certain forms of mental activity, which showed itself at so early a period as to exclude the notion that it could have been acquired by the experiences of the individual.

It might be noted that this commentary sounds like an almost verbatim transcription from Plato's *Meno*.[40]

A term that sounds much like ancestral memory is "cellular" memory. Graham Farrant uses this term to explain the phenomenon of children who claim to recall prenatal trauma (like attempted induced abortions). David Chamberlain expands the boundaries of memory even further, crediting patients' accounts of their own conception. He stops shy of particular hypotheses other than to quote research that "it is not possible to demonstrate the isolated localization of a memory trace any-where within the nervous system" and to assert that some kind of self-awareness transcends and predates any physical basis for memory. He adds the suggestive observation, based on his own clinical research, that "memories, at whatever age you tap into them, always show mature and humane qualities."[41]

Ancestral or cellular memory may be fuzzy science, but Chamberlain's invocation of hypnotic regression and Treffert's almost desperate bid for a theory suggest that the urgency of the question first posed by Plato—how do we know what we shouldn't reasonably know?—has changed little in two millennia, and his theory of preexistence continues its many transmogrifications: "Whether called ancestral, genetic, or racial memory, or intuitions or congenital gifts, the concept of a genetic transmission of sophisticated knowledge, well beyond 'instincts,' is necessary to explain how prodigious savants particularly can know things they never learned."[42]

Memory, of course, is only one of the human insolubles that the concept of preexistence presumes to illuminate. The preoccupation with memory as a focus of linguistic, psychological, historical, and evolutionary approaches may be traced back to the shattering tenet of modernity that consciousness is but a stream of mental perceptions; the unity with which memory welds together present and past perceptions, rather than an independently existing entity, is commonly held to constitute one's sense of a coherent identity. More than memory goes into personality, of course, and here again, preexistence illuminates questions of the human self that modern philosophy has yet to resolve fully. One example of this is the study of human behavior. As Steven Pinker summarizes, "The three laws of behavioral genetics may be the most important discovery in the history of psychology." The first two state, "all human behavioral traits are heritable," and "the effect of being raised in the same family is smaller than the effect of the genes." But what he calls the third discovery is actually the absence of a discovery: "A substantial portion of the variation in complex human behavioral traits is not accounted for by the effects of genes or families." In fact, he continues, a conventional estimate "is that about half of the variation in intelligence, personality, and life outcomes is heritable—a correlate or an indirect product of the genes." What other factors constitute the formative influences on human behavior is a considerable mystery. Pinker continues:

> [T]here must be causes that are neither genetic *nor* common to the family that make identical twins different and, more generally, make people what they are....Something is happening here, but we don't know what it is....If *anything* that parents do affects their children in *any* systematic way, then children growing up with the same parents will turn out more similar than children growing up with different parents. But they don't.[43]

Pinker finds himself drawn to the work of Judith Rich Harris, who argues that the "elusive environmental shaper of personality" is socialization by the peer group (group socialization theory).[44] Unfortunately, Pinker concludes, research has shown that some identical twins who grow up together have common genes, family environments, and, it turns out, peer groups, "but the correlations between them are only around 50 percent. Ergo, neither genes nor families nor peer groups can explain what makes them different." And so, we find Pinker concluding that neither nature nor nurture, singly or in tandem, can explain the mystery of human personality. Chance, he writes with a kind of wistful resignation, may be the only alternative. "A cosmic ray mutates a stretch of DNA" or "one twin lies one way in the womb" while "the other has to squeeze around her."[45]

Pinker's summary of the nature-nurture debate—and its insufficiencies—is instructive not because it leads us to any particular solution, but because it clearly admits the need for another hypothetical influence to fill the void and add a third leg to the wobbly nature-nurture stool. Modern psychologists have not been the only observers to sense that an unrecognized dimension to the shaping of identity has always been at work. The philosopher J. M. E. McTaggart argued for these "other considerations" as bearing directly on the theory of preexistence:

> As a man grows up certain tendencies and qualities make themselves manifest in him. They cannot be entirely due to his environment, for they are often very different in people whose environment has been very similar. We call these the man's natural character, and assume that he came into existence with it. Now when we look at these differentiations, which we call the natural characters of men, we find that they have a very great resemblance to those differentiations which we learn[ed] by direct experience can be produced in the course of a single life.... Here, then, we have characteristics which are born with us, which are not acquired in our present lives, and which are strikingly like characteristics which, in other cases, we know to be due to the condensed results of experience. Is it not probable that the innate characteristics are also due to the condensed results of experience—in this case, of experience in an earlier life?[46]

An early twentieth-century proponent of preexistence made the same argument, neatly foreshadowing Pinker's three-legged approach, though substituting free will for genetics:

> Some great men have said that one-third of an individual's character is formed before he comes into the world: that the prenatal influences which have gone into the building up of his personality have predisposed him to certain lines of thought and activity, after he has been born among

the children of men. It is said, also, that one-third of one's character is
due to his own self-effort: the things that he accomplishes, or strives to
accomplish, go into the making of his character: and that one-third of his
being is made up from the environment with which he is associated during his sojourn here upon the earth: that men with whom he associates
and whom he meets from day to day, have some influence in the shaping
of his character.[47]

It may not be great science. But as religious scholar Matthew Spinka argues, "the
belief in the preexistence of souls is perhaps as logical as any other theory which
attempts to account for the origin of human personality."[48]

No contemporary philosopher of note promotes preexistence as a solution
to the enigma of the human mind or rationality itself. But some—even avowed
atheists like Thomas Nagel—find scientific physicalism and evolutionary theory in
particular to deliver less than they promise as general accounts of the self. Nagel at
the same time recognizes the discomfort that a concept of independent and eternal
human intelligence can engender:

I am denying that what rationality is can be understood through the theory of natural selection. What it is, what it tells us, and what its limits
are can be understood only from inside it. But that leaves the question,
how can we integrate such an attitude toward reason with the fact that we
are members of a biological species whose evolution has been shaped by
the contingencies of natural selection? To this I don't have a proper positive response.... [But] the physical story, without more, cannot explain the
mental story, including consciousness and reason.

This is not to say, he hastens to point out, that our only alternative is a religious
one. The difficulty is that fear of such recourse to religion to explain the mystery of
human consciousness may extend by way of overreaction "far beyond the existence
of god, to include any cosmic order of which the mind is an irreducible and nonaccidental part."[49]

A mind that is "irreducible" and "nonaccidental" and an etiology of mental
existence that runs independently of an evolutionary story line seem to flirt with a
self that borders on the transcendent and timeless. And indeed, Nagel's preface to
this whole discussion is an approving reference to C. S. Peirce's "Platonism," including this "morsel":

The soul's deeper parts can only be reached through its surface. In this
way the eternal forms, that mathematics and philosophy and the other
sciences make us acquainted with will by slow percolation reach the very

core of one's being, and will come to influence our lives; and this they will do...because they [are] ideal and eternal verities.

No wonder Nagel fears the "quasi-religious" ring to his efforts to salvage "mind" from evolution's nearly total dominion as a master heuristic. He does not mean to inculcate belief in either God or a "world soul," he says tellingly. Still, in the end, we find once again that science has yet to definitively account for the origins of the human self, after Plato's fallen angels have been expelled from heaven and academia alike. And though he is loath to invoke a Supreme Being, the roots of human identity seem to him beyond either natural or proximate origins.:

> We are simple examples of minds, and...the existence of mind is certainly a *datum* for the construction of any world picture: At the very least, its *possibility* must be explained. And it hardly seems credible that its appearance should be a natural accident, like the fact that there are mammals.[50]

Epilogue

One scholar has this to say about the Neo-Platonic Christian bishop
Synesius and his belief in the pre-mortal origins of the human soul: his
"affirmation of the inherent divinity (and therefore immortality) of
the human soul, which makes possible its return to the divine under its
own power, is a clear indication of an essentially pagan faith."[1] That's a
somewhat striking and revealing claim. Even with the important qualifier
"under its own power," this may be a Pelagian, but hardly a pagan,
position. In any case, salvational self-reliance is certainly not a dominant
feature in Synesius's religious conception, and the best illustration the
scholar cites of his claim is the bishop's reference to that blessed one "who
fleeing the devouring bark of matter and earth, raises us and with a leap
of the spirit presses on his path to God."[2] Surely this sounds as much
like any medieval mystic as a pagan or even a Pelagian. The quickness
of the critic to slide from mystic ascent to pagan theurgy may be an
utterly revealing tendency that explains a great deal about the decline of
preexistence in Western thought. The sovereignty of God, as it came to be
constructed, implied quite literal conceptions of a jealous God. Thinkers
as far back as Tertullian have jumped into the breach to protect God's
remoteness, to maintain with fear and fervor the Creator-creature divide.

But such concerns may be a projection onto the divine of
human ideas about sovereignty and hierarchy. Plato's conception of
deity suggests the possibility of an alternative to such models. Plato
envisioned a God whom he couldn't even describe as generous—not
because he was impersonal, but because generosity might imply a

self-conscious triumph of condescension over patent superiority. His God seems somehow nobler. "He who framed this whole universe...was good, and one who is good can never become jealous of anything. And so, being free of jealousy, he wanted everything to become as much like himself as was possible."[3] In that cosmology or, more important, in that axiology, no danger is to be feared from divine origins that intimate apotheosis nor from a conception of apotheosis that may reasonably suggest divine, and therefore immortal, origins.

Other developments beside the fashioning of a jealous God of absolute transcendence combined to overthrow the older philosophical universe which made possible and sustained the doctrine of preexistence. With the centering of grace in Christian theology, it became a specially dispensed gift that precluded most if not all capacity for self-elevation. With the entrenchment of sin, inherited guilt, and depravity in the face especially of Pelagian inroads, divine sparks and heavenly antecedents to the human personality were effectively precluded. With creation *ex nihilo* as evidence of God's further sovereignty, preexistence was increasingly, logically incompatible with a Creator God. And to the extent that, as with Augustine's capitulation, theodicy was made to bow to the mysterious workings of God, rational resolution of the scandal of human pain and misery no longer required an explanatory prologue to the human condition. For all of these reasons, preexistence lost its allure. For a brief moment in the seventeenth century, when human possibilities found exuberant expression alongside Neo-Platonic resurgence, the idea gained a new foothold. Then again, when the century of reform in the age of Romanticism ushered in a new social conscience and a less powerful and less medieval church and as poets and intellectuals, free of all imaginative constraints, again plumbed the depths of Faustian yearning, the idea flourished once more. And interspersed throughout the Christian centuries, mystics, Kabbalists, prophets, and poets turned their attention to ancient sources to reimagine even older worlds and kept alive an idea too potent in its explanatory powers to relinquish. Still, the tide of theological currents dating to the turn of the fifth century was, ultimately, decisive. The twin condemnation of Pelagius and Origen, writes one scholar, ensured the supremacy "of a Christian theology whose central concerns were human sinfulness, not human potentiality; divine determination, not human freedom and responsibility; God's mystery, not God's justice. Christianity was perhaps poorer for their suppression."[4]

Unlike many paradigms that have succumbed to philosophical or scientific critique, preexistence was not really vanquished in a contest of ideas. Even in the realm of religious inquiry, where no prima facie dismissal of angelic realms and pre-mortal glories would seem warranted, the careless and nervous avoidance of genuine intellectual engagement suggests that the idea was more a victim of collateral damage, a casualty of the theological and political battles that raged throughout the early Christian world. Actual, direct confrontation with the essential idea was relatively rare. A respected biblical commentary is, in this regard, entirely emblematic of the long history we have surveyed. Commenting on the clear allusion to preexistence in chapter 9 of John, where the disciples inquire about pre-mortal sin, the scholar acknowledges the appeal of such anthropologies, which posit a relationship between present circumstance and prior existence:

> In such a view there are no enigmas and no baffling problems of providence to puzzle and confuse the mind. It is all clear, and understandable, and absolutely just....And what we are today, our circumstances, what befalls us in our present existence, and the like, these are not chance-blown, but are the fruit of what we were and did....All the disabilities that beset us arise from our own mistakes and wrongdoings in the past....We have no possible grievance against anyone or anything....There is something majestic in this conception of a fundamental justice woven into the very web of life, running through all things, and working itself out in everything that happens to us: a conception which leaves no room for whimpering, or whining, or self-pity, or railing against fate.

The most vexing religious challenge of the Western tradition, theodicy, or the vindication of God's justice in the face of evil, pain, and suffering, is hereby solved definitively, or so it would seem. Nevertheless, the commentator concludes with unexpected curtness, "surely it is much too crude and easy a solution."[5]

A Cambridge classical scholar could well have had this commentator in mind when he wrote, "however many readers...believe that their soul will survive death, rather few, I imagine, believe that it also pre-existed their birth. The religions that have shaped Western culture are so inhospitable to the idea of pre-existence that you probably reject the thought out of hand, for no good reason."[6] Of course, he then pointed out slyly, the same Pythagoras that taught the pre-mortality of the human soul also taught his followers to spit on their nail and hair clippings, to wash the left foot before the right, and that the sea consists of the tears of Cronus. The scholar's statement may be true. Unfortunately, it misses the fact that some beliefs meet a demise as definitive as their implausibility. Others persist with uncommon tenacity across millennia and across cultures, a tribute, if not to their truth, at least to their powerful satisfaction of logical, moral, and aesthetic imperatives.

Acknowledgments

My good friend the Milton scholar John Tanner was a collaborator in spirit if not in fact, as we originally hoped, overwhelmed as he was by the task of running a university. Cynthia Read at Oxford was an indefatigable advisor, supporter, and friend through the process. I have come to appreciate her keen judgment on matters large and small. Marcia Whitehead was an invaluable resource from the project's inception to the very end. Friends and colleagues Anthony Russell and Louis Schwartz were invigorating sounding boards. Ben Huff was a frequent source of ideas and feedback, and James McLachlan steered me in some productive directions. Nathaniel Givens helped to hash out a number of philosophical issues, while Brad Kramer helped to track down arcane Hebrew sources. Justin Collins and Justin White both did valuable work as research assistants. Zina Peterson gave me leads I would have overlooked and provided helpful and at times provoking feedback. Roger Minert and Martin Sulzer-Reichel performed a great service to me in translating difficult nineteenth-century German texts, as Stephen Bay did with Latin quotations. Ronan Head lent his good will and Assyrian expertise. My good friend David Bokovoy, another scholar of Akkadian, was an especially helpful and encouraging resource, and I express special appreciation for his role in moving me and the project along. Cory Crawford was very generous in sharing his knowledge about preclassical traditions, as were Paul Hoskisson, Dan Belnap, and Aaron Schade. Ariel Bybee contributed a number of useful suggestions, and Tyler Petrey was especially critical in good and productive ways. John Gee read early sections and provided his typically erudite comments. John Armstrong kindly lent his expertise in classical philosophy. John Welch made helpful suggestions along the way, and Rosaylnde Welch offered useful criticisms. Rachael Givens and Elin Roberts were perceptive proofreaders, and, as usual, my most exacting critic was my wife, Fiona.

Notes

PROLOGUE

1. Thomas Moore, preface to "The Loves of the Angels," in *The Poetical Works of Thomas Moore*, ed. A. D. Godley (London: Oxford University Press, 1915), 537.

2. Plato, *Phaedrus*, 246c, trans. Alexander Nehamas and Paul Woodruff, in *Plato: Complete Works*, ed. John M. Cooper (Indianapolis, Ind.: Hackett, 1997), 524.

3. Origen, *De Principiis*, I.8, in *Origen on First Principles, Being Koetschau's Text of the De Principiis*, trans. G. W. Butterworth (New York: Harper & Row, 1966), 72–73.

4. Leo Steinberg provides a sweeping overview of interpretations of the fresco's figures in "Who's Who in Michelangelo's *Creation of Adam*: A Chronology of the Picture's Reluctant Self-Revelation," *Art Bulletin* 74.4 (December 1992): 553, including the one cited from E. Steinmann, *Die Sixtinische Kapelle* (Munich, 1905). The other scholarly positions described here are all included, with sources, in his essay. In a subsequent piece, Steinberg traces (while dismantling) the Sophia interpretation from Julien Klaczko's *Rome et la Renaissance* (1898) to Rudolf Kuhn's *Michelangelo: Die sixtinische Decke* (1975). See Marcia Hall and Leo Steinberg, "Who's Who in Michelangelo's *Creation of Adam* Continued," *Art Bulletin* 75.2 (June 1993): 340–44.

INTRODUCTION

1. Friedrich Schiller, *The Robbers*, I.i. trans. F. J. Lamport, in *The Robbers; Wallenstein* (New York: Penguin, 1979), 33.

2. Spirit and soul (*pneuma* and *psyche* in Greek; *ruach* or *neshamah* and *nephesh* in Hebrew), representing at times very different concepts, are each

possessed of a long, complex history of meanings. An account of these would necessarily constitute a separate work. For our purposes and for many, though by no means all, ancient writers, the two are usually interchangeable. Each constitutes what is held to be the immaterial and immortal part of the human being. Plato, for example, considers the soul to be the principle of life. As the essence of self-action and manifestation of an autonomous will, the soul is the true self and core of identity. Whereas some consider the soul unitary, many treat it as complex. For Plato, it comprises three parts: the *logos* or rational soul, the source of higher intellectual activities, located in the brain; the *thymos* or emotional soul, the locus of the higher emotions, situated in the thorax; and the *pathos* or carnal soul, the source of gross appetites, housed in the abdomen. Among ancient thinkers, Aristotle's use of the word soul is entirely unlike Plato's and Christian usages generally. For Aristotle, the soul is the form a living body takes, not a separate entity that animates the body (it is not the sailor who works the ship of the body, in his metaphor) (*De Anima*, II.1). Since it cannot exist independently of the body, any conception of preexistence is thereby immediately precluded. The Hebrew case, as we shall see, is somewhere between these conceptions. In this book, I will use the terms soul and spirit interchangeably unless the original or present context requires differentiation.

3. See the treatment by P. B. T. Bilaniuk, "Traducianism," *New Catholic Encyclopedia*, 2nd ed. (Detroit: Gale, 2003), 14:140. J. E. Royce and J. Furton, however, point out that, though the ordinary magisterium teaches creationism, "there is no solemn teaching of the Church concerning the origin of the human soul." "Soul, Human, Origin of," *New Catholic Encyclopedia*, 13:353–56.

4. G. R. S. Mead, "The Doctrine of Reincarnation Ethically Considered," *International Journal of Ethics* 22.2 (January 1912): 159.

5. Geddes MacGregor, *Reincarnation in Christianity* (Wheaton, Ill.: Quest, 1978), 94.

6. Mead cites a study by Robert Eisler, *Weltenmantel und Himmelszelt: Religionsgeschichtliche Untersuchungen zur Urgeschichte des antiken Weltbildes* (Munich: Beck, 1910), which begins with a comparison of Indian and Greek forms of the doctrine in the seventh and sixth centuries BCE and traces their common root back to a "high cult of Chronos-Adrasteia (or of the Æon) of Ionian Asia Minor," and from there back to Iranian traditions and eventually to an origin in Central Asia. Mead, "Doctrine of Reincarnation," 163–64.

7. Fred B. Craddock, *The Pre-Existence of Christ in the New Testament* (Nashville, Tenn.: Abingdon, 1968), 27, cited in R. G. Hamerton-Kelly, *Pre-Existence, Wisdom, and the Son of Man* (Cambridge: Cambridge University Press, 1973; repr., Eugene, Ore.: Wipf and Stock, 2000), 5.

8. Hamerton-Kelly, *Pre-Existence*, 5.

9. See, in this regard, Ian Barbour, who describes the function of religious language as providing models that "are used in the interpretation of experience." *Myths, Models, and Paradigms: A Comparative Study in Science and Religion* (New York: Harper & Row, 1971), 57.

10. Hamerton-Kelly, *Pre-Existence*, 6–7, paraphrasing W. Norman Pittenger's discussion of Rudolf Bultmann. See Pittenger, *The Word Incarnate* (New York: Harper, 1959), 131.

11. These positions are represented by Adolf Harnack, Sigmund Mowinckel, and Fred Craddock, respectively. See Hamerton-Kelly, *Pre-Existence*, 3–4.

12. Simon J. Gathercole, *The Pre-Existent Son: Recovering the Christologies of Matthew, Mark, and Luke* (Grand Rapids, Mich.: Eerdmans, 2006), is a survey of the idea as it pertains to Christ's preexistence. The most comprehensive work on the subject of preexistence to date is Hamerton-Kelly, *Pre-Existence, Wisdom, and the Son of Man: A Study of the Idea of Pre-Existence in the New Testament.* The subtitle notwithstanding, the book has an important section on precursors to the idea in Jewish thought.

13. Richard H. Popkin, "Newton's Biblical Theology and His Theological Physics," in *Newton's Scientific and Philosophical Legacy*, ed. Paul B. Scheurer and G. Debrock (Dordrecht: Kluwer, 1988), 82.

14. Friedrich Nietzsche, preface to *Genealogy of Morals*, in *Genealogy of Morals and Ecce Homo*, trans. Walter Kaufmann and R. J. Hollingdale (New York: Vintage, 1989), 19, 17.

15. The expression "trailing clouds of glory" is from William Wordsworth, "Ode: Intimations of Immortality." In *Poetical Works*, ed. Thomas Hutchinson and Ernest de Selincourt (New York: Oxford University Press, 1989), 460–62.

CHAPTER 1

1. Paul E. Davies, "The Projection of Pre-Existence," *Biblical Research* 12 (1967): 36, 34.

2. Jean Bottéro, *Religion in Ancient Mesopotamia*, trans. Teresa Lavender Fagan (Chicago: University of Chicago Press, 2001), vii.

3. W. G. Lambert and A. R. Millard, *Atra-hasis: The Babylonian Story of the Flood* I.2–6 (Winona Lake, Ind.: Eisenbrauns, 1999), 43. Akkadian is the earliest known Semitic language, spoken in Mesopotamia by the Assyrians and Babylonians. Scholars assign the date 1700 BCE to the best preserved text of *Atrahasis*; Abusch gives a date of 2000–1600 BCE for the original composition. Tzvi Abusch, "Ghost and God: Some Observations on a Babylonian Understanding of Human Nature," in *Self, Soul and Body in Religious Experience*, ed. A. I. Baumgarten, J. Assmann, and G. G. Stroumsa (Leiden: Brill, 1998), 364.

4. Lambert and Millard, *Atra-hasis*, I:210–28 (59).

5. Bottéro, *Religion*, 100.

6. Tzvi Abusch, "Etemmu," in *Dictionary of Deities and Demons in the Bible*, 2nd ed., ed. Karel van der Toorn, Bob Becking, and Pieter W. van der Horst (Boston: Brill, 1999), 309. See also S. A. Geller, "Some Sound and Word Plays in the First Tablet of the Old Babylonian *Atrahasis* Epic," in *The Frank Talmage Memorial Volume*, 2 vols., ed. B. Walfish (Haifa: Haifa University Press, 1993), 1:62–63.

7. Abusch, "Ghost and God," 372.

8. Benjamin Foster's translation has "the inspiration" for *temu*. See "Atra-Hasis," in *The Context of Scripture: Canonical Compositions from the Biblical World*, ed. William W. Hallo (Leiden: Brill, 1997), 1:451. The term is rendered "personality" in the standard English version of Lambert and Millard, *Atra-hasis*, 59. Bottéro, *Religion*, renders it simply "spirit." In all versions, however, it is the god's "spirit" that is mixed with the clay to form the human (ll. 215, 217, 228, 230).

9. Bottéro, *Religion*, 100.

10. Lambert and Millard, *Atra-hasis*, 22. Abusch, however, refers to other creation accounts that at least allude to humans' origin in "the remains of a slain god" and their subsequent constitution out of "divine elements." See G. Pettinato, *Das altorientalische*

Menschenbild und die sumerischen und akkadischen Schöpfungsmythen (Heidelberg: Carl Winter, 1971), cited in Abusch, "Ghost and God," 369.

11. Abusch, "Ghost and God," 366–67.

12. Bottéro, *Religion*, 100–101.

13. This and all subsequent biblical citations are from the New Revised Standard Version (Anglicized edition), except where indicated.

14. Dexter E. Callender, Jr., *Adam in Myth and History: Ancient Israelite Perspectives on the Primal Human* (Winona Lake, Ind.: Eisenbrauns, 2000), 212.

15. Dana M. Pike discusses several examples of election in ancient Near Eastern texts, including the Hammurabi prologue, in "Before Jeremiah Was: Divine Election in the Ancient Near East," in *A Witness for the Restoration: Essays in Honor of Robert J. Matthews*, ed. Kent P. Jackson and Andrew C. Skinner (Provo, Utah: Religious Studies Center, Brigham Young University, 2007), 33–59.

16. The code was produced late in the reign of Hammurabi (1792–1750). Since the date of the actual composition of *Atrahasis* is uncertain and may have been as early as 2000 BCE, we have no way of knowing which was written first.

17. Martha T. Roth, *Law Collections from Mesopotamia and Asia Minor*, vol. 6 of *Writings from the Ancient World* (Atlanta, Ga.: Scholars, 1995), 76–77.

18. Phillip J. Johnston, *Shades of Sheol: Death and Afterlife in the Old Testament* (Downers Grove, Ill.: InterVarsity, 2002), 109.

19. *The Assyrian Dictionary of the Oriental Institute of the University of Chicago*, 21 vols., ed. Martha T. Ross (Chicago: Oriental Institute, 1958), 4:308.

20. G. del Olmo Lete and J. Sanmartín, *Dictionary of the Ugaritic Language in the Alphabetic Tradition*, 2 vols. (Leiden: Brill, 2004), 1:106. I am indebted to David Bokovy for this discussion of etymologies.

21. E. Theodore Mullen, *The Divine Council in Canaanite and Early Hebrew Literature* (Missoula, Mont.: Scholars, 1986), 204–5.

22. Ronald S. Hendel, "When the Sons of God Cavorted with the Daughters of Men," in *Understanding the Dead Sea Scrolls*, ed. Herschel Shanks (New York: Random House, 1992), 170, 172. The older wording is preserved in Qumran manuscripts.

23. "When Jews of this period read the passages commented on above they now understood them to refer, not to divine beings, but to angels." S. B. Parker, "Sons of (the) God(s)," in *Dictionary of Deities and Demons*, 798.

24. "Other nations, moreover, are called a part of the angels" is how Origen glossed the passage. Origen, *De Principiis*, I.5.2 trans. Frederick Crombie, in *The Ante-Nicene Fathers*, ed. Alexander Roberts and James Donaldson (Grand Rapids, Mich.: Eerdmans, 1977), 4:256 (hereafter, *ANF*).

25. Origen, *De Principiis*, I.8.4 (*ANF* 4:266).

26. Adolf Harnack, *History of Dogma*, 7 vols., trans. from 3rd German ed. by Neil Buchanan (London: Williams & Norgate, 1894), 1:103n.

27. Cyrus Gordon long ago disputed the effort to translate the offending term *elohim* as "rulers" or "judges" in "Elohim in Its Reputed Meaning of Rulers, Judges," *Journal of Biblical Literature* 54 (1935): 139–44. More recently, Michael Heiser provides convincing reasons for reading the word as "gods" or "heavenly beings," in "Deuteronomy 32:8 and the Sons of God," *Bibliotheca Sacra* 158.629 (January–March 2001): 52–74.

28. Julian Morgenstern, "The Mythological Background of Psalm 82," *Hebrew Union College Annual* 14 (1939): 73.

29. Hamerton-Kelly relates this "primal man" to the preexistent Wisdom, since they appear together both here and in Proverbs 8. *Pre-Existence*, 28.

30. Mullen, *Divine Council,* 192–93.

31. E. Theodore Mullen, Jr., "Divine Assembly," in *Anchor Bible Dictionary*, 6 vols., ed. David Noel Freedman (Garden City, N.Y.: Doubleday, 1992), 2:214.

32. Mullen, "Divine Assembly," 2:216.

33. P. W. Coxon, paraphrasing Moses Aberbach, in "Nephilim," in *Dictionary of Deities and Demons*, 619.

34. Coxon, "Nephilim," 619.

35. Moshe Halbertal and Avishai Margalit, *Idolatry*, trans. Naomi Goldblum (Cambridge, Mass.: Harvard University Press, 1992), 4.

36. Bottéro, *Religion*, 214.

37. Frank Chamberlain Porter, "The Pre-Existence of the Soul in the Book of Wisdom and in the Rabbinical Literature," *American Journal of Theology* 12.1 (January 1908): 57.

38. Porter, "Pre-Existence of the Soul," 57–58.

39. Harnack, *History of Dogma*, 1:319–20.

40. Harnack, *History of Dogma*, 1:318–19.

41. Paul E. Davies, "The Projection of Pre-Existence," *Biblical Research* 12 (1967): 29.

42. R. G. Hamerton-Kelly, *Pre-Existence, Wisdom, and the Son of Man: A Study of the Idea of Pre-Existence in the New Testament* (Cambridge: Cambridge University Press, 1973; repr., Eugene, Ore.: Wipf and Stock, 2000), 16.

43. Hamerton-Kelly cites in this regard Norman Perrin, *Rediscovering the Teaching of Jesus* (London: SCM, 1967); Morna D. Hooker, *The Son of Man in Mark* (Montreal: McGill University Press, 1967); Hamerton-Kelly, *Pre-Existence*, 9.

44. Gerald Bostock, "The Sources of Origen's Doctrine of Pre-Existence," in *Origeniana Quarta: Die Referate des 4. Internationalen Origenskongresses*, ed. Lothar Lies (Innsbruck: Tyrolia, 1987), 261.

CHAPTER 2

1. H. Wheeler Robinson, "The Council of Yahweh," *Journal of Theological Studies* 45.45 (1944): 151.

2. Werner Jaeger, "The Greek Ideas of Immortality: The Ingersoll Lecture for 1958," *Harvard Theological Review* 52.3 (July 1959): 136–37.

3. Thomas Taylor, ed. and trans., *The Works of Plato*, 5 vols. (London: R. Wilks, 1804; repr., New York: Garland, 1984), 1:xliii–xliv.

4. W. K. C. Guthrie, *Orpheus and Greek Religion: A Study of the Orphic Movement* (London: Methuen, 1952; repr., New York: Norton, 1966), 218.

5. Richard A. Norris, "Soul," *Encyclopedia of Early Christianity*, 2nd ed., ed. Everett Ferguson (New York: Garland, 1998), 1079.

6. Aristotle, *De Anima*, I.3, 5 (407b, 410b–411a), in *Aristotle's On the Soul and On Memory and Recollection*, trans. Joe Sachs (Santa Fe.: Green Lion, 2001), 64, 75.

7. Aristotle, *De Anima*, III.5 (430a); *On the Soul*, 142–43.

8. Robert Parker, "Early Orphism," in *The Greek World*, ed. Anton Powell (New York: Routledge, 1995), 484–86.

9. Plato, *Cratylus*, 400c, trans. C. D. C. Reeve, in *Plato: Complete Works*, ed. John M. Cooper (Indianapolis, Ind.: Hackett, 1997), 119.

10. One exception is Harold Cherniss who, in correcting one typical instance of this conflation, writes, "The evidence fails to show that the Pythagoreans…had any notion at all of pre-existent knowledge…. Neither does Plato state the theory of recollection as a 'deduction from the idea of transmigration.' On the contrary, the pre-existence of the soul is deduced as a necessary consequence of anamnesis [recollection]." Review of Alister Cameron, "The Pythagorean Background to the Theory of Recollection," *American Journal of Philology* 60 (1940): 361, 364.

11. Walter Burkert, *Lore and Science in Ancient Pythagoreanism*, trans. Edwin L. Minar, Jr. (Cambridge, Mass.: Harvard University Press, 1972), 126.

12. Jaeger, "Greek Ideas of Immortality," 142.

13. Empedocles, "On Purification," no. 383, in *Fragments*, in *Selections from Early Greek Philosophy*, ed. Milton Nahm (Englewood Cliffs, N.J.: Prentice-Hall, 1964), 128.

14. Empedocles, "On Purification," no. 390, 128.

15. Burkert, *Lore and Science*, preface.

16. Burkert exploded a number of myths associated with Pythagoras that pervade modern treatments nonetheless. See, in this regard, M. F. Burnyeat, "Other Lives," *London Review of Books* 29.4 (22 February 2007).

17. R. J. Hawkins, "Pythagoreanism," in *Oxford Companion to Philosophy*, ed. Ted Honderich (Oxford: Oxford University Press, 1995), 734.

18. Burkert, *Lore and Science*, 120.

19. Guthrie, *Orpheus and Greek Religion*, 217.

20. Augustine, *The City of God against the Pagans*, VIII.4, trans. R. W. Dyson (Cambridge: Cambridge University Press, 1998), 316.

21. Plato, *Meno*, 80d–e, trans. G. M. A. Grube, in *Plato*, 879–80.

22. Plato, *Meno*, 81a–c, in *Plato*, 880.

23. Plato, *Meno*, 85e–86a, in *Plato*, 886.

24. As I indicated in the introduction, the focus of this book is the sweep and permutations of a seminal idea in Western thought—not the degree of faith commitment of its purveyors. But I do find this remark by Dominic Scott apt:

> We should not try to purge the theory of any commitment to pre-existence and literal recollection by claiming that Plato was only speaking metaphorically. This fails to do justice to the fact that in the *Phaedo* Plato sets out to prove the pre-existence of the soul, for which he needs to claim quite literally that the soul was once in possession of its innate knowledge. Even in the *Meno*, where the emphasis is more epistemological, there is still a short argument for the claim that the soul has been in existence from eternity.

Recollection and Experience: Plato's Theory of Learning and Its Successors (Cambridge: Cambridge University Press, 1995), 17.

25. Plato, *Meno*, 86b, in *Plato*, 886.

26. Plato, *Phaedo*, 70c, trans. G. M. A. Grube, in *Plato*, 61.

27. Plato, *Phaedo*, 72e–73a, in *Plato*, 63.

28. John Armstrong makes a compelling case for another dimension to Plato's thought related to his ideal of apotheosis. "Rather than fleeing from the sensible world, becoming like this god commits one to improving it," he writes. See "After the Ascent: Plato on Becoming like God," *Oxford Studies in Ancient Philosophy* 26 (Summer 2004): 171–83.

29. Plato, *Phaedo*, 66c–d, in *Plato*, 57–58.

30. Plato, *Phaedo*, 74d, in *Plato*, 65.

31. Plato, *Phaedo*, 75b–d, 76c, in *Plato* 66–67.

32. Plato, *Phaedrus*, 246b, trans. Alexander Nehamas and Paul Woodruff, in *Plato*, 524.

33. Plato, *Phaedrus*, 246c, in *Plato*, 524.

34. Plato, *Phaedrus*, 248c, in *Plato*, 526.

35. Plato, *Phaedrus*, 250a, in *Plato*, 527.

36. Plato, *Phaedrus*, 250b–c, in *Plato*, 528.

37. Plato, *Phaedrus*, 249b–c, in *Plato*, 527.

38. Plato, *Republic*, X.617e, trans. G. M. A. Grube, rev. C. D. C. Reeve, in *Plato*, 1220.

39. Plato, *Republic*, X.618d, in *Plato*, 1221.

40. Plato, *Symposium*, 192c–d, trans. Alexander Nehamas and Paul Woodruff, in *Plato*, 475.

41. *The Revelation of Adam,* trans. George W. MacRae, adapted by Willis Barnstone, in *The Gnostic Bible*, ed. Barnstone and Marvin Meyer (Boston: Shambhala, 2003), 181.

42. Plato, *Phaedrus*, 250d–51b, in *Plato*, 528.

43. Plato, *Timaeus*, 27a, trans. Donald J. Zeyl, Alexander Nehamas, and Paul Woodruff, in *Plato*, 1234.

44. Plato, *Timaeus*, 29e, 30b, 34c, in *Plato*, 1236, 1239.

45. Plato, *Timaeus*, 30c, 40b, 38c, 41c, 41d–42a, 43a, in *Plato*, 1236, 1243, 1242, 1244–45, 1246.

46. Plato, *Timaeus*, 41e, 42b, 90a, in *Plato*, 1245, 1288–89.

47. *The Exegesis on the Soul*, trans. William C. Robinson, Jr., in *The Nag Hammadi Library in English*, ed. James Robinson (San Francisco: Harper & Row, 1977), 180–81.

48. The subject of gendered souls in Gnostic thought is addressed in Michael A. Williams, "Varieties in Gnostic Perspectives on Gender," in *Images of the Feminine in Gnosticism*, ed. Karen L. King (Harrisburg, Pa.: Trinity, 2000), 2–22. An excellent study of the subject in classical philosophy is Giulia Sissa, "The Sexual Philosophies of Plato and Aristotle," in *A History of Women in the West*, 5 vols., trans. Arthur Goldhammer (Cambridge, Mass.: Harvard University Press, 1992), 1:46–82.

49. Plato, *Phaedo*, 114d, in *Plato*, 97.

50. Plato, *Timaeus*, 29c–d, in *Plato*, 1235–36.

51. David Sedley, "The Ideal of Godlikeness," in *Plato: Ethics, Politics, Religion, and the Soul*, 2 vols., ed. Gail Fine (Oxford: Oxford University Press, 1999), 2:309.

52. Plato, *Theaetetus*, 176a, trans. M. J. Levett, rev. Myles F. Burnyeat, in *Plato*, 195.

CHAPTER 3

1. Werner Foerster, *From the Exile to Christ: A Historical Introduction to Palestinian Judaism*, trans. Gordon E. Harris (Philadelphia: Fortress, 1964), 19.

2. Edwin Hatch, *The Influence of Greek Ideas on Christianity* (Gloucester: Peter Smith, 1970), 128–29.

3. Philo, *De Plantatione* [*Concerning Noah's Work as a Planter*], II (6), in *The Works of Philo*, trans. C. D. Yonge (Peabody, Mass.: Hendrickson, 1993), 191.

4. David T. Runia, *Exegesis and Philosophy: Studies on Philo of Alexandria* (Aldershot, England: Variorum, 1990), 8.

5. Gerhard May, *Creation ex Nihilo: The Doctrine of "Creation Out of Nothing" in Early Christian Thought*, trans. A. S. Worrall (Edinburgh: Clark, 1994), 10. Antonia Tripolitis sees more ambiguity on this issue: "Concerning the origin of matter from which the world was made, Philo is inconsistent. In some passages it is considered as created by God, and in other passages as coeternal with God." See *The Doctrine of the Soul in the Thought of Plotinus and Origen* (New York: Libra, 1978), 7. This position seems to arise from confusion surrounding Philo's reference to God creating out of "nonbeing" (*ek mei ontos*). But he always takes for granted the eternity of matter, and the Greek expression is simply "an unreflective way of saying that through the act of creation something arose which did not previously exist." See May, *Creation ex Nihilo*, 16–18, 21.

6. Philo, *De Somniis* [*On Dreams*], II.6 (45), in Yonge, *Works of Philo*, 391.

7. Philo, *De Opificio Mundi* [*On the Creation*], V (22), in Yonge, *Works of Philo*, 5.

8. In some cases, the denial of preexistence in the plain sense of the word can involve some intellectual calisthenics. David Winston, for example, concludes that "the many passages in which Philo speaks of creation in temporal terms are not to be taken literally, but only as accommodations to the biblical idiom." Faced with such clearly difficult cases as Philo's explicit statement "there was a time when the world was not," Winston simply asserts, "Philo did not hesitate to use locutions that explicitly negated his precise technical position." Philo of Alexandria, *The Contemplative Life, the Giants, and Selections*, ed. and trans. David Winston (New York: Paulist, 1981), 17. Philo himself recurrently expressed distress with those who considered allegorical truth to be a substitute for, rather than a complement to, the literal truth it embodied. He singled out as examples of this lamentable misunderstanding circumcision and Jewish festivals, which he saw as "symbols of things appreciable by the intellect," while insisting that to consider such things as only symbols and therefore to annul their literal importance would be grievous error. See Philo, *On the Migration of Abraham* (89–93). See the discussion of this concern in Philo by David M. Scholer, "Foreword," in Yonge, *Works of Philo*, xiii–xiv.

9. Philo, *Contemplative Life*, 17. Winston is citing Philo, *De Cherubim*, XVIII (58–60).

10. The reference to a time when the world did not exist is from *De Decalogo* [*The Decalogue*], XII (58).

11. Plato, *Republic*, X.596–99.

12. Aristotle, *On the Generation of Animals*, I.19.30 (727b), I.21.13–20 (729b–30a), II.4 (739b), trans. A. L. Peck (Cambridge, Mass.: Harvard University Press, 1943), 101, 113–14, 117, 191.

13. Aristotle, *Generation of Animals*, II.4.25 (738b) (185). Aquinas will adopt this position verbatim. See *Summa Theologica*, III:Q32, art. 4.

14. Philo, *Opificio Mundi*, IV (17–20), in Yonge, *Works of Philo*, 4.

15. Philo, *De Gigantibus* [The Giants], II (7–10), in Winston, *Contemplative Life*, 62.

16. Philo, *De Gigantibus*, III (12–14), in Winston, *Contemplative Life*, 63.

17. Philo, *Plantatione*, IV (14), in Yonge, *Works of Philo*, 192.

18. *Somniis*, I.22 (134–40), in Yonge, *Works of Philo*, 377.

19. *Somniis*, I.22 (137), in Yonge, *Works of Philo*, 377.

20. Philo, *Quis Rerum Divinarum Heres Sit* [*Who Is the Heir of Divine Things*], XLIX (239–40), in Winston, *Contemplative Life*, 118–19.

21. Philo, *Quaestiones et Solutiones in Genesin* [*Questions and Answers on Genesis*], IV (74), in Winston, *Contemplative Life*, 119.

22. Philo, *Legum Allegoriarum* [*Allegorical Interpretation*], III.20 (68), in Winston, *Contemplative Life*, 227.

23. Philo, *Quaestiones*, I (53), in Yonge, *Works of Philo*, 802.

24. Philo, *Quaestiones*, IV (4), in Winston, *Contemplative Life*, 164.

25. Philo, *De Migratione Abrahami* [*On the Migration of Abraham*], 1–4, in Winston, *Contemplative Life*, 167.

26. Philo, *Migratione*, 7–12; *Rerum Divinarum*, 69–70, in Winston, *Contemplative Life*, 168–69.

27. Philo, *Quod Deterius Potiori Insidiari Soleat* [*That the Worse Is Wont to Attack the Better*], 89–90, in Winston, *Contemplative Life*, 172.

28. "Pre-existence," in R. J. Zwi Werblowsky and Geoffrey Wigoder, eds., *The Encyclopedia of the Jewish Religion* (New York: Adama, 1986), 308.

29. F. I. Andersen, introduction to *2 (Slavonic Apocalypse of) Enoch*, in *The Old Testament Pseudepigrapha*, 2 vols., ed. James H. Charlesworth (Garden City, N.Y.: Doubleday, 1983), 1:94–95.

30. *2 Enoch* XXIII.4–5, trans. F. I. Andersen, in Charlesworth, *Old Testament*, 1:140.

31. *Prayer of Joseph*, fragment A 2–3, trans. J. Z. Smith, in Charlesworth, *Old Testament*, 2:713.

32. Origen, *Commentary on John*, II.25, trans. Allan Menzies, in *The Ante-Nicene Fathers*, ed. Alexander Roberts and James Donaldson (Grand Rapids, Mich.: Eerdmans, 1977), 10:341 (hereafter, *ANF*).

33. *Prayer of Joseph*, fragment C, trans. J. Z. Smith, in Charlesworth, *Old Testament*, 2:713. Charlesworth notes the difficulty of establishing a basis for Origen's reading.

34. Charlesworth, *Old Testament*, 2:713n.

35. *Testament of Moses*, I.14, trans. J. Priest, in Charlesworth, *Old Testament*, 1:927; *Assumption of Moses*, I.14, trans. R. H. Charles, in R. H. Charles, *The Apocrypha and Pseudepigrapha of the Old Testament*, 2 vols. (Oxford: Clarendon, 1968), 2:415.

36. Charles, *Apocrypha and Pseudepigrapha*, 2:415n.

37. *Jubilees*, II.2, trans. O. S. Wintermute, in Charlesworth, *Old Testament*, 2:55.

38. *Apocalypse of Abraham*, XXI.7–XXII.5, trans. R. Rubinkiewicz, in Charlesworth, *Old Testament*, 1:699–700.

39. *The Fourth Book of Ezra*, trans. B. M. Metzger, in Charlesworth, *Old Testament*, 1:523.

40. *Fourth Book of Ezra*, IX.13, VII.127–28, 132, 78, in Charlesworth, *Old Testament*, 1:541, 539.

41. Helmer Ringgren, *Word and Wisdom: Studies in the Hypostatization of Divine Qualities and Functions in the Ancient Near East* (Lund: Ohlssons, 1947), 91–92.

42. R. G. Hamerton-Kelly, *Pre-Existence, Wisdom, and the Son of Man* (Cambridge: Cambridge University Press, 1973; repr., Eugene, Ore.: Wipf and Stock, 2000), 19.

43. Roland E. Murphy, "Wisdom in the OT," in *Anchor Bible Dictionary*, 6 vols., ed. David Noel Freedman (Garden City, N.Y.: Doubleday, 1992), 6:926.

44. Ringgren, *Word and Wisdom*, 104.

45. Ringgren, *Word and Wisdom*, 108.

46. Adolf Harnack, *History of Dogma*, 7 vols., trans. from 3rd German ed. by Neil Buchanan (London: Williams & Norgate, 1894), 1:103n–104n.

47. George A. Barton, "On the Jewish-Christian Doctrine of the Pre-Existence of the Messiah," *Journal of Biblical Literature* 21.1 (1902): 79.

48. Harnack, *History of Dogma*, 1:324.

49. Simon J. Gathercole, *The Pre-Existent Son: Recovering the Christologies of Matthew, Mark, and Luke* (Grand Rapids, Mich.: Eerdmans, 2006), 31.

50. H.-C. Kammler, *Die Präexistenzaussagen im Neuen Testament* (Frankfurt am Main: Lang, 1990), 421, cited in Gathercole, *Pre-Existent Son*, 31.

51. Gerald Bostock, "The Sources of Origen's Doctrine of Pre-Existence," in *Origeniana Quarta: Die Referate des 4. Internationalen Origenskongresses*, ed. Lothar Lies (Innsbruck: Tyrolia, 1987), 259.

52. Origen, *De Principiis*, II.6.3, trans. Frederick Crombie (*ANF* 4:282). Jerome's version comes from his epistle to Avitus (Letter 124), cited in *ANF* 4:282n.

53. J. A. Dorner, *History of the Development of the Person of Christ*, trans. D. W. Simon (Edinburgh: Clark, 1862), 2:138.

54. H. Wheeler Robinson, "The Council of Yahweh," *Journal of Theological Studies* 45.45 (1944): 156–57.

55. *2 Baruch* IV.2–7, in Charles, *Apocrypha and Pseudepigrapha*, 2:482; Bostock, "The Sources," 262.

56. Harnack, *History of Dogma*, 1:103n.

57. *Pastor of Hermas*, I.1.1, 2.4, trans. F. Crombie (*ANF* 2:9, 12).

58. *Pastor of Hermas*, I.3.5, 9 (*ANF* 2:14, 16).

59. See note to Irenaeus, *Against Heresies* IV.20.2 (*ANF* 1:488).

60. "The So-Called Second Letter of Clement," XIV.1–2, in *The Apostolic Fathers*, trans. Edgard J. Goodspeed (New York: Harper, 1950), 91.

61. "The So-Called Second Epistle of S. Clement to the Corinthians," trans. J. B. Lightfoot, in *The Apostolic Fathers* (1890; repr., Peabody, Mass.: Hendrickson, 1989), 247n.

62. James Charlesworth dissents from this view. See his "The Odes of Solomon—Not Gnostic," *Catholic Biblical Quarterly* 31 (1969): 357–69.

63. *Odes of Solomon*, VII.9, trans. J. H. Charlesworth, in Charlesworth, *Old Testament*, 2:740.

64. *Odes of Solomon*, VIII.13–14, XXIII.2–3, in Charlesworth, *Old Testament*, 2:742, 755.

65. Hamerton-Kelly, *Pre-Existence*, 193, 152.

66. Albert Schweitzer, *The Mysticism of Paul the Apostle*, trans. W. Montgomery (London: Black, 1931), 116, cited in Hamerton-Kelly, *Pre-Existence*, 9.

67. Bostock, "The Sources," 262.

68. L. Cerfaux, *The Church in the Theology of St. Paul*, trans. Geoffrey Webb and Adrian Walker (New York: Herder and Herder, 1963), 360.

69. Origen, *De Principiis*, I.6.2 (*ANF* 4:261).

70. Henri Crouzel, *Origen*, trans. A. S. Worrall (San Francisco: Harper & Row, 1989), 206.

71. Walter Kasper, "On the Church," *America: The National Catholic Weekly* 184:14 (23 April 2001); online edition: www.americamagazine.org/content/article.cfm?article_id=1569.

72. To this end, Ratzinger quotes Rudolf Bultmann, who agrees about "the precedence of the universal church [and] could certainly never be accused of Platonism." Joseph Ratzinger, "The Local Church and the Universal Church," *America: The National Catholic Weekly Magazine* 185:16 (19 November 2001); online edition: www.americamagazine.org/content/article.cfm?article_id=1250.

73. Hamerton-Kelly, *Pre-Existence*, 154. He is citing William Sanday and A. C. Headlam, *The Epistle to the Romans* (Edinburgh: Clark, 1902), 217.

74. John Peter Lange, *Commentary on the Holy Scriptures: Critical, Doctrinal, and Homiletical*, trans. Philip Schaff (1871; repr., Grand Rapids, Mich.: Zondervan, 1978), 9:306.

75. Adam Clarke, *The Holy Bible: Containing the Old and New Testaments with a Commentary and Critical Notes*, 6 vols. (1811–25) (Nashville, Tenn.: Abingdon, n.d.), 5:584.

76. Matthew Henry, *Matthew Henry's Commentary in One Volume* (Grand Rapids, Mich.: Zondervan, 1961), 1557.

77. Josephus, *Wars of the Jews*, II.8.11, in *The Life and Works of Flavius Josephus*, trans. William Whiston (Philadelphia: David McKay, n.d.), 675.

78. "Hymn," 1QH V.13–14, in *The Dead Sea Scrolls Translated: The Dead Sea Texts in English*, 2nd ed., ed. Florentino García Martínez, trans. Wilfred G. E. Watson (Leiden: Brill, 1996), 319.

79. Hans Jonas, *The Gnostic Religion: The Message of the Alien God and the Beginnings of Christianity*, 2nd ed. (Boston: Beacon, 1963), xiii.

80. Michael Allen Williams, *Rethinking "Gnosticism": An Argument for Dismantling a Dubious Category* (Cambridge, Mass.: Harvard University Press, 1996), 51.

81. Karen L. King, *What Is Gnosticism?* (Cambridge, Mass.: Harvard University Press, 2003), 6.

82. Jonas, *Gnostic Religion*, 33, 147.

83. Elaine Pagels, *The Gnostic Gospels* (New York: Random House, 1979), xxi.

84. James Robinson, ed., *The Nag Hammadi Library in English* (New York: Harper & Row, 1977), 3.

85. For a critique of James Robinson's "arbitrary conjectures" in regard to the authorship and context behind the Nag Hammadi texts, see Robert A. Kraft and Janet A. Timbie, "Review of *The Nag Hammadi Library in English*," *Religious Studies Review* 8.1 (January 1982): 32–52.

86. Kurt Rudolph, *Gnosis: The Nature and History of Gnosticism*, trans. and ed. Robert McLachlan Wilson (San Francisco: HarperSanFrancisco, 1987), 55.

87. Williams, *Rethinking "Gnosticism,"* 51.

88. Pagels, *Gnostic Gospels*, xix.

89. Robinson, *Nag Hammadi*, 2.

90. Walter Bauer, *Orthodoxy and Heresy in Earliest Christianity*, ed. Robert A. Kraft and Gerhard Krodel (Philadelphia: Fortress, 1971), xxiii.

91. *Excerpta ex Theodoto of Clement of Alexandria*, 78.2 trans. Robert Pierce Casey (London: Christophers, 1934), 89.

92. Rudolph, *Gnosis*, 55.

93. *Gospel of Truth*, trans. Robert M. Grant, Harold W. Attridge, and George W. MacRae; adapted by Willis Barnstone and Marvin Meyer, in *The Gnostic Bible*, ed. Barnstone and Meyer (Boston: Shambhala, 2003), 245, 249, 255.

94. *Excerpta ex Theodoto*, 50 (75).

95. Rudolph, *Gnosis*, 57.

96. Rudolph, *Gnosis*, 66.

97. Rudolph, *Gnosis*, 94–95. The redeemer myth that Rudolph reconstructs is not found as such in any one text.

98. Rudolph, *Gnosis*, 92, 93.

99. Hans Jonas, *Gnosis und spätantiker Geist*, I, Ergänzungsheft, 383, cited in Rudolph, *Gnosis*, 93.

100. Bentley Layton, *The Gnostic Scriptures: A New Translation with Annotations and Introductions* (Garden City, N.Y.: Doubleday, 1987), 366.

101. *The Song of the Pearl*, trans. Han J. W. Drijvers, Robert M. Grant, Bentley Layton, and Willis Barnstone, in Barnstone and Meyer, *Gnostic Bible*, 388–94.

102. *Gospel of Philip*, trans. Wesley W. Isenberg, in Robinson, *Nag Hammadi*, 132–33. See the review by Robert A. Kraft and Janet A. Timbie of *The Nag Hammadi Library in English* wherein they cite this passage in particular as a reference to "the pre-existent church." *Religious Studies Review* 8.1 (January 1982): 45.

103. *A Valentinian Exposition*, trans. John D. Turner, in Robinson, *Nag Hammadi*, 437.

104. Rudolph, *Gnosis*, 207.

105. *The Tripartite Tractate*, trans. Harold W. Attridge and Dieter Mueller, in Robinson, *Nag Hammadi*, 59.

106. *The Secret Book of John*, trans. Marvin Meyer, in Barnstone and Meyer, *Gnostic Bible*, 146, 156–57, 159, 160.

107. *Revelation of Adam*, trans. George W. MacRae, adapted by Willis Barnstone, in Barnstone and Meyer, *Gnostic Bible*, 182, 185. The implication, writes Bentley Layton, is that Seth's descendants "received a spirit from a different kingdom." Layton, *The Gnostic Scriptures* (Garden City, N.Y.: Doubleday, 1995), 59n.

108. *The Exegesis on the Soul*, trans. William C. Robinson, Jr., in Robinson, *Nag Hammadi*, 181.

109. This stage of self-movement is crucial, because for Plato it was the first defining characteristic of the human soul: "So what's the definition of the thing we call the soul? Surely we can do nothing but use our formula of a moment ago: 'motion capable of moving itself.'" *Laws*, X.896a, trans. Trevor J. Saunders, in *Plato: Complete Works*, ed. John M. Cooper (Indianapolis, Ind.: Hackett, 1997), 1552.

110. *Exegesis on the Soul*, in Robinson, *Nag Hammadi*, 185.

111. The philosophical usage of "hypostasis" emphasizes the true essence of a thing. In Christian thought, the term evolves to suggest, according to one authority, the "quasi-personification of certain attributes proper to God, occupying an intermediate position between personalities and abstract beings," or "a personification of qualities, functions, limbs, etc., of a higher god." W. O. E. Oesterley and G. H. Box, *Religion and Worship of the Synagogue* (London: Pitman, 1911), 169; Sigmund Mowinckel, "Hypostase," in *Religion in Geschichte und Gegenwart*, cited in Ringgren, *Word and Wisdom*, 8.

112. C. S. Lewis, *Perelandra* (New York: Scribner's, 1996), 24.

113. *Hypostasis of the Archons*, trans. Bentley Layton, in Robinson, *Nag Hammadi*, 158–59.

114. *On the Origin of the World*, trans. Hans-Gebhard Bethge and Orval S. Wintermute, in Robinson, *Nag Hammadi*, 163–79.

115. Codex VI from Nag Hammadi contains an original work, the *Discourse on the Eighth and Ninth*, along with a prayer and a portion of the "Perfect Sermon," which derives from *Asclepius*, which is considered a foundational text of hermeticism.

116. Frances A. Yates, *Giordano Bruno and the Hermetic Tradition* (Chicago: University of Chicago Press, 1964), 4–5.

117. D. P. Walker, *The Ancient Theology: Studies in Christian Platonism from the Fifteenth to the Eighteenth Century* (Ithaca, N.Y.: Cornell University Press, 1972), 1.

118. Although the idea is an old one, Walker claims to have "launched" the term *prisca theologia*. See his *Ancient Theology*, 1.

119. "The Key," *Corpus Hermeticum*, X.7, 15, in *Hermetica*, trans. Brian P. Copenhaver (Cambridge: Cambridge University Press, 1992), 31, 33.

120. Adolf Erman was the first to point to parallels between the book of Proverbs and the Egyptian *Instruction of Amenemope* that were too close to deny. "Eine ägyptische Quelle der 'Sprüche Salomos,'" *Sitzungsberichte der Preussischen Akademie der Wissenschaften* 15 (1924): 86–95, cited in Stuart Weeks, *Early Israelite Wisdom* (Oxford: Clarendon, 1994), 6.

121. Augustine, *The City of God against the Pagans* VIII.4, trans. R. W. Dyson (Cambridge: Cambridge University Press, 1998), 347–48.

122. Lactantius, *On the Anger of God*, XI; *The Divine Institutes*, I.6 (*ANF* 7:269, 15).

123. *Poimandres*, trans. Willis Barnstone, in Barnstone and Meyer, *Gnostic Bible*, 505–6.

124. *Poimandres*, in Barnstone and Meyer, *Gnostic Bible*, 509.

125. Albert Taylor Bledsoe, *A Theodicy; or, Vindication of the Divine Glory, as Manifested in Constitution and Government of the World* (New York: Carlton & Porter, 1856), 182.

126. Pagels, *Gnostic Gospels*, xx.

127. Larry Hurtado, "What Do We Mean by 'First-Century Jewish Monotheism'?" in *Society of Biblical Literature: 1993 Seminar Papers*, ed. Eugene H. Lovering, Jr. (Atlanta, Ga.: Scholars, 1993), 354.

128. Hans Freiherr von Campenhausen, *Lateinische Kirchenväter* (Stuttgart: Kohlhammer, 1960), 24, cited in Rudolph, *Gnosis*, 15–16.

CHAPTER 4

1. Tertullian, *On Prescription against Heretics*, VII, trans. Peter Holmes, in *The Ante-Nicene Fathers*, ed. Alexander Roberts and James Donaldson (Grand Rapids, Mich.: Eerdmans, 1977), 3:246 (hereafter, *ANF*).

2. Philosophers refer to the period between 130 BCE and Plotinus as the era of Middle Platonism.

3. Lucas Siorvanes, *Proclus: Neo-Platonic Philosophy and Science* (New Haven, Conn.: Yale University Press, 1996), ix.

4. Plotinus, *The Enneads* V.2.1, trans. A. H. Armstrong, 7 vols. (Cambridge, Mass.: Harvard University Press, 1966–88), 5:59.

5. Plotinus, *Enneads*, IV.1.1, 3.6, 2.1.

6. Plotinus, *Enneads*, I.1.8, 12.

7. Plotinus, *Enneads*, I.3.1.

8. Porphyry, *On the Life of Plotinus and the Order of His Books*, II, in Plotinus, *Enneads*, 1:7.

9. Porphyry, *Life of Plotinus*, XXIII, in *Enneads*, 1:71.

10. "The soul is evil when it is thoroughly mixed with the body and shares its experiences and has all the same opinions." Plotinus, *Enneads*, I.2.3.

11. Porphyry, *Life of Plotinus*, I, in *Enneads*, 1:3.

12. Plotinus, *Enneads*, IV.3.9.

13. Plotinus, *Enneads*, IV.3.12.

14. Plotinus, *Enneads*, II.9.8.

15. Plotinus, *Enneads*, IV.3.12–13.

16. Plotinus, *Enneads*, IV.8.4.

17. Plotinus, *Enneads*, IV.8.4–5, 3.13; R. T. Wallis, *Neo-Platonism* (London: Duckworth, 1995), 78.

18. Plotinus, *Enneads*, IV.3.13–15.

19. Plotinus, *Enneads*, IV.3.16–17.

20. This same argument occurs in Aristotle, Philo, Proclus, and others. See Wallis, *Neo-Platonism*, 103n.

21. Gerhard May, *Creation ex Nihilo: The Doctrine of "Creation Out of Nothing" in Early Christian Thought*, trans. A. S. Worrall (Edinburgh: Clark, 1994), 19. Philo's statement is May's paraphrase of *De Opificio Mundi* [*On the Creation*], III (13).

22. Plotinus, *Enneads*, III.7.4.

23. Proclus, *On the Eternity of the World (De Aeternitate Mundi)*, trans. Helen S. Lang and A. D. Macro (Berkeley: University of California Press, 2001), 69.

24. Porphyry's analogy is cited—without source—in Samuel Parker, *An Account of the Nature and Extent of the Divine Dominion and Goodnesse especially as They Refer to the Origenian Hypothesis Concerning the Preexistence of Souls...* (Oxford: W. Hall, 1666), 52.

25. Iamblichus, *De Mysteriis*, 269.1–270.12; *Stobaeus*, I.371.6–8, 368.1–6. These references, with a full discussion, are in Gregory Shaw, *Theurgy and the Soul: The Neo-Platonism of Iamblichus* (University Park: Pennsylvania State University Press, 1995), 108ff.

26. Martin Laird, *Gregory of Nyssa and the Grasp of Faith: Union, Knowledge, and Divine Presence* (Oxford: Oxford University Press, 2004), 9.

27. Shaw, *Theurgy and the Soul*, 5.

28. Plato, *Theaetetus*, 176a, trans. M. J. Levett, rev. Myles F. Burnyeat, in *Plato: Complete Works*, ed. John M. Cooper (Indianapolis, Ind.: Hackett, 1997), 195.

29. Plotinus, *Enneads*, I.2.1, cited and discussed in Aharon Lichtenstein, *Henry More: The Rational Theology of a Cambridge Platonist* (Cambridge, Mass.: Harvard University Press, 1962), 46.

30. Lichtenstein, *Henry More*, 46.

31. Edwin Hatch, *The Influence of Greek Ideas on Christianity* (Gloucester: Peter Smith, 1970), 133, 1.

32. Hatch, *Influence of Greek Ideas*, 131–32.

33. Justin Martyr, *The First Apology of Justin*, XX (*ANF* 1:169).

34. Augustine may have been the first to invoke this parallel. Platonic truths, he wrote, should be claimed from the philosophers "as it were from owners who have no right to

them," as gold taken from the ancient Egyptians by Israelites. *Doctrina Christiana*, II.144, trans. R. P. H. Green (Oxford: Clarendon, 1995), 125.

35. Justin, *First Apology*, LIX (*ANF* 1:182).

36. Clement of Alexandria, *The Stromata; or, Miscellanies*, I:2 (*ANF* 2:334–35).

37. Clement, *Stromata*, II.1 (*ANF* 2:347).

38. Tertullian, *Apology*, XLVII (*ANF* 3:51).

39. Augustine, *The City of God against the Pagans* VIII.11, trans. R. W. Dyson (Cambridge: Cambridge University Press, 1998), 327. See also *On the Christian Doctrine*, XI.28.

40. Augustine, *City of God*, VIII.5–6.

41. Augustine, *Retractions*, I.12.3, trans. Mary Inez Brogan (Washington, D.C.: Catholic University of America Press, 1968), 54.

42. Philo of Alexandria, *The Contemplative Life, the Giants, and Selections*, ed. and trans. David Winston (New York: Paulist, 1981), 4.

43. Adolf Hilgenfeld, cited in "Introductory Notice," *Recognitions of Clement* (*ANF* 8:73).

44. Clement, *Recognitions*, I.1, 28 (*ANF* 8:77, 85).

45. Clement, *Recognitions*, III.24, 26 (*ANF* 8:120–21).

46. Justin Martyr, *Dialogue with Trypho*, II (*ANF* 1:195).

47. This is the verdict, for example, of both nineteenth- and twentieth-century reference works like *Fessenden & Co.s Encyclopedia of Religious Knowledge* (Brattleboro, Vt.: Fessenden, 1836), 964, and the article on preexistence in *Encyclopedia Britannica*, 11th ed. (New York: 1910), 22:277 (which also opines that the doctrine is "the natural correlative of a belief in immortality").

48. Justin Martyr, *Dialogue with Trypho*, IV–V (*ANF* 1:197–98).

49. Clement of Alexandria, *The Instructor*, III.12 (*ANF* 2:296).

50. Clement, *Stromata* [*Miscellanies*], V.14 (*ANF* 2:465).

51. Henry Chadwick, *Early Christian Thought and the Classical Tradition* (Oxford: Clarendon, 1984), 46–47.

52. Clement, *Stromata*, I.5 (*ANF* 2:305).

53. Clement, *Stromata*, I.7 (*ANF* 2:308).

54. Clement, *Stromata*, I.15 (*ANF* 2:315).

55. Henry More, "Preface General," in *A Collection of Several Philosophical Writings of Dr. Henry More* (London: James Flesher, 1662; repr., New York: Garland, 1978), xx; Jaroslav Pelikan, *The Christian Tradition: A History of the Development of Doctrine*, vol. 1: *The Emergence of the Catholic Tradition 100–600* (Chicago: University of Chicago Press, 1989), 96.

56. Clement of Alexandria, *Stromata*, I.15 (*ANF* 2:315).

57. Clement of Alexandria, *Exhortation to the Heathen*, I (*ANF* 2:173).

58. Clement of Alexandria, *Fragments*, "Comments on the First Epistle of Peter," I.1, trans. William Wilson (*ANF* 2:572, 571).

59. Tertullian, *Treatise on the Soul*, XXI (*ANF* 3:202).

60. Irenaeus, *Against Heresies*, II.34.2; "Fragments from the Lost Writings," XLIX (*ANF* 1:411, 576).

61. Clement of Alexandria, *Stromata*, VII.1 (*ANF* 2:523).

62. *Excerpta ex Theodoto of Clement of Alexandria*, 78.2, trans. Robert Pierce Casey (London: Christophers, 1934), 89.

63. Clement of Alexandria, *Instructor*, I.7 (*ANF* 2:224).

64. Clement of Alexandria, *Instructor*, I.6 (*ANF* 2:217).

65. Tertullian, *On Prescription against Heretics*, VII, XIII, trans. Peter Holmes (*ANF* 3:246, 249).

66. Tertullian, *Treatise on the Soul*, XXIII, trans. Peter Holmes (*ANF* 3:203).

67. Tertullian, *Treatise on the Soul*, III (*ANF* 3:183).

68. Tertullian, *Treatise on the Soul*, IV, XXV (*ANF* 3:184, 205).

69. Tertullian, *Treatise on the Soul*, XXVII, XL, XLI (*ANF* 3:208, 220).

70. Tertullian, *On Prescription against Heretics*, VII (*ANF* 3:246).

71. Tertullian, *Treatise on the Soul*, XXIII (*ANF* 3:203).

72. Tertullian, *Treatise on the Soul*, XXIV (*ANF* 3:203–4).

73. Tertullian, *Treatise on the Soul*, IV (*ANF* 3:184).

74. Tertullian, *Treatise on the Soul*, XXIV (*ANF* 3:203).

75. Adolf Harnack, *History of Dogma*, 7 vols., trans. from 3rd German ed. by Neil Buchanan (London: Williams & Norgate, 1894), 1:318–19.

76. Augustine, *Confessions*, IV.15, trans. F. J. Sheed (Indianapolis, Ind.: Hackett, 1993), 63.

77. Joseph Campbell, *The Masks of God: Creative Mythology* (New York: Viking, 1968), 148.

78. Tertullian, *Treatise on the Soul*, XXIII, XXVII (*ANF* 3:203, 207–8).

79. Tertullian, *The Soul's Testimony*, I, trans. S. Thelwall (*ANF* 3:175).

80. Tertullian, *On the Resurrection of the Flesh*, XLV, trans. Peter Holmes (*ANF* 3:578).

81. Paul Johnson, *A History of Christianity* (New York: Simon & Schuster, 1976), 59.

82. Mark Julian Edwards, for example, insists that "a careful examination of the sources will reveal two Origens, [and] two Ammonii"; *Origen against Plato* (Aldershot, England: Ashgate, 1988), 54. (Edwards's argument is also notable for holding that Origen's theories of the pre-mortal soul have been misconstrued and misrepresented.) The two-Origen hypothesis emerged in the seventeenth century, according to Henri Crouzel, and "many students of Origen are unconvinced." Crouzel, *Origen*, trans. A. S. Worrall (San Francisco: Harper & Row, 1989), 11–12. Joseph Wilson Trigg outlines the most compelling reasons behind the two-Origen hypothesis, concluding that they both studied with Ammonius Saccas, but two decades apart. *Origen: The Bible and Philosophy in the Third-century Church* (Atlanta, Ga.: John Knox, 1983), 259–60. Another complicating factor in Origen studies is the fact that his most important work, *De Principiis*, survives only in a Latin translation by Rufinus, who admits it is loose and includes both omissions and interpolations from other works. And those fragments translated elsewhere by Jerome are most likely marked by the biases of this ideological opponent.

83. Edwards, *Origen against Plato*, 1.

84. Crouzel, *Origen*, xi.

85. Crouzel, *Origen*, xi. Crouzel's assessment is entirely typical.

86. Philip Schaff, *History of the Christian Church*, 8 vols. (Grand Rapids, Mich.: Eerdmans, 1910), 3:699.

87. Trigg, *Origen*, 8.

88. Chadwick, *Early Christian Thought*, 72.

89. Origen's *Peri Archon* exists in the original Greek only in scattered fragments. It was translated into Latin as *De Principiis* by Rufinus, who in many cases altered the text to

avoid flagrant breaches with orthodoxy. It is therefore unlikely that the work's extensive rationale for and description of spiritual preexistence—already disputed by Tertullian and others—were invented or exaggerated by the cautious Rufinus. Henri de Lubac's remark that refusing to make use of the imperfect translations would be "excessive purism" is for this reason especially apt here. I therefore utilize Frederick Crombie's translation of Rufinus and, where appropriate, I have relied upon Paul Koetschau's recuperation of Greek portions—though his procedure was itself often based on doubtful conjecture. Lubac, "Introduction," in *Origen on First Principles, Being Koetschau's Text of the De Principiis*, trans. G. W. Butterworth (New York: Harper & Row, 1966), ix.

90. Origen, *De Principiis*, trans. Frederick Crombie, 3 (*ANF* 4:239).

91. Origen, *De Principiis*, 4–5 (*ANF* 4:240).

92. Origen, *De Principiis*, 10 (*ANF* 4:241).

93. Mark Edwards makes a case that Origen never advocated human preexistence, in spite of overwhelming opinion to the contrary. It is true, for example, that the famous passage of Origen in chapter 4 that refers to the soul's defection out of satiety is not explicitly placed in a pre-mortal setting. I am arguing that such pre-mortality is understood by Origen as the explanation for a diverse order that is already present in the created world. As for Edwards's point that Origen was never explicitly censured "simply for maintaining the pre-existence of the soul," he points out himself that it is likely that "the bare hypothesis of a pre-existent soul, without the corollary of transmigration or a fall from heaven, was not a heresy." And regarding his argument that he could never have derived a preexistent fall "from scripture or the catholic traditions of the Church," Origen acknowledged precisely that fact and then explicitly invoked reasonable conjecture and deduction as providing acceptable, alternative bases for his theorizing. Absent scriptural foundation, he wrote, one must deduce doctrine "by closely tracing out the consequences and following a correct method." Other arguments of Edwards also merit consideration. See Edwards, *Origen against Plato*, 89–90. Given the suspicious textual history of Origen's works, especially *De Principiis*, Frederick Norris notes that "the strong case for Origen teaching the most heretical doctrines has been laid aside on historical-critical textual grounds." "Apokatastasis," in *The Westminster Handbook to Origen*, ed. John Anthony McGuckin (Louisville, Ky.: Westminster John Knox, 2004), 61.

94. Origen, *De Principiis*, I.3.8 (*ANF* 4:255).

95. Origen, *De Principiis*, I.6.2 (*ANF* 4:260).

96. Origen, *De Principiis*, I.3.8 (*ANF* 4:255).

97. Origen, *De Principiis*, I.8.1; *Koetschau's Text*, 67.

98. Origen, *De Principiis*, I.7.4 (*ANF* 4:263–64).

99. Origen, *Against Celsus*, IV.40 (*ANF* 4:516).

100. Origen, *De Principiis*, I.8; *Koetschau's Text*, 72–73. These portions derive from Gregory of Nyssa's account of Origen's teachings.

101. Elizabeth A. Clark agrees that Origen's motive in writing *De Principiis* was "the need to construct a polemic against Gnostic and astrological determinism that would 'save' human free will and God's justice." *The Origenist Controversy: The Cultural Construction of an Early Christian Debate* (Princeton, N.J.: Princeton University Press, 1992), 7.

102. Origen, *De Principiis*, II.9.3, 5 (*ANF* 4:290–91).

103. Origen, *De Principiis*, II.9.6 (*ANF* 4:292).

104. Origen, *De Principiis*, III.3.5 (*ANF* 4:337).

105. Origen, *De Principiis*, II.9.7 (*ANF* 4:292).

106. Origen, *De Principiis*, II.9.8 (*ANF* 4:293).

107. Crouzel, *Origen*, 208.

108. Origen, *De Principiis*, I.6.3 (*ANF* 4:261).

109. Origen, *De Principiis*, I.5.5 (*ANF* 4:260).

110. Origen, *De Principiis*, I.2.9 (*ANF* 4:249).

111. Origen, *De Principiis*, I.2.10 (*ANF* 4:249–50).

112. Origen, *De Principiis*, I.3.1 (*ANF* 4:251).

113. Origen, *De Principiis*, I.2.11 (*ANF* 4:251).

114. Origen, *Commentary on the Gospel of Matthew*, trans. John Patrick, XIII:1 (*ANF* 10:474).

115. Geddes MacGregor, *Reincarnation in Christianity* (Wheaton, Ill.: Quest, 1978), 54.

116. Thomas Aquinas, *On the Power of God* [*Quaestiones Disputatae de Potential Dei*], trans. English Dominican Friars (Westminster, Md.: Newman, 1952), 165.

117. Origen, *De Principiis*, III.6.1 (*ANF* 4:344).

CHAPTER 5

1. Rufinus associates all of these people with Origenist ideas, including preexistence, and imputes their denunciation to Jerome, who has sharply distanced himself from Origenism. *Apology*, I.43, in Philip Schaff and Henry Wace, eds., *Nicene and Post-Nicene Fathers* (Peabody, Mass.: Hendrickson, 1994) 2nd ser., 3:458 (hereafter, *NPNF*).

2. Jay Bregman, *Synesius of Cyrene* (Berkeley: University of California Press, 1982), 1.

3. Arnobius, *Against the Heathen*, trans. Hamilton Bryce and Hugh Campbell, II.15 in *The Ante-Nicene Fathers*, ed. Alexander Roberts and James Donaldson (Grand Rapids, Mich.: Eerdmans, 1977), 6:440 (hereafter, *ANF*).

4. Arnobius, *Against the Heathen*, I.28 (*ANF* 6:420).

5. Arnobius, *Against the Heathen*, I.29 (*ANF* 6:420).

6. R. T. Wallis, *Neo-Platonism* (London: Duckworth, 1995), 103.

7. Henry Chadwick, *Early Christian Thought and the Classical Tradition* (Oxford: Clarendon, 1984), 166.

8. Tertullian, *Treatise on the Soul*, XXXIV (*ANF* 3:215).

9. Gregory of Nyssa, *De hominis opificio*, 29, cited in Nicholas Costas, "'To Sleep, Perchance to Dream': The Middle State of Souls in Patristic and Byzantine Literature," in *Dumbarton Oaks Papers* 55, ed. Alice-Mary Talbot (Washington, D.C.: Harvard University Press, 2001), 97.

10. Cyril of Jerusalem, Catechesis, IV.19, in Edward Yarnold, *Cyril of Jerusalem* (London: Routledge, 2000), 104.

11. Cyril, Catechesis, IV.20, in Yarnold, *Cyril of Jerusalem*, 104.

12. J. P. Landis, "Matter—Eternal or Created?" *Old Testament Student* 4.4 (December 1884): 146.

13. Justin Martyr, *The First Apology*, X (*ANF* 1:165).

14. Empedocles, *Fragments*, 36, 45, in *Selections from Early Greek Philosophy*, ed. Milton C. Nahm (Englewood Cliffs, N.J.: Prentice-Hall, 1964), 117.

15. Gerhard May, *Creatio ex Nihilo*, trans. A. S. Worrall (Edinburgh: Clark, 1994), xi.

16. Philo of Alexandria, *The Contemplative Life, the Giants, and Selections*, ed. and trans. David Winston (New York: Paulist, 1981), 11.

17. Menasseh ben Israel, *The Conciliator* (New York: Hermon, 1972), 14.

18. May, *Creation ex Nihilo*, 57.

19. May, *Creation ex Nihilo*, 4.

20. May, *Creation ex Nihilo*, 73–75.

21. Irenaeus, *Against Heresies*, II.10.3–4 (*ANF* 1:370).

22. Henri Irénée Marrou, "Synesius of Cyrene and Alexandrian Neo-Platonism," in *The Conflict between Paganism and Christianity in the Fourth Century*, ed. Arnaldo Momigliano (Oxford: Clarendon, 1963), 126.

23. Gregory of Nazianzus, *Oration*, 37:15, in *Select Orations of Saint Gregory Nazianzen*, trans. Charles Gordon Brown and James Edward Swallow (New York: Christian Publishing, 1894; repr., Peabody, Mass.: Hendrickson, 1999), 342.

24. Michael O'Laughlin, "The Anthropology of Evagrius Ponticus and Its Sources," in *Origen of Alexandria: His World and His Legacy*, ed. Charles Kannengiesser and William L. Petersen (Notre Dame, Ind.: University of Notre Dame Press, 1988), 364–65.

25. See, in this regard, Elizabeth A. Clark, *The Origenist Controversy: The Cultural Construction of an Early Christian Debate* (Princeton, N.J.: Princeton University Press, 1992).

26. Richard A. Layton, *Didymus the Blind and His Circle in Late-Antique Alexandria: Virtue and Narrative in Biblical Scholarship* (Urbana: University of Illinois Press, 2004), 1.

27. Layton, *Didymus the Blind*, 72. Twentieth-century knowledge of Didymus's teachings derives from the World War II era discovery of the Tura papyri, comprising almost 2,000 pages of his commentary. Citations are from those papyri, as quoted in Layton.

28. Layton, *Didymus the Blind*, 73.

29. Layton, *Didymus the Blind*, 109.

30. Layton, *Didymus the Blind*, 152.

31. Arnobius, *Against the Heathen*, I.29 (*ANF* 6:420).

32. Arnobius, *Against the Heathen*, II.47, 51 (*ANF* 6:451–53).

33. Augustine, *On Free Choice of the Will*, III.21, trans. Thomas Williams (Indianapolis, Ind.: Hackett, 1993), 111.

34. Synesius, "Letter 105: To His Brother," in *Letters of Synesius of Cyrene*, trans. Augustine Fitzgerald (Oxford: Oxford University Press, 1926), 197, 200.

35. R. D. Hampden, *The Scholastic Philosophy Considered in Its Relation to Christian Theology in a Course of Lectures* (London: Simpkin, Marshall, 1848), 467.

36. Synesius had a pedigree without equal "in the history of mankind," according to Edward Gibbon. Quoted in Bregman, *Synesius of Cyrene*, 3.

37. Nemesius, *De natura hominis*, II.17, cited in Chadwick, *Early Christian Thought*, 166.

38. Augustine, *On Free Choice*, III.20.

39. Augustine, *On Free Choice*, III.21.

40. Augustine, *On Free Choice*, III.21.

41. Augustine, *The Soliloquies*, II.20.34, in John H. S. Burleigh, *Augustine's Earlier Writings* (Philadelphia: Westminster, 1953), 61–62.

42. Augustine, *Retractions*, I.4.4, in Burleigh, *Augustine's Earlier Writings*, 18. As we will see, Augustine moves further away from Platonic recollection in *Trinitate*.

43. Augustine, *Two Books on Genesis against the Manichees* [*De Genesi adversus Manichaeos*], II.3.4–5, in *On Genesis*, trans. Roland J. Teske (Washington, D.C.: Catholic University of America Press, 1990), 96–98.

44. Augustine, *On the Literal Interpretation of Genesis* [*De Genesi ad litteram*], III.8, in Teske, *On Genesis*, 150.

45. Augustine, *Confessions* I.6–7, trans. F. J. Sheed (Indianapolis, Ind.: Hackett, 1993), 7–9.

46. Augustine, *Confessions*, X.20–21.

47. Augustine, *Confessions*, X.8.

48. Augustine, *Confessions*, X.16.

49. Augustine, *Confessions*, X.18.

50. Augustine, *Confessions*, X.20.

51. Robert J. O'Connell, *The Origin of the Soul in St. Augustine's Later Works* (New York: Fordham University Press, 1987), 192, 198. O'Connell's work is a meticulously argued treatise in which he claims, contra received wisdom, that Augustine does not simply jettison preexistence in his later years. For an opposing view, see Gerald O'Daly, who insists that "nowhere in his early writings does he unequivocally assert the soul's preexistence." *Augustine's Philosophy of Mind* (Berkeley: University of California Press, 1987), 199. Much of his argument hinges on the distinction between a fall into mortality and a fall into corporeality. György Heidl reviews the controversy over O'Connell's position in *Origen's Influence on the Young Augustine: A Chapter in the History of Origenism* (Louaize, Lebanon: Gorgias, 2003), 171ff.

52. Jaroslav Pelikan, *The Christian Tradition: A History of the Development of Doctrine*, vol. 1: *The Emergence of the Catholic Tradition 100–600* (Chicago: University of Chicago Press, 1989), 279–80. Pelikan cites Niebuhr, *The Nature and Destiny of Man* (New York: Scribner's, 1941), 1:241; and Augustine, *De Prædestinatione Sanctorum* XIV.27, and *De Dono Perseverantiae*, II.4.

53. O'Connell, *Origin of the Soul*, 11–12.

54. "Traducianism," in *Oxford Dictionary of the Christian Church*, ed. F. L. Cross and E. A. Livingstone (Oxford: Oxford University Press, 1997), 1636.

55. Etienne Gilson, *The Christian Philosophy of Saint Augustine*, trans. L. E. M. Lynch (New York: Random House, 1960), 50. Gilson cites Epistle 166:2, 3.

56. Augustine, Letter 143 (to Marcellinus), in *The Works of Saint Augustine: A Translation for the 21st Century: Letters 100–155*, trans. Roland Teske (Hyde Park, N.Y.: New City Press, 1990), pt. II, 2:305.

57. Augustine, Letter 144 (to Optatus, as numbered in the Jerome collection), in W. H. Fremantle, trans., *The Principal Works of St. Jerome*, in *NPNF* 6:287.

58. Clark, *Origenist Controversy*, 86.

59. Clark, *Origenist Controversy*, 96.

60. Rufinus, *Apology* (to Apronianus), I.27–28 (*NPNF* 3:449–50). Most of Jerome's words in support of Origen and preexistence derive from his *Commentary on Ephesians*, which was heavily indebted to Origen's commentary on the same work. See the parallel edition by Ronald E. Heine, *The Commentaries of Origen and Jerome on St. Paul's Epistle to the Ephesians* (Oxford: Oxford University Press, 2002).

61. Rufinus, *Apology*, I.28 (*NPNF* 3:472).

62. Rufinus, though hardly a disinterested source, paraphrases the essence of Jerome's retraction in *Apology*, I.43 (*NPNF* 3:458).

63. Jerome, Letter 84 (to Pammachius and Oceanus), in Fremantle, *Principal Works of St. Jerome* (*NPNF* 6:180).

64. Jerome, Letter 126.1 (to Marcellinus and Anapsychia) (*NPNF* 6:252). Fremantle gives the date as 412; other sources assign the date 410.

65. Clark, *Origenist Controversy*, 105. Clark's is the most thorough study of the crisis; a brief overview is found in John Anthony McGuckin, ed., *The Westminster Handbook to Origen* (Louisville, Ky.: Westminster John Knox, 2004), 164–65.

66. Philip Schaff, *History of the Christian Church*, 8 vols. (Grand Rapids, Mich.: Eerdmans, 1910), 3:831.

67. On this point, O'Connell concurs that Augustine's acquiescence to the condemnation of Origen was noncommittal regarding preexistence. His "instincts of revulsion [toward Origenism] bear...on its cyclic and 'fantastic' account of creation and of God's motive for creating the visible world" (O'Connell, *Origin of the Soul*, 323).

68. Wallis, *Neo-Platonism*, 104. Wallis cites in support Gilson, *Christian Philosophy*, 50–51, 275.

69. The expression was "sed vicit Dei gratia," in Augustine, *Retractions*, trans. Mary Inez Bogan (Washington, D.C.: Catholic University of America Press, 1968), II.27 (120); Robert J. O'Connell, *Images of Conversion in St. Augustine's Confessions* (New York: Fordham University Press, 1996), 305.

70. Augustine, *Reconsiderations*, 1.9, in *On Free Choice of the Will*, trans. Thomas Williams (Indianapolis, Ind.: Hackett, 1993), 127, 125.

71. Augustine, *To Simplician On Various Questions*, trans. John H. S. Burleigh, in *Augustine: Earlier Writings* (Philadelphia: Westminster, 1953), 386, 397–98, 406.

72. Tertullian, *On Prescription against Heretics*, XIV, trans. Peter Holmes (*ANF* 3:250).

73. Pietro Vermigli, *Most Learned and Fruitfull Commentaries...upon the Epistle of S. Paul to the Romanes* (London: Daye, 1568), 85b, cited in "traduce," *Oxford English Dictionary*, 2nd ed. (Oxford: Clarendon, 1989), 18:355.

74. Augustine, *The City of God against the Pagans* XIII.14, trans. R. W. Dyson (Cambridge: Cambridge University Press, 1998), 555–56.

75. Edward Beecher, *The Conflict of Ages; or, The Great Debate on the Moral Relations of God and Man* (Boston: Phillips, Sampson, 1853), 297–98.

76. O'Connell, *Origin of the Soul*, 16.

77. O'Connell, *Origin of the Soul*, 324.

78. O'Connell, *Origin of the Soul*, 326.

79. Beecher, *Conflict of Ages*, 301.

80. Augustine, *De trinitate*, XIV.15.21, trans. Stephen McKenna, in Augustine, *On the Trinity: Books 8–15*, ed. Gareth B. Matthews (Cambridge: Cambridge University Press, 2002), 159.

81. Lodi Nauta, "The Pre-existence of the Soul in Medieval Thought," *Recherches de Théologie ancienne et médiévale* 63 (1996): 102.

82. Schaff, *History*, 3:831–32.

83. Leo the Great, Letter 15 ("To Turribius, Bishop of Asturia, upon the Errors of the Priscillianists"), XI (10), trans. Charles Lett Feltoe, in *The Letters and Sermons of Leo the Great* (*NPNF* 12:23). This letter is considered spurious by some scholars. See K. Künstle, *Antepriscilliana* (Freiburg, 1905).

84. Leo the Great, Letter 35 ("To Julian, Bishop of Cos") (*NPNF* 12:48).

85. Brian E. Daley, *The Hope of the Early Church: A Handbook of Patristic Eschatology* (Cambridge: Cambridge University Press, 1991), 191.

86. Maria E. Colonna, *Theophrastus sive de immortalitate animae* (Naples: 1958), translated and cited by Alexander Alexakis, "Was There Life Beyond the Life Beyond?: Byzantine Ideas on Reincarnation and Final Restoration," in *Dumbarton Oaks Papers* 55, ed. Alice-Mary Talbot (Washington, D.C.: Harvard University Press, 2001), 164.

87. Evagrius Scholasticus, *Ecclesiastical History*, IV.38 trans. Michael Whitby (Liverpool, England: Liverpool University Press, 2000), 249.

88. Gregory of Nazianzus and Basil of Caesarea, *The Philocalia of Origen* XXV.2, trans. George Lewis (Edinburgh: Clark, 1911), 210.

89. Samuel Parker, *An Account of the Nature and Extent of the Divine Dominion and Goodnesse…* (Oxford: W. Hall, 1666), 109.

90. Joseph Priestly, *Disquisitions Relating to Matter and Spirit: To Which Is Added the History of the Philosophical Doctrine Concerning the Origin of the Soul…* (Birmingham, England: Pearson and Rollason, 1782), 347.

91. Crouzel, *Origen*, 177. See also the account in E. M. Harding, "Origenist Crises," in McGuckin, *Westminster Handbook to Origen*, 165–66.

92. Evagrius, *Ecclesiastical History*, IV.38.

93. Leo Donald Davis, *The First Seven Ecumenical Councils (325–787)* (Collegeville, Minn.: Liturgical Press, 1990), 226.

94. Henry R. Percival, *The Seven Ecumenical Councils of the Undivided Church* (New York: Scribner's, 1900), 320.

95. "Edict of Justinian," in *Creeds and Confessions of Faith in the Christian Tradition*, ed. Jaroslav Pelikan and Valerie Hotchkiss (New Haven, Conn.: Yale University Press, 2003), 1:129.

96. Percival, *Seven Ecumenical Councils*, 316.

97. Believing that the local synod of 544 had sufficiently dealt with Origenism, Schaff thinks that even the mention of Origen in the council's eleventh anathema is a later interpolation. *History*, 3:771.

98. Adolf Harnack, *History of Dogma*, 7 vols., trans. from 3rd German ed. by Neil Buchanan (London: Williams & Norgate, 1894), 4:249, 348.

99. Percival, *Seven Ecumenical Councils*, 318–19; Percival also reprints the eleven anathemas of the council and the nine "anathematisms" of Justinian (312–20).

100. Daley, *Hope of the Early Church*, 87.

101. Boethius, *The Consolation of Philosophy*, trans. W. V. Cooper (New York: Random House, 1943), 75.

102. Boethius, *Consolation*, 75.

103. Bede, *A History of the English Church and People* II.13 (New York: Dorset, 1968), 127.

104. Pelikan and Hotchkiss, *Creeds and Confessions*, 1:153, 219, 235.

105. "Exact Exposition of the Orthodox Faith," II.12, in Frederic H. Chase, Jr., *Saint John of Damascus* (New York: Fathers of the Church, 1958), 235.

106. Photius, *Bibliotheca*, in "A Section of the Writings of Pierius" (*ANF* 6:157). Photius is in the context referring more immediately to Pierius, the late third-century Alexandrian presbyter and head of the catechetical school there. He was apparently so enamored of Origen's teachings on preexistence and other topics that he was called "Little Origen."

107. Adolf Harnack, "Origen," in *Encyclopedia Britannica*, 11th ed. (New York: 1910), 20:270.

108. Cited by A. Bronson Alcott, *Concord Days* (1872; repr., Philadelphia: Albert Saifer, 1962), 84n.

109. Gerald Bostock, "The Sources of Origen's Doctrine of Pre-Existence," in *Origeniana Quarta: Die Referate des 4. Internationalen Origenskongresses*, ed. Lothar Lies (Innsbruck: Tyrolia, 1987), 263.

CHAPTER 6

1. "The Treasury of Souls," in Howard Schwartz, *The Tree of Souls: The Mythology of Judaism* (Oxford: Oxford University Press, 2004), 166. Schwartz traces the origin of the myth of the *guf* to the Talmud (Yevamot 62a), but does not clearly attribute the particular apocalyptic version given here.

2. Parashah 1, Midrash 4, in *The Creation According to the Midrash Rabbah*, trans. and comm. Wilfred Shuchat (Jerusalem: Devora, 2002), 15–16.

3. Pesahim 54a; Nedarim 39b.

4. Plato, *Phaedo*, trans. G. M. A. Grube, in *Plato: Complete Works*, ed. John M. Cooper (Indianapolis, Ind.: Hackett, 1997), 76c (67).

5. *Bereshith Rabba*, trans. W. Wynn Westcott et al., in *The Sacred Books and Early Literature of the East*, 14 vols., ed. Charles F. Horne (New York: Parke, Austin, and Lipscomb, 1917), 4:42.

6. Meir Zlotowitz, *Bereishis/Genesis: A New Translation with a Commentary Anthologized from Talmudic, Midrashic and Rabbinic Sources* (New York: Mesorah, 1977), 31.

7. Menasseh ben Israel, *Conciliador*, cited in Johannes van den Berg, "Menasseh ben Israel, Henry More, and Johannes Hoornbeeck on the Pre-Existence of the Soul," in *Religious Currents and Cross-Currents: Essays on Early Modern Protestantism*, ed. Jan de Bruijn, Pieter Holtrop, and Ernestine van der Wall (Leiden: Brill, 1999), 66.

8. Parashah 8, Midrash 7, in Shuchat, *The Creation*, 305–6.

9. Genesis Rabbah, 8.7, in Schwartz, *Tree of Souls*, 162.

10. Schwartz, *Tree of Souls*, 161.

11. *Midrash Tanhuma Pekude*, III.11, in *The Metsudah Midrash Tanchuma: Shemos II*, trans. Avrohom Davis (New York: Judaica Press, 2004), pt. 2, 2:402.

12. *2 Baruch*, XXIII.3–5, trans. R. H. Charles, in R. H. Charles, *The Apocrypha and Pseudepigrapha of the Old Testament*, 2 vols. (Oxford: Clarendon, 1968), 2:495.

13. *Hagigah* 12b, in *The Babylonian Talmud*, 4 vols., ed. Isidore Epstein (London: Soncino, 1938), 4:72.

14. *Yebamoth* 62a, in *Babylonian Talmud*, 1:415; see also *Niddah* 13b.

15. Menasseh ben Israel, *De Creatione Problemata*, XXX, cited in van den Berg, "Menasseh ben Israel," 66. For his reliance upon the verse in Deuteronomy, see Schwartz, *Tree of Souls*, 164.

16. *Midrash Tanhuma Pekude*, III.14–15; *Metsudah Midrash Tanchuma*, pt. 2, 2:404–5.

17. Rodolphe Kasser, Marvin Meyer, and Gregor Wurst, eds., *The Gospel of Judas from Codex Tchacos* (Washington, D.C.: National Geographic, 2006), 35–36.

18. Aristotle, *Metaphysics*, XII.5–8.

19. Stephen Bemrose, *Dante's Angelic Intelligences: Their Importance in the Cosmos and in Pre-Christian Religion* (Rome: Edzioni De Storia e Letteratura, 1983), 35.

20. Bemrose, *Dante's Angelic Intelligences*, 34–37.

21. William B. Hunter, Jr., *The English Spenserians* (Salt Lake City: University of Utah Press, 1977), 417n. More enumerates the sprites in "The Præexistency of the Soul," in *Philosophical Poems* (1647; repr., Menton, England: Scolar, 1969), st. XXXVII.

22. Bemrose, *Dante's Angelic Intelligences*, 42–51.

23. Eadmer, *The Life of St Anselm: Archbishop of Canterbury*, trans. R. W. Southern (Oxford: Clarendon, 1972), 142.

24. Peter Lombard, *Sentences*, II, D. 18; Thomas Aquinas, *Summa Theologica*, I:Q47, art. 2; Q90, art. 4.

25. Brian Stock, *Myth and Science in the Twelfth Century: A Study of Bernard Silvester* (Princeton, N.J.: Princeton University Press, 1972), 203.

26. Stock, *Myth and Science*, 165.

27. The weeping-souls scene is cited in C. S. Lewis, *The Discarded Image* (Cambridge: Cambridge University Press, 1976), 156.

28. Hildegard of Bingen, *Scivias*, I.iv.1–8 trans. Columba Hart and Jane Bishop (New York: Paulist, 1990), 109–16.

29. Julian of Norwich, *Showings*, ed. Denise N. Baker (New York: Norton, 2005), XIV.51 (70).

30. Julian, *Showings*, XIV.51.

31. Even without the additional Neo-Platonic underpinnings, Julian's editor finds sufficient evidence in the allegory just discussed to conclude that Julian "believes in the preexistence of the soul before its union with the body and its fall into the material world." Julian, *Showings*, xv.

32. Henry Denzinger, *The Sources of Catholic Dogma*, 30th ed., 348 trans. Roy J. Deferrari (St. Louis, Mo.: Herder, 1954), 142.

33. Julian, *Showings*, XIV.54, 58.

34. As Denise N. Baker clarifies, "substance" in Julian's usage reflects the scholastic meaning of "the essence of a being, the permanent and unchanging substratum of an entity." Julian, *Showings*, xvi.

35. Julian, *Showings*, XIV.58.

36. P. Alexander, "Introduction," to *3 (Hebrew Apocalypse of) Enoch*, trans. P. Alexander, in *The Old Testament Pseudepigrapha*, 2 vols., ed. James H. Charlesworth (Garden City, N.Y.: Doubleday, 1983), 1:232.

37. *3 Enoch* XLIII.1–3, in Charlesworth, *Old Testament*, 1:293–94.

38. Charles, *Apocrypha and Pseudepigrapha*, 2:444n.

39. Moses Cordovero, *Shi'ur Qomah*, quoted in Daniel C. Matt, *The Essential Kabbalah: The Heart of Jewish Mysticism* (San Francisco: HarperSanFrancisco, 1995), 27.

40. "The Key," *Corpus Hermeticum*, X.7, in Brian P. Copenhaver, trans., *Hermetica* (Cambridge: Cambridge University Press, 1992), 31–32.

41. Daniel Chanan Matt, trans., *Zohar: The Book of Enlightenment* (New York: Paulist, 1983), 34.

42. Matt, *Zohar*, 36–37.

43. Moses de León, *Sefer ha-Mishqal*, ed. Jochanan H. A. Wijnhoven (Ph.D. diss., Brandeis University, 1964), 46–47, cited in Matt, *Essential Kabbalah*, 148.

44. Adolphe Franck, *The Kabbalah; or, The Religious Philosophy of the Hebrews*, trans. I. Sossnitz (New York: Kabbalah Publishing, 1926), 194–95.

45. De León's widow, for one, insisted that "he wrote it entirely from his own head." Matt, *Zohar*, 4.

46. Matt, *Zohar*, 60–61. "Soul-breath" is from the Hebrew *neshamah*, which is generally translated as "breath" in the Bible but refers in the *Zohar* to "a spiritual essence, the highest level of soul" (218).

47. Matt, *Zohar*, 99.

48. Christina Baldwin, *The Seven Whispers* (Navato, Calif.: New World Library, 2002), 40. A typical, if shortened, Hasidic version is also found in Louis I. Newman, *The Hasidic Anthology: Tales and Teaching of the Hasidim* (New York: Bloch, 1944), 306. Howard Schwartz recounts an oral tradition, in which it is God who touches the child's upper lip. *Tree of Souls*, 140.

49. *Midrash Tanhuma Pekude*, III.23, in Louis Ginzberg, *Legends of the Jews*, 7 vols., trans. Henrietta Szold (Philadelphia: Jewish Publication Society, 1913), 1:58.

50. Clement of Alexandria, *Excerpts of Theodotus; or, Selections from the Prophetic Scriptures* [*Prophetic Eclogues*], L, trans. William Wilson, in *The Ante-Nicene Fathers*, ed. Alexander Roberts and James Donaldson (Grand Rapids, Mich.: Eerdmans, 1977), 8:49 (hereafter, *ANF*). Clement's authorship of these writings is disputed, and in any case, they are not to be confused with the *Excerpta ex Theodoto*, cited above.

51. The story is from *Bereshith Rabbah*, XXIV, recounted by Menasseh ben Israel in his *De Resurrectione Mortuorum*. See Johannes van den Berg, "Menasseh ben Israel, Henry More, and Johannes Hoornbeeck on the Pre-Existence of the Soul," in *Religious Currents and Cross-Currents: Essays on Early Modern Protestantism*, ed. Jan de Bruijn, Pieter Holtrop, and Ernestine van der Wall (Leiden: Brill, 1999), 68–69.

52. Daniel Chanan Matt, trans. and annotator, *Zohar: Annotated and Explained* (Woodstock, Vt.: Skylight, 2002), 22–23.

53. Cited in Franck, *Kabbalah*, 197.

54. Jacob Boehme, *Forty Questions of the Soul and the Clavis*, trans. John Sparrow (London: John M. Watkins, 1911), 135.

55. Jacob Boehme, *The Three Principles of the Divine Essence*, in *Jacob Boehme*, ed. Robin Waterfield (Berkeley, Calif.: North Atlantic, 2001), 91.

56. Boehme, *Forty Questions*, 302–3.

57. Boehme, *Three Principles*, 109.

58. Boehme, *Forty Questions*, 75.

59. N. A. Berdyaev, "Studies Concerning Jacob Boehme: Etude 1. The Teaching about the Ungrund and Freedom" (1939, #349), *Journal Put'* 20 (February 1930): 47–79, www
.berdyaev.com/berdiaev/berd_lib/1930_349.html#s.

60. Berdyaev, "Studies."

CHAPTER 7

1. Richard Montagu, *Acts and Monuments of the Church before Christ Incarnate* (London: Flesher and Young, 1642), 409.

2. Augustine, *The City of God against the Pagans*, VIII.4, trans. R. W. Dyson (Cambridge: Cambridge University Press, 1998), 316.

3. Frances A. Yates, *Giordano Bruno and the Hermetic Tradition* (Chicago: University of Chicago Press, 1964), 11.

4. Anselm, *Proslogion*, I, in *Monologion and Proslogion*, trans. Thomas Williams (Indianapolis, Ind.: Hackett, 1996), 99.

5. "Formula of Concord," in *Creeds and Confessions of Faith in the Christian Tradition*, ed. Jaroslav Pelikan and Valerie Hotchkiss (New Haven, Conn.: Yale University Press, 2003), 2:173.

6. C. A. Patrides, ed., *The Cambridge Platonists* (London: Edward Arnold, 1969), 10.

7. "Dr. Tuckney to Dr. Whichcot," 8 September 1651, in *The Cambridge Platonists: A Brief Introduction, with Eight Letters of Dr. Antony Tuckney and Dr. Benjamin Whichcote*, ed. Tod E. Jones (Dallas: University Press of America, 2005), 71.

8. "Dr. Whichcote's First Letter: In Answer" (1651), in Jones, *Cambridge Platonists*, 76.

9. Philip C. Almond, *Heaven and Hell in Enlightenment England* (Cambridge: Cambridge University Press, 1994), 6.

10. Patrides, *Cambridge Platonists*, 4.

11. Henry More, "Preface General," *A Collection of Several Philosophical Writings of Dr. Henry More* (London: James Flesher, 1662; repr., New York: Garland, 1978), xxi.

12. Henry More, "Brief Discourse of Enthusiasm," LXIII, in *Philosophical Writings*, 45.

13. Benjamin Whichcote, *Several Discourses*, 4 vols., ed. John Jeffery (London: Knapton, 1701–1707), 2:407, cited in Patrides, *Cambridge Platonists*, 7.

14. Whichcote, *Several Discourses*, 2:25–50, cited in Patrides, *Cambridge Platonists*, 22.

15. Pico della Mirandola, *Oration on the Dignity of Man*, in *The Renaissance Philosophy of Man*, ed. Ernst Cassirer, Paul Oskar Kristeller, and John Herman Randall (Chicago: University of Chicago Press, 1967), 223, 226.

16. Henry More, *An Explanation of the Grand Mystery of Godliness* (London, 1660), 51, in Patrides, *Cambridge Platonists*, 13.

17. Whichcote, *Several Discourses*, 2:400, in Patrides, *Cambridge Platonists*, 13.

18. Ernst Cassirer, *The Platonic Renaissance in England*, trans. James P. Pettegrove (Austin: University of Texas Press, 1953), 27–28, cited in Jones, *Cambridge Platonists*, 20.

19. Aharon Lichtenstein, *Henry More: The Rational Theology of a Cambridge Platonist* (Cambridge, Mass.: Harvard University Press, 1962), 45.

20. Norman Russell, *The Doctrine of Deification in the Greek Patristic Tradition* (Oxford: Oxford University Press, 2004), 1.

21. John Smith, "The Excellency and Nobleness of True Religion," in Patrides, *Cambridge Platonists*, 167.

22. Benjamin Whichcote, "The Manifestation of Christ and the Deification of Man," in Patrides, *Cambridge Platonists*, 70.

23. Athanasius, *De Incarnatione Verbi Dei*, LIV, cited by Ralph Cudworth, "A Sermon Preached before the House of Commons," in Patrides, *Cambridge Platonists*, 101.

24. Henry More, *Antimonopsychia*, XXV, cited in Patrides, *Cambridge Platonists*, 18.

25. Henry More, *Grand Mystery of Godliness*, I.16.6; *Conjectura Cabbalistica*, "Preface to the Reader," III, cited in Lichtenstein, *Henry More*, 47.

26. Sterling P. Lamprecht, "Innate Ideas in the Cambridge Platonists," *Philosophical Review* 35.6 (November 1926): 572–73.

27. Henry More, *An Antidote against Atheism*, I.3, 5, in *Philosophical Writings*, 1:13, 17.

28. Henry More, "Preface General," in *Philosophical Writings*, ix.

29. More, *Antidote*, I.6, in *Philosophical Writings*, 18–19.

30. Nathanael Culverwel, *An Elegant and Learned Discourse on the Light of Nature* (1652), cited in E. T. Campagnac, *The Cambridge Platonists* (Oxford: Clarendon, 1901), 255.

31. Culverwel, *Elegant and Learned Discourse*, in Campagnac, *Cambridge Platonists*, 285.

32. Culverwel, *Elegant and Learned Discourse*, in Campagnac, *Cambridge Platonists*, 290.

33. Culverwel, *Elegant and Learned Discourse*, in Campagnac, *Cambridge Platonists*, 293.

34. Joseph Glanvill, *Lux Orientalis*, in Joseph Glanvill [and George Rust], *Two Choice and Useful Treatises: The One Lux Orientalis…the Other, a Discourse on Truth* (London: James Collins and Samuel Lowndes, 1682; repr., New York: Garland, 1978), 17–18; [Henry More], *Annotations upon Lux Orientalis…*, 19, in Glanvill [and Rust], *Two Choice and Useful Treatises*.

35. Whichcote, *Sermons*, 3:18, cited in Dominic Scott, "Reason, Recollection, and the Cambridge Platonists," in *Platonism and the English Imagination*, ed. Anna Baldwin and Sarah Hutton (Cambridge: Cambridge University Press, 1996), 145.

36. Ralph Cudworth, *Treatise Concerning Eternal and Immutable Morality* (London, 1731), 128, cited in Scott, "Reason," 145.

37. Ralph Cudworth, *Intellectual System of the Universe*, 2:105–6, cited in Sterling P. Lamprecht, "Innate Ideas in the Cambridge Platonists," *Philosophical Review* 35.6 (November 1926): 570.

38. More, "Preface General," in *Philosophical Writings*, xx.

39. Henry More, "Preface to the Reader," of "The Præexistency of the Soul," in *Philosophical Poems* (1647; repr., Menton, England: Scolar, 1969), 254, 253.

40. Some commentators connect the allusion here to Spenser through Aristo as an assumed version of "Ariosto." But Aristo was the name of Plato's father, and the explicit allusion to Plotinus a few lines later, if the title itself weren't sufficient, clinches the case. See M. J. Edwards, "The Proem to Henry More's *The Præexistency of the Soul*," *Notes and Queries* 44.3 (1997): 185.

41. [More], *Annotations*, 9, in Glanvill [and Rust], *Two Choice and Useful Treatises*.

42. Richard Ward, *The Life of the Pious and Learned Henry More* (London, 1710), 169, cited in Sarah Hutton, *Anne Conway: A Woman Philosopher* (Cambridge: Cambridge University Press, 2004), 54.

43. More, "Preface General," in *Philosophical Writings*, xxv; *Immortality of the Soul*, in *Philosophical Writings*, 2:110.

44. More, *Immortality of the Soul*, in *Philosophical Writings*, 2:111.

45. Joel R. Primack and Nancy Ellen Abrams, *The View from the Center of the Universe* (New York: Riverhead, 2006), 94.

46. More, *Immortality of the Soul*, in *Philosophical Writings*, 2:111–12.

47. More, *Immortality of the Soul*, in *Philosophical Writings*, 2:112.

48. Macrobius, *Commentary on the Dream of Scipio by Macrobius*, trans. William Harris Stahl (New York: Columbia University Press, 1990), 185.

49. Cicero, *Tuscan Disputations*, I.27; *Consolation*, cited by Lactantius, *On the Anger of God*, XI, in *The Ante-Nicene Fathers*, ed. Alexander Roberts and James Donaldson (Grand Rapids, Mich.: Eerdmans, 1977), 7:267 (hereafter, *ANF*).

50. See David E. Hahm, *The Origins of Stoic Cosmology* (Columbus: Ohio State University Press, 1977), 140, 151.

51. James Mark Baldwin, ed., *Dictionary of Philosophy and Psychology*, 3 vols. (New York: Macmillan, 1902), 2:270. See also Ernest Fortin, "The *Viri Novi* Arnobius and the Conflict between Faith and Reason in the Early Christian Centuries," in *The Birth of Philosophic Christianity: Studies in Early Christian and Medieval Thought*, ed. J. Brian Benestad (Lanham, Md.: Rowman & Littlefield, 1996). Fortin also claims that Arnobius opposed Platonic recollection, which he calls "inseparable from the notion of the soul's pre-existence" (176). For these Cambridge Platonists, as we see, the link is not a necessary one.

52. Stephen Bay's translation, from More, "Preface General," in *Philosophical Writings*, xiii.

53. More, "Preface General," in *Philosophical Writings*, xxv.

54. Letter of Henry More to Anne Conway, 12 May [1668], cited in Hutton, *Anne Conway*, 60.

55. Franciscus Palaeopolitanus [Henry More], *Divine Dialogues, Containing Sundry Disquisitions and Instructions Concerning the Attributes of God and His Providence in the World*, 2 vols. (London: James Flesher, 1668), 1:440–42.

56. More, *Divine Dialogues*, 2:449, 452–53.

57. More, *Divine Dialogues*, 2:471.

58. More, *Divine Dialogues*, 2:491.

59. More, *Annotations*, 19, in Glanvill [and Rust], *Two Choice and Useful Treatises*.

60. The Kabbalistic midrash referred to is the *Midrash ha-Ne'lam*. See Johannes van den Berg, "Menasseh ben Israel, Henry More, and Johannes Hoornbeeck on the Pre-Existence of the Soul," in *Religious Currents and Cross-Currents: Essays on Early Modern Protestantism and the Protestant Enlightenment*, ed. Jan de Bruijn, Pieter Holtrop, and Ernestine van der Wall (Leiden: Brill, 1999), 67.

61. Allison P. Coudert, *The Impact of the Kabbalah in the Seventeenth-Century: The Life and Thought of Francis Mercury van Helmont (1614–1698)* (Leiden: Brill, 1999), xix, 115.

62. Coudert, *Impact of the Kabbalah*, chs. 3 and 6.

63. Coudert, *Impact of the Kabbalah*, 222.

64. Richard H. Popkin, "The Spiritualist Cosmologies of Henry More and Anne Conway," in *Henry More (1614–1687): Tercentenary Studies*, ed. Sarah Hutton (Dordrecht: Kluwer, 1990), 105.

65. The attack took the form of a 1675 letter by Herman Rose, cited in Coudert, *Impact of the Kabbalah*, 115.

66. Coudert, *Impact of the Kabbalah*, 196.

67. Coudert, *Impact of the Kabbalah*, xvi.

68. Anne Conway, *The Principles of the Most Ancient and Modern Philosophy Concerning God, Christ and the Creatures* VI, ed. and trans. Allison P. Coudert and Taylor Corse (Cambridge: Cambridge University Press, 1996), 39.

69. Conway, *Principles*, II, 12.

70. Conway, *Principles*, VII, 43.

71. Conway, *Principles*, VII, 42.

72. [George Rust], *A Letter of Resolution Concerning Origen and the Chief of His Opinions* (London, 1661; repr., New York: Columbia University Press, 1933), 14. Though the letter is generally attributed to Rust, the evidence is not conclusive.

73. Rust, *Letter of Resolution*, 23–26.

74. Rust, *Letter of Resolution*, 29–31, 37.

75. Rust, *Letter of Resolution*, 51.

76. Rust, *Letter of Resolution*, [ii].

77. Charles F. Mullett, "Letter by Joseph Glanville [*sic*] on the Future State," *Huntington Library Quarterly* 1.4 (July 1938): 447–56.

78. Glanvill [and Rust], *Two Choice and Useful Treatises*, B2.

79. Glanvill [and Rust], *Two Choice and Useful Treatises*, [xiii, vii, x].

80. Cited in Marjorie Hope Nicolson, ed., *Conway Letters: The Correspondence of Anne, Viscountess Conway, Henry More, and Their Friends, 1642–1684* (New Haven, Conn.: Yale University Press, 1930), 323n.

81. Glanvill [and Rust], *Two Choice and Useful Treatises*, 7, 12, 15; [More], *Annotations*, 17, in Glanvill [and Rust], *Two Choice and Useful Treatises*.

82. John Davies, "The Original [*sic*], Nature, and Immortality of the Soul" (1599), cited in "traduce," *Oxford English Dictionary*.

83. Glanvill [and Rust], *Two Choice and Useful Treatises*, 22, 25, 31.

84. Glanvill [and Rust], *Two Choice and Useful Treatises*, 52.

85. Glanvill [and Rust], *Two Choice and Useful Treatises*, 42, 43.

86. E. W. [Edward Warren], *No Præexistence; or, A Brief Dissertation against the Hypothesis of Humane Souls, Living in a State Antecedaneous to This* (London: Samuel Thomson, 1667).

87. Warren, *No Præexistence*, 2–4.

88. Warren, *No Præexistence*, 7, 8, 24.

89. Edmund Spenser, *Faerie Queene*, bk. III.6, st. 31–32, in *Edmund Spenser's Poetry*, ed. Hugh Maclean (New York: Norton, 1981), 272.

90. Coudert, *Impact of the Kabbalah*, 221.

91. Thomas Vaughan, *The Magical Writings of Thomas Vaughan*, ed. Arthur Edward Waite (London: George Redway, 1888), 5, 9, 23.

92. Vaughan, *Magical Writings*, 30–31.

93. Henry Vaughan, "Man in Darkness; or, A Discourse of Death," in *The Mount of Olives*, in *The Works of Henry Vaughan*, ed. Leonard Cyril Martin (Oxford: Clarendon 1914), 1:169, 173.

94. Thomas Traherne, "The Salutation," in *Selected Writings of Thomas Traherne*, ed. Dick Davis (Manchester: Fyfield, 1980), 19–20.

95. Traherne, "Wonder," *Selected Writings*, 20.

96. Traherne, "The Preparative," *Selected Writings*, 26.

97. "Psalm 139," in *The Collected Works of Mary Sidney Herbert, Countess of Pembroke*, ed. Margaret P. Hannay, Noel J. Kinnamon, and Michael G. Brennan (Oxford: Clarendon, 1998), 2:235.

98. Traherne, "Dumbness," *Selected Writings*, 28–30.

99. Traherne, "Eden," *Selected Writings*, 23.

100. Traherne, "Innocence," *Selected Writings*, 24–26.

101. Traherne, "My Spirit," *Selected Writings*, 35.

102. [Abel Evans?], "Pre-Existence," in *Poems Imitative of Spenser: And, in the Manner of Milton*, ed. John Bell (London: John Bell, 1790). Scholars have assumed that the author was Abel Evans, but there are several problems with such attribution, as Justin White has indicated in "'Pre-Existence': A Poem in Imitation of Milton: A Discussion of Authorship," unpublished manuscript, author's files.

103. Evans, "Pre-Existence," 124, 129.

104. Evans, "Pre-Existence," 130.

105. Evans, "Pre-Existence," 131, 134, 136.

106. Edward Moore, "Origen of Alexandria and *Apocatastasis*: Some Notes on the Development of a Noble Notion," *Quodlibet: Online Journal of Christian Theology and Philosophy* 5.1 (January 2003), www.quodlibet.net/articles/moore-origen.shtml.

107. Joseph Wilson Trigg, *Origen: The Bible and Philosophy in the Third-century Church* (Atlanta, Ga.: John Knox, 1983), 40.

108. Evans, "Pre-Existence," 128.

109. "An Impartial Inquirer after Truth," *A Miscellaneous Metaphysical Essay; or, An Hypothesis Concerning the Formation and Generation of Spiritual and Material Beings*...(London: A. Millar, 1748), 68.

110. Evans, "Pre-Existence," 136.

111. Alvin Boyd Kuhn, *The Lost Light: An Interpretation of Ancient Scriptures*, www.theosophical.ca/LostLight1.htm#colonists.

112. Laurence Dermott, *Ahiman Rezon; or, A Help to a Brother Shewing the Excellency of Secrecy and the First Cause or Motive of the Institution of Free Masonry*...(London: Laurence Dermott, 1756), [v].

113. Harry F. Robins, *If This Be Heresy: A Study of Milton and Origen* (Urbana: University of Illinois Press, 1963), esp. 60ff.

114. John Milton, *Christian Doctrine* VII, trans. Charles Richard Sumner (Cambridge: Cambridge University Press, 1825), 189.

115. John Milton, *Comus*, ll. 256, 467–75.

116. This attribution is called an error in Leslie Stephen, ed., *Dictionary of National Biography* (New York: Macmillan, 1887), 12:280.

117. Impartial Inquirer, *Miscellaneous Metaphysical Essay*, v, 49.

118. Andrew Michael Ramsay, *The Travels of Cyrus: To Which Is Annexed, a Discourse upon the Theology and Mythology of the Pagans* (Boston: Manning and Loring, 1795), 220.

119. Impartial Inquirer, *Miscellaneous Metaphysical Essay*, iv, 153–54.

120. Impartial Inquirer, *Miscellaneous Metaphysical Essay*, 274–76.

121. "A Layman," *The Certainty of the Origin of Evil in the World, and the Probable Pre-Existence of Mankind in the Fallen Angels, Cast Out of Heaven…* (London: John W. Parker, 1842; repr., Whitefish, Mont.: Kessinger, 2005), 2.

122. A Layman, *Certainty of the Origin*, 96.

123. A Layman, *Certainty of the Origin*, 102–4.

124. A Layman, *Certainty of the Origin*, 131, 31, 257, 109.

125. Impartial Inquirer, *Miscellaneous Metaphysical Essay*, 65, 68–69.

126. Impartial Inquirer, *Miscellaneous Metaphysical Essay*, 177.

127. Impartial Inquirer, *Miscellaneous Metaphysical Essay*, 60–61.

128. Impartial Inquirer, *Miscellaneous Metaphysical Essay*, 61–62, 64.

129. The general consensus is that the telescope came first, though Pieter Harting argued in the nineteenth century that the order should be reversed. See the literature referred to in Edward G. Ruestow, *The Microscope in the Dutch Republic: The Shaping of Discovery* (Cambridge: Cambridge University Press, 1996), 227.

130. Ruestow, *Microscope*, 218.

131. Ruestow, *Microscope*, 226.

132. John Cook, *An Anatomical and Mechanical Essay on the Whole Animal Oeconomy*, 2 vols. (London, 1730), 1:12, quoted in Dennis Todd, "'One Vast Egg': Leibniz, the New Embryology, and Pope's *Dunciad*," *English Language Notes* 26.4 (June 1989): 27.

133. Augustine, *On Free Choice of the Will*, III.20, trans. Thomas Williams (Indianapolis, Ind.: Hackett, 1993), 108.

134. Nicolas Malebranche, *The Search after Truth*, cited in J. Needham, *A History of Embryology* (Cambridge: Cambridge University Press, 1959), 169.

135. Henry Baker, *The Universe: A Poem* (London, 1734?), 23, cited in Todd, "One Vast Egg," 28.

137. Impartial Inquirer, *Miscellaneous Metaphysical Essay*, 65.

137. Impartial Inquirer, *Miscellaneous Metaphysical Essay*, 64–66.

CHAPTER 8

1. Benjamin Franklin to Jane Mecom, cited in *The Works of Benjamin Franklin*, 10 vols., ed. Jared Sparks (Boston: Hilliard, Gray, 1840), 7:58–59. Sparks does not date the letter.

2. Franklin to Mecom, in *Works of Franklin*, 7:59.

3. Andrew Michael Ramsay, *The Travels of Cyrus: To Which Is Annexed, a Discourse upon the Theology and Mythology of the Pagans* (Boston: Manning and Loring, 1795), xv.

4. Ramsay, *Travels of Cyrus*, 152–53.

5. Ramsay, *Travels of Cyrus*, 220.

6. Ramsay, *Travels of Cyrus*, 230.

7. *National Union Catalog Pre-1956 Imprints* (London: Mansell, 1976), 480, 409–12.

8. René Descartes, *Meditations*, III, trans. Elizabeth S. Haldane and G. R. T. Ross, in *Discourse on Method and Meditations on First Philosophy*, ed. David Weissman (New Haven, Conn.: Yale University Press, 1996), 73, 75–76, 82.

9. John Locke, *Essay Concerning Human Understanding*, I.1.8–2.1, ed. Peter H. Nidditch (Oxford: Clarendon, 1975), 48.

10. Locke, *Essay*, I.2.2, 5 (49–50).

11. Locke, *Essay*, II.27.14 (338–39).

12. Augustine, *On Free Choice of the Will*, III.21 trans. Thomas Williams (Indianapolis, Ind.: Hackett, 1993), 113.

13. G. W. Leibniz, *Discourse on Metaphysics*, XXVI, trans. George R. Montgomery (Chicago: Open Court, 1908), 44–45.

14. Leibniz, *Discourse*, XXVI,45.

15. G. W. Leibniz, "Preface," in *New Essays Concerning Human Understanding*, trans. Alfred G. Langley (Chicago: Open Court, 1916), 42–43.

16. Jeffrey Andrew Barash, "The Sources of Memory," *Journal of the History of Ideas* 58.4 (October 1997): 711.

17. Leibniz, *Discourse*, XXVI,45.

18. See, in this regard, Barash, "Sources of Memory," 712.

19. Locke, *Essay*, II.27.9 (335).

20. Barash, "Sources of Memory," 713.

21. David Hume, *Treatise of Human Nature* I.4.6, ed. David Fate Norton and Mary J. Norton (Oxford: Clarendon, 2007), 165.

22. As Herbert Wilson Carr interprets Leibniz, "According to the degree of clearness in their perceptions the monads are graded. When the perceptions…have some degree of clearness accompanied by consciousness they are *souls*, when they have knowledge of necessary truths, they are *rational souls*." G. W. Leibniz, *Monadology*, intro. and essays by Herbert Wilson Carr (London: Favil, 1930), 23.

23. Leibniz, *New Essays*, I.1 (70).

24. Roy Sorensen, *Paradox: Philosophy and the Labyrinths of Mind* (New York: Oxford University Press, 2003), 240.

25. Sorensen, *Paradox*, 240.

26. Dennis Todd, "'One Vast Egg': Leibniz, the New Embryology, and Pope's *Dunciad*," *English Language Notes* 26.4 (June 1989): 30.

27. G. W. Leibniz, *Theodicy: Essays on the Goodness of God, the Freedom of Man, and the Origin of Evil* 1, 38, 41–42, ed. Austin Farrer, trans. E. M. Huggard (La Salle, Ill.: Open Court, 1985), 123, 144–47.

28. Leibniz, *Theodicy*, 151.

29. Leibniz, *Theodicy*, 7.

30. Leibniz, *Theodicy*, 90–91; Leibniz reasserts this idea in his *Monadology*, 74.

31. Leibniz, *Monadology*, 74.

32. Leibniz, *Theodicy*, 91.

33. Edward Search [Abraham Tucker], *Freewill, Foreknowledge and Fate: A Fragment* (London, 1763; repr., Bristol, England: Thoemmes, 1990), 169.

34. Search, *Freewill,*, 170–71.

35. Tertullian, *A Treatise on the Soul*, XXIV, in *The Ante-Nicene Fathers*, 10 vols., ed. Alexander Roberts and James Donaldson (Grand Rapids, Mich.: Eerdmans, 1977), 3:203 (hereafter, *ANF*).

36. Perhaps the only history of the idea of preexistence ever written, Bruch's study was limited largely to patristic and German philosophical sources. I am indebted to Roger Minert and Martin Sulzer-Reichel for translation assistance with this important text.

A paraphrased and abridged version was published in *Bibliotheca Sacra* 20.80 (October 1863): 681–733.

37. James Ward, *The Realm of Ends; or, Pluralism and Theism: The Gifford Lectures... 1907–10* (Cambridge: Cambridge University Press, 1920), 404n. Ward cites in support of his claim Max Heinze, *Vorlesungen Kant's über Metaphysik* (1894), 547.

38. Immanuel Kant, *Critique of Practical Reason* I.1 trans. Werner Pluhar (Indianapolis, Ind.: Hackett, 2002), 121.

39. Kant, *Critique of Practical Reason*, I.1.

40. Immanuel Kant, *Grounding for the Metaphysic of Morals*, III (452) trans. James W. Ellington (Indianapolis, Ind.: Hackett, 1993), 53–54.

41. Kant, *Grounding*, III (457).

42. Immanuel Kant, *Religion within the Limits of Reason*, trans. Theodore M. Greene (Chicago: Open Court, 1934), 20.

43. Kant, *Religion*, 36.

44. Kant, *Religion*, 36–37.

45. Kant, *Religion*, 44–45.

46. Kant, *Religion*, 35. He found the doctrine equally unpersuasive whether argued from biological, legalistic, or theological grounds. See 35n–36n.

47. Stephen Mulhall, *Philosophical Myths of the Fall* (Princeton, N.J.: Princeton University Press, 2005), 15.

48. Immanuel Kant, *Critique of Pure Reason* B76, trans. Paul Guyer and Allen W. Wood (Cambridge: Cambridge University Press, 1998), 193–94.

49. W. T. Jones, *A History of Western Philosophy*, 5 vols. (New York: Harcourt Brace Jovanovich, 1975), 4:9.

50. Kant argued that analytic judgments like the rose is a flower rely for evidence upon "the law of contradiction."

51. Kant, *Critique of Pure Reason*, B43–45.

52. For an analysis of Platonic recollection in the light of Kant's theory of intuitions and concepts, see Dominic Scott, "Platonic Recollection," in *Plato: Metaphysics and Epistemology*, ed. Gail Fine (Oxford: Oxford University Press, 1999), 93–124.

53. Kant, *Critique of Pure Reason*, B807–8.

CHAPTER 9

1. J. Friedrich Bruch, *Die Lehre von der Präexistenz* (Strasburg: Treuttel und Würz, 1859), 24. Translation by Roger Minert.

2. Edward Allen Beach, *The Potencies of God(s): Schelling's Philosophy of Mythology* (Albany: State University of New York Press, 1994), 59.

3. F. W. J. Schelling, *Of Human Freedom*, trans. James Gutmann (Chicago: Open Court, 1936), 61.

4. Schelling, *Human Freedom*, 63.

5. Schelling, *Human Freedom*, 65–66.

6. Schelling, *Human Freedom*, 64.

7. Immanuel Hermann von Fichte, *Anthropologie* (1860), par. 119, cited in Rudolf Steiner, *The Riddle of Man*, trans. William Lindeman (Spring Valley, N.Y.: Mercury, 1990), 51.

8. Fichte, *Anthropologie*, paraphrased in Bruch, *Die Lehre von der Präexistenz*, 52–56.

9. Wilhelm Benecke, *An Exposition of St. Paul's Epistle to the Romans*, trans. Friedrich Wilhelm (London: Longman, Brown, Green, and Longmans, 1854), xii–xiii.

10. Paul Johnson, *A History of Christianity* (New York: Simon and Schuster, 1976), 39.

11. Benecke, *Exposition of St. Paul's Epistle*, 31.

12. See, in this regard, the dissenting comments of prominent Calvinist churchman Charles Hodge, who wrote his own *Commentary on the Epistle to the Romans* (1835; repr., Grand Rapids, Mich.: Eerdmans, 1994), 145.

13. Bruch, *Die Lehre von der Präexistenz*, 40.

14. Charles Hodge, *Systematic Theology*, 3 vols. (Grand Rapids, Mich.: Eerdmans, 1970), 2:215.

15. Benecke, *Exposition of St. Paul's Epistle*, 455–56.

16. Hermann Olshausen, *Biblical Commentary on the New Testament*, 6 vols. (New York: Sheldon, Blakeman, 1857), 3:576.

17. Adolf Harnack, *History of Dogma*, 7 vols., trans. from 3rd German ed. by Neil Buchanan (London: Williams & Norgate, 1894), 1:319.

18. J. B. Turner, *Mormonism in All Ages; or, The Rise, Progress, and Causes of Mormonism* (New York: Platt & Peters, 1842), 241–42. Turner adds that Mormons concealed their belief in preexistence after its unpopular reception, but it was consistently taught from the pulpit and in print from the 1830s.

19. Stan Larson, "The King Follett Discourse: A Newly Amalgamated Text," *BYU Studies* 18.2 (Winter 1978): 203–4.

20. A good treatment of the doctrine's origins and evolution in Mormon history is Blake Ostler, "The Idea of Pre-Existence in the Development of Mormon Thought," *Dialogue: A Journal of Mormon Thought* 15.1 (Spring 1982): 59–78.

21. Moses 6:51, in *Pearl of Great Price* (Salt Lake City, Utah: Church of Jesus Christ of Latter-day Saints, 1981) (hereafter, *PGP*). Some Mormons see Alma 13 in the Book of Mormon as referring to human preexistence. Joseph Smith and his contemporaries, however, apparently did not.

22. *Doctrine and Covenants* (Salt Lake City, Utah: Church of Jesus Christ of Latter-day Saints, 1981), 93:29–30 (hereafter, *D&C*). Smith claimed that the revelation was received on 6 May 1833.

23. Julius Müller, *The Christian Doctrine of Sin*, 2 vols., trans. William Urwick (Edinburgh: Clark, 1868), 2:157.

24. Plato, *Laws*, X.896a, trans. Trevor J. Saunders, in *Plato: Complete Works*, ed. John M. Cooper (Indianapolis, Ind.: Hackett, 1997), 1552.

25. Abraham 3:22–23, in *PGP*.

26. S. B. Parker, "Council," in *Dictionary of Deities and Demons in the Bible*, 2nd ed., ed. Karel van der Toorn, Bob Becking, and Pieter W. van der Horst (New York: Brill, 1999), 204–8.

27. Larson, "King Follett Discourse," 202.

28. Abraham 3:24, *PGP*.

29. Moses 4:1; Abraham 3:24, 27, 28, *PGP*.

30. Orson Hyde gave a definitive gloss on the subject, commenting on 1 Cor. 6:3:

Is it possible that we, the servants of God, are going to judge angels? When we lay [these mortal bodies] off we shall remember…the scenes of those early times.…The Saints will say to their fallen brethren, You were arrayed under the command of Lucifer, and fought against us; we prevailed, and it now becomes our duty to pass sentence against you, fallen spirits.…The Saints shall judge angels, even those spirits who kept not their first estate.

Hyde, *Journal of Discourses,* 26 vols., reported by G. D. Watt et al. (Liverpool: F.D and S. W. Richards, et al., 1851–1886; repr. Salt Lake City: n.p., 1974), 1:128.

31. A 1789 dictionary defines the term as "spirit or unembodied mind." Thomas Sheridan, *Complete Dictionary of the English Language* (London: Charles Dilly, 1789). Webster's 1828 dictionary gives as definition 4, "a spiritual being; as a *created intelligence,*" and adds, "it is believed that the universe is peopled with innumerable superior *intelligences.*" Noah Webster, *An American Dictionary of the English Language* (New York: S. Converse, 1828).

32. John L. Brooke, *The Refiner's Fire: The Making of Mormon Cosmology, 1644–1844* (Cambridge: Cambridge University Press, 1994), xiii.

33. Harold Bloom, *The American Religion: The Emergence of the Post-Christian Nation* (New York: Simon & Schuster, 1992), 101.

34. Bloom, *American Religion*, 99, 105. An overview of these developments is found in Lance S. Owens, "Joseph Smith and Kabbalah: The Occult Connection," *Dialogue: A Journal of Mormon Thought* 27.3 (Fall 1994): 116–94.

35. No written text or full transcript of the sermon exists, though at least four auditors took notes. The best record is the composite document produced by Larson, "King Follett Discourse," 193–208.

36. Joseph Fielding Smith, ed., *Teachings of the Prophet Joseph Smith* (Salt Lake City, Utah: Deseret, 1973), 354n. Charles Harrell concurs that, based on Smith's use of the term "organization" elsewhere, "the only organization of intelligences envisioned by the Prophet in these statements is a social organization and not an organization of intelligence into intelligences." "The Development of the Doctrine of Preexistence, 1830–1844," *BYU Studies* 28.2 (Spring 1988): 86.

37. James E. Talmage, *The Vitality of Mormonism* (Boston: Gorham, 1919), 241.

38. Orson Whitney, "Man's Origin and Destiny," *Contributor* 3.9 (June 1882): 269–70.

39. Bruce R. McConkie, *Mormon Doctrine*, 2nd ed. (Salt Lake City, Utah: Bookcraft, 1966), 750.

40. Susa Young Gates, "Reminiscences of Brigham Young," *Improvement Era* 11.8 (June 1908).

41. *D&C* 131:7.

42. Joseph Glanvill [and George Rust], *Two Choice and Useful Treatises: The One Lux Orientalis…the Other, a Discourse on Truth* (London: James Collins and Samuel Lowndes, 1682; repr., New York: Garland, 1978), 49.

43. Anne Conway, *The Principles of the Most Ancient and Modern Philosophy Concerning God, Christ and the Creatures*, ed. and trans. Allison P. Coudert and Taylor Corse (Cambridge: Cambridge University Press, 1996), 49.

44. B. H. Roberts, "Religious Faiths," *Improvement Era* 1.11 (September 1898): 827–28.

45. *D&C* 93:38.

46. Abraham 3:26, *PGP*.

47. "When they had revolted from their former blessedness they were endowed with bodies in consequence of the fall from their first estate." Origen, *De Principiis*, 1.8.1, Greek text, in Butterworth, *Origen on First Principles*, 67.

48. Roberts, "Religious Faiths," 827–28.

49. Larson, "King Follett Discourse," 196.

50. Larson, "King Follett Discourse," 202.

51. Joseph F. Smith, John R. Winder, and Anthon H. Lund, "The Origin of Man," First Presidency statement, in *Messages of the First Presidency of the Church of Jesus Christ of Latter-day Saints*, 6 vols., comp. James R. Clark (Salt Lake City, Utah: Bookcraft, 1965–1975), 4:206.

52. Charles Edward Stowe and Lyman Beecher Stowe, *Harriet Beecher Stowe: The Story of Her Life* (Boston: Houghton Mifflin, 1911), 44.

53. Cited in Robert Meredith, *The Politics of the Universe: Edward Beecher, Abolition, and Orthodoxy* (Nashville, Tenn.: Vanderbilt University Press, 1968), 27.

54. Meredith, *Politics*, 40. Meredith relies, for Catherine's question and Beecher's response, on Stowe and Stowe, *Harriet Beecher Stowe*.

55. Charles Beecher, "Life of Edward Beecher," 38–41. Unpublished manuscript in the Illinois College Library, Jacksonville. A microfilm copy is at the Abraham Lincoln Presidential Library in Springfield, Illinois.

56. Augustine, *On Free Choice of the Will*, III.20, trans. Thomas Williams (Indianapolis, Ind.: Hackett, 1993), 109.

57. Augustine, *On Free Choice*, 107.

58. Beecher, "Life," 204.

59. Edward Beecher, *The Conflict of Ages; or, The Great Debate on the Moral Relations of God and Man* (Boston: Phillips, Sampson, 1853), 6; Beecher, "Life," preface.

60. Beecher, *Conflict*, iii, 2–3.

61. Beecher, *Conflict*, 46, 60, 98, 107.

62. Beecher, *Conflict*, 110–11, 5.

63. Beecher, *Conflict*, 196, 211.

64. Moses Ballou, *The Divine Character Vindicated: A Review* (New York: Redfield, 1854), vii, 50–52.

65. Beecher, *Conflict*, 221, 242.

66. Beecher, *Conflict*, 242, 228–33.

67. Beecher, *Conflict*, 222–23.

68. Letter to Henry Acland, 24 May 1851, in John Ruskin, *Works*, 39 vols., ed. E. T. Cook and Alexander Wedderburn (London: George Allen, 1903–1912), 36:115.

69. Beecher, *Conflict*, 239.

70. Beecher, *Conflict*, 231–32, 552.

71. Green's article appeared in *Christian Advocate* 3 (1825): 530. The delayed protest took fifteen years to hit the pages of the *Christian Observer* 19.32 (6 August 1840), which printed excerpts of the article.

72. Duffield's words, from his *Spiritual Life; or, Regeneration* (Carlisle, Pa.: George Fleming, 1832), 395, were cited in the *Christian Observer* article, along with the editor's and a reader's.

73. Blurb from "Notices of the Press," appended to Jacob Blain, *Death Not Life; or, The Destruction of the Wicked* (Buffalo, N.Y.: Author, 1870).

74. H. B., "Review of *The Divine Character Vindicated*," *Universalist Quarterly and General Review* (April 1855).

75. "Notices of the Press," in Blain, *Death Not Life*.

76. Advertisement in Blain, *Death Not Life*, 2.

77. Cited in Edward Beecher, *Concord of Ages* (New York: Derby & Jackson, 1860), 405.

78. Beecher, *Concord*, 381, 404–5.

79. Stowe and Stowe, *Harriet Beecher Stowe*, 49.

80. These names are given by Meredith, *Politics*, 146.

81. Ballou, *Divine Character*, v–viii.

82. Ballou, *Divine Character*, viii–ix, xv.

83. H. B., "Review."

84. H. B., "Review."

85. Cited in Blain, *Death Not Life*, 1.

86. Anonymous reviewer, *Christian Review* (January 1854).

87. Beecher, "Life."

88. John Beecher to President Hudson, 11 March 1950. Letter introducing the manuscript copy of "Life of Edward Beecher"; original in Illinois College Library.

89. Oliver Wendell Holmes, "The One-Hoss Shay," in *The Wonderful "One-Hoss-Shay" and Other Poems* (New York: Stokes, 1897), 11, 42.

90. Cited in Debby Applegate, *The Most Famous Man in America: The Biography of Henry Ward Beecher* (Garden City, N.Y.: Doubleday, 2006), 300.

91. "The Sacredness of Life," in *Phillips Brooks: Selected Sermons*, ed. William Scarlett (New York: Dutton, 1949), 19. Brooks is quoting Alexander Pope's poem "The Messiah: A Sacred Eclogue."

92. "Sacredness of Life," in *Phillips Brooks: Sermons*, 21.

93. Virgil, *Aeneid*, VI, ll. 913–14, from the translation by Robert Fitzgerald (New York: Vintage, 1990), 183.

94. Alexander Pope, *Essay on Man* I.3, ll. 77–80, 97, in *Collected Poems*, ed. Bonamy Dobrée (London: Dent, 1975), 184.

95. "The Candle of the Lord," in *Phillips Brooks: Sermons*, 39.

96. Alexander V. G. Allen, *Phillips Brooks* (New York: Dutton, 1907), 64, 66.

97. George MacDonald, Poem No. 1, in his 366-poem sequence, *Diary of an Old Soul* (Minneapolis, Minn.: Augsburg, 1975), 6.

98. Though Mill is better remembered today as an apostle of freedom (the Mill of *On Liberty*, written in 1859), he also argued for a deterministic view of human nature, which he called "invariability" (in his *Examination of Sir W. Hamilton's Philosophy* in 1865). The reference is from Julius Müller, *The Christian Doctrine of Sin*, 2 vols., trans. William Urwick (Edinburgh: Clark, 1868), 1:vii.

99. Ballou, *Divine Character*, 62.

100. Müller, *Christian Doctrine*, 2:70–73.

101. Müller, *Christian Doctrine*, 2:72–73.

102. Müller, *Christian Doctrine*, 2:69.

103. Its title notwithstanding, Edwards's *Freedom of the Will*, with its tortuous accommodation of freedom to a deterministic world view, strikes Urwick as a prime instance of a failed attempt to rectify an ill-considered overreaction to the Pelagian celebration of human will. Müller, *Christian Doctrine*, 2:76n.

104. J. P. Romang, *System der natürlichen Religionslehre*, cited in Müller, *Christian Doctrine*, 2:74n.

105. Müller, *Christian Doctrine*, 2:74.

106. Müller, *Christian Doctrine*, 2:76.

107. The actual title of Herschel's work was *Preliminary Discourse on the Study of Natural Philosophy* (1830).

108. John F. W. Herschel, *A Preliminary Discourse on the Study of Natural Philosophy* (Chicago: University of Chicago Press, 1987), 360.

109. Andréa Pizzani, *Pre-existence and Future Existence; or, The Soul Created in the Image of God…* (London: William Ridgeway, 1864?), 16–17.

110. Norman Pearson, "Before Birth," *Nineteenth Century* (September 1886): 340–63.

CHAPTER 10

1. William Wordsworth, *The Excursion*, IV.395–96, in *Poetical Works*, ed. Thomas Hutchinson and Ernest de Selincourt (New York: Oxford University Press, 1989), 630.

2. Augustine, *Confessions*, trans. F. J. Sheed (Indianapolis, Ind.: Hackett, 1993), IV.16 (66).

3. George Herbert, "The Pulley," in *The Poems of George Herbert* (Oxford: Oxford University Press, 1979), 150–51.

4. Thomas Taylor, ed. and trans., *The Works of Plato*, 5 vols. (London: R. Wilks, 1804). Taylor made use of Floyer Sydenham's prior translation of nine of the dialogues.

5. Taylor, *Works of Plato*, 1:iv, xxiii, xxxv, xc.

6. Burton Feldman writes that "the Enlightenment…had generally ignored the Neoplatonists and also lopped off Plato's 'supernatural speculations' and theory of Ideas." "Introduction," Taylor, *Works of Plato*, 1:vi.

7. Taylor, *Works of Plato*, 1:lxv–lxvii, lxiii.

8. Taylor, *Works of Plato*, 1:lxxix–lxxx; lxvi–lxvii.

9. Feldman, "Introduction," in Taylor, *Works of Plato*, 1:vii, v.

10. Algernon Charles Swinburne, *William Blake: A Critical Essay* (London: John Camden Hotten, 1868), 41.

11. Letter of William Blake to John Flaxman, 21 September 1800, in *The Letters of William Blake*, ed. Geoffrey Keynes (Cambridge, Mass.: Harvard University Press, 1968), 41–42.

12. Blake to Flaxman, in *Letters of William Blake*, 42.

13. Emanuel Swedenborg, *The Spiritual Diary*, 5 vols., trans. George Bush and John H. Smithson (London: John Speirs, 1883), 2591 (2:292); Swedenborg, *The True Christian Religion*, 2 vols. (New York: Swedenborg Foundation, 1965), 171 (1:257).

14. Swedenborg, *Spiritual Diary*, 2793 (2:350).

15. William Blake, "The Book of Thel," in *The Complete Poetry and Prose of William Blake*, ed. David V. Erdman (Berkeley: University of California Press, 1982), 4–5.

16. William Blake, "The Little Black Boy," in *Complete Poetry*, 9.

17. Samuel Taylor Coleridge, "Sonnet on Receiving Letters," in *The Complete Poems*, ed. William Keach (New York: Penguin, 1997), 121.

18. Letter to John Thelwall (19 November 1796) and Letter to Thomas Poole (1 November 1796), in *Collected Letters of Samuel Taylor Coleridge*, 6 vols., ed. E. L. Griggs (Oxford: Clarendon, 1956), 1:260–61 and 1:246. Irene H. Chayes makes the case that Coleridge came to the idea of preexistence by way of Ramsay's *Philosophical Principles*, which he had been reading, in "Coleridge, Metempsychosis and 'Almost All the Followers of Fenelon,'" *English Literary History* 25.4 (December 1958): 290–315.

19. William Wordsworth, "Sonnet XXX," in *Poetical Works*, 205. The poem was composed in 1802 but not published until 1807; the child referred to was Caroline, his natural child by the French woman Annette Vallon.

20. Stephen Banfield, "The Immortality Odes of Finzi and Somervell," *Musical Times* 116.1588 (June 1975): 528.

21. Wordsworth, *The Excursion*, IV, ll. 140, 179–83. In *Poetical Works*, 627.

22. Lord Byron, *Cain*, in *Byron*, ed. Jerome J. McGann (New York: Oxford University Press, 1986), II.i, ll. 50–51 (902).

23. Robert Browning, "Two in the Campagna," in *Robert Browning's Poetry*, ed. James F. Loucks (New York: Norton, 2007), 266.

24. Wordsworth, *The Excursion*, IV, ll. 330–31. In *Poetical Works*, 629. Wordsworth is here quoting the earlier poet Samuel Daniel.

25. Wordsworth, "Ode: Intimations of Immortality from Recollections of Early Childhood," in *Poetical Works*, 460–62.

26. Jonathan Wordsworth, M. H. Abrams, and Stephen Gill, "The Texts: History and Presentation," in William Wordsworth, *The Prelude 1799, 1805, 1850*, ed. Jonathan Wordsworth, M. H. Abrams, and Stephen Gill (New York: Norton, 1979), 524.

27. See Terryl L. Givens and Anthony P. Russell, "Romantic Agonies: Human Suffering and the Ethical Sublime," in *Romanticism across the Disciplines*, ed. Larry H. Peer (Lanham, Md.: University Press of America, 1998), 231–53.

28. Letter to Thomas Poole, 1 November 1796, in Griggs, *Collected Letters*, 1:246.

29. Samuel Taylor Coleridge, *Biographia Literaria*, ed. J. Shawcross (Oxford: Oxford University Press, 1907), 2:120–21.

30. Chayes, "Coleridge," 291; Griggs, *Collected Letters*, 1:278. Chayes argues that Coleridge never resolved the tension: "imagination and emotions were attached to doctrines and beliefs his critical intellect and increasingly orthodox theological convictions impelled him to reject" (313).

31. Jared Curtis, ed., *The Fenwick Notes of William Wordsworth* (London: Bristol Classical, 1993), 61–62. The *Fenwick Notes* derive from oral commentary Wordsworth delivered on his poetry to his friend Isabella Fenwick in 1843.

32. Robert Zimmer, *Clairvoyant Wordsworth: A Case Study in Heresy and Critical Prejudice* (San Jose, Calif.: Writers Club Press, 2002), xiv. Zimmer's book makes an extended

case for a perverse obliviousness on the part of Romanticism scholars especially to the genuine unorthodoxies of Wordsworth's poetry.

33. Stephen Gill, *William Wordsworth: A Life* (Oxford: Oxford University Press, 1989), 227.

34. Quoted in Banfield, "Immortality Odes," 527.

35. J. K. Mathison, "Wordsworth's Ode: Intimations of Immortality from Recollections of Early Childhood," *Studies in Philology* 46 (1949): 439, cited in Banfield, "Immortality Odes," 529.

36. Augustine, *The City of God against the Pagans* X.31, trans. R. W. Dyson (Cambridge: Cambridge University Press, 1998), 441.

37. David Hume, "On the Immortality of the Soul," in *Of the Standard of Taste and Other Essays*, ed. John W. Lenz (Indianapolis, Ind.: Bobbs-Merrill, 1965), 162.

38. Menasseh ben Israel, *De Resurrectione Mortuorum*, cited in Johannes van den Berg, "Menasseh ben Israel, Henry More, and Johannes Hoornbeeck on the Pre-Existence of the Soul," in *Religious Currents and Cross-Currents: Essays on Early Modern Protestantism*, ed. Jan de Bruijn, Pieter Holtrop, and Ernestine van der Wall (Leiden: Brill, 1999), 68.

39. Percy B. Shelley, "On a Future State," in *Essays and Letters by Percy Bysshe Shelley*, ed. Ernest Rhys (London: Walter Scott, n.d.), 81–82.

40. Thomas Jefferson Hogg, *The Life of Percy Bysshe Shelley* (London: Routledge, 1906), 147–48.

41. Percy Bysshe Shelley, "Prince Athanase," ll. 91–92, in *Complete Poetical Works*, ed. Thomas Hutchinson (New York: Oxford, 1933), 161.

42. Shelley, *Epipsychidion*, ll. 417–23, 453–56, in *Complete Poetical*, 420–21.

43. Shelley, *Epipsychidion*, ll. 131–37, in *Complete Poetical*, 414.

44. Byron, *Cain*, I.1.549–52; II.1.175–76, in *Byron*, 900, 906.

45. English version of Mikhail Lermontov, "The Angel," from Carol Zaleski and Philip Zaleski, *The Book of Heaven: An Anthology of Writings from Ancient to Modern Times* (New York: Oxford University Press, 2000), 369.

46. Thomas Carlyle, *Sartor Resartus* (Chicago: Scribner's, 1921), 63.

47. Goethe, *Faust*, I, ll. 1112–17, in the translation of Walter Arndt (New York: Norton, 1976), 27.

48. Sarah Austin, ed. and trans., *Characteristics of Goethe, from the German of Falk, von Müller, &c.*, 3 vols. (London: Effingham Wilson, 1833), 1:78–84.

49. John R. Williams, *The Life of Goethe: A Critical Biography* (Oxford: Blackwell, 2001), 201. Only slightly different is Dan Latimer's view that Homunculus represents "this new Goethean doctrine of the spirit unfolding itself and reaching its fulfillment in the mortal and material." "Homunculus as Symbol: Semantic and Dramatic Functions of the Figure in Goethe's *Faust*," *Modern Language Notes* 89.5 (October 1974): 814.

50. Goethe, *Faust*, II.2, l. 7858.

51. Alfred, Lord Tennyson, "To —," in *Poetic and Dramatic Works* (Boston: Houghton Mifflin, 1898), 24.

52. Alfred, Lord Tennyson, "The Two Voices," ll. 364–84, in *Poetic and Dramatic*, 34.

53. This passage is not universally read as referring to mortal humans and their preexistence, but one critic who disagrees admits that it is a defensible reading and adds,

"the idea of pre-existence is not infrequent in Tennyson." See Andrew Cecil Bradley, *A Commentary on Tennyson's In Memoriam* (New York: Macmillan, 1930), 130.

54. Alfred, Lord Tennyson, *In Memoriam*, XLIV, in *Poetic and Dramatic*, 173.

55. Alfred, Lord Tennyson, "Crossing the Bar," in *Poetic and Dramatic*, 753.

56. Dante Gabriel Rossetti, "Sudden Light," in *Complete Poetical Works*, ed. William M. Rossetti (Boston: Roberts Brothers, 1894), 260.

57. Robert Browning, "Rabbi ben Ezra," ll. 159–68, in *Browning's*, 291.

58. Francisco Sellén, "Pre-existence," trans. Helen S. Conant, *Current Literature* 5.3 (September 1890): 234.

59. Andrew Jackson Davis, *Memoranda of Persons, Places, and Events* (Boston: William White, 1868), 338.

60. Robert Southey, "Letters," cited in Davis, *Memoranda*, 339.

61. Sir Walter Scott, *The Journal of Sir Walter Scott: From the Original Manuscript at Abbotsford* (New York: Harper, 1891), 355.

62. Davis, *Memoranda*, 342.

63. Paul Hamilton Hayne, "Pre-existence," in *Avolio: A Legend of the Island of Cos: With Poems Lyrical, Miscellaneous, and Dramatic* (Boston: Ticknor and Fields, 1890), 73.

64. Paul Hamilton Hayne, "Pre-existence," in *Poems of Paul Hamilton Hayne* (Boston: D. Lothrop, 1882), 204–5.

65. Austin Warren, "The Orphic Sage: Bronson Alcott," *American Literature* 3.1 (March 1931): 13.

66. "The first thing we have to say, respecting what are called *new views* here in New England, at the present time, is, that they are not new, but the very oldest of thoughts cast into the mold of these new times." "The Transcendentalist," in Ralph Waldo Emerson, *The Complete Writings of Ralph Waldo Emerson* (New York: Wise, 1929), 101.

67. Octavius Frothingham, *George Ripley* (Boston: Houghton Mifflin, 1882), 84–85.

68. Ralph Waldo Emerson, *Journals*, 10 vols., ed. Edward Waldo Emerson and Waldo Emerson Forbes (Boston: Houghton Mifflin, 1909), 3:341.

69. Emerson, "Compensation," in *Complete Writings*, 164.

70. Emerson, "History," in *Complete Writings*, 132–33.

71. Emerson, "History," in *Complete Writings*, 134–35.

72. Emerson, "The Over-Soul," in *Complete Writings*, 206.

73. Friedrich Nietzsche, "On the Uses and Disadvantages of History for Life," in *Untimely Meditations*, ed. Daniel Breazeale, trans. R. J. Hollindale (Cambridge: Cambridge University Press, 1997), 122.

74. Nietzsche, "Uses and Disadvantages," 73.

75. Nietzsche, "Uses and Disadvantages," 76.

76. Nietzsche, "Uses and Disadvantages," 63.

77. Nietzsche, "Uses and Disadvantages," 61.

78. Emerson, "The Over-Soul," in *Complete Writings*, 207–8.

79. Oliver Wendell Holmes, *Ralph Waldo Emerson*, in *The Works of Oliver Wendell Holmes*, 13 vols. (Boston: Houghton Mifflin, 1892), 11:302.

80. Arthur McCalla, "The Structure of French Romantic Histories of Religions," *Numen* 45.3 (1998): 279.

81. Holmes, *Emerson*, 304.

82. Holmes, *Emerson*, 304.

83. Frederic Henry Hedge, *The Ways of the Spirit and Other Essays* (Boston: Roberts Brothers, 1878), 358–62.

84. Hedge, *Ways of the Spirit*, 360.

85. William Rounseville Alger attributes these lines to "Dr. Hedge," in *The Destiny of the Soul: A Critical History of the Doctrine of a Future Life*, 10th ed. (Boston: Roberts Brothers, 1880), 6.

86. Cyrus Augustus Bartol, *Radical Problems* (Boston: Roberts Brothers, 1872), 93.

87. Bartol, *Radical Problems*, 167, 234.

88. Warren, "Orphic Sage," 3.

89. A. Bronson Alcott, *Concord Days* (1872; repr., Philadelphia: Albert Saifer, 1962), 83–84.

90. A. Bronson Alcott, "Orphic Sayings," *Dial* 1.3 (January 1841): 361.

91. Alcott, "Orphic Sayings," *Dial* 1.1 (July 1840): 87.

92. Amos Bronson Alcott, *Table-Talk* (Boston: Roberts Brothers, 1877), 175.

93. Alcott, *Table-Talk*, 141. He may have in mind Plato's statement in *Laws* that "it has been proved up to the hilt that the soul…is the most ancient thing there is." Plato, *Laws*, X.896b–c, trans. Trevor J. Saunders, in *Plato: Complete Works*, ed. John M. Cooper (Indianapolis, Ind.: Hackett, 1997), 1553.

94. Alcott, *Table-Talk*, 111, 144.

95. Raymond L. Bridgman, ed., *Concord Lectures on Philosophy* (Cambridge: Moses King, 1883), 149.

96. The schedule of lectures for the first five years, for example, lists under Hiram K. Jones, "Preexistence," in 1879; "The Eternity of the Soul and Its Preexistence," in both 1880 and 1881; and "The Platonic Idea of the Soul," in 1883. Bridgman, *Concord Lectures*, 8–12.

97. Bridgman, *Concord Lectures*, 149.

98. Austin Warren, "The Concord School of Philosophy," *New England Quarterly* 2.2 (April 1929): 216.

99. Bridgman, *Concord Lectures*, 121.

100. Bridgman, *Concord Lectures*, 121.

101. Plotinus, *The Enneads*, 7 vols., trans. A. H. Armstrong (Cambridge, Mass.: Harvard University Press, 1966–1988), VI.9.7 (7:331).

102. Alcott, "Orphic Sayings," *Dial* 1.1 (July 1840): 87.

103. Plotinus, *Enneads*, VI.9.8, 11.

104. Alcott, *Table-Talk*, 146.

105. Alcott, *Table-Talk*, 116–17.

106. Alcott, *Table-Talk*, 136.

107. Alcott, *Table-Talk*, 165.

108. Amos Bronson Alcott, "Ion," VIII, cited in Warren, "Orphic Sage," 12–13.

109. Holmes, *Emerson*, 394.

110. Cited in Rutherford B. Hayes, *Diary and Letters*, 5 vols., ed. Charles R. Williams (Columbus: Ohio State Archaeological and Historical Society, 1922–1926), 1:301–3, cited in Applegate, *Most Famous Man*, 273.

111. Henry More, "Preface General," in *A Collection of Several Philosophical Writings of Dr. Henry More* (London: James Flesher, 1662; repr., New York: Garland, 1978), vii.

112. W. L. Nichols, "The Sense of Pre-Existence," *Notes and Queries*, 2nd ser., no. 55 (17 January 1857): 50–52. The sources from which Nichols quotes are cited incompletely or not at all.

113. Alger, *Destiny of the Soul*, 4.

114 Alger, *Destiny of the Soul*, 6–7.

115 Alger, *Destiny of the Soul*, 8.

116 Alger, *Destiny of the Soul*, 8.

117. Moses Ballou, *The Divine Character Vindicated: A Review* (Redfield, N.Y., 1854), 62–63.

118. Alger, *Destiny of the Soul*, 9.

CHAPTER 11

1. J. E. Littlewood, *Littlewood's Miscellany*, ed. Béla Bollobás (Cambridge: Cambridge University Press, 1986), 135–36.

2. Charles E. Raven, *Good News of God* (New York: Harper, n.d.), 98–99, cited in Matthew Spinka, "Berdyaev and Origen: A Comparison," *Church History* 16.1 (March 1947): 3.

3. Spinka, "Berdyaev and Origen," 13.

4. Hieromonk Patapios, "Book Review: *The Orthodox Way*," online review at *Orthodox Christian Information Center*, www.orthodoxinfo.com/phronema/review_tow.aspx. The Synesios (Synesius) reference is from Johannes Quasten, *Patrology* (Westminster, Md.: Christian Classics, 1992), 3:107.

5. "Theologian Is the One Who Verily Prays," *Ecumenism—A Path to Perdition*, http://ecumenizm.tripod.com/ECUMENIZM/id18.html.

6. Paul Tillich, cover blurb of Nicholas Berdyaev, *The Beginning and the End* (New York: Harper, 1952).

7. Edward Moore, "Origen of Alexandria," *Internet Encyclopedia of Philosophy*, www.iep.utm.edu.

8. Nicholas Berdyaev, *The Beginning and the End*, trans. R. M. French (New York: Harper, 1952), IV.9.2 (240–41).

9. Berdyaev, *Beginning and the End*, IV.8.1 (206–7).

10. D. P. Walker, "Eternity and the Afterlife," *Journal of the Warburg and Courtauld Institutes* 27 (1964): 243.

11. "The concept of time has no meaning before the beginning of the universe." Stephen Hawking, *A Brief History of Time* (New York: Bantam, 1988), 8.

12. Berdyaev, *Beginning and the End*, IV.9.2 (241).

13. Berdyaev, *Beginning and the End*, IV.9.2 (241).

14. Berdyaev, *Beginning and the End*, IV.8.1 (207).

15. Nicholas Berdyaev, *The Destiny of Man* (London: Geoffrey Bles, 1948), 46, 52, 61.

16. Jacob Boehme, *The Forty Questions of the Soul and the Clavis*, trans. John Sparrow (London: John M. Watkins, 1911), 1–2.

17. This title was first bestowed by Count Keyserling in a preface to a German translation of Berdyaev's *Meaning of History*, according to Spinka, who seconds the epithet. Spinka, "Berdyaev and Origen," 9.

18. Julius Müller, *The Christian Doctrine of Sin*, 2 vols., trans. William Urwick (Edinburgh: Clark, 1868), 2:100.

19. F. W. J. Schelling, *Of Human Freedom*, trans. James Gutman (Chicago: Open Court, 1936), 32.

20. N. O. Lossky, *History of Russian Philosophy* (New York: International Universities Press, 1951), 236. Berdyaev's word for this freedom, meonic, is from the Greek *mei on*, meaning literally "not being" or "nonexistent." Meonic freedom is thus a primordial freedom or potentiality prior even to God. Lossky's quoted passages are from Berdyaev's *Destiny of Man*.

21. George M. Marsden, *Jonathan Edwards: A Life* (New Haven, Conn.: Yale University Press, 2003), 444.

22. Thomas Nagel, *Moral Questions* (Cambridge: Cambridge University Press, 1979), 33, 35.

23. McTaggart created categories of A-series and B-series time, which are especially useful in discussing the impact of relativistic theory on our understanding of time. See Palle Yourgrau, *A World without Time: The Forgotten Legacy of Gödel and Einstein* (New York: Basic, 2005), 124ff.

24. J. M. Ellis McTaggart, *Some Dogmas of Religion* (London: Edward Arnold, 1906), 165.

25. Marsden, *Jonathan Edwards*, 453.

26. Thomas Aquinas, "Whether Man Has Free Will," Objection 3 and Response to Objection 3, in *Summa Theologica*, 7 vols. (New York: Benziger Brothers, 1947), 1:418. (Aquinas is quoting Aristotle's *Metaphysics*, I.2.) Aquinas escapes the quagmire by simply asserting in his response that "it does not of necessity belong to liberty that what is free should be the first cause of itself."

27. J. M. Ellis McTaggart, "Human Pre-Existence," *International Journal of Ethics* 15.1 (October 1904): 83–85.

28. John Wisdom, *Problems of Mind and Matter* (Cambridge: Cambridge University Press, 1963), 130.

29. Helen M. Smith, "Pre-Existence and Free Will," *Analysis* 3.3 (January 1936): 41.

30. Roderick Chisholm, "Human Freedom and the Self," quoted in Daniel Dennett, *Elbow Room: The Varieties of Free Will Worth Wanting* (Cambridge, Mass.: MIT Press, 1984), 76.

31. Dennett, *Elbow Room*, 76. The expression is originally from P. F. Strawson.

32. William James, *The Varieties of Religious Experience* (Cambridge, Mass.: Harvard University Press, 1985), 112.

33. David Paulsen, "The God of Abraham, Isaac, and (William) James," *Journal of Speculative Philosophy* 13.2 (1999): 124. Paulsen notes that, although James in this context did not identify what he meant by co-original entities or principles, in a 1904 statement he explicitly included "agencies and their activities" among the ultimate spiritual realities. See Henry James, ed., *The Letters of William James*, vol. 2 (Boston: Atlantic Monthly Press, 1920), 213.

34. See, for example, Archimandrite Alexander Mileant, *The Greatness of God and the Triviality of Gods*, missionary leaflet E66b, trans. Ana P. Joyce and Barbara Olson (Los Angeles: Holy Protection Russian Orthodox Church, 1999). This tract singles out many of

the names and philosophies specifically associated with preexistence as prime culprits in "making a bridge between Creator and creature," including Pythagoras, Gnostics, Neo-Platonists, Boehme, Schelling, Joseph Smith, Berdyaev, and others.

35. Arthur Henry King, *The Abundance of the Heart* (Salt Lake City, Utah: Bookcraft, 1986), 25.

36. Walter Burkert, *Lore and Science in Ancient Pythagoreanism*, trans. Edwin L. Minar, Jr. (Cambridge, Mass.: Harvard University Press, 1972), 136.

37. John Knox, "Pre-Existence, Survival, and Sufficient Reason," *American Philosophical Quarterly* 32.2 (April 1995): 175, 167, 170, 169, 171.

38. Plotinus, *The Enneads*, trans. A. H. Armstrong, 7 vols. (Cambridge, Mass.: Harvard University Press, 1966–1988), VI.9.8 (7:333).

39. Knox, "Pre-Existence," 176n.

40. Walker, "Eternity and the Afterlife," 246.

41. Walker, "Eternity and the Afterlife," 248.

42. McTaggart, "Human Pre-Existence," 87.

43. Roy Sorensen, *A Brief History of Paradox: Philosophy and the Labyrinths of the Mind* (New York: Oxford University Press, 2003), 1.

44. G. R. S. Mead, "The Doctrine of Reincarnation Ethically Considered," *International Journal of Ethics* 22.2 (January 1912): 159.

45. Mead, "Doctrine of Reincarnation," 162.

46. Sylvia Cranston, *The Extraordinary Life and Influence of Helena Blavatsky: Founder of the Modern Theosophical Movement* (New York: Putnam's, 1994), xviii.

47. H. P. Blavatsky, *Isis Unveiled: A Master-Key to the Mysteries of Ancient and Modern Science and Theology*, 2 vols. (Pasadena, Calif.: Theosophical University Press, 1950), 2:406.

48. Blavatsky, *Isis Unveiled*, 1:316–17.

49. H. P. Blavatsky, "Theories about Reincarnation and Spirits," *Path* (November 1886), reprinted in *Isis Unveiled*, 2:appendix 44.

50. G. K. Chesterton, *Orthodoxy* (1908; repr., New York: Dover, 2004), 73.

51. Marcel Proust, *Remembrance of Things Past*, trans. G. K. Scott Moncrieff (New York: Random House, 1927), 2:509–10. Of this passage, Gabriel Marcel writes, "We are probably at first tempted to refer back to the Platonic myth which underlies this. There is, however, every reason to think that we should be making a serious mistake if we put the accent here on the word myth." *Homo Viator: Introduction to a Metaphysic of Hope*, trans. Emma Craufurd (Chicago: Regnery, 1951), 8

52. Maurice Maeterlinck, *The Blue Bird*, trans. Alexander Teixeira de Mattos (New York: Dodd, Mead, 1944), 32.

53. Maeterlinck, *Blue Bird*, 214, 218.

54. Maeterlinck, *Blue Bird*, 218–19, 235.

55. Maeterlinck, *Blue Bird*, 241.

56. Robert Frost, "Trial by Existence," first published in *A Boy's Will* (New York: Henry Holt, 1913).

57. Frances Cornford, "Preexistence," in *Modern British Poetry*, ed. Louis Untermeyer (New York: Harcourt, Brace, 1921), 184–85.

58. Wislawa Szymborska, "A Version of Events," in *People on a Bridge*, trans. Adam Czerniawski (London: Forest, 1990), 62–64.

59. Vladimir Nabokov, *Speak Memory: An Autobiography Revisited* (New York: Random House, 1967), 19.

60. Kathleen Norris, *Mother: A Story* (New York: Macmillan, 1912), 156.

61. Joseph Chaikin and Sam Shepard, *The War in Heaven: Angel's Monologue*, in Sam Shepard, *A Lie of the Mind: A Play in Three Acts* (New York: New American Library, 1987), 137, 138, 143, 153.

62. Interview quoted in Alan Keele, *In Search of the Supernal: Preexistence, Eternal Marriage, and Apotheosis in German Literary, Operatic, and Cinematic Texts* (Münster: Agenda, 2003), 27.

63. Elizabeth M. Carman and Neil J. Carman, *Cosmic Cradle: Souls Waiting in the Wings for Birth* (Fairfield, Iowa: Sunstar, 1999), i, 7, 55, 57.

64. Elisabeth Hallett, *Soul Trek: Meeting Our Children on the Way to Birth* (Hamilton, Mont.: Light Hearts, 1995). A sequel followed, *Stories of the Unborn Soul: The Mystery and Delight of Pre-Birth Communication* (Lincoln: Writers Club Press, 2002).

65. Sarah Hinze, *Coming from the Light: Spiritual Accounts of Life before Life* (New York: Pocket, 1997), 64–71.

66. Sam Parnia, *What Happens When We Die* (Carlsbad, Calif.: Hay House, 2006), 14, 62.

CHAPTER 12

1. John Dryden, "Dedication of the Aeneis," in *Virgil's Aeneid*, trans. John Dryden (New York: Collier, 1909), 37.

2. Jorge Luis Borges, "A Vindication of Basilides the False," quoted in Marvin Meyer, introduction, *The Gospel of Judas from Codex Tchacos*, ed. Rodolphe Kasser, Marvin Meyer, and Gregor Wurst (Washington, D.C.: National Geographic, 2006), 8.

3. Thomas Hobbes, *Leviathan* eds. Richard E. Flathman and David Johnson (New York: Norton, 1997), I.13 (70).

4. John Rawls, *A Theory of Justice* (Cambridge, Mass.: Harvard University Press, 1971), 11–12.

5. Quoted in Adam Gopnik, "Rewriting Nature," *New Yorker* 82.34 (23 October 2006): 52.

6. Quoted in P. J. Bowler, *Charles Darwin: The Man and His Influence* (Cambridge: Cambridge University Press, 1990), 85.

7. William S. Walsh, *Paradoxes of a Philistine* (Philadelphia: Lippincott, 1889), 151–52.

8. Mortimer Mishkin and Tim Appenzeller, "The Anatomy of Memory," *Scientific American* 256.6 (June 1987): 80.

9. Jerry Fodor, "The Selfish Gene Pool: Mother Nature, Easter Bunnies, and Other Common Mistakes," review of David J. Buller's *Adapting Minds: Evolutionary Psychology and the Persistent Quest for Human Nature*, in *Times Literary Supplement* (29 July 2005).

10. Sigmund Freud, *Dora: An Analysis of a Case of Hysteria* (New York: Collier, 1963), 27.

11. Sigmund Freud, *Civilization and Its Discontents*, trans. James Strachey (New York: Norton, 1989), 18.

12. C. G. Jung, "New Paths in Psychology," 263. This essay, originally published in 1912, and "The Structure of the Unconscious," 1916, were more fully developed and published later in translation as C. G. Jung, *Two Essays on Analytic Psychology*, trans. R. F. C. Hull (New York: Meridian, 1956). Citations from "New Paths" come from the original version,

which was published as an appendix in *Two Essays*. Citations from "Structure of the Unconscious" also come from the original essay, also in an appendix, which was translated by Philip Mairet from the French of M. Marsen's translation.

13. Freud, *Civilization*, 11.

14. Freud, *Civilization*, 13–15.

15. Jung, "Structure of the Unconscious," 277.

16. Jung, "Structure of the Unconscious," 277–79.

17. Jung, "Structure of the Unconscious," 282.

18. Jung, "Structure of the Unconscious," 282.

19. Carl Jung, *Dreams*, trans. R. F. C. Hull (Princeton, N.J.: Princeton University Press, 1974), 295.

20. Carl Jung, *Psychological Types*, trans. H. G. Baynes, rev. R. F. C. Hull, in *Collected Works of C. G. Jung* (Princeton, N.J.: Princeton University Press, 1971), 6:443–45, 202.

21. Carl Jung, *Man and His Symbols* (New York: Dell, 1964), 58.

22. Jung, "On the Psychology of the Unconscious," in *Two Essays*, 76.

23. Jung, "Psychology of the Unconscious," 87.

24. Jung, "Psychology of the Unconscious," 76.

25. Jung, "Psychology of the Unconscious," 75.

26. Carl Jung, *Memories, Dreams, Reflections*, rec. and ed. Aniela Jaffé (New York: Pantheon, 1963), 291.

27. Samuel Butler, *Unconscious Memory* (London: Cape, 180), 174; Butler, *Life and Habit* (London: Cape, 1878), 297. Rupert Sheldrake refers to both studies in *The Presence of the Past: Morphic Resonance and the Habits of Nature* (Rochester, Vt.: Park Street, 1995), 15.

28. Robert Anton Wilson, jacket blurb for Sheldrake, *Presence of the Past*.

29. Sheldrake, *Presence of the Past*, xvii, 99, 157.

30. Sheldrake, *Presence of the Past*, 71.

31. Sheldrake, *Presence of the Past*, 177–81.

32. Thomas De Quincy, *The Collected Writings of Thomas De Quincey*, ed. David Masson, 14 vols. (New York: AMS, 1968), 13:346. The passage was quoted in "Sense of Pre-Existence," *American Notes and Queries* (n.d.), and then reprinted in the *New York Times*'s "Current Literature" column, 1.3 (September 1888).

33. Richard Dawkins, *The Selfish Gene* (New York: Oxford University Press, 1976), 206.

34. Daniel C. Dennett, *Darwin's Dangerous Idea* (New York: Simon & Schuster, 1995), 368.

35. Dennett, *Darwin's Dangerous Idea*, 368. Dennett has in mind, respectively, Jerry Fodor's *Modularity of Mind* (1983) and Colin McGinn's *Problem of Consciousness* (1991).

36. Noam Chomsky, *Language and the Problems of Knowledge* (Cambridge, Mass.: MIT Press, 1988), 34. The "purged of the error" allusion is to Leibniz's *Essay on Metaphysics* XXVI.

37. Noam Chomsky, *Cartesian Linguistics: A Chapter in the History of Rationalist Thought* (New York: Harper & Row, 1966), 63. The Cordemoy passage is from *Discours Physique de la Parole* (1666), 59.

38. Steven Pinker, *The Language Instinct* (New York: Morrow, 1994), 333. The Chomsky passage is from *Language and Mind* (New York: Harcourt Brace Jovanovich, 1968), 97–98, cited in Pinker, *Language Instinct*, 355.

39. Darold A. Treffert, *Extraordinary People: Understanding "Idiot Savants"* (New York: Harper & Row, 1989), 220.

40. Treffert, *Extraordinary People*, 181. Treffert is here quoting Dr. William Carpenter as cited in A. A. Brill, "Some Peculiar Manifestations of Memory with Special Reference to Lightning Calculators," *Journal of Nervous and Mental Diseases* 92 (1940): 709–26.

41. Graham Farrant, "Cellular Consciousness," *Aesthema: Journal of the International Primal Association* 7 (1986): 28–39, cited in David B. Chamberlain, "The Expanding Boundaries of Memory," *Pre- and Peri-Natal Psychology* 4.3 (Spring 1990): 179–84.

42. Darold A. Treffert, "'Ancestral' or 'Genetic' Memory: Factory Installed Software," *Savant Syndrome: Islands of Genius*, www.wisconsinmedicalsociety.org/savant_syndrome/savant_articles/genetic_memory. Treffert's use of the term "genetic memory" should not be confused with the mechanism in DNA that goes by precisely that name. See Marshall Nirenberg, "Genetic Memory," *Journal of the American Medical Association* 206.9 (25 November 1968): 1973–77.

43. Steven Pinker, *The Blank Slate: The Modern Denial of Human Nature* (New York: Penguin, 2002), 372–74, 380, 384.

44. Pinker, *Blank Slate*, 390. See, on this topic, Judith R. Harris, *The Nurture Assumption: Why Children Turn Out the Way They Do* (New York: Free Press, 1998).

45. Pinker, *Blank Slate*, 396.

46. J. M. Ellis McTaggart, "Human Pre-Existence," *International Journal of Ethics* 15.1 (October 1904): 86–87.

47. Milton H. Welling, *Conference Report of the Church of Jesus Christ of Latter-day Saints* (April 1913), 43.

48. Matthew Spinka, "Berdyaev and Origen: A Comparison," *Church History* 16.1 (March 1947): 11.

49. Thomas Nagel, *The Last Word* (New York: Oxford University Press, 1997), 137–38, 133.

50. C. S. Peirce, *Reasoning and the Logic of Things*, ed. Kenneth Laine Ketner (Cambridge, Mass.: Harvard University Press, 1992), 112; Nagel, *Last Word*, 132.

EPILOGUE

1. Jay Bregman, *Synesius of Cyrene* (Berkeley: University of California Press, 1982), 34.

2. Synesius, Hymn 1, in Bregman, *Synesius of Cyrene*, 34.

3. Plato, *Timaeus*, 29e, trans. Donald J. Zeyl, in *Plato: Complete Works*, ed. John M. Cooper (Indianapolis, Ind.: Hackett, 1997), 1236.

4. Elizabeth A. Clark, *The Origenist Controversy: The Cultural Construction of an Early Christian Debate* (Princeton, N.J.: Princeton University Press, 1992), 250.

5. George Arthur Buttrick, ed., *The Interpreter's Bible*, 12 vols. (New York: Abingdon, 1952), 8:611.

6. M. F. Burnyeat, "Other Lives," *London Review of Books* 29.4 (22 February 2007).

Index

Note: Page numbers in bold indicate illustrations

Crookes, William, 290
Cudworth, Ralph, 152, 154
Culverwel, Nathanael, 153, 154
Cyril of Jerusalem, 103

Dante, 23, 71, 177
Darwin, Charles, 2, 237, 271, 305, 306
Darwinism, 236, 237, 271, 274
Davies, John, 168
Davies, Paul, 20
Davis, Andrew Jackson, 260
Dawkins, Richard
    The Selfish Gene, 312–13
divine assembly, 49
Dead Sea Scrolls, 59
deification, 12, 37, 53, 78, 98, 140, 151–52,
    213, 220, 255–56, 268, 270, 310
Demetrius, 80
demiurge, 35, 62, 67, 72
Dennett, Daniel, 284, 313
Descartes, René, 7, 28, 152–154, 157, 185,
    187, 191–95, 203, 205, 218, 305
    Passions of the Soul, 185
    Treatise on Man, 185
Deuteronomy, Book of, 15, 132
Dial, 267, 268
Diderot, Denis, 256
Didymus, 99, 106, 107, 117, 127
Diogenes Laertius, 26
Dionysus, 23
divine assembly, 9–10, 12–17, 51, 53, 67,
    130, 139, 216
Dryden, John, 303
dualism, anthropological, 12, 22, 23, 42
dualism, metaphysical, 30, 51, 62
Duffield, George, 227

Ea, 13
Eadmer, 134
Eastern Orthodox Church, 2
Ecclesiasticus, 50
Echecrates, 27
Eden, 1, 12, 34, 62, 129, 131–32, 139, 141,
    172–75, 247, 253, 303, 305

Edersheim, Alfred, 52
Edict of Milan, 99
Edison, Thomas, 290
Edwards, Jonathan, 282–83
Edwards, Mark Julian, 342–43
Edwin, King of Northumbria, 126
Egypt, 4, 60, 68, 71, 80, 147, 190, 264, 290
Einstein, Albert, 6, 290
Elijah, 139
Eliphaz, 13, 49
Ellis, George, 228
emanations, 3
embryology, 42, 164, 174, 184–87, 197
Emerson, Ralph Waldo, 71, 228,
    263–67, 272
Empedocles, 24, 25, 104
    "On Purification," 24
Empiricism, 203
Enki, 10, 12
Enlil, 13
Ennemoser, Joseph, 274
Ennoia, 62
Enoch, 47, 68, 140
Enuma Elish, 216
Ephesians, Letter to the, 54, 56, 67
Epinoia, 65
Epiphanius of Salamis, 117
epistrophe, 66
Er, 32
Eratosthenes, 39
Erman, Adolf, 339
Ernesti, Johann August, 200
Eros, 33
Esdras, 80
Essenes, 58–59
Euclid, 39
Eurydice, 23
Eusebius, 91
Eutyches, 122
Evagrius Ponticus, 106, 116, 118, 127, 217
Evagrius Scholasticus, 124
Evangelist, 228
Evans, Abel, 178–80, 356
    "Pre-Existence: A Poem," 178–80